APEX COURTS AND THE COMMON LAW

Apex Courts and the Common Law

EDITED BY PAUL DALY

UNIVERSITY OF TORONTO PRESS
Toronto Buffalo London

Toronto Buffalo London
utorontopress.com

ISBN 978-1-4875-0443-4

Library and Archives Canada Cataloguing in Publication

Title: Apex courts and the common law / edited by Paul Daly.
Names: Daly, Paul, 1983– editor.
Description: Includes bibliographical references.
Identifiers: Canadiana 20190049375 | ISBN 9781487504434 (hardcover)
Subjects: LCSH: Constitutional courts. | LCSH: Common law.
Classification: LCC K3370 .A64 2019 | DDC 347/.035—dc23

University of Toronto Press acknowledges the financial assistance to its publishing program of the Canada Council for the Arts and the Ontario Arts Council, an agency of the Government of Ontario.

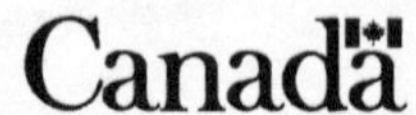

Contents

Acknowledgments vii

Introduction 3
PAUL DALY

Part I: Decision Making by Common Law Apex Courts

1 The Role of the Supreme Court of Canada in Shaping the Common Law 25
BEVERLEY McLACHLIN

2 Apex Courts and the Development of the Common Law 36
BRICE DICKSON

3 The Common Law, the High Court of Australia, and the United States Supreme Court 66
PETER CANE

4 Against All Odds: Numbers Sitting in the UK Supreme Court and Really, Really Important Cases 94
JAMES LEE

5 The Reference Jurisdiction of the Supreme Court of Canada 140
CARISSIMA MATHEN

Part II: Public Law Issues

6 Judicial Review in the American States 169
ROBERT F. WILLIAMS

7 The Common Law, the Constitution, and the Alien 192
AUDREY MACKLIN

8 Administrative Law and Rights in the UK House of Lords and Supreme Court 225
JASON N.E. VARUHAS

9 The Continuing Significance of *Dr Bonham's Case* 279
HAN-RU ZHOU

Part III: Common Law Concepts

10 The Development of an Obligation to Perform in Good Faith 303
ANGELA SWAN AND JAKUB ADAMSKI

11 Cause and Courts 342
SANDY STEEL

12 What Is Happening to the Law of Unjust Enrichment? 365
STEVE HEDLEY

13 The Supreme Court, Fundamental Principles of Property Law, and the Shaping of Aboriginal Title 385
BRUCE ZIFF

Afterword 405
WILLIAM B. EWALD

Contributors 413

Acknowledgments

The papers contained in this collection were initially presented at a conference held at the Université de Montréal's Cyberjustice Laboratory on 27 May 2016. The conference title was "Supreme Courts and the Common Law." The proceedings have been archived and can be accessed at the following address: http://commonlaw.umontreal.ca/videos/.

The facilities provided by the Cyberjustice Laboratory and the Centre de recherche en droit public at the Université de Montréal contributed to a memorable event. In particular, the webcasting, which reached a global audience, would not have been possible without their support. My colleague in the Faculté de droit's Common Law Programme, Matthew Harrington, helped a great deal in organizing the conference and conceptualizing this project.

Florian Martin-Bariteau went above and beyond the call of duty in revising and redrafting a funding application that ultimately influenced the content and structure of this collection. I was extremely fortunate to have Sarah Richert as my executive assistant at the time: she took care of travel, accommodation, and nourishing the conference participants. On the day of the conference, Dominique Payette ensured that the event ran smoothly.

Apart from the in-kind contributions from the Faculté de droit, the Centre de recherche en droit public, and the Cyberjustice Laboratory, the event and this publication were supported by a Connection grant from the Social Sciences and Humanities Research Council of Canada. Further financial support from the Yorke Fund at the University of Cambridge and Queens' College, Cambridge allowed this book to see the light of day.

My editor at the University of Toronto Press, Daniel Quinlan, has been excellent in guiding the project through the production process. The anonymous peer reviewers read the draft manuscript assiduously and provided many thoughtful comments, which the contributors and I have taken on board. I am also indebted to Stephanie Stone for her thoroughly professional copy editing. Breanna Muir has also been invaluable in preparing the book for market.

On a personal level, Marie-France, Liam, Lorna, and Luke have been a source of support and delight throughout the production process.

APEX COURTS AND THE COMMON LAW

Introduction

PAUL DALY

The overarching theme of this collection is the influence of apex courts on the development of the common law[1] – in particular, how the institutional position of apex courts causes them to shape the common law and, conversely, how the traditions of the common law shape the way in which apex courts conceive of their role. Contributors from around the common law world address the overarching theme in three different contexts: first, the particular characteristics of the apex courts of several selected jurisdictions; second, the influence, if any, of constitutionalism and bills of rights on apex courts' relationships to the common law; and third, how apex courts have treated core concepts such as causation, restitution, good faith, and property. Former chief justice Beverley McLachlin's essay on the role of the Supreme Court of Canada provides a useful starting point; Canada's apex court features prominently in the subsequent chapters – although always in comparative perspective – as do the apex courts of the United States, the United Kingdom, and Australia. The resulting study of the common law as shaped by apex courts, and apex courts as shaped by the common law, represents a novel contribution to the literature on judicial decision making in the common law tradition, one that will interest students, legal practitioners, and academics.

1 In this collection, *apex court* is preferred to *supreme court* because it better captures the institutional position of a court at the top of the judicial hierarchy in a given jurisdiction and because many first-instance courts – e.g., in New York (United States), British Columbia (Canada), and Victoria (Australia) – are labelled *supreme* on the basis that they have inherent jurisdiction, and that word is liable to create misunderstandings.

The contributors to this collection set out with a common goal: to better understand how the institutional role of apex courts influences the common law and vice versa. For the most part, the contributors apply traditional common law methodology, using judicial decisions as the building blocks for arguments about the nature of legal reasoning and subjecting those decisions to close analysis for doctrinal and theoretical consistency. This is especially evident in the contributions in part III, which focus on core common law concepts. However, the contributors have not closed their eyes to related academic disciplines (an influential feature of the study of apex courts).[2] To take two examples, Audrey Macklin's discussion of the common law of immigration draws on political science, philosophy, and history; and Peter Cane's comparative analysis of the Supreme Court of the United States and the High Court of Australia is informed by concepts drawn from political science.

In this introductory chapter, I will trace two major themes that bind this volume together – first, common law method; and second, the role of apex courts – before providing a brief overview of the individual contributions.

Common Law Method

For centuries, courts across the common law world have developed their systems of law by building bodies of judicial decisions. By deciding individual cases, common law courts settle litigation and move the law in new directions. Apex courts, which sit at the apex of common law systems, fulfil these standard dispute-resolution and law-development functions, but they also have a unique institutional position. By virtue of their place at the top of the judicial hierarchy, their decisions and, in particular, the language used in those decisions, resonate through the legal system. Moreover, members of the legal community – judges, lawyers, legal academics, students, and laypeople – often look to apex courts for general guidance.[3] Accordingly, the institutional position of apex courts

2 See eg L. Epstein, W. Landes, and R. Posner, *The Behavior of Federal Judges: A Theoretical and Empirical Study of Rational Choice* (Cambridge, MA, Harvard University Press, 2013).

3 See eg P. Strauss, "One Hundred Fifty Cases per Year: Some Implications of the Supreme Court's Limited Resources for Judicial Review of Agency Action" (1987) 87 *Columbia Law Review* 1093.

may nudge them away from incremental development of the law based on the resolution of individual cases and towards the elaboration of general principles that can unify large areas of the law and provide meaningful guidance to the legal community and the general public.

When venturing into the domain of common law methodology, one must tread carefully. As William Ewald reminds readers in his concluding essay, what common lawyers mean by *common law* is not always clear (beyond agreement, as Peter Cane explains in his contribution, that common law jurisdictions share a medieval heritage).

The term can refer to *core common law subjects*, such as torts, contracts, property, and (perhaps) restitution or, more generally, to a body of decided cases; these meanings are not especially prominent in the present collection. Bruce Ziff's chapter stands out in this regard, perhaps, given its detailed explanation of how Aboriginal title to land might be shaped by ancient common law concepts such as adverse possession, as does Macklin's account of how the common law's traditional approach to migrants has influenced the Supreme Court of Canada's interpretation of fundamental rights.

The term can also refer to a *method of constitutional interpretation* – although, in the American constitutional tradition, common law constitutionalism is generally taken to mean judicial decision making that relies more (or entirely) on ensuring the conformity of decisions to previous constitutional cases than on conformity to the constitutional text itself[4] – whereas elsewhere in the common law world, common law constitutionalism (which features prominently in the contributions by Han-Ru Zhou and Jason Varuhas) usually refers to the process of judges drawing constitutional norms from sources recognized as valid by common lawyers.[5] It is sometimes thought that the common law constitution is inevitably progressive or pro-individual: Zhou's careful tracing of Coke's jurisprudence on judicial control of executive action points very much in this direction, as does Varuhas's critical analysis of recent developments in the United Kingdom, the upshot of which is that the Supreme Court of the United Kingdom risks altering, in favour of the judges, the balance of power between the judiciary and the political branches of government.

---

4 See eg D. Strauss, *The Living Constitution* (Oxford, Oxford University Press, 2010).

5 See generally T. Poole, "Back to the Future? Unearthing the Theory of Common Law Constitutionalism" (2003) 23 *Oxford Journal of Legal Studies* 435.

Yet Macklin's account of the relationship between immigration law and the Canadian Charter of Rights and Freedoms casts some doubt on received wisdom: immigration law, with its insistence on the prerogative of the state to control migration flows, allows the subordination of the individual to the collective; here, the Supreme Court of Canada's approach to setting out general principles in respect of fundamental rights has been influenced by its common law heritage. Notably, both Macklin and Zhou suggest that apex courts' institutional positions (as explainers of modern rights instruments and expounders of fundamental norms) should influence how they approach common law constitutionalism. Varuhas, by contrast, warns of the danger of judicial self-aggrandizement: the rooting out of general principles by an apex court keen to take a prominent place in the constitutional ecosystem may upset the delicate balance between the judicial and political branches of government.[6]

Finally, *common law* can refer to *methodology*: the way common lawyers reason. Yet here, too, there may be ambiguity. On the one hand, common law reasoning can be understood as the practice of an "interpretive community,"[7] with an agreed set of norms about what count as valid and persuasive arguments about the law; Cane recalls A.W.B. Simpson's memorable articulation of this view, which is worth quoting here:

> [T]he common law system is properly located as a customary system of law in this sense, that it consists of a body of practices observed and ideas received by a caste of lawyers, these ideas being used by them as providing guidance in what is conceived to be the rational determination of disputes litigated before them, or by them on behalf of clients, and in other contexts. These ideas and practices exist only in the sense that they are accepted and acted upon within the legal profession, just as customary practices may be said to exist within a group in the sense that they are observed, accepted as appropriate forms of behaviour, and transmitted both by example and precept as membership of the group changes.[8]

---

6 See also P. Daly, "A Supreme Court's Place in the Constitutional Order: Contrasting Recent Experiences in Canada and the United Kingdom" (2015) 41 *Queen's Law Journal* 1.

7 S. Fish, *Is There a Text in This Class? The Authority of Interpretive Communities* (Cambridge, MA, Harvard University Press, 1982).

8 "The Common Law and Legal Theory" in A.W.B. Simpson (ed), *Oxford Essays in Jurisprudence (Second Series)* (Oxford, Clarendon Press, 1973) 77 at 94.

It may be thought to follow, as Cane outlines, that different communities of lawyers might differ in their approach to the law, from the classically legalistic approach of the Australians,[9] pursuant to which questions of *common law* are in the judicial province, to the realistic approach of the Americans,[10] whereby *law* (including common law) and *policy* run into each other, especially in the Supreme Court of the United States, "standardly considered to be a political institution." Australians and Americans are common lawyers,[11] but their approach to the common law is shaped by different constitutional traditions – and the account in the previous paragraph of the divergences among Macklin, Zhou, and Varuhas bears further witness to the importance (and contestability) of interpretive traditions.

Cane's reminder of the importance of the potentially endless particularities of history and tradition is underscored by James Lee's account of how the UK Supreme Court is adapting its practices (and perhaps decisions) to its new role, and Robert F. Williams's illuminating discussion of how the supreme courts in the American states, which differ markedly from the Supreme Court of the United States, cannot be understood in isolation from the functions they have been asked to perform. Some readers will no doubt conclude that, with history and tradition playing such a prominent role, issues of common law methodology should be approached with extreme caution.

On the other hand, one might try to define *common law reasoning* in terms of its "bottom-up" quality by opposition to civil law reasoning, typically thought to be "top down" in nature.[12] Where the common law treats cases as primary sources and recognizes no principles save those that can be found in the jurisprudence, civil lawyers are cabined by their code, which sets out general principles to which previous cases

---

9 See eg O. Dixon, "Concerning Judicial Method" in *Jesting Pilate* (Melbourne, Law Book Company, 1965) at 152. Of course, the "Dixonian" legacy is controversial.

10 See eg K. Llewellyn, *The Common Law Tradition – Deciding Appeals* (Boston, MA, Little Brown, 1960).

11 Although one should here mention the civil law state of Louisiana, described in J.T. Hood, Jr, "The History and Development of the Louisiana Civil Code" (1958–59) *Tulane Law Review* 7.

12 See further text to nn 18–21 below.

are merely helpful guideposts.[13] Beverley McLachlin offers a "modest challenge" to the utility of the oppositional concepts in her contribution – noting that bottom-up common law courts have always been willing to reason from the top down to bring coherence to the law or bring the law into line with social developments – but she stops short of driving a stake through their hearts. Indeed, although she identifies significant convergence in common law and civilian approaches in recent times, she also acknowledges that there *are* differences – rooted in history and the conceptual bases of adjudication – in the ways common law and civil law courts approach the task of deciding cases.

However, for reasons of history and tradition (now memorialized in law),[14] these differences may be less obvious in the Canadian context. For one thing, the Supreme Court of Canada – composed of six judges drawn from common law provinces and three drawn from the civil law province of Quebec – sits in appeal from both common law and civil law courts, a feature that, all things considered, must lead to some cross-fertilization of methodology.[15] For another, Quebec is probably better regarded as a mixed system than a purely civilian one: its public law is common law[16] and, critically, so is its civil procedure, such that adversarial argument and reasoned judgments combine to make case law a primary source of law.[17]

More generally, however, the concepts of top-down and bottom-up reasoning reappear throughout this volume, not necessarily as paradigms derived from a comparison between the civil law and common law but as representations of different predispositions on the part of

13 This is a simplification, of course (see eg W. Tetley QC, "Mixed Jurisdictions: Common Law vs Civil Law (Codified and Uncodified)" [1999] *Uniform Law Review* 591 (Part I) and 887 (Part II), but there are important differences between the common law and the civil law traditions. See also Peter Cane's contribution to this volume (ch 3), noting the different locations of the power to make law in common law and civilian jurisdictions, with the judges and legislature in the one, with the legislature alone in the other (at least as far as the code is concerned).

14 Supreme Court Act, RSC 1985, c S-26; *Reference re Supreme Court Act, ss 5 and 6* [2014] 1 SCR 433.

15 See eg L. LeBel and P.-L. Saunier, "L'interaction du droit civil et de la common law à la Cour suprême du Canada" (2006) 47 *Les Cahiers de droit* 179.

16 *Attorney General of Quebec v Labrecque* [1980] 2 SCR 1057.

17 As Angela Swan and Jakub Adamski emphasize in their contribution (see ch 10), these are important constraints on what common law judges may do in individual cases.

different lawyers. Angela Swan and Jakub Adamski's contribution can usefully be read in contrast with Steve Hedley's in this respect. Whereas Swan and Adamski, in their treatment of good faith in contract law, emphasize the desirability of apex courts setting out clear, general principles for the guidance of others in the legal community (on any view, a top-down approach), Hedley decries the flight to principle in the area of unjust enrichment, which, for him, is marked by outgrowths that must be addressed on a case-by-case basis (a bottom-up approach if ever there was one); to the extent that apex courts have attempted to distil the essence of restitution to a readily citable and applicable statement of principle, they have created only confusion. This is not to say that Hedley has a *philosophical* predisposition to this sort of reasoning: as he explains, his approach is derived from his perception of the characteristics of this area of the law. So it may be that common lawyers are not a homogeneous interpretive community at all, but many and varied interpretive communities, depending on the area of law in which they work, where they work, and whether they work at the apex of, or elsewhere in, the judicial hierarchy.

Apex Courts as Common Law Courts

If one accepts that there is a legitimate distinction to be made between top-down and bottom-up reasoning – either because it is inherent to the common law or because lawyers are predisposed to prefer one or the other – institutional considerations may introduce a tension between them. The development of the common law has typically been seen as a bottom-up exercise, with courts proceeding by analogy from case to case without guidance from tablets of stone delivered from on high. By contrast, a top-down approach is designed "to organize, criticize, accept or reject, explain or explain away, distinguish or amplify the existing decisions to make them conform to the theory and generate an outcome in each new case as it arises that will be consistent with the theory and with the canonical cases, that is, the cases accepted as authoritative within the theory."[18]

18 R. Posner, "Legal Reasoning from the Top Down and from the Bottom Up: The Question of Unenumerated Constitutional Rights" (1992) 59 *University of Chicago Law Review* 433 at 433.

Although this distinction has found judicial favour, most notably on the High Court of Australia,[19] it is hotly contested.[20] Common law judges and scholars who advocate principled reasoning as a means of bringing coherence to a mass of decided cases often note that the principles must be drawn from the cases, an approach that is arguably as much "bottom up" as it is "top down."[21] Nevertheless, an apex court's position at the apex of its national legal system may push it to prefer a top-down approach designed to achieve coherence in the application of law by lower courts.

The UK Supreme Court is a fascinating case study in this regard. As a young body – although one steeped in history as the successor to the Appellate Committee of the House of Lords[22] – it has, in some respects, been finding its way as an apex court, as Lee explains. From determining how to assign more important cases to larger panels (which, in theory, can then give a relatively more definitive account of the law) to figuring out how best to engage a wider audience, the UK Supreme Court has gradually changed its practices. The halting incrementalism in this respect is in contrast with the UK Supreme Court's bold embrace of common law constitutionalism, as described by Varuhas.

In Brice Dickson's view, recent decades have been marked by a preference on apex courts for general statements of principle revolving around

---

19 See eg *McGinty v Western Australia* (1996) 186 CLR 140 (HCA) at 231–2 (McHugh J); *Roxborough v Rothmans of Pall Mall (Australia) Ltd* (2001) 208 CLR 516 (HCA) at 543–5 (Gummow J).

20 For a recent overview, see C. Conte, "From Only the 'Bottom Up'? Legitimate Forms of Judicial Reasoning in Private Law" (2015) 35 *Oxford Journal of Legal Studies* 1. See generally E. Bant and M. Harding (eds), *Exploring Private Law* (Cambridge, Cambridge University Press, 2010), especially the chapter by K. Mason, "Do Top-Down and Bottom-Up Reasoning Ever Meet?" 19.

21 See eg A. Beever and C. Rickett, "Interpretive Legal Theory and the Academic Lawyer" (2005) 68 *Modern Law Review* 320. As has been said, in defence of the metaphor of "mapping" in private law:

> An explorer, as opposed to a planner, or even a Utopian visionary, must map what he sees from the ground, feeling his way where he must as well as taking the bird's eye view where he can. In this sense, the explorer brings order to chaos, but not by turning away from the chaos, and not by refusing to bear the responsibility of imposing order.
>
> E. Bant and M. Harding, "Introduction" in E. Bant and M. Harding (eds), *Exploring Private Law* (Cambridge, Cambridge University Press, 2010) 3.

22 See generally Constitutional Reform Act, 2005, c 4.

abstract concepts such as fairness and proportionality. Articulating the meaning of fairness and proportionality – to take just two examples – is a task to which an apex court will typically be well suited: not only can it resolve the case before it, but it can also elaborate a framework for the application of the general concept by lower courts. But this formulation is question-begging as the foregoing would be true of any time, not just our own. The interesting question is, Why now?

Some tentative answers might be found in Beverley McLachlin's contribution. Many common law jurisdictions now have judicially enforceable, written constitutions or bills of rights whose provisions are often cast in general terms.[23] Principled reasoning has, of necessity, become a feature of the common law landscape. In the area of public law, there is a strong demand for apex courts to develop a coherent set of principles that can guide the legal community in the development of the law. And, as Williams reminds us, the "statutorification" of the common law can also push courts to reason in a top-down manner as they interpret statutory codes.[24] Constitutionalism may, alongside common law apex courts' institutional positions and the rise of codification (especially in the United States), push judges further towards a decision-making approach dominated by general principles.

Similarly, as McLachlin recounts, the internationalization of legal discourse may contribute to the lowering of common lawyers' intellectual trade barriers.[25] True, common law judges have long been accustomed to seeking inspiration from their brothers and sisters in other jurisdictions. But technological change has made cross-border research and in-person discussion much easier. Judicial decisions and scholarly work are now available at several clicks of a button from anywhere in the world. Moreover, the low price of international travel and communication has permitted the growth of academic and judicial networks in which jurists from various jurisdictions are in regular contact.[26]

---

23 As Bruce Ziff observes in his contribution (see ch 13), "The language of any bill of rights is designed to be open-textured."

24 On the diminishing judicial hostility to statutory intervention in the common law, see R. Munday, "The Common Lawyer's Philosophy of Legislation" (1983) 14 *Rechtstheorie* 191.

25 See also R. Hirschl, *Towards Juristocracy: The Origins and Consequences of the New Constitutionalism* (Cambridge, MA, Harvard University Press, 2004).

26 See also A.-M. Slaughter, *A New World Order* (Princeton, NJ, Princeton University Press, 2004).

How, then, do apex courts go about this task of setting out general principles? Has their *modus operandi* had an influence on common law methodology? Answers can be found in the contributions by Carissima Mathen and James Lee. Mathen's essay on the Supreme Court of Canada's reference function sheds light on the decline in importance of the distinction between *ratio decidendi* and *obiter dicta*. Technically, references are non-binding statements of judicial opinion (so much so that the constitutional appropriateness of their character was once doubted),[27] but, in practical terms, they have shaped much of modern Canadian legal practice. Significantly, the Supreme Court of Canada is so comfortable adjudicating in generalities and setting out broad principles that there no longer seems to be any material difference between references (formulated for the Court by politicians) and *inter partes* litigation. This is consistent with a breakdown in the distinction between *ratio decidendi* and *obiter dicta*. Where once it was thought that "a case is only authority for what it actually decides,"[28] modern apex courts have tended to follow a more flexible approach:

> All *obiter* do not have, and are not intended to have, the same weight. The weight decreases as one moves from the dispositive *ratio decidendi* to a wider circle of analysis which is obviously intended for guidance and which should be accepted as authoritative. Beyond that, there will be commentary, examples or exposition that are intended to be helpful and may be found to be persuasive, but are certainly not "binding" in the sense the *Sellars* principle [that whatever was said in a majority judgment of the Supreme Court of Canada was binding, no matter how incidental to the main point of the case or how far it was removed from the dispositive facts and principles of law] in its most exaggerated form would have it. The objective of the exercise is to promote certainty in the law, not to stifle its growth and creativity. The notion that each phrase in a judgment of this Court should be treated as if enacted in a statute is not supported by the cases and is inconsistent with the basic fundamental principle that the common law develops by experience.[29]

27 *Reference Re Criminal Code (Canada)*, s 873(A) (1910) 43 SCR 434.
28 *Quinn v Leathem* [1901] AC 495 (HL) at 506.
29 *R v Henry* [2005] 3 SCR 609 at para 57.

Even in Australia, home of formalism and legalism, similar sentiments have been expressed, the High Court of Australia admonishing courts to pay due regard to its "seriously considered dicta."[30] Plainly, this approach – on one reading a "profound shift in the rules of judicial engagement"[31] – gives apex courts much more leeway to expound general principles intended to guide (or even bind) lower courts, even if these principles are not strictly necessary to the decision at hand. It does bear noting, however, that the concern of the High Court of Australia was just as much about perceived top-down reasoning by an intermediate appellate court as about its own ability to expound general principles.[32]

A particularly interesting point raised by Lee is the apparent reduction in the use of seriatim judgments in the United Kingdom. Where readers of a case once had to be careful to trace the *ratio decidendi* through several speeches delivered by judges "who are forever disagreeing, often at inordinate length,"[33] they are now guided by the UK Supreme Court's own identification of the leading, concurring, and dissenting reasons. This is no small matter – as Cane suggests, the American preference for judgments of the court, as opposed to Australian-style seriatim opinions, might reflect the respective constitutional positions of the bodies concerned – and further underscores the possibility raised by Varuhas that the UK Supreme Court's position might be shifting.

Beyond the constitutional question, one might think that setting out a majority judgment assists in setting out the law in clear terms, but there is a venerable tradition in the common law of providing concurring or dissenting reasons (although Cane cautions that reasons of history and tradition may account for divergences in this regard, certainly as between American and Australian apex court judges).[34] In a trenchant essay, Dyson Heydon, formerly of the High Court of Australia, argued in forthright terms for seriatim judgments:

30 *Farah Constructions v Say-Dee* (2007) 230 CLR 89 (HCA) at 150–1.

31 K. Mason, "President Mason's Farewell Speech" (2008) 82 *Australian Law Journal* 768 at 769.

32 See generally M. Harding and Ian Malkin, "The High Court of Australia's Obiter Dicta and Decision-Making in Lower Courts" (2012) 34 *Sydney Law Review* 239.

33 Simpson, above n 8 at 90.

34 For a useful discussion, see J. Lee, "A Defence of Concurring Speeches" [2009] *Public Law* 305.

> One course is to produce a succession of judgments containing separate assenting and dissenting opinions that expose the difficulty of a particular point and alert the profession to possible future changes in the law. The other is to produce a series of seemingly (but not actually) unanimous judgments followed by a sudden new decision that without any prior warning revolutionises the law and damages those who have acted in the expectation that the law would not change. The former course enables the profession to warn about the risks and give advice about contracts and other measures accommodating them. The latter does not. The practice of those who earlier disagreed with majorities, sullenly or otherwise, while withholding their true opinions, may lead eventually to something which was not foreseen: "an uncontrollable expostulation against a whole line of cases in which the dissenter has hitherto concealed his disagreement."[35]

Whatever one thinks of Heydon's proposal, he raises squarely the issue of judicial craft. Apex courts, by virtue of their position at the top of the judicial hierarchy in a given jurisdiction, have a super-added obligation to provide clear guidance to those below them. If an apex court provides no clarity, intermediate appellate courts, first-instance courts, lawyers, and litigants will find themselves mired in uncertainty.

Judicial craft features prominently in Bruce Ziff's and Sandy Steel's contributions to this volume. Ziff's topic is property, with a particular focus on Aboriginal title. As he explains, defining the concept of *property* requires significant juridical skill. Although common law judges

35 J.D. Heydon, "Judicial Independence: The Enemy Within" (2013) 129 *Law Quarterly Review* 205 at 211, citing L. Blom-Cooper and G. Drewry, *Final Appeal: A Study of the House of Lords in Its Judicial Capacity* (Oxford, Clarendon Press, 1972) at 84. See also Heydon at 215:

> Compromise can be misleading, because a compromise is a decision which no party to it believes to be entirely correct. The course by which judges avoid compromise and instead state, after conscientious consideration, what they believe, can be superior to expressing agreement with what they actually disbelieve. While many executive decisions do not have to be explained, all significant judicial decisions do. The powers possessed by judges are capable of causing vast harm, and reasons for judgment explain to the parties and the people how and why those powers have been used. The explanation should state the position of all judges, not just a majority. If in truth the law is unclear in the sense that judges disagree about its content, it is preferable that the truth about this disagreement be communicated, not concealed.

are not formally encumbered by the *numerus clausus* principle to the same extent as their civilian counterparts, they are keenly aware that a proliferation of property rights could easily cause significant uncertainty and – by raising transaction costs – inefficiency.[36] Accordingly, they do not create new property rights lightly. The Supreme Court of Canada found itself in a position, however, where it *had to* consider the law governing the recognition and extinction of Aboriginal title.[37] Yet, as Ziff recalls, it was derelict in its duty, failing in the 1970s – "a missed opportunity" – to lay out any clear definition of the concept, a failure that held back development of the law (and good faith negotiation between the state and First Nations) for decades. Perhaps ironically, *Calder* failed to set out any vision because the case was decided by a 3–3–1 split, a swing vote that was cast on the narrowest possible grounds.

Steel assails apex courts for their failure to articulate coherent causation principles in the law of torts. This failure is rooted, in part, in what seems to be a desire to do justice in individual cases. Examples abound, but the most notorious is the UK House of Lords' decision in *Fairchild v Glenhaven Funeral Services*,[38] of which Lord Hoffmann (then a member of the House) later said, "I think the most satisfactory outcome would have been for their Lordships in their judicial capacity to have adhered to established principle, wrung their hands about the unfairness of the outcome in the particular case, and recommended to the Government that it pass appropriate legislation."[39]

Swan and Adamski also touch on the question of judicial attitude, which may be favourable to injured parties in some circumstances, although they are careful to specify that common law judges, even on apex courts, operate under constraints imposed by the adversarial process. In general, as Steel demonstrates, responding to the felt necessities

36 See eg T.W. Merrill and H.E. Smith, "Optimal Standardization in the Law of Property: The Numerus Clausus Principle" (2000) 110 *Yale Law Journal* 1.

37 Constitution Act, 1982, Schedule B to the Canada Act 1982 (UK), 1982, c 11, s 35, although the issue of the nature of Aboriginal title had come up before: see *St Catherine's Milling and Lumber Co v The Queen* (1888) 14 AC 46 (PC) and *Calder v Attorney-General of British Columbia* [1973] SCR 313.

38 [2003] 1 AC 32 (HL).

39 "*Fairchild* and After" in A. Burrows, D. Johnston, and R. Zimmerman (eds), *Judge and Jurist: Essays in Memory of Lord Rodger of Earlsferry* (Oxford, Oxford University Press, 2013) 63 at 68.

of an individual case causes problems because (inevitably) legal principles are bent out of shape: "If some change in the law would immediately require a large number of further changes in order for the law to be in a desirable condition, ... courts should be wary of making the initial change."

Dickson, too, touches upon this theme – noting that the multi-factorial tests that characterize the jurisprudence of modern apex courts may make the application of the law in individual cases uncertain – as does Varuhas – decrying the failure of the UK Supreme Court to adequately map out the respective territories of *human rights* and *common law judicial review*, a failure that has led to a distinct lack of clarity in the law. These contributions suggest that judicial craft alone may not be enough for those who sit on apex courts, but that it must be applied with a sense of duty (informed by the importance of legal certainty) as to how an apex court judge ought to act in shaping the law.[40]

Detailed Overview of Contributions

The contributions have been divided into three sections. The first section focuses on individual apex courts, while the second and third focus on selected, substantive areas of law developed and applied by apex courts: the second on public law and the third on private law.

In the first section, Beverley McLachlin discusses apex courts and the common law in general terms but from a Canadian perspective. Moving from the particular to the general, she draws lessons from her experience as chief justice of the Supreme Court that apply more broadly. In Canada and elsewhere, "the incidence of top-down reasoning in common law courts has accelerated in recent decades," for several reasons: the adoption of constitutional codes, which require principled elaboration by the judiciary; the changing mandate of apex courts, from error correction to establishment of broad principles; and internationalization.

That common law adjudication has indeed become more principleled and reliant on broad concepts such as fairness and proportionality is confirmed by Brice Dickson's contribution. Dickson identifies two

40 See also K. Hayne, "Letting Justice Be Done without the Heavens Falling" (2001) 27 *Monash University Law Review* 12 at 17–18: "Faithful application of precedent is at the heart of the judicial task."

important trends in decision making by apex courts across the common law world: the narrowing of areas of non-justiciability and the introduction of multi-factorial tests for deciding cases. Dickson gives a cautious welcome to these trends on the basis that they bring a greater degree of transparency to common law adjudication, and, although he acknowledges that the price of transparency in this context is increased uncertainty, he suggests that it is one worth paying.

With James Lee's chapter on the UK Supreme Court, the focus shifts somewhat: Lee's interest here is in this body as an institution and how it has begun to develop its own identity. Lee is occasionally critical, highlighting, for instance, the difficulty of discerning meaningful criteria for the assignment of cases to five-, seven-, and nine-judge panels – which is often "erratic" – and questioning the Court's forays into social media as a means of publicizing its decisions – which is inconsistent and in tension with its practice of assigning cases to smaller or larger panels. The lesson is that in determining and carrying out their mandates, apex courts have to give careful consideration to issues of internal institutional structure.

Institutional considerations are central to Peter Cane's comparative analysis of the High Court of Australia and the Supreme Court of the United States, two bodies that share much because they are courts of last resort in constitutional issues, but operate very differently. In Cane's view, these significant divergences are best explained by historical and institutional factors – that is, the location of "the *foundational* (or *autonomous*) power (and obligation) to make law." In Australia, authoritative judicial interpretations have the "full force of law," whereas in the United States, "the Supreme Court's role in the constitutional design was not to make law (that was to be the job of Congress and the president), but rather to enforce the Constitution and, in so doing, maintain the constitutional balance of power between the other branches (and itself)." Several consequences follow, including the relative politicization of American judicial appointments and the relative jealousy the courts have for maintaining an interpretive monopoly on questions of law.[41]

41 Compare *Chevron USA, Inc v Natural Resources Defense Council, Inc* 467 US 837 (1984) (SCOTUS) (deference to administrative interpretations of law) with *City of Enfield v Development Assessment Committee* (2000) 199 CLR 135 (HCA) (no deference on questions of law).

Cane's contribution is followed by Carissima Mathen's chapter on the Supreme Court of Canada's reference function, in which she traces the relationship between references and common law judging. The function expressly takes the Court away from the resolution of individual cases and requires it to answer hypothetical questions in a principled manner, but, as Mathen recounts, in both reference cases and ordinary cases, the line between case-by-case decision making and decisions that set out the law in an abstract, general way has recently become blurred. Reference cases now have, it seems, as much authority as ordinary *inter partes* litigation. Indeed, some politicians and commentators have suggested that the reference role should be expanded to provide scrutiny of proposed legislation in the manner of a civilian constitutional court. For Mathen, this expanded role would be a bridge too far, but the suggestion nonetheless represents a further breakdown in the clear distinctions between common law and civilian systems.

In the second and third sections of this volume, which in turn feature public law and private law, several areas of apex court decision making are put under the spotlight.

Some readers will be surprised to learn that the reference function plays an important role in the United States – not at the federal level, where Article III of the US Constitution provides for judicial power to be exercised only in respect of "cases or controversies," but at the state level. Indeed, Williams is explicit in stating that the reference function causes state supreme courts to operate like European constitutional courts. In this, as in the other ways he describes, the function of state supreme courts diverges significantly from that of federal courts: "the two regimes of American judicial review operate separately from each other."

Again, history and tradition go a long way towards explaining how and why they do so. Their constitutional origins are different; state courts tend to be more concerned with whether powers were legitimately exercised than whether the powers actually existed; state constitutions are infinitely more malleable and have often changed significantly over time, whereas the federal Constitution is notoriously difficult to amend; more materials about the reasons that particular provisions were introduced are available to state supreme courts than to the Supreme Court of the United States, which is limited to contemporary accounts of the eighteenth-century drafting process; state constitutions often protect positive rights, which are unknown to the federal Constitution; and state constitutions "are much longer and more detailed than the more familiar American federal Constitution."

Jason Varuhas examines the resurgence of common law constitutionalism in the UK Supreme Court. Identifying first the emergence of a unique *public* law, which required, in turn, a conception of *judicial review*, Varuhas recounts how English law developed down parallel tracks in the early years of this century: on one track, the Human Rights Act, 1998; on the other, the common law of judicial review. But, recently, the tracks have begun to cross, creating, on Varuhas's telling, a jurisprudential muddle that could have been avoided had the judges spent more time mapping the terrain they had to traverse. Moreover, that proportionality now rides on the judicial review track poses a risk to the balance of power among the branches of government.

For their part, both Audrey Macklin and Han-Ru Zhou critically analyse common law constitutionalism as a constraint on administrative and legislative action, respectively, again with a view to highlighting the methodological implications of public law adjudication for the whole of the common law; Macklin focuses on the relationship between fundamental rights and the common law's historical approach to immigration, whereas Zhou examines the use by courts of last resort across the Commonwealth of principles first enunciated by Chief Justice Coke in the seventeenth century.[42] For Macklin, apex courts need to make a fresh start using fundamental rights instruments, which represent a popular or legislative desire to make a break with problematic aspects of the history and tradition of the common law. For Zhou, there is a rich seam of common law norms for apex courts to mine, and how they do so will be informed by their conception of their institutional role.

The third section of the volume concerns particular common law concepts. Leading experts on causation, restitution, good faith, and property examine how apex courts around the common law world have treated concepts that continue to provoke academic debate. The chapter on each concept is, in essence, a case study in the relationship between apex courts' institutional positions and the nature of common law adjudication. By picking apart apex court decisions on these fundamental concepts, Swan and Adamski, Hedley, Steel, and Ziff place them in a broad, international perspective and draw out more general lessons about the development of the common law by apex courts.

Swan and Adamski examine the role of good faith as an organizing principle in the law of contract. They are generally satisfied that good

42 *Dr Bonham's Case* (1610) 8 Co Rep 114 (Court of Common Pleas).

faith should play a central role and single out the Supreme Court of Canada for particular praise for its decision in *Bhasin v Hrynew*.[43] Good faith in contract law permits Swan and Adamski to illustrate the larger point that apex courts have an obligation to set out general principles to guide other members of the legal community. They point out, "Judgments, particularly at the appellate level, must … reflect how they will be used by trial judges and subsequent courts." Setting out general principles "makes the job that judges do easier and provides a basis for those who advise clients, comment on the law, or try to foresee what it might become or how it might develop."

By contrast, Hedley – through the prism of Canadian law – sees restitution as irreducible to a neat statement of principle and criticizes apex courts that have attempted to formulate a single master principle of restitution. The situations in which restitution will be appropriate "are likely to be one-off, and while, no doubt, a court will do its best to achieve a satisfactory resolution of each case, it hardly sounds as if any deep principle is likely to be involved." In the end, "the controversy over the nature and extent of unjust enrichment is not one that can be resolved simply by authoritative rulings from the highest court." Rather, the establishment of a "more rigorous framework" is more a matter for academic debate than for judicial decision.

In his contribution, Steel attacks what he sees as a series of weak judgments delivered by common law courts that have made exceptions to the general rule of *but-for* causation.[44] In his view, apex courts have been veering from case to case, either trying to do justice to unfortunate victims or trying desperately to explain how pro-individual decisions can be reconciled with previous authority. In response to this failure of judicial duty to set out clear, coherent principles in the area of causation, Steel proposes five principles that ought to guide apex courts in the future: transparency, necessity, non-arbitrariness, rationality, and competence. Exceptions to the general rule can be recognized, on Steel's approach, but in a way that is analytically rigorous.

Finally, Ziff paints an account of the Supreme Court of Canada's jurisprudence on Aboriginal title, where it has been able to make its mark on the law of property, on a broad canvas constructed of apex courts' general reluctance to recognize new property rights. The Court

43 [2014] 3 SCR 494.

44 See generally *Barnett v Chelsea & Kensington Hospital* [1969] 1 QB 428 (HC).

has classified Aboriginal title as *sui generis*, which is "theoretically problematic and prone to inducing unwarranted distinctions between common law and Aboriginal perspectives." For Ziff, "the jurisprudence is marred by an imprecise, unsubtle, and unhelpful approach when principles of Canadian property law have been engaged in the creation of a distinct set of legal principles applicable to Aboriginal rights claims." Analogies to the common law of waste and occupation have proved to be inappropriate. It is best, in Ziff's view, to recognize that the Court's efforts in this area are essentially "a mediation of competing political positions."

Conclusion

Although legal academics and scholars from related disciplines such as political science have studied individual apex courts in some detail,[45] a survey of the interrelationship between the common law and the institutional position of apex courts is novel[46] and will, I hope, become a reference point not only for lawyers but also for academics from other disciplines who are interested in judicial adjudication and the influence of institutional considerations on decision making.

45 See eg L. Blom-Cooper, G. Drewry, and B. Dickson (eds), *The Judicial House of Lords* (Oxford, Oxford University Press, 2009); S. Grossi, *The US Supreme Court and the Modern Common Law Approach* (Cambridge, Cambridge University Press, 2015); M.E.K. Hall, *The Nature of Supreme Court Power* (Cambridge, Cambridge University Press, 2013); D.E. Klein and G. Mitchell (eds), *The Psychology of Judicial Decision Making* (Oxford, Oxford University Press, 2010); J. Lee (ed), *From House of Lords to Supreme Court: Judges, Jurists and the Process of Judging* (Oxford, Hart Publishing, 2011); F. Maltzman, J.F. Spriggs II, and P.J. Wahlbeck, *Crafting Law on the Supreme Court: The Collegial Game* (Cambridge, Cambridge University Press, 2000).

46 See also B. Dickson (ed), *Judicial Activism in Common Law Supreme Courts* (Oxford, Oxford University Press, 2007).

PART I

Decision Making by Common Law Apex Courts

1 The Role of the Supreme Court of Canada in Shaping the Common Law

BEVERLEY McLACHLIN

Modern legal systems throughout the world tend to divide themselves into two classes – civilian legal systems and common law legal systems. The two systems are distinguished, it is said, by two discrete forms of legal reasoning.

Civilian systems are characterized by a written code, which sets out general legal principles. To apply these general principles to the particular fact patterns that come before them, judges rely first on *la loi* ("the code"), second on *la jurisprudence* ("the cases"), and last on *la doctrine* ("the academic commentary"). This reasoning process from principle to particular is sometimes described as "top-down" reasoning.

Common law systems initially possessed no written code of principles. The decision in a case did not flow from principle; rather, it emerged from cases previously decided by judges. Judges looked to precedents – descriptions of past cases – to decide cases. Over time, a course of cases on a particular subject might produce a principle. This process of reasoning – from particular cases to general principle – is sometimes described as "bottom-up" reasoning.

We tend to view civilian, top-down reasoning and common law, bottom-up reasoning as occupying two separate water-tight compartments. And this informs our normative notions of correct judging. We say that it is wrong for civilian judges to reason bottom up from precedents because it may lead to adulteration of the principles set out in the code. Similarly, we say it is wrong for common law judges to reason top down because, without a code, they are compelled to invent their own principles and rules, risking arbitrary decisions and inappropriate judicial law-making. Judge Richard Posner opines that the common law judge engaged in top-down reasoning "invents or adopts a theory about an area of law" and "uses it to organize, criticize, accept or reject, explain or explain away, distinguish or amplify the existing decisions to make them conform to the theory and generate an outcome in each new case as it arises that will be consistent with the theory and with the canonical cases, that is, the cases accepted as authoritative within the theory."[1]

Today, focusing on final, or *apex*, courts, I propose to offer a modest challenge to the distinction between civilian top-down reasoning and common law bottom-up reasoning, and the normative expectations the distinction produces. I will suggest that the distinction between the types of reasoning employed by civilian judges on the one hand and common law judges on the other, viewed historically, is not as absolute as we sometimes think. I will go on to suggest that the incidence of top-down reasoning in common law courts has accelerated in recent decades. I will also suggest that bottom-up reasoning figures in decision making under the Quebec Civil Code. Finally, I will ask whether, in view of this blurring, the traditional criticisms for courts that stray are still valid.

My modest thesis is this: top down and bottom up are generalizations, grounded in theory and historical reality. However, the distinction between the two types of reasoning, while relevant and useful, may lead us to oversimplify the complex process of judicial reasoning in both the common law and the civilian legal systems.

A Historical Look at Bottom-Up Reasoning in Common Law Courts

In its origins, the common law was widely viewed as absolutely bottom up.[2] Two philosophical strands supported the view that judges took the law as it was found. The first was the natural law idea that the common law was pre-existing, or "natural," and that a judge's only task was to discover the law – not to change it. As Montesquieu, the French civil lawyer and political philosopher, put it, the judge was but

1 R. Posner, "Legal Reasoning from the Top Down and from the Bottom Up: The Question of Unenumerated Constitutional Rights" (1992) 59 *University of Chicago Law Review* 433 at 433.

2 The view was widespread, but even from its beginning, the common law was never entirely hostile to principle-based reasoning. Lord Mansfield in the eighteenth century wrote that the law "does not consist of particular cases but of general principles, which are illustrated and explained by these cases" and that "the reason and spirit of cases make law; not the letter of particular precedents" (*R v Bembridge* (1783) 3 Dougl 327, 99 ER 679 (KB) at 681; and *Fisher v Prince* (1762) 3 Burr 1364, 97

the mouth of the law.[3] The second and related philosophical strand was concern – understandable in the absence of a written code – that judges not be seen to be making up the law. *Stare decisis* – the principle that courts must abide by decided cases – was understood as a safeguard against judicial arbitrariness. Thus, Blackstone's *Commentaries* state that "to keep the scale of justice even and steady, and not liable to waver with every new judge's opinion ... [the judge] is sworn to determine, not according to his own private judgment, but according to the known laws and customs of the land; not delegated to pronounce a new law, but to maintain and expound the old one."[4]

Notwithstanding the common law's early insistence that the law was not a matter of applying principles but something to be discovered by the judge, by the early part of the twentieth century it was evident that common law judges of apex courts were prepared, where necessary, to alter the law by top-down reasoning. Let me offer a few examples.

My first example is the 1930 decision of the Judicial Committee of the Privy Council in *Edwards v A.G. Canada* – the famous *Persons Case*.[5] At the time, English common law provided that women were not "persons" for purposes of holding public office. The Supreme Court of Canada – which was not yet Canada's apex court – dutifully applied the English precedents. But the Judicial Committee in England held that the changing position of women in society necessitated a change in the law – the constitution, Viscount Sankey famously pronounced, was "a living tree capable of growth within its natural limits." The time had come to grow a new branch – the right of women to hold public office. The judges were prepared to accept changing social circumstances as a legitimate reason for refusing to accept the law as they found it, and to change it.[6]

ER 876). More recently, Lord Scarman noted that "[t]he mark of the great judge from Coke through Mansfield to our day has been the capacity and the will to search out principle, to discard the detail appropriate (perhaps) to earlier times, and to apply principle in such a way as to satisfy the needs of their own time" (*Gillick v West Norfolk and Wisbech Health Authority* [1986] 1 AC 112 (HL) at 183).

3 Montesquieu, *De l'esprit des lois* (Paris, Éditions Garnier Frères, 1961).

4 Sir W. Blackstone, *Commentaries on the Laws of England*, Book One, 4th edn (Oxford, Clarendon Press, 1770) at 69, cited in *R v Salituro* [1991] 3 SCR 654 at 665.

5 *Edwards v AG Canada* [1930] AC 123.

6 For a competing view, see B.W. Miller, "Origin Myth: The Persons Case, the Living Tree, and the New Originalism" in G. Huscroft and B.W. Miller (eds), *The Challenge of Originalism: Theories of Constitutional Interpretation* (New York, Cambridge University Press, 2011) at 120.

My second example is *Donoghue v Stevenson*[7] – the famous snail-in-the-bottle-of-ginger-beer case – where the House of Lords in 1932 sought to clear up the clutter of actions on the case by introducing a general negligence principle to, in the immortal words of Lord Atkin, "take reasonable care to avoid acts or omissions which you can reasonably foresee would be likely to injure your neighbour."[8] This decision marked a turning point in the law of torts, expanding the scope of negligence liability so that the tort of negligence would no longer depend on the existence of precedents and be confined to situations where a duty of care had already been held to exist. The justification for this abandonment of bottom-up reasoning, once again, was the need to keep with the times. Lord Atkin explained, "I do not think so ill of our jurisprudence as to suppose that its principles are so remote from the ordinary needs of civilized society and the ordinary claims it makes upon its members as to deny a legal remedy where there is so obviously a social wrong."[9]

The same concern to "clean up the clutter" and bring the law up to date drove changes to the law of hearsay later in the century – my third example. Historically, the hearsay rule was understood as an absolute prohibition with limited exceptions. In *Ares v Venner*,[10] the Supreme Court of Canada held that old categories were no longer exclusive and that hearsay evidence that did not fall within one of the traditional exceptions could be received. The Court created a new exception for hospital records in light of changes in the business environment that could not have been foreseen at the time the hearsay rule was developed. Not only that, the rules of evidence were unfairly restricting litigants' right to bring relevant and helpful evidence before a court, and this undermined the courts' mandate to find the truth and do justice.

The Supreme Court's 1982 decision on the accomplice-warning rule in *Vetrovec v The Queen*[11] offers another example of top-down reasoning. Noting that the law was unnecessarily complex and technical, and that an accomplice's evidence was not automatically untrustworthy, the court departed from established precedent and changed the law. To do otherwise, it observed, would amount to "blind and empty formalism."[12]

7 *Donoghue v Stevenson* [1932] AC 562.
8 Ibid at 580.
9 Ibid at 583.
10 *Ares v Venner* [1970] SCR 608.
11 *Vetrovec v The Queen* [1982] 1 SCR 811.
12 Ibid at 823.

Finally, I cannot conclude my list of examples without mentioning the evolution of the concept of the law on the equitable remedies of restitution and unjust enrichment in the common law world. Concerned about unfair treatment of common law spouses and the untidy and unpredictable state of the law, courts gradually transformed a set of unstructured, fact-specific categories into a single set of uniform and coherent rules.[13]

These are but a few examples of common law apex courts changing the law on the basis of overarching considerations. The judges involved did not always fully acknowledge this departure from traditional common law dogma. Viscount Sankey did not enunciate the principle of gender equality, to be sure. Yet the neighbour test for liability for negligently caused injury is, by any other name, a general principle, as was the necessity-reliability principle for the admission of hearsay evidence.

By 1991, we had reached the point where the Supreme Court of Canada could openly acknowledge the legitimacy of judicial changes to the law. In *R. v Salituro*, Justice Iacobucci stated what was implicit in a host of prior cases – "[j]udges can and should adapt the common law to reflect the changing social, moral and economic fabric of the country."[14] And, one may add, to bring coherence to the legal system.

In summary, common law judges of apex courts in the first three-quarters of the twentieth century were prepared to depart from precedent and apply top-down, principle-based reasoning for either or both of two reasons: the need to adapt the law to changed social conditions and the need to bring coherence to the legal system. In more recent decades, three other factors accelerated the frequency and openness of top-down reasoning in common law apex courts – the adoption of constitutional codes and bills of rights, heightened mandates for apex courts, and internationalization of the law.

Three Recent Factors that Support Top-Down Reasoning

Adoption of Constitutional Codes

The latter part of the twentieth century saw the introduction of constitutional or quasi-constitutional codes into common law systems – to name two, the Canadian Charter of Rights and Freedoms and the UK

13 *Peel (Regional Municipality) v Canada; Peel (Regional Municipality) v Ontario* [1992] 3 SCR 762 at 784.

14 *R v Salituro* [1991] 3 SCR 654 at 670.

Human Rights Act 1998. Like all legal codes, these instruments employ a civilian method – they lay out general principles and ask judges to apply them in particular cases. This insertion of civilian methodology into common law systems has directly and indirectly moved apex courts towards top-down reasoning.

It has directly pushed courts in this direction by requiring them to engage in top-down reasoning from principle. The rights are set out as a series of principles, cast in the broad language associated with civil codes. Apex courts are required to refine and define these principles and, in the case of the Canadian Charter, to determine whether breaches are justified having regard to another broad principle – the principle of proportionality.

The insertion of civilian codes like the Charter into common law systems has indirectly pushed courts to carry out top-down thinking, not only with respect to the documents themselves but also in private areas of the law where reasoning up from precedent was once the only option. As discussed earlier, courts had concluded pre-Charter that it was their role to change the law in keeping with evolving social values. Then the Charter – the ultimate statement of social values – came along. It followed that the common law should be altered where necessary to conform to the Charter.

This is what happened in *WIC Radio Ltd. v Simpson*,[15] a defamation case solidly anchored in common law waters. Viewing the common law problem through the Charter lens, the Court weighed the competing values of freedom of expression and the worth and dignity of individuals, whose reputation may be their most valued asset, and reconciled them by modifying the defence of fair comment in the tort of defamation.

More broadly, the very nature of constitutional cases may influence the legal method of reasoning adopted by apex courts. The Supreme Court recently ruled in *Canada v Bedford*[16] that the common law principle of *stare decisis* is subordinate to the Constitution and cannot require a court to uphold a law that is unconstitutional. In plain words, an apex court may depart from constitutional precedent if this is necessary to keep pace with changing societal norms and values. Professor Hogg argues that this is justified since "[i]n non-constitutional cases, there

---

15 *WIC Radio Ltd v Simpson* 2008 SCC 40, [2008] 2 SCR 420.

16 *Canada (Attorney General) v Bedford* 2013 SCC 72, [2013] 3 SCR 1101.

is always a legislative remedy if the doctrine developed by the courts proves undesirable: the unwanted doctrine can simply be changed by the competent legislative body. That is not true of constitutional doctrine, which after its establishment by the Court can be altered only by the difficult process of constitutional amendment."[17]

The Mandate of Modern Apex Courts

A second factor that has amplified resort to top-down reasoning in common law courts is linked to the emerging mandate of these courts not only to resolve disputes but also to settle issues of legal principle. This is certainly true for the Supreme Court of Canada, which is instructed by s. 40(1) of the Supreme Court Act to decide questions of "public importance."[18]

This was not always the case. Before 1949, when appeals to the Judicial Committee of the Privy Council were abolished, the focus of the Court in most cases was the correction of error. In the decades following the abolition of appeals to London, the focus shifted more and more to settling the principles that guided the law. In 1981, Chief Justice Laskin pronounced that a seminal duty of the Supreme Court was "to settle the law on public or national issues for the whole of Canada."[19] The adoption of the Charter a year later completed the transformation of the mandate of the Supreme Court from a court concerned primarily with correcting errors to a court concerned primarily with settling principles of law: principle-based reasoning, from the top down.

Internationalization

The third development that has given impetus to top-down, principle-based reasoning in common law courts is the *internationalization* of law. In this brave, new global world, there is no escaping the influence of law from other jurisdictions, be they national or international. This influence takes a number of forms.

17 P.W. Hogg, *Constitutional Law of Canada*, student edn (Scarborough, Carswell, 2015) at 8-25 and 8-26.

18 Supreme Court Act, RSC 1985, c S-26, s 40(1).

19 "Address to the Empire Club of Toronto, 1981," quoted in H. Brown, *Supreme Court of Canada Practice 2015* (Toronto, Carswell, 2014) at 19.

First, courts interpret statutes and Charter guarantees in accordance with international norms that Canada has adopted. Recently, in *Appulonappa*, the Supreme Court stated that "[a]s a matter of statutory interpretation, legislation is presumed to comply with Canada's international obligations, and courts should avoid interpretations that would violate those obligations. Courts must also interpret legislation in a way that reflects the values and principles of customary and conventional international law."[20] And time and time again, the Supreme Court has relied on Canada's international human rights obligations to interpret and define the principles and values underlying the Charter.[21]

At a macro level, second, apex courts may make decisions that foster the inclusion of international principles in domestic law. The 1977 decision of the English Court of Appeal in *Trendtex Trading*,[22] where the court changed the common law rules of sovereign immunity to reflect the development of restrictive immunity in customary international law, provides an example. The issue was whether international law became part of English law by "transformation," which required recognition by the House of Lords, or "incorporation," under which the rules of international law were automatically considered to be part of English law unless they came into conflict with an Act of Parliament. Lord Denning, never one to shy away from principle, held that the doctrine of incorporation should prevail so that domestic law would change in sync with international law.

Third, the Canadian Supreme Court has not infrequently altered domestic law to harmonize it with the law of other relevant jurisdictions. In *Bow Valley*, it lifted the bar on contributory negligence in Canadian maritime law to align Canadian law with that of jurisdictions like the United States, Australia, and England.[23] Recently, in *Bhasin v Hrynew*,[24] the Court recognized that good faith contractual performance was a general organizing principle of the common law of contracts. This principle entailed a common law duty to act honestly in the performance of contractual obligations. The Court noted that acknowledging

---

20 *R v Appulonappa* 2015 SCC 59, [2015] 3 SCR 754 at para 40.

21 See eg *R v Keegstra* [1990] 3 SCR 697; *Baker v Canada (Minister of Citizenship and Immigration)* [1999] 2 SCR 817.

22 *Trendtex Trading Corporation v Central Bank of Nigeria* [1977] 2 WLR 356.

23 *Bow Valley Husky v Saint John Shipbuilding* [1997] 3 SCR 1210 at 1265–6.

24 *Bhasin v Hrynew* 2014 SCC 11, [2014] 3 SCR 494.

this change was just, that it accorded with the reasonable expectations of commercial parties, and that the new duty was sufficiently precise to enhance commercial certainty. Tellingly, the pre-existing approach that was the subject of the change was found to be "out of step with the civil law of Quebec and most jurisdictions in the United States."[25]

Bhasin illustrates a form of domestic internationalization. Quebec civil law may influence the common law of other provinces and vice versa. This brings me to my final observation on top-down and bottom-up legal reasoning.

Bottom-Up Reasoning in Civil Law

Because *la jurisprudence* ("the cases") is one of the sources of the civil law, alongside *la loi* ("the code") and *la doctrine* ("the academic commentary"), it should come as no surprise that a form of reasoning akin to common law bottom-up reasoning is alive and well in the civil law.

In his book on legal epistemology, Christian Atias proposes a thought experiment that shows just how essential precedents are to civil law judging.[26] Imagine that a legislature adopted a law that forbade judges from mentioning precedents in their judgments. Would their decisions be as convincing? What would the consequences of such a measure be on legal knowledge? How could judges tasked with applying general principles of civil law like *bonne foi* and *abus de droit* solve cases effectively? Inevitably, the broad principles that form the basis of the civil law system are inextricably bound with the cases and corresponding fact patterns that help ascertain their meaning. In short, principles and precedents are symbionts.

But the similarities with common law methodology go further than acknowledging that cases play a central part in judicial reasoning. Codes like the Civil Code of Québec and the Code Napoléon are institutions built to last, and society does not stay still. Like the common law judge, the civil law judge is sometimes required to keep the law in step with the evolution of society.[27]

Two cases from the Supreme Court illustrate how civil law principles can be altered on the basis of an evolution of society.

25 Ibid at para 32.
26 C. Atias, *Épistémologie juridique*, 1st edn (Paris, Dalloz, 2002) at 124.
27 J. Carbonnier, *Droit civil: Introduction*, 25th edn (Paris, PUF, 1997) at 31.

The first is *Houle v Banque canadienne nationale*,[28] the seminal Quebec civil law case on abuse of a contractual right. The case, decided in 1990, involved a bank liquidating a company's assets only three hours after demanding payment of the company's loan. The bank was aware at the time of the shareholders' negotiations to sell their shares, and the bank's prompt liquidation of assets had resulted in the shares being sold at a reduced price. Before this case was decided, a stringent test of malice and absence of good faith had been used to establish liability resulting from an abuse of contractual rights. The Supreme Court ruled that a less stringent standard should be used. What mattered was whether the contractual right of the bank had been exercised reasonably and whether the bank had adopted the "conduct of the prudent and reasonable individual."[29] The basis for this change to principle was a need for evolution long expressed in Quebec doctrine and jurisprudence.

A second, more recent example of judicial modification of civil law principles by a form of bottom-up reasoning is *St. Lawrence Cement Inc. v Barrette*.[30] People living near a cement plant sued for dust and noise pollution. The Civil Code, at Article 976, provided that neighbours were required to "suffer the normal neighbourhood annoyances that are not beyond the limit of tolerance they owe each other." This was argued to attract a fault-based regime – had the polluter gone further than the normal limit of tolerance? However, relying on case law and commentaries from before and after the enactment of the Civil Code, the Court opted for a no-fault scheme, ruling that liability would be based on the extent of the annoyances suffered by the victim rather than on whether the conduct of the person who allegedly caused them exceeded the limits of tolerance. The Court noted that resorting to no-fault liability in the context of neighbourhood disturbances was "also consistent with the approaches taken in Canadian common law and in French civil law, and with general policy considerations."[31]

These cases suggest that bottom-up, case-based reasoning is important under the Civil Code. Principles are prime. But placing particular fact patterns within a principle may change that principle for the future.[32]

---

28 *Houle v Canadian National Bank* [1990] 3 SCR 122.

29 Ibid at 155.

30 *St Lawrence Cement Inc v Barrette* 2008 SCC 64, [2008] 3 SCR 392.

31 Ibid at para 75.

32 F. Ost and M. van de Kerchove, "L'interprétation du droit" in *Jalons pour une théorie critique du droit*, fourth part (Bruxelles, Publications des Facultés universitaires Saint-Louis, 1987).

Conclusion

Both bottom-up and top-down judicial reasoning are acceptable techniques that depend on the nature of a case. While common law reasoning retains its primary focus on precedent and the past, top-down reasoning from principle is becoming more and more common in common law courts on common law issues. In a parallel movement in the opposite direction, while top-down reasoning still dominates the civil law, cases and precedents are used more and more often to calibrate the just result and bring certainty and harmony to the law, not only as it is written but also as it is applied in practice.

Faced with this methodological cross-fertilization, what is a judge to do? Karl Llewellyn offered this advice to common law judges in his treatise, *The Common Law Tradition*: "(1) a court ought always to be slow in *uncharted* territory, and, in such territory, ought to be narrow, again and again, in any ground for decision. [...] (2) [...] *once there is clearish light*, a court should make effort to state an ever broader line for guidance. And (3) so long as each such line is promptly and overtly checked up and checked on and at need rephrased on each subsequent occasion of new illumination, such informed questing after broader lines is of the essence of good appellate judging."[33]

The same precepts, modified to fit, may guide a civilian judge. Move slowly in altering doctrine on settled principle. Once there is a clearish light, structure lines of guidance to delineate the departure. Finally, keep checking and adjusting to ensure that the rule is working well.

Whether at common law or civil law, measured development of the law is the watchword. Neither precedent nor doctrine should easily undermine the courts' mandate to find the truth and do justice.[34] At the same time, they must not be jettisoned. Courts must "strike an appropriate balance between predictability in the law and justice in the individual case,"[35] "choose a middle course between the extremes of inflexible rules and case by case 'palm tree' justice."[36] Whether we reason from the bottom up or the top down, measured justice that works in the real world should be the goal.

33 K.N. Llewellyn, *The Common Law Tradition: Deciding Appeals* (Boston, Little, Brown, 1960) at 389.

34 *R v Seaboyer* [1991] 2 SCR 577 at 622.

35 *Peel (Regional Municipality) v Canada; Peel (Regional Municipality) v Ontario* [1992] 3 SCR 762 at 802.

36 Ibid.

2 Apex Courts and the Development of the Common Law

BRICE DICKSON

One of the distinguishing features of common law courts – especially apex courts – is that they make new law. Unlike courts in civil law countries, where judicial law-making is not meant to happen and is at times expressly forbidden or accorded merely a complementary role,[1] common law courts can create new causes of action, award new remedies, develop new legal principles, and lay down authoritative interpretations of legislation. The myth that, in common law countries, judges do not create law, but merely discover it, has been well and truly debunked.[2] More particularly, in recent years, there has been a particularly noticeable rise in the idea of common law constitutionalism, which holds that common law courts should strive to uphold certain constitutional values, such as the rule of law, the principle of legality, and fundamental human rights. Even in a country such as the United Kingdom, where the highest principle of the unwritten constitution is that Parliament is absolutely sovereign, there have been intimations from some senior judges that, in the appropriate circumstances, courts might set aside

1 Eg Art 5 of the *Code civil* in France: "Il est défendu aux juges de prononcer par voie de disposition générale et réglementaire sur les causes qui leur sont soumises" and Art 1(6) of the Spanish *Codigo civil*: "La jurisprudencia complementará el ordenamiento jurídico con la doctrina que, de modo reiterado, establezca el Tribunal Supremo al interpretar y aplicar la ley, la costumbre y los principios generales del derecho."

2 Lord Reid, "The Judge as Lawmaker" (1972) *Journal of Public Teachers of Law* 22; Lord Mackay, "Can Judges Change the Law?" (1987) 73 *Proceedings of the British Academy* 285; A. Mason, "The Judge as Law-Maker" (1996) 3 *James Cook University Law Review* 1.

a provision in an Act of Parliament if it is in violation of one of those constitutional values.[3]

In tandem with this development in the field of public law, it is arguable that we are witnessing a florescence of the common law in the field of private law. More particularly, in contract and tort law there seems to have been a move towards a more values-based approach.[4] There is also evidence, certainly in England, that in private law the courts are more willing to rely upon comparisons with other common law countries rather than be influenced by the principles of the European Court of Human Rights (ECtHR) or even the Court of Justice of the European Union.[5]

Of course, contract and tort law are fields that have traditionally been relatively free from legislative interference, thereby leaving more scope for judicial creativity. They are also areas where the inventiveness of the common law has been apparent not just for decades but for centuries. Nevertheless, one of the features of contract and tort law in today's world is that judges in common law courts are emphasizing much more frequently the aims of the law and the values that underpin it. They often do this by resorting to adjudicative principles that are open-textured in nature. These principles set the framework of analysis by specifying, for example, that the preferred solution to a problem should be "fair," "reasonable," "proportionate," or "just," but they leave the practical outworking of the principles to the discretion of individual judges.

The thesis of this short chapter is that such an approach, while every bit as worthy as that adopted in public law, is in both settings a double-edged sword. On the one hand, it enhances the credibility of the law and provides judges with a strategic approach to guide their thinking around particular facts; on the other hand, it leaves significant areas of the law in a state of some uncertainty: individuals and their legal advisers cannot always predict what a court might say about their past or proposed course of action.

---

3 Eg in *R (Jackson) v Attorney General* [2005] UKHL 56, [2006] 1 AC 262 at para 102 per Lord Steyn, paras 104–8 per Lord Hope, and para 159 per Lady Hale. See too Lord Neuberger, "The Supreme Court and the Rule of Law," the Conkerton Lecture, 9 October 2014 at para 9, www.supremecourt.uk/docs/speech-141009-lord-neuberger.pdf.

4 I would submit that there is evidence of the trend in property and family law too, but lack of space prohibits development of that point here.

5 P. Giliker, "The Influence of EU and European Human Rights Law on English Private Law" (2015) 64 *International and Comparative Law Quarterly* 237.

In the next section, I will attempt to provide evidence for two central propositions. First, common law courts are becoming more interventionist in the sense that they are ever more reluctant to decline to adjudicate upon matters that they would previously have shunned. Second, in making their adjudications, common law courts are more readily resorting to principles that require judges to weigh up a multiplicity of factors before deciding how best to resolve a dispute in legal terms: the weighing of factors is appealing to the average observer and enhances the impression that there is a consistency to the law.

In the subsequent section, I will suggest that there is a welcome dimension to these two trends in that they entail judges engaging more reflectively in their role: they have to justify their decisions in a more structured manner, thereby satisfying the public that the legal system is coherent and comprehensible. But I will then highlight a downside to the trends in that they result in a lack of clarity as to what weight will be given to the different factors in particular contexts and what, therefore, will ultimately swing a court in favour of one side to the dispute rather than the other. This makes life difficult for all individuals and organizations, whether public or private. In advance of undertaking a course of action, they are unlikely to be able to predict where the line will ultimately be drawn between conduct that is legal and conduct that is not.

The First Trend: The Preference for Justiciability

In illustrating this first trend, the chapter can only scratch the surface of what is a large topic. My choice of cases inevitably suffers from selection bias, but I will refer to three areas in which I believe the trend to be discernible. Counter-examples could have been cited, but I maintain that the prevailing direction of travel is firmly in line with my hypothesis. After considering the tendency to promote constitutional values, specifically the protection of fundamental rights, I touch upon cases raising political issues and cases dealing with novel causes of action. It could be argued that what we are witnessing in these three areas is nothing new: that courts in common law countries have always had to move with the times because new social movements and technologies always lead to novel claims. But even if this is correct, it still seems clear that today's common law courts are more willing than ever to engage openly with such matters and, as a result, play a notable role in driving forward a values-based legal system.

Constitutional Values and Human Rights

If we take *justiciability* as referring not just to whether a particular set of questions is even appropriate for judicial involvement in the first place but also to whether courts take the opportunity to develop the law when the legislators are not doing so, it is abundantly clear that top judges in common law countries have been spreading their wings for decades. In common law countries with written constitutions, it is not at all unusual for judges to emphasize particular words in those documents to promote certain values that they consider to be fundamental to their interpretative role. The US Supreme Court has dwelt on the reference to "due process of law" in the Fifth and Fourteenth Amendments to the Constitution and has thereby developed a huge jurisprudence on what is required for a fair trial in both civil and criminal cases.[6] The Supreme Court of Canada has made great use of a comparable provision in the Canadian Charter of Rights and Freedoms, where the phrase "principles of fundamental justice" is substituted for "due process of law,"[7] and the same Court has laid out a set of principles that it says have characterized the evolution of the country's Constitution – namely, "adherence to the rule of law, respect for democratic institutions, the accommodation of minorities, insistence that governments adhere to constitutional conduct and a desire for continuity and stability."[8] The Supreme Court of Ireland has focused on Article 40.3.1° of the country's Constitution to develop a series of "unenumerated" constitutional rights.[9]

The Supreme Court of India, in *Kesavananda Bharati v State of Kerala*,[10] likewise identified the "basic structures" of India's 1950 Constitution,

6 Those two amendments refer to, among other things, the duty of the United States (Amendment 5) and of any one of those states (Amendment 14) not to "deprive any person of life, liberty, or property, without due process of law." See eg R. Williams, "The One and Only Substantive Due Process Clause" (2010–11) 120 *Yale Law Journal* 408.

7 Constitution Act 1982, s 7, which reads, "Everyone has the right to life, liberty and security of the person and the right not to be deprived thereof except in accordance with the principles of fundamental justice." See eg Ian Greene, *The Charter of Rights and Freedoms* (Toronto, James Lorimer, 2014) esp. ch 5.

8 *Reference re Secession of Quebec* [1998] 2 SCR 217 at para 48. See too the text at n 34 ff below.

9 Article 40.3.1° reads, "The state guarantees in its laws to respect, and, as far as practicable, by its laws to defend and vindicate the personal rights of the citizen." See G. Hogan, G. Whyte, D. Kenny, and R. Walsh, *Kelly: The Irish Constitution*, 5th ed. (Dublin: Bloomsbury Professional, 2018) at 1645–788.

10 *Kesavananda Bharati v State of Kerala* AIR 1973 SC 1461.

which, it ruled, could not be altered by any constitutional amendment. Among the basic features listed by Chief Justice Sikri were the country's republican and democratic form of government, secularism, and the separation of powers doctrine, while other judges added, for example, the dignity of the individual secured by the various rights and freedoms mentioned in Part III of the Constitution, the duty to build a welfare state (as indicated by Part IV – Directive Principles of State Policy), and egalitarianism.[11] In a later case, *IR Coelho v State of Tamil Nadu*,[12] the Supreme Court reinforced this position by ruling that even when Parliament had agreed to include certain provisions in the Ninth Schedule to the Constitution,[13] thereby supposedly immunizing them from judicial review, the courts could still assess whether those provisions deserved to be so included, given the basic structures of the Constitution.[14] In a separate stream of case law, the Supreme Court of India has constructed a large set of unenumerated rights on the basis of the protection given to the right to life by Article 21 of the Constitution.[15]

The outlier in this sphere is the High Court of Australia, which has no obvious hook within the country's 1900 Constitution on which to hang a set of principles protective of human rights or some other values. Yet Australia is a liberal democracy, with national and state parliaments that have passed numerous laws to safeguard human rights. In their interpretation of that legislation, the courts have shown themselves willing to build upon principles deriving from democracy, tolerance,

11 See generally O.C. Reddy. *The Court and the Constitution of India: Summits and Shallows* (Oxford, Oxford University Press, 2008) ch 7.

12 AIR 2007 SC 861.

13 There are currently 284 such provisions, mostly concerning land reform.

14 This is in spite of the explicit wording of Art 31B of the Constitution, which was the first amendment made to the Constitution in 1951, that "none of the Acts and Regulations specified in the Ninth Schedule nor any of the provisions thereof shall be deemed to be void, or ever to have become void, on the ground that such Act, Regulation or provision is inconsistent with, or takes away or abridges any of the rights conferred by, any provisions of this Part [of the Constitution]."

15 Art 21 reads, "No person shall be deprived of his life or personal liberty except according to procedure established by law." For a critique of so-called public interest litigation in India, see V. Iyer, "The Supreme Court of India" in B. Dickson (ed), *Judicial Activism in Common Law Supreme Courts* (Oxford, Oxford University Press, 2007) at 141–54.

and fairness.[16] There is, as a result, a thriving common law of human rights in Australia (although there is room for improvement, as there is elsewhere). As Williams and Hume put it, "Human rights do not jump off Chapter III's pages: they are often protected in round-about ways and appear only after reading the many thousands of pages of the Commonwealth Law Reports in which the High Court has considered Chapter III."[17]

New Zealand, unlike its larger neighbour, does not have a written constitution, but it does have a reasonably comprehensive piece of legislation on human rights, the New Zealand Bill of Rights Act 1990.[18] This seeks to incorporate the United Nations' International Covenant on Civil and Political Rights into domestic law. However, while one section of the Act requires courts to give a meaning to enactments that is consistent with the Bill of Rights (if there is any doubt about the meaning),[19] another section forbids courts from treating any provision in an enactment passed before or after the Bill of Rights as in any way invalidated by its inconsistency with that bill.[20] Moreover, the 1990 Act does not make any remedies available for violations of the rights it guarantees.

Some commentators believe that New Zealand's courts, including the relatively new Supreme Court, established in 2004, have been reasonably activist in applying the Bill of Rights.[21] But, although judges were

16 For details, see G. Williams and D. Hume, *Human Rights under the Australian Constitution,* 2nd edn (Oxford, Oxford University Press, 2013); also H. Patapan, *Judging Democracy: The New Politics of the High Court of Australia* (Cambridge, Cambridge University Press, 2000) ch 3.

17 Williams and Hume, *Human Rights under the Australian Constitution* at 325. Ch III of the Constitution deals with "The Judicature."

18 See A. Butler and P. Butler, *The New Zealand Bill of Rights Act: A Commentary,* 2nd edn (Toronto, Lexis Nexis, 2015).

19 New Zealand Bill of Rights Act 1990 at s 6.

20 Ibid at s 4.

21 P. Butler, "15 years of the NZ Bill of Rights: Time to Celebrate, Time to Reflect, Time to Work Harder?" (2006) 4 *Human Rights Research Journal* 1 at 6–20; also Butler and Butler, above n 18. For a contrary view, see eg J. Allen, "Turning Clark Kent into Superman: The New Zealand Bill of Rights Act 1990" (2000) 9 *Otago Law Review* 613. A more recent evaluation concludes that the Act has not had a "transformative effect": C. Geiringer, "Mr Bulwark and the Protection of Human Rights" (2014) 45 *Victoria University of Wellington Law Review* 367 at 385. See too Sir Geoffrey Palmer's views in an address given to the New Zealand Bar Association, 15 September 2015, www.lawsociety.org.nz/lawtalk/lawtalk-archives/issue-873/make-bill-of-rights-supreme-law.

prepared to give "indications" that a piece of legislation was inconsistent with the Bill of Rights, it was not until 2015 that any court in New Zealand formally declared such inconsistency,[22] and in *Chapman* the Supreme Court recently denied compensation to a man who had not been accorded a proper right of appeal against what turned out to be a wrongful conviction for sex offences.[23] On the other hand, in that case New Zealand's judges did at least accept that it was within their power to award damages for a violation of rights and (as in Australia) they have elsewhere hinted that, in the right circumstances, they too, like British judges, might be willing to declare that an Act of Parliament cannot be enforced to the extent that it violates particularly fundamental rights.[24]

In the United Kingdom, judicial statements concerning the underlying tenets of the unwritten constitution have abounded since the late 1990s, both in decisions by the top courts and in extrajudicial pronouncements.[25] They have occurred in several cases connected with the devolution of powers to the three regional legislatures in Scotland, Wales, and Northern Ireland.[26] They have also featured prominently in numerous court decisions on the reach of the Human Rights Act 1998, which, to all intents and purposes, incorporates most of the rights set

---

22 *Taylor v Attorney-General* [2015] NZHC 1706: Heath J held that a blanket ban on prisoners voting in parliamentary elections, contained in s 80(1)(d) of the Electoral Act 1993, as amended in 2010, was inconsistent with the Bill of Rights. In 2017, the Court of Appeal dismissed an appeal against this decision: [2017] NZCA 215.

23 *Attorney-General v Chapman* [2011] NZSC 110, [2012] 1 NZLR 462.

24 M. Kirby, "Deep Lying Rights: A Constitutional Convention Continues" (2005) 3 *New Zealand Journal of Public and International Law* 195, where he agrees with the former president of the New Zealand Court of Appeal, Robin (later Lord) Cooke, that the common law should be able to trump Parliament in certain situations.

25 For a sample of the latter, see these lectures by Lord Neuberger, the president of the UK Supreme Court: "The Constitutional Role of the Supreme Court in the Context of Devolution in the UK" (14 October 2016); "Magna Carta: The Bible of the English Constitution or a Disgrace to the English Nation?" (18 June 2015); "'Judge Not, That Ye Be Not Judged': Judging Judicial Decision-Making" (29 January 2015); "The UK Constitutional Settlement and the Role of the UK Supreme Court" (10 October 2014). All are available at https://www.supremecourt.uk/news/speeches.html.

26 Eg *AXA General Insurance Ltd v Lord Advocate* [2011] UKSC 46, [2012] 1 AC 868; *In re Agricultural Sector (Wales) Bill* [2014] UKSC 43, [2014] 1 WLR 2622; *Robinson v Secretary of State for Northern Ireland* [2002] UKHL 32, [2002] NI 390.

out in the European Convention on Human Rights (ECHR) into the domestic law of all parts of the United Kingdom.[27] Recently, they were to the fore in what was possibly the most highly publicized case ever heard by the country's highest court, the *Miller* case,[28] which turned on whether Brexit could be triggered by the national government or only by legislation passed by the national Parliament – by eight to three, the Supreme Court justices favoured the latter position.

Political Issues

In the first half of the twentieth century, there was a predominant conservatism within common law supreme courts. In the third quarter, a degree of liberalism reared its head, perhaps symbolized most eloquently in the decision of the US Supreme Court in *Brown v Board of Education*,[29] where the Court unanimously struck down the practice of educating young people along racially segregated lines. In the last quarter of the century, liberalism became the norm. More particularly, judges became more willing to adjudicate upon matters that would previously have been deemed too political for them to handle. Obviously, the extent of such judicial involvement may be dictated by what the country's Constitution or legislation says about the role of the courts, but in cases where there is no such clear guidance, judges in common law countries now seem willing to contribute their tuppence worth, even if this extends only to laying down some general principles, while leaving the ultimate solution to politicians.

In the United States, the Supreme Court had previously adhered to the *political question doctrine*, whereby, in politically sensitive cases, even if technically it did have jurisdiction, it would tend to decline it in favour of a solution hammered out by politicians. This position was softened in *Baker v Carr*,[30] when the Court intervened to ensure greater equality among the number of representatives elected by voting districts

27 *A v Secretary of State for the Home Dept* [2004] UKHL 56, [2005] 2 AC 68; *Smith v Ministry of Defence* [2013] UKSC 41, [2014] AC 52; *Beghal v DPP* [2015] UKSC 49, [2016] 1 AC 88; *Belhaj v Straw* [2017] UKSC 3, [2017] AC 964.

28 *R (Miller) v Secretary of State for Exiting the European Union* [2017] UKSC 5, [2018] AC 61.

29 347 US 483 (1954).

30 369 US 186 (1962).

in Tennessee, but it was maintained in the 1980s, when unsuccessful attempts were made to ask the Supreme Court to hear cases alleging that the war in Vietnam or US military involvement in El Salvador was unconstitutional.

Then came the seminal decision in *Bush v Gore*,[31] where the Supreme Court played a determinative role in deciding the outcome of the presidential election of November 2000. Four of the justices held that the issue in that case was one that the Supreme Court should *not* deal with: they thought it should be left to Congress or to the state of Florida (where the outcome of the vote depended on whether certain ballot papers should be considered valid).[32] But the other five justices were content not just to deal with the issue but also to decide it by ruling that no further recounting of the votes cast in Florida should take place, thereby handing victory in the election to the Republican candidate, George W. Bush. The case calls into question the continued existence of the political question doctrine and is strong evidence that, in the United States, top judges are now prepared to rush in where their predecessors feared to tread.[33]

In Canada, the last decades of the twentieth century were marked by the repatriation of the Constitution and the enactment of the Canadian Charter of Rights and Freedoms in 1982. One of the issues taken to the Supreme Court in the early life of the Charter was *Operation Dismantle v The Queen*,[34] where the judges were asked to rule that, in allowing the US government to test cruise missiles over Canadian territory, the Canadian government was violating the right to life, liberty, and security of people in Canada.[35] Here the Court ruled that the issue was justiciable but that there was no breach of the Charter. Wilson J said that it would not be appropriate for the courts to "second guess" the government on matters of defence but that the courts had a duty to respond if asked to decide whether any particular act of the government violated the rights of citizens.[36] Webber puts this well when he writes, "The Court will not

---

31 531 US 98 (2000).

32 Justices Breyer, Ginsburg, Souter, and Stevens.

33 See the collection of opinions collated in E.J. Dionne and W. Kristol (eds), *Gore v Bush: The Court Cases and the Commentary* (Washington, DC, Brookings Institution Press, 2001).

34 [1985] 1 SCR 441.

35 Protected by s 7 of the Canadian Charter of Rights and Freedoms: see above n 7.

36 Above n 34 at para 64.

shy away from a genuine question of law simply because that question is politically charged."[37]

The role of the Canadian Supreme Court was again in question more than a decade later. The Constitution had been repatriated without the consent of the province of Quebec, where a referendum in 1980 had revealed that there was 40 per cent support for the province's secession from the federation. In a second referendum in 1995, support for secession rose to 49.4 per cent, and this prompted the federal government to refer to the Supreme Court the question whether Canadian or international law conferred a right on Quebec's legislature or government to bring about secession unilaterally. The Supreme Court first confirmed that the question asked of it was indeed justiciable, even the part relating to the content of international law.[38] It held that the matter was not a "political question" in the sense used in the United States because the points raised did not require the Court to usurp any democratic decision that the people of Quebec might be called upon to make: the Court's role was limited to considering aspects of the legal framework within which that democratic decision was to be made.[39]

In its collective judgment, which has been described as "adroit" and "a masterstroke,"[40] the Supreme Court ruled that neither Canadian nor international law granted Quebec the right to secede but that, if Quebec continued to press for secession on the back of winning a provincial referendum on the matter, then negotiations should take place between the Quebec government and the federal government on how to proceed. This is a classic example of courts judiciously self-limiting their role in governance: the judges clarified the legal framework within which politicians had to operate but then bowed out in favour of whatever solution could be politically negotiated within that framework. Martin, however, maintains that the influence of the Canadian Supreme Court on the country's democracy has been anything but benign.[41]

---

37 J. Webber, *The Constitution of Canada: A Contextual Analysis* (Oxford, Hart Publishing, 2015) at 127.

38 *Reference re Secession of Quebec* [1998] 2 SCR 217 at paras 24–31.

39 Ibid at para 27.

40 Webber, above n 37 at 53.

41 R. Martin, *The Most Dangerous Branch: How the Supreme Court of Canada Has Undermined Our Law and Our Democracy* (Montreal and Kingston, McGill-Queen's University Press, 2005).

In the United Kingdom, the last decade has seen some intensely politicized issues come before the Supreme Court. In *R (Gentle) v The Prime Minister*,[42] the mothers of British soldiers who had died in Iraq sought a full investigation into their deaths under Article 2 of the ECHR (the right-to-life provision). In the end, the claim was rejected because, in the Court's view, the duty to investigate arises only if there has been a breach of the substantive right to life in going to war in the first place, a breach that had not been established in this case. If there had been such a breach, the Court would have had jurisdiction. Indeed, in the words of Lady Hale,

> As I understand it, it is now common ground that if a Convention right requires the court to examine and adjudicate upon matters which were previously regarded as non-justiciable, then adjudicate it must.[43]

The mothers in question probably derived small comfort from the fact that a later public enquiry into the invasion of Iraq did conclude that the invasion was unnecessary.[44] UK law, any more than Canadian law, has never adopted a political question doctrine in the explicit way in which the US Supreme Court has done, but it is hard to imagine the House of Lords in years gone by adjudicating on any aspect of the deployment of British troops abroad.

In *R (Bancoult) v Secretary of State for Foreign and Commonwealth Affairs*,[45] former residents of the Chagos Islands in the Indian Ocean sought a remedy for having been evicted from their homeland by their imperial masters in the late 1960s and early 1970s. Again the claim failed, but only by a vote of 3–2 in the Appellate Committee of the House of Lords. It later transpired that not all relevant information had been disclosed to the court before it reached its decision, so an attempt was

---

42 [2008] UKHL 20, [2008] AC 1356.

43 Ibid at para 60.

44 This more general enquiry was commenced in June 2009, charged with examining the decisions taken in relation to Iraq between 2001 and 2009, with a view to identifying lessons that could be learned. It finally reported in July 2016 and found, among other things, that the war in 2003 was unnecessary: peaceful alternatives to war had not been exhausted, the United Kingdom and United States had undermined the authority of the UN Security Council, and the legal basis for the invasion had not been satisfactorily demonstrated. See *The Report of the Iraq Inquiry*, chaired by Sir John Chilcot, www.iraqinquiry.org.uk/the-report/.

45 [2008] UKHL 61, [2009] 1 AC 453.

made to vacate the earlier judgment. This, too, failed by a majority of 3–2, but it would have succeeded if one of the judges who had previously dissented, Lord Mance, had maintained his position in the subsequent case.[46] As has been well observed by Twomey,[47] the case had the potential to revive the idea that there are certain things that parliaments cannot do if they violate fundamental human rights, but not enough justices of the UK Supreme Court were prepared to grasp that nettle.[48]

As a final example of political issues being adjudicated upon in the United Kingdom, we can cite *R v Chaytor*, where the Supreme Court held that neither the Bill of Rights 1689 nor the doctrine of the exclusive jurisdiction of the House of Commons should prevent the trial of former members of Parliament for falsely claiming parliamentary expenses.[49]

In South Africa, the Constitutional Court recently ordered President Zuma to pay some of the costs involved in making alterations to his country home, thereby revoking a resolution by the National Assembly that had excused him from having to pay anything at all.[50] In stirring words, Chief Justice Mogoeng opened the Court's judgment by proclaiming that "constitutionalism, accountability and the rule of law constitute the sharp and mighty sword that stands ready to chop the ugly head of impunity off its stiffened neck."[51] The same Court has flexed its political muscles in several other cases. In *United Democratic Movement v President of the Republic of South Africa* it considered the constitutionality of floor-crossing legislation, which the claimants argued was contrary to fundamental values in South Africa's 1996 Constitution because, they said, the rights to vote and to have proportional representation were part of the basic structure of the Constitution and therefore could not be amended at all.[52] The Constitutional Court dismissed the claim

46 *R (Bancoult (No 2)) v Secretary of State for Foreign and Commonwealth Affairs* [2016] UKSC 35, [2017] AC 300.

47 A. Twomey, "Fundamental Common Law Principles as Limitations upon Legislative Power" (2009) 9 *Oxford University Commonwealth Law Journal* 47.

48 For an excellent account of the neo-colonialism evident in the Supreme Court's decision, see C. Murray and T. Frost, "The Chagos Islands Cases: The Empire Strikes Back" (2015) 66 *Northern Ireland Legal Quarterly* 263.

49 [2011] UKSC 52, [2011] 1 AC 68.

50 *Economic Freedom Fighters v Speaker of the National Assembly Cases* CCT 143/15 and CCT 171/15, [2016] ZACC 11, 2016 (3) SA 580 (CC).

51 Ibid at para 1.

52 Case CCT 23/02, [2002] ZACC 33, 2003 (1) SA 488 (CC).

but did agree that the mechanism used for amending the Constitution in this instance was unconstitutional.

In the field of socio-economic rights, the Constitutional Court has been world-leading, although its initial enthusiasm for devising mechanisms to ensure that the government's socio-economic policies were consistent with international human rights standards – in the *Grootboom*[53] and *Treatment Action Campaign*[54] cases – appeared to dim slightly in its more recent decision about payment for water, the *Phiri* case.[55] It is too soon to know whether the tide has turned again as a result of the decision in *Daniels v Scribante*,[56] where a majority on the Constitutional Court ruled that the owner of residential property owed a positive obligation to ensure that occupiers of the property were living in conditions that afforded them their human dignity. As Nolan has observed, this suggests a more activist approach than before to the horizontal application of the duty to protect socio-economic rights.[57]

By way of contrast, the Supreme Court of Ireland has to date played an understated role, particularly in the context of claims to social and economic rights. Thus, in *Sinnott v Minister for Education*, it refused to grab the opportunity to vindicate the right of disabled adults to receive education,[58] and in *TD v Minister for Education* it refused to pay much regard to the right of children in care to have secure residential facilities.[59] In *Maguire v Ardagh*, the Supreme Court ruled that the national Parliament had no power to set up an enquiry and compel the attendance of witnesses,[60] a decision that was later endorsed in a referendum by a majority of 53 per cent to 47 per cent. In *Pringle v Government of*

---

53 *Government of the Republic of South Africa v Grootboom*, Case CCT 11/00, [1996] ZACC 26, 1996 (4) SA 744 (CC).

54 *Minister of Health v Treatment Action Campaign*, Case CCT 8/02, [2002] ZACC 15, 2002 (5) SA 721 (CC).

55 *Mazibuko v City of Johannesburg*, Case CCT 39/09, [2009] ZACC 28, 2010 (4) SA 1 (CC).

56 [2017] ZACC 13.

57 A. Nolan, *Daniels v Scribante: South Africa Pushes the Boundaries of Horizontality and Social Rights*, *International Journal of Constitutional Law* (blog), 27 June 2017, http://www.iconnectblog.com/2017/06/daniels-v-scribante-south-africa-pushes-the-boundaries-of-horizontality-and-social-rights.

58 [2001] 2 IR 545.

59 [2001] 4 IR 259 (a 4–1 decision).

60 [2002] 1 IR 385.

Ireland, the Supreme Court ruled that the Irish government could ratify the treaty setting up the European Stability Mechanism without needing to put it to a referendum,[61] and a year later, the Court of Justice of the European Union agreed with that position.[62] Most recently, a unanimous, seven-judge Supreme Court issued a seminal decision holding that Ireland's ban on asylum seekers from looking for work was unconstitutional, although it allowed the government a six-month period to consider how to rectify the matter.[63]

New Causes of Action

In today's world, it is perhaps to be expected that novel claims will emerge that challenge senior judges to devise new principles reflecting current expectations. As well, judges have to interpret legislation devised for novel fields. As a result of UK membership of the European Union (EU), UK courts have had to accept that rights conferred under EU law must take priority even over provisions in UK Acts of Parliament, whenever made.[64] In the realm of public law, additional grounds for judicial review have been accepted, among which is the doctrine of legitimate expectations, with its obligation on public bodies to consult widely on proposed changes to policy.[65]

As far as human rights are concerned, I have argued elsewhere that the UK's Human Rights Act 1998 has prompted top UK judges to belatedly develop a "common law of human rights," one that may well need to play a greater role if, as the current British government has promised will happen, the Human Rights Act is repealed.[66] But there are still limits to how far the UK Supreme Court is willing to go in this context. While it will allow police forces to be sued for not protecting a victim's right to

---

61 [2012] IESC 47, [2013] 3 IR 1.

62 *Pringle v Government of Ireland* Case 370/12 [2013] 2 CMLR 2.

63 *NVH v Minister for Justice and Equality* [2017] IESC 35.

64 *R (Factortame Ltd) v Secretary of State for Transport (No 2)* [1991] 1 AC 603, where the House of Lords "disapplied" provisions in the Merchant Shipping Act 1988.

65 For a recent account of the current state of English law on this matter, see P. Leyland and G. Anthony, *Administrative Law*, 8th edn (Oxford, Oxford University Press, 2016) ch 15.

66 B. Dickson, "Repeal the Human Rights Act and Rely on the Common Law?" in K. Ziegler, E. Wicks, and L. Hodson (eds), *The UK and European Human Rights: A Strained Relationship?* (Oxford, Hart Publishing, 2015) ch 7.

life,[67] it still refuses to impose a duty of care on police forces towards potential victims of crime.[68] It is also content to protect people's right to confidentiality but has stopped short of endorsing a full-blown right to privacy.[69] It has adopted more generous rules on causation and time limits.[70] In contract law, it has recognized new heads of damages,[71] but it has still not accepted that there are general duties to contract in good faith and to act fairly.[72] It has granted recognition to claims based on the presumption against unjust enrichment.[73]

In Canada, one recent example of a new cause of action is the 2014 decision of the Supreme Court in *Bhasin v Hrynew*,[74] where the Court unanimously concluded that one of the general organizing principles of Canadian contract law is the principle that parties to a contract owe a duty of good faith to each other when performing that contract. This contrasts with the refusal of the UK Supreme Court to countenance such a principle, despite the growing criticism that English contract law is in dire need of some such overarching rationale that could embrace the range of distinct protections (such as the doctrine of undue influence) that have arisen to date on a piecemeal basis.[75]

---

67 *Van Colle v Chief Constable of Hertfordshire Police* [2008] UKHL 50, [2009] 1 AC 225 (although on its facts the claim failed).

68 *Smith v Chief Constable of Sussex Police* [2008] UKHL 50, [2009] 1 AC 225 (reported alongside *Van Colle*, ibid); *Michael v Chief Constable of South Wales* [2015] UKSC 2, [2015] AC 1732. But in *Commissioner of Police of the Metropolis v DSD* [2018] UKSC 11, [2018] 2 WLR 895, a police force was found liable under the Human Rights Act 1998 to pay compensation for its failure to thoroughly investigate serious sexual crimes, even though no duty of care was otherwise owed to the victims.

69 *Campbell v MGN Ltd* [2004] UKHL 22, [2004] 2 AC 457.

70 *Fairchild v Glenhaven Funeral Services Ltd* [2002] UKHL 22, [2003] 1 AC 32; *Abdulla v Birmingham City Council* [2013] UKSC 47, [2013] 1 All ER 649.

71 *Ruxley Electronics and Construction Ltd v Forsyth* [1996] 1 AC 344 (recovery of the "consumer surplus"); *Malik v Bank of Credit and Commerce International SA* [1998] AC 20 (recovery for loss of reputation); *Farley v Skinner* [2001] UKHL 49, [2002] 2 AC 732 (recovery for inconvenience and distress).

72 *Watford v Miles* [1992] 2 AC 128.

73 *Lipkin Gorman v Karpnale Ltd* [1991] 2 AC 548; *Benedetti v Sawiris* [2013] UKSC 50, [2014] AC 938.

74 2014 SCC 71. See too ch 11 in this volume.

75 See the brave judgment of Leggatt J in *Yam Seng Pte Ltd v International Trade Corp* [2013] EWHC 111. The fact that the Consumer Rights Act 2015 has created an obligation on traders to act fairly towards consumers has ratcheted up the pressure on judges to adopt a similar principle in general contract law.

In another decision in 2014, *Sattva Capital Corp v Creston Moly Corp*,[76] the Canadian Supreme Court adhered to the line adopted in a significant House of Lords decision concerning the method to be used when interpreting contracts, *Investors Compensation Scheme Ltd v West Bromwich Building Society*,[77] itself an attempt by Lord Hoffmann to introduce greater consistency and practicality into this vital area of private law and one that he repeated a decade later.[78] This new, interpretative approach is focused on treating contractual interpretation not as a question of law; instead, it favours relying on the interpretation that a reasonable observer would have come to had he or she witnessed the pre-contract negotiations between the parties. But the UK Supreme Court made it clear in a subsequent case that such an approach did not necessarily mean that the words explicitly used by contracting parties could be ignored, even if they had resulted in an extremely one-sided bargain.[79] To that extent, as in Canada, the UK courts are prepared to leave parties to make what for them turn out to be very bad bargains.

Canada has also greatly developed its law on unjust enrichment in recent years. It has moved beyond the approach preferred by other common law countries by opting to allow recovery in situations where, D having received a benefit and P having suffered a loss corresponding to that benefit, P can claim the benefit from D if there was no "juristic reason" for the benefit and loss. In one fairly recent decision by the Supreme Court, the principle was applied to calculate how much each of two previously cohabiting people should be able to claim from the other for the benefits they had conferred on each other during their relationship.[80] This is comparable to the "fairness" approach adopted by the UK Supreme Court when ruling on how the jointly owned property of a formerly cohabiting couple should be distributed.[81]

In tort law, speaking generally, both the United Kingdom and Canada have recently developed rules that make it more difficult to make

76 2014 SCC 53, [2014] 2 SCR 633. See further Ryan Krushelnitzky and Sandra Corbett, "Recent Developments in the Canadian Law of Contract," www.fieldlaw.com/articles/DRI_Recent_Developments_Canadian_Law_Contract.pdf?utm_source=Mondaq&utm_medium=syndication&utm_campaign=View-Original.

77 [1998] 1 All ER 98.

78 *Chartbrook Ltd v Persimmon Homes Ltd* [2009] UKHL 38, [2009] 1 AC 1101.

79 *Arnold v Britton* [2015] UKSC 36, [2015] AC 1619.

80 *Kerr v Baranow* 2011 SCC 10, [2011] 1 SCR 269.

81 *Jones v Kernott* [2011] UKSC 53, [2012] 1 AC 776 at para 51 (per Lady Hale).

successful claims.[82] In Australia, the courts have opted for their own specific approach to determining whether a duty of care should exist in novel circumstances. This was recently confirmed by the Court of Appeal of New South Wales in *Makawe Pty Limited v Randwick City Council*,[83] where the claimant was the purchaser of a building whose underground parking lot had flooded because, allegedly, the council had neglected to impose a condition on the construction of the building at a time when it was aware of the risk of flooding. In holding that there was no duty of care owed by the council to the purchaser, the court applied the "salient features" test, which had been endorsed by the High Court of Australia some years earlier in *Sullivan v Moody*.[84] This was a deliberate abandonment of the previous test, which depended on foreseeability, proximity, and policy.[85] It allows a range of connecting factors to be taken into account before imposing a duty of care.

In the area of unjust enrichment law, the High Court of Australia has also departed from the common law norm by maintaining that the calculation of whether an enrichment still exists is to be made in accordance with general equitable principles rather than principles governing defences to claims of unfair enrichment.[86]

The Second Trend: The Preference for Multifactorial Tests

Running in tandem with the first trend, where courts are showing themselves ever more willing to promote a values-based approach to adjudication, there has been a noticeable second trend, where, in both public law and many areas of private law, top common law courts have couched their preferred tests for upholding these values in terms that are open-textured, flexible, and (to be frank) rather vague. They have tended to enunciate a plethora of considerations that need to be borne in mind when the tests are being applied – what makes an administra-

---

82 See the entertaining lecture by Justice Allen Linden, "The Triumphs and Trials of Canadian Tort Law" (2007), www.mjswm.com/JPM/Torts.2/files/The_Triumphs_and_Trials_of_Canadian_Tort_Law.pdf.

83 [2009] NSWCA 412.

84 (2001) 207 CLR 562.

85 See C. Witting, "Tort Law, Policy and the High Court of Australia" (2007) 31 *Melbourne Law Review* 569.

86 *Australian Financial Services and Leasing Pty Ltd v Hills Industries Ltd* [2014] HCA 14, (2014) 307 ALR 512.

tive decision unreasonable, for example, or when it would be "just" to impose a duty of care on an organization, or what circumstances are relevant to whether a contractual agreement is "fair." Such multi-factorial tests have proliferated, but the judges have understandably refrained from indicating which factors should carry more weight than others. Consequently, it is frequently impossible to discern why exactly the judges have come down in favour of one side to a dispute rather than the other.

In adopting such an approach, the judges have been following in famous footsteps. Perhaps the most noteworthy exemplar in the public law field is the judgment of Lord Greene MR in the English Court of Appeal case of *Associated Provincial Picture Houses Ltd v Wednesbury Corporation*,[87] where he ruled that a body that had been granted a discretionary power by Parliament could not decide to exercise that power in a way that was so unreasonable that no reasonable authority would ever have considered doing so.[88] In the subsequent seventy years, there have been thousands of challenges based on this "*Wednesbury* unreasonableness" ground, and there are long sections in administrative law books pointing out the factors that should be borne in mind by a court when applying the test.[89]

In private law, the archetypal flexible standard is the one laid down by the House of Lords in *Donoghue v Stevenson* in 1932, where Lord Atkin and his brethren stated that an essential requirement that needed to be satisfied before a defendant could be sued for negligence was that the defendant owed the claimant a duty of care. A duty of care was said to exist if the defendant could reasonably have foreseen that his or

---

87 [1948] 1 KB 223.

88 On the facts of the case, the Court of Appeal ruled that the corporation had not acted unreasonably in allowing cinemas to open on Sundays on condition that no child under the age of 15 years could be admitted, even if accompanied by an adult.

89 Eg M. Fordham, *Judicial Review Handbook*, 6th edn (Oxford, Hart Publishing, 2012) at 569–77; J. Auburn, J. Moffett, and A. Sharland, *Judicial Review: Principles and Procedure* (Oxford, Oxford University Press, 2013) at 384–401. In *Council of Civil Service Unions v Minister for the Civil Service* [1985] AC 374, the House of Lords "unpacked" *Wednesbury* unreasonableness, labelled it "irrationality," and set it alongside two other grounds for judicial review, "illegality" and "procedural impropriety." It also held that decisions taken under the Crown prerogative were not immune from judicial review but that courts should not second-guess decisions based on "national security."

her acts or omissions would be likely to injure a neighbour – that is, a person so closely and directly affected by the act or omission that the defendant ought reasonably to have had that person in contemplation when directing his or her mind to the act or omission in question.

The progeny of this ruling is even more numerous than that of the *Wednesbury* principle, and the legal literature on when such injury can be reasonably foreseen is vast. The common, open-textured word in those two famous rulings is *reasonable*. It has been adopted in many other spheres of the law, too, and has been joined by a host of other such terms, which equally provide the courts with a large amount of discretion when seeking to arrive at what they perceive to be the appropriate conclusion on a given set of facts. These terms include *equitable*, *fair*, *proportionate*, and *just*. By definition, a conclusion that has been given such a label must have been reached only after all relevant factors have been weighed in the balance and a determination made as to which combination of factors finds most favour with the judges.

Across common law countries, the law on judicial review of administrative action has now developed to such an extent that to maintain the shibboleth that such review is all about whether the right procedures have been adopted by the decision-making body and not about the merits of the decision being challenged is somewhat disingenuous. The growing acceptance that public bodies must now act in a way that complies with human rights standards, and the creeping penetration of the doctrine of proportionality in this context, are evidence that the line between procedure and merits has become blurred almost to the point of invisibility. In the United Kingdom, justices of the Supreme Court have recently refused to sign up wholeheartedly to the doctrine of proportionality, even in a case where protection of the right to life was in play,[90] but to all intents and purposes the doctrine is already applied when the judges have to decide whether a measure taken in breach of a right was unreasonable because a less interfering measure would have been just as effective.[91] In New Zealand, the courts have tended to follow the English approach to judicial review,[92] but, from time to time

90 *R (Keyu) v Secretary of State for Foreign and Commonwealth Affairs* [2015] UKSC 69, [2016] AC 1355.

91 *R (Daly) v Secretary of State for the Home Dept* [2001] UKHL 26, [2001] 2 AC 532.

92 *New Zealand Fishing Industry Association Inc v Minister of Agriculture and Fisheries* [1988] 1 NZLR 544.

as in England, variations of the grounds for review come to the fore.[93] Australia, again an outlier, has tended to stick to a rather formalistic approach, which applies the *Wednesbury* formulation in a traditional manner.[94]

In Canada, until recently, the Supreme Court was insistent that the courts should apply three discrete standards of judicial review, depending on the pragmatic and functional dimensions to the issue in question.[95] These were (a) whether the decision being reviewed was correct, (b) whether it was reasonable, and (c) whether it was patently unreasonable.[96] But this approach was altered by the Court in 2008 when, in *Dunsmuir v New Brunswick*,[97] it reduced the types of review to two (doing away with patent unreasonableness) and changed the basis on which the choice between the remaining two standards is made to the appropriateness or not of showing deference to the decision maker in question, given the nature of the matter being decided.

This latter change may not be that different from the previous "pragmatic and functional" approach, but it does have the merit of focusing attention on whether courts *should* be second-guessing the merits of decisions taken by bodies that may have more democratic and experiential credentials.[98] Nevertheless, some commentators believe that *Dunsmuir* has rendered Canadian administrative law unstable and have argued for reforms.[99] A recent study suggests, moreover, that in the years since it adopted this new approach the Supreme Court of

93 See the treatment in D. Knight, *Vigilance and Restraint in the Common Law of Judicial Review: Scope, Grounds, Intensity, Context* (PhD diss, London School of Economics, 2014) at 99–108, http://etheses.lse.ac.uk/3100/1/Knight_Vigilance_and_Restraint.pdf.

94 Ibid at 46–8.

95 *Baker v Canada (Minister of Citizenship and Immigration)* [1999] 2 SCR 817.

96 Ibid at para 55 (per L'Heureux-Dubé J).

97 2008 SCC 9, [2008] 1 SCR 190.

98 For further discussion on this, see eg M. Lewans, "Deference and Reasonableness since Dunsmuir" (2012–13) 38 *Queen's Law Journal* 59; P. Daly, "Dunsmuir's Flaws Exposed: Recent Decisions on Standards of Review" (2012) 58 *McGill Law Journal* 483.

99 D. Stratas, "The Canadian Law of Judicial Review: A Plea for Doctrinal Coherence and Consistency" (2016) 42 *Queen's Law Journal* 27; P. Daly, "Struggling towards Coherence in Canadian Administrative Law? Recent Cases on Standard of Review and Reasonableness" (2016) 62 *McGill Law Journal* 527.

Canada has shown itself to be more deferential to decision-making bodies than it was under the previous test.[100]

In Ireland, too, the courts have not exactly covered themselves in glory as far as the adoption of clear standards of judicial review is concerned. Not wanting to be seen to be relying on the English precedent of *Wednesbury*, which was not even cited by the Irish Supreme Court until 1986, Irish judges have opted for an even more open-textured test. In *The State (Keegan) v Stardust Victims' Compensation Tribunal*,[101] Henchy J put it thus:

> I would myself consider that the test of unreasonableness or irrationality in judicial review lies in considering whether the impugned decision plainly and unambiguously flies in the face of fundamental reason and common sense. If it does, then the decision-maker should be held to have acted *ultra* vires.[102]

This "common sense" approach – which might appeal to non-lawyers – has not made the task of Irish lawyers any easier when advising clients as to whether an administrative decision is challengeable or not. The picture has since been made more complex by the willingness of the Supreme Court, in *Meadows v The Minister for Justice, Equality and Law Reform*,[103] to qualify the *Keegan* approach when determining the reasonableness of an administrative decision affecting constitutional or fundamental rights: in such cases, the courts can overturn the decision if they think it is "disproportionate" in the circumstances. In its most recent comments on the "effectiveness" of judicial review as a remedy, the Supreme Court of Ireland, in *AAA v Minister for Justice*,[104] has made it clear that, in some circumstances, the intensity of judicial review can bring the process very close to that of an appeal on the merits.[105]

---

100 R. Danay, "Quantifying *Dunsmuir*: An Empirical Analysis of the Supreme Court of Canada's Jurisprudence on Standard of Review" (2016) 66 *University of Toronto Law Journal* 555.

101 [1986] IR 642.

102 Ibid at 658.

103 [2010] IESC 3, [2011] 2 ILRM 157.

104 [2017] IESC 80.

105 Paul Daly, "Substantive Review in the Common Law World: *AAA v Minister for Justice* in Comparative Perspective" [2018] *Irish Supreme Court Review* (forthcoming).

In private law, the most obvious example of the amplification of an already vague test into an even vaguer one is the way in which the courts have explained when a duty of care arises in the law of tort. It was in *Caparo Industries plc v Dickman* that the House of Lords determined that whether a duty of care existed depended on whether it would be "fair, just and reasonable" for such a duty to be imposed.[106]

A more recent example of the same phenomenon is the way in which the courts have extended the reach of the doctrine of vicarious liability in tort law. This doctrine used to apply only in a master-servant context, where an employer could be allocated the responsibility for losses caused by an employee because the employer was more likely to be insured against such losses and, in any event, would have a deeper pocket out of which to pay compensation if not insured. Today the doctrine applies to all situations where a defendant can be said to be in a better position to bear the risk, principally because he or she created the situation in which some other person used an opportunity and, as a result, caused loss to another. This is what the UK Supreme Court effectively held in *Various Claimants v Catholic Child Welfare Society*[107] ("the Christian Brothers case") and further developed in *Cox v Ministry of Justice*,[108] a legal reform that has been described as showing that vicarious liability is "on the move."[109] In Lord Reed's words,

> The essential idea is that the defendant should be liable for torts that may fairly be regarded as risks of his business activities, whether they are committed for the purpose of furthering those activities or not.[110]

That such an approach is in tune with wider thinking on responsibilization is apparent from the case of *O'Keeffe v Hickey*, which came before Ireland's Supreme Court in 2008 and again involved sexual abuse by a

106 [1990] 2 AC 605.

107 [2012] UKSC 56, [2013] 2 AC 1.

108 [2016] UKSC 10, [2016] 1 AC 660.

109 Above n 107 at para 19, per Lord Phillips; above n 108 at para 1, per Lord Reed. See too P. Morgan, "Vicarious Liability on the Move" (2013) 129 *Law Quarterly Review* 139.

110 Above n 108 at para 23. More generally see J. Morgan, "Liability for Independent Contractors in Contract and Tort: Duties to Ensure That Care Is Taken" [2015] *Cambridge Law Journal* 109.

schoolteacher. The Supreme Court held that the state could not be vicariously liable either for the abuse itself or for the failure of the "manager" of the school, a church appointee, to take any effective steps to investigate it.[111] But when the applicant took her complaint to the ECtHR, she won.[112] The Grand Chamber held by 11–6 that there had been a violation of Article 3 of the ECHR (the right not to be ill treated) and also of Article 13 as regards the failure of Irish law to provide an effective domestic remedy for the violation of Article 3 in this type of situation. Unusually, one of the Irish Supreme Court justices subsequently published a piece in which he strongly criticized the ECtHR for ignoring its own rules on the need for applicants to exhaust domestic remedies before proceeding to Strasbourg.[113]

English contract law is also moving, it could be argued, towards the adoption of principles that require a variety of factors to be taken into account before the outworkings of the principles can be determined. In *Cavendish Square Holding BV v Talal El Makdessi*, the UK Supreme Court held that whether a liquidated damages clause was enforceable depended on what was an appropriate balance between the interests of the conflicting parties.[114] English contract law still clings fairly tightly to the doctrines of consideration and frustration and, as already noted, has yet to succumb to the temptation to develop a general principle of fairness in contract law, but, increasingly, it is favouring principles that allow for a degree of flexibility in deciding whether a defendant should be held liable to pay damages. In the particular subset of contract law governing employment relationships, the Supreme Court has favoured a "realistic" approach to whether a worker is, in law, an employee or an independent contractor[115] and to whether a former employee is prohibited from using

---

111 [2008] IESC 72.

112 (2014) 59 EHRR 15 (GC). See too D. Ryan, "'Close Connection' and 'Akin to Employment': Perspectives on 50 Years of Radical Developments in Vicarious Liability" [2016] *Irish Jurist* 239.

113 Adrian Hardiman, "The Jurisdiction of the European Court of Human Rights and the Case of *O'Keeffe v Hickey*" in L. Cahillane, J. Gallen, and T. Hickey, *Judges, Politics and the Irish Constitution* (Manchester, Manchester University Press, 2017) ch 6. Hardiman's position is countered by Conor O'Mahony in ch 7 of the same book.

114 [2015] UKSC 67, [2016] AC 1172.

115 *Autoclenz Ltd v Belcher* [2011] UKSC 41, [2011] 4 All ER 745; *Pimlico Plumbers Ltd v Smith* [2018] UKSC 29. The textbooks speak explicitly about a multifactorial test in this context: see eg Gwyneth Pitt, *Pitt's Employment Law*, 10th edn (London, Sweet & Maxwell, 2016) at 100–7.

any knowledge obtained from prior work experience to make money for him- or herself in a separate subsequent venture.[116]

Furthermore, the legislation on unfair dismissal in English law expressly states that the determination of the question whether a dismissal is fair or unfair "(a) depends on whether in the circumstances (including the size and administrative resources of the employer's undertaking) the employer acted reasonably or unreasonably in treating it as a sufficient reason for dismissing the employee, and (b) shall be determined in accordance with equity and the substantial merits of the case."[117] This again confers considerable discretion on first-instance judges to decide cases by pitting one set of factors against another and plumping for the one that is most in touch with their instincts. This is not quite palm-tree justice, but it does make outcomes (and appeals against them) somewhat unpredictable.

The United States[118] and Canada[119] have witnessed a similar growth in the reach of vicarious liability, although the High Court of Australia has been more conservative.[120] In the context of employment law, several jurisdictions have held employers to be liable for the sexual harassment or other forms of discrimination suffered by their employees at the hands of third parties such as fellow employees, customers, and clients.[121]

The Positive Aspect to the Two Trends: Greater Transparency

In general, we should welcome the fact that top courts in common law countries are adjudicating new types of issues and developing multifactorial tests to resolve them. It suggests that the judges are more

---

116 *Vestergaard Frandsen A/S v Bestnet Europe Ltd* [2013] UKSC 31, [2013] 1 WLR 1556. The justices stressed that former employees should not be disincentivized from using their initiative.

117 Employment Rights Act 1998, s 98(4).

118 *Meyer v Holley* 527 US 280 (2003), although, on the facts, the Court held that there was no liability.

119 *Bazley v Curry* [1999] 2 SCR 534; B. Feldthusen, "Civil Liability for Sexual Assault in Aboriginal Residential Schools: The Baker Did It" (2007) 22 *Canadian Journal of Law and Society* 61.

120 *Prince Alfred College Inc v ADC* [2016] HCA 37; D. Ryan, "From Opportunity to Occasion: Vicarious Liability in the High Court of Australia" [2017] *Cambridge Law Journal* 14.

121 See eg *Vance v Ball State University* 570 US 1 (2013); C. MacKinnon, "In Their Hands: Restoring Institutional Liability for Sexual Harassment in Education" (2015–16) 125 *Yale Law Journal* 2038.

conscious of the important role they play in the governance of society and of the expectation that the public has that they will explain their judgments in a detailed and convincing manner. If public trust in judges is to be maintained at the high level that it currently occupies in these countries, judges will have to continue to demonstrate not just impartiality and incorruptibility but also a talent for consistency and transparency. If they are to trespass into areas, especially political or moral areas, that they previously avoided, they will have to be able to justify doing so.

It is difficult for them to do so if legislators have deliberately refused to make laws in a particular field, as is the case with most legislatures, for instance, regarding assisted suicide. In *R (Nicklinson) v Ministry of Justice*,[122] five of the nine justices who sat in the UK Supreme Court thought that they did have constitutional authority to make a declaration that the general prohibition on assisted suicide in s. 2 of the Suicide Act 1961 was incompatible with Article 8 of the ECHR; of these, however, three would have declined the declaration,[123] while only two would have granted it.[124] The other four judges thought that the matter was best left to Parliament's assessment.[125] The Irish Supreme Court has reached a similar conclusion,[126] but the Canadian Supreme Court has been bolder, striking down the prohibition on assisted suicide as contrary to the right-to-life provision in the Canadian Charter of Rights and Freedoms.[127] It suspended its declaration of invalidity for twelve months to allow the government to bring about a change to the legislation.

At times, the very divisiveness of an issue can provide a tenable excuse for a top court to provide what it deems to be the appropriate

---

122 [2014] UKSC 38, [2015] AC 657.

123 Lords Neuberger, Mance, and Wilson.

124 Lady Hale and Lord Kerr.

125 Lords Sumption, Hughes, Clarke, and Reed. When the issue was debated in the House of Commons fifteen months later, MPs voted 330–118 to reject the Assisted Dying Bill, proposed as a private member's bill: see www.dignityindying.org.uk/news/parliament-ignores-public-votes-assisted-dying-bill/.

126 *Fleming v Ireland* [2013] IESC 19, [2013] 2 IR 417.

127 *Carter v Canada (Attorney General)* 2015 SCC 5, [2015] 1 SCR 331; for the wording of s 7 see n 7 above.

solution. It is not unreasonable to suppose that individual legislators, and maybe even political parties, would prefer judges to intervene in some situations because it takes the pressure off the politicians to adopt positions that may not be immediately attractive to their usual support base. As an instance of this one could point to the decisions by the South African Constitutional Court and the US Supreme Court concerning the constitutional right to enter into same-sex marriage.[128]

The very act of adopting multifactorial tests as methods for resolving contentious issues means that judges are challenging themselves to engage in more nuanced reasoning when delivering their judgments. They are duty-bound to explicitly take into account the factors that they have previously listed as relevant to the matter at hand, and they are required to justify their assessment that, taken in the round, the factors lead to one conclusion rather than another. If the court issuing the decision is a first-instance or intermediate appellate court, the judges will be anxious to protect themselves against being overturned on appeal and will therefore seek to be assiduous in their balancing exercise. If the court is a final appeal court, it too will want to be sure that its assessment of where the balance lies is fully rationalized.[129] The judges may be conscious that if the legislators do not agree with their assessment, it can be overturned, but if an inability to reach consensus among the legislators is one of the reasons for the court becoming involved in the first place the wait for legislative correction may be a long one. In countries such as the United Kingdom and Ireland, which are subject to oversight by the ECtHR, judges will also be conscious that if their assessment is reviewed by the Court in Strasbourg the judges there will apply the checklist of values and principles that it has developed over the last fifty-nine years.[130]

128 *Minister for Home Affairs v Fourie* CCT 60/04, [2005] ZACC 19, 2006 (1) SA 524 (CC), where the Court gave the South African Parliament one year to come up with appropriate legislation, which it did: Civil Union Act 17 of 2006; *Obergefell v Hodges* 576 US (2015) (14-556).

129 In the UK, the Judicial Power Project has been undertaken by a right-leaning think tank, Policy Exchange. It seeks to discredit our top judges for their law-making tendencies, but I think unfairly so. In my view, we should applaud our top judges for the care they put into rationalizing the common law, even if they can be shown to have got it wrong sometimes.

130 The first judgment of the ECtHR was issued in 1960.

The Negative Aspect to the Two Trends: Less Certainty

There is, however, a significant downside to the enhanced willingness of top courts to enter new pastures and enunciate new, pluralistic tests. It is that individuals, and businesses, who want to plan their activities in a way that ensures they do not transgress the law may find it much more difficult to do so because they may not be able to anticipate what view a court will ultimately take of their approach. The more factors that are eligible to be taken into account in an assessment of legality, the less easy it will be for anyone, including legal advisers, to reach a reliable view as to what will be deemed legally acceptable. To try to immunize themselves against accusations of illegality, individuals and businesses may seek more and more legal advice, but lawyers could reasonably disagree as to how a court might look upon a situation. The result could be more litigation than is really necessary, with all the consequential wasted time and expenditure. In turn, this could tend to bring the whole legal system into disrepute, and the motivation of lawyers even more so.

Still, this negative aspect to recent trends should not be overemphasized. For a start, there will always be an element of uncertainty in any adjudication concerning the legality of actions or omissions. For every civil wrong (and most crimes) there are defences. It is the job of lawyers to represent their clients to the best of their ability, and they will therefore exploit potential defences to the full. More importantly, the multi-varied nature of the factors that are to be taken into account under many of the new tests means that defendants should have just as great a chance of winning their cases as the claimants who are initiating the litigation. If the test is one that stresses the need for fairness, equity, or justice, there is no *a priori* reason why a defendant should not benefit from those goals just as much as a claimant. Indeed, such goals may allow both parties to raise points that, under the previous law, may not have been deemed relevant. In any event, in most legal systems, it is still the claimant who carries both the burden of proof and the risk as regards costs. This disincentive will not be alleviated by the uncertainty of the law; in fact, it will be increased.

Conclusion

Judges who sit in a common law country's top court are frequently confronted with very difficult legal problems. Rather than finding facts and applying clear law to those facts, which is the main task facing judges in lower tiers of the judiciary, judges at the top spend nearly all their time considering what the law *should* be on particular issues. As the rule of law becomes an ever more deeply entrenched value in democracies,[131] an inevitable corollary is that courts are seen as the appropriate fora for resolving all manner of disputes that, for whatever reason, have not managed to be dealt with through negotiation, arbitration, mediation, or conciliation.[132]

Litigation at the Supreme Court level is usually, therefore, a high-stakes affair. Quite apart from the costs involved, the way in which the judges decide a dispute could have huge consequences not just for the parties to the litigation but also for countless other players in society, including private businesses, public bodies, and the state itself. The reasoning given for a decision, because of the fundamental role played by the doctrine of precedent in common law systems, is crucial: the principles enunciated need to be clear and nuanced enough to be readily applicable in similar future disputes. This could be depicted as the "top-down" approach to judicial reasoning referred to by Daly in his Introduction to this book.

This chapter has sought to demonstrate, albeit through a self-serving selection of cases plucked from the databases of various common law Supreme Courts around the world, that top judges are increasingly willing to play a role in solving novel legal problems and that, in doing so, they are keen to display an awareness that a multitude of considerations need to be taken into account before conclusions are reached on appropriate solutions.[133] Sometimes this resort to cataloguing the relevant factors to consider may occur because judges are responding to difficulties that they have encountered in reconciling existing precedents; at other times, it may be the result of the ingenious argumentation of the lawyers who have pleaded in front of the judges.

As modern living becomes more complex, as subtle distinctions become more necessary, and as competing interests become more heterogeneous, the challenges facing top judges grow correspondingly

131 T. Bingham, *The Rule of Law* (London, Penguin Books, 2010).

132 See generally A. Barak, *The Judge in a Democracy* (Princeton, NJ, Princeton University Press, 2006).

133 An analogy could be drawn here to the work of Elaine Mak in identifying what makes top judges refer to foreign or international legal sources; see her *Judicial Decision-Making in a Globalised World: A Comparative Analysis of the Changing Practices of Western Highest Courts* (Oxford, Hart Publishing, 2015) ch 6; see too B. Flanagan and S. Ahern, "Judicial Decision-Making and Transnational Law: A Survey of Common Law Supreme Court Judges" (2011) 60 *International and Comparative Law Quarterly* 1.

greater. They have different audiences to satisfy, they have their own judicial oath to obey, and they have their consciences to live with. They know that their decisions will be closely scrutinized not just by parties to the litigation but also by many others, whether professionally qualified in the law or not. It should hardly be surprising, then, that when enunciating their decisions, judges in apex courts should seek to do so in a way that indicates precisely why they favoured solution A over solutions B, C, or D. In doing so, they see the advantage in identifying particular features of a case that pull in favour of solution A. Features that would be more aligned with solutions B, C, or D are often mentioned precisely to underscore the difference that those features make and why they are not as persuasive as those favouring solution A.

I submit that top common law judges are today more conscious than ever of their importance in the development of their legal system. Aware that they are also more accountable than ever, they are keen to justify their decisions in ways that are easily understood by laypeople and less susceptible to subversion by legal professionals who are disappointed by the result.[134] Announcing that solution A is the one that is reasonable, fair, or just – because (e.g.) the combined persuasive weight of factors 1, 2, 3, and 4 is greater than that of factors 1, 3, 5, and 6 – is a clever way of deflecting outright negative criticism. It may also be a genuine reflection of the thought processes at work in the judges' minds.

Most of us, when pondering the pros and cons of a proposition, can see merit on both, or all, sides, and what makes us opt for one side rather than another is the combination of factors pulling us in that direction. Even if we cannot quantify the relative weight of the various pros and cons, we can somehow calculate the optimum choice. Our subconscious may be operative during this decision-making process, as may factors such as our wish to be consistent with what we have decided in the past or our desire not to appear out of step with our current colleagues.[135] This particularization of the factors that have swung a decision a certain way is perhaps an illustration of what Daly, in his Introduction,

134 See R. Posner, *How Judges Think* (Cambridge, MA, Harvard University Press, 2008) esp ch 2 ("The Judge as Labor-Market Participant").

135 See A. Paterson, *Final Judgment: The Last Law Lords and the Supreme Court* (Oxford, Hart Publishing, 2013) at 130–67; P. Darbyshire, *Sitting in Judgment: The Working Lives of Judges* (Oxford, Hart Publishing, 2011) at 414–23.

refers to as a "bottom-up" approach to judicial reasoning. In my view, judges in apex courts are today increasingly engaging in a mixture of top-down and bottom-up reasoning because they see the combination of approaches as giving the whole judicial process enhanced legitimacy.

Whatever mental processes are at work, the outcome is a series of judicial forays that, while treading new ground and producing greater transparency, are also making the ground in question less firm and the pathways across it more treacherous. The best judges are those who are able to explore unknown territory, while leaving reliable footsteps, which can be followed by those who come after. Whether the successors will arrive at the same destination as their predecessors will depend on other environmental features prevalent at the time. In such a fashion is the legal map of every country constantly being redrawn to an ever-larger scale.

3 The Common Law, the High Court of Australia, and the United States Supreme Court

PETER CANE*

This chapter compares and contrasts the High Court of Australia and the Supreme Court of the United States.[1] It argues, first, that although both the Australian (federal) legal system and the US (federal) legal system may be described as members of the common law family of legal systems, and although both the High Court and the Supreme Court may be described as "common law courts," the two courts are not common law courts in the same sense as one another. Second, it will argue that although both Australia and the United States are federal systems of government, they distribute power vertically in significantly different ways and that this affects the respective roles of the High Court and the Supreme Court as common law courts. Third, it will argue that although both the Australian Constitution and the US Constitution formally separate judicial power from legislative and executive power, and confer federal judicial power on the High Court and the Supreme Court, respectively, the High Court and the Supreme Court occupy very different positions and perform very different roles in their respective systems of government vis-à-vis the other branches. The general conclusion will be that although the two courts are similar in various ways, such similarities conceal very significant differences.

---

* Many thanks to James Stellios for extremely penetrating and helpful comments and suggestions. Thanks also to Colm McGrath and an anonymous reviewer.

1 The choice of these two courts is of no particular significance beyond the fact that both are sufficiently similar to each other to make comparison meaningful and sufficiently different from each other to make it fruitful. It would be possible and, no doubt, enlightening to put other courts into the mix, as Carissima Mathen does in her contribution to this volume (see ch 5, n 78).

The High Court and the Supreme Court as Common Law Courts

Some history will help us to understand the concept of a "common law court." The High Court can trace its lineage back to the Norman Conquest. Among the first governmental institutions to be established by the invaders were courts staffed by members of the King's Council.[2] Their main function was to resolve disputes, initially by applying the existing laws of the conquered peoples. At this time, adjudication of disputes was perhaps the most important service provided by the monarch to the people and, apart from military might, the main foundation of royal authority, and the prime guarantor of law and order. Put differently, adjudication was effectively a form of royal administration. Gradually, the King's Courts developed the patchwork of more-or-less local, inherited laws into a system of common law – "common" in the sense of a single law for the whole realm. Despite the growth, over the succeeding centuries, of legislation as a mode of law-making, judges arguably remained the most important lawmakers in England until the nineteenth century.

By the seventeenth century, the structure of the secular, central courts had developed to a point where it was possible to distinguish among the Chancery Court, the conciliar courts (notably the Court of Star Chamber), and the common law courts (notably, the Court of Common Pleas and the Court of King's/Queen's Bench) – "common law" in the sense that both Chancery (which had developed a supplementary set of "equitable" norms) and the conciliar courts (which specialized in what we could now call "public law") operated within a basic legal framework established by "the royal justices."

In the medieval period, the royal justices were regularly engaged not only in resolving disputes but also in the legislative activities of the monarch and Parliament and in executive affairs of state as all-purpose, legal functionaries. Clear distinctions were not drawn among legislative, administrative, and judicial functions or among legislature, executive, and judiciary. The royal justices were servants of the monarch in much more than a technical sense: they depended on the sovereign for their elevation to and maintenance in judicial office.

---

2 For a suggestive account, see M. Shapiro, *Courts: A Comparative and Political Analysis* (Chicago, Chicago University Press, 1981) at 65–108.

As a result of the Revolution of 1688, the monarch ceased to be personally involved in performing judicial functions and was forced to cede to Parliament the power to dismiss royal justices – although, henceforth, that could be done only "for cause." As a result, the justices were no longer all-purpose legal functionaries of the Crown, involved in the day-to-day affairs of government, but agents – albeit quite independent agents – of the new, "sovereign" Parliament. Their role as agents was to interpret and apply statute law in the context of resolving disputes; and as a sort of *quid pro quo* for their marginalization from the everyday affairs of government, they effectively gained a monopoly over the authoritative performance of the interpretive function. In this way, at the same time as the Revolution reduced the "common law judges" to the role of "subordinate" agents of Parliament,[3] it also gave them a unique role as interpreters of "the (Parliamentary sovereign's) law" – its "guardians," if you like.[4]

In the mid-eighteenth century, Montesquieu marked the new status of the common law judges by recognizing the judicial function as one of the three powers that, in a well-functioning polity, were allocated to different institutions.[5] In this, he departed from John Locke, who, in the previous century, had treated the exercise of judicial power as it had originally been utilized: as an aspect and instrument of administration, not a distinct governmental function.[6] However, where Montesquieu got things seriously wrong was in depicting the courts as "crude mechanicals," in the process failing to notice that, since the Conquest, the judges had been the major lawmakers in the English system. The

3 The conciliar courts were abolished in 1641, but thereafter, the Privy Council acquired very significant overseas jurisdiction as a consequence of the acquisition of empire. The Chancery Court survived more or less in its traditional form until the nineteenth century. From the middle of the seventeenth century, the House of Lords consolidated its position as the ultimate domestic court of appeal.

4 For an argument that a similar process played out in America in the transition from colonialism to post-colonial constitutionalism, see G.S. Wood, "Comment" in A. Gutmann (ed), *A Matter of Interpretation: Federal Courts and the Law* (Princeton, NJ, Princeton University Press, 1997) at 49–63.

5 Baron de Montesquieu, *The Spirit of the Laws* was first published in 1757. A useful modern edition is D.W. Carrithers (ed), *The Spirit of the Laws by Montesquieu* (Berkeley, CA, University of California Press, 1977).

6 M.J.C. Vile, *Constitutionalism and the Separation of Powers*, 2nd edn (Indianapolis, IN, Liberty Fund, 1998) at 63–74.

Revolution did not significantly diminish the law-making role of the courts; rather, it relocated the judges from the centre of government to a sort of limbo between the state and civil society, and it redefined their relationship with the sovereign, following Parliament's ousting of the monarch from that position. Henceforth, they were to be independent enforcers of Parliament's sovereign will (with tenure and guaranteed salary), not dependent, all-purpose legal functionaries of the sovereign monarch. This change had implications for their role as lawmakers. Previously, the courts had been law-making agents of the monarch, and it was their relationship with the monarch that legitimized their law-making. Now, they were law-applying agents of Parliament, and judicial law-making lacked an obvious, institutional source of legitimacy. The advent of democracy aggravated this problem, and the legitimacy of judicial law-making remains a topic of ongoing discussion and debate.

The Anglo-Australian legal system sprang into existence in 1788. The colonial system of government developed gradually over the course of the nineteenth century. Responsible government came to Australia in the 1850s, somewhat in advance of its maturation in Britain. The courts were generally modelled on, and inherited the jurisdiction of, the English courts, but with at least one very significant qualification. From the 1820s to the 1850s, one of the functions of the New South Wales Supreme Court was to decide whether colonial legislation conflicted with legislation of the Imperial Parliament – an early form of judicial review of legislation.[7]

By the end of the nineteenth century, it had become very widely accepted that the Australian colonies would benefit from entering into a federal arrangement. For the basic design of the federal government, the founders adopted the English model, with colonial modifications. For the design of the federation and the Constitution, they looked to the United States. One important result of this dual inheritance was the creation of a strong upper house of the Commonwealth Parliament – the Senate, originally designed to protect the interests of the smaller states against the larger.[8] A second important result was that a formal, constitutional separation of legislative, executive, and judicial powers was

7 Unlike the English Parliament, the colonial parliaments were not sovereign.

8 The Australian Senate is not quite as strong as the US Senate; but in 1901, neither was it as strong as the House of Lords – the Parliament Act 1911 was still a decade away.

superimposed on a system of responsible government. As we will see later, this unique combination of responsible government, federalism, and separation of powers has had profound effects on the development of the judicial function in Australia and, more specifically, on the role of the High Court.

The design of the US system of government was deeply influenced by the English system and by Montesquieu's account of that system. However, although the Founders contemplated that the Supreme Court would be the weakest of the three branches, they modelled it as "coordinate" with the other two branches, not subordinate to either but, like each of them, a direct delegate of the sovereign people. The main role apparently contemplated for the Court in the system of government was to enforce the Constitution against the other branches on behalf of the people.[9] This needs some elaboration.

The basic constitutional-design principle adopted by the Founders was (what may be called) "diffusion" of power. This entailed not only that different types of power would be allocated to different branches. It meant, too, that while each branch would exercise a characteristic type of power (legislative, executive, or judicial), it would also have a share in the powers characteristic of the other branches. The purpose of this design was to create a "balance" of power among the various branches of government, thus enabling each branch to "check" exercises of their respectively characteristic powers by the other branches. The expectation was that organs that shared one and the same power would have to cooperate and coordinate in the exercise of that power. In this way, the Founders hoped to protect the citizenry by making it more difficult for the federal government to encroach on the interests of the individual on the one hand and the states on the other. Bruised by their colonial experience not only of the English monarch and Parliament but also of populist colonial legislatures, Americans wanted to avoid creating a new federal government that could dominate citizens and their local governments.

The idea of checks and balances found early judicial expression in 1803 in *Marbury v Madison*, in which the (federalist-dominated) Supreme Court assumed the power to check Congress by testing legislation for

9 On the implications of this shift from subordinate to coordinate status on statutory interpretation, see eg C.E. Gonzalez, "Reinterpreting Statutory Interpretation" (1976) 74 *North Carolina Law Review* 585.

its constitutionality and to control the president by reviewing exercises of executive power. (Other manifestations of the idea in the Constitution itself included the presidential, qualified, legislative veto, and the involvement of the Senate in treaty-making and in the appointment of judges and senior government officials.) The *Marbury* incident also made it clear for all to see that one corollary of the checks-and-balances system would be "politicization" of the Court, in the sense that the president and the Senate would have strong incentives to appoint ideologically "reliable" justices and to "curb" the Court if, and when, it strayed too far from the policies preferred by the incumbent president and Senate. Because the Court enjoys a share of the powers of the other branches (just as the other branches enjoy a share of judicial power), neither the president nor Congress can afford to allow the Court to have complete freedom of action. The Court needs a significant measure of independence[10] to maintain its legitimacy as a delegate of the people, but cannot be allowed too much independence by the other branches lest it dominate them.

In the late nineteenth century, as a result of the ratification of the Fourteenth Amendment in 1868 (subjecting the states to the Bill of Rights), and the rapid increase in (federal) governmental economic and social regulation in response to the Industrial Revolution, the power of the Court started to grow significantly relative to that of the other branches. The Court took the opportunity presented by these new circumstances first (in the name of the Constitution) to champion common law rights of property and contract – "common law" rights in the sense that they were derived from (English law through) state law and existed independently of statute.[11] Such solicitude on the part of the Court, for the financial interests of individuals affected by governmental regulation, reached a climax in the 1930s in response to the New Deal. As is

10 Note that here, and throughout this chapter, independence, when referring to the judiciary, identifies a structural feature of courts, not a quality (impartiality) of sound judicial reasoning.

11 In modern terminology, "constitutional common law." Because such rights were read into the constitution through the Due Process Clause, they came to be referred to as "substantive due process." This technique is often referred to as "activism" or "non-originalist interpretation." For a useful discussion, see J.M. Beermann, "The Supreme Common Law Court of the United States" (2008) 18 *Public Interest Law Journal* 119.

well known, Franklin D. Roosevelt's controversial Court-packing plan was made redundant by the Court's sudden and unexpected bow to the inevitability of strong, interventionist federal government – the famous "stitch in time that saved nine." Thereafter, the Court redirected its activism to protecting the civil and political rights of groups such as blacks, criminal defendants, religious minorities, and voters. More recently, it has increasingly espoused individual autonomy in areas such as abortion and sexual life choices.

As we have seen, in seventeenth-century England, the common law courts were distinguishable from the Chancery Court and the conciliar courts. In one of its numerous senses, common law was the law developed and administered by the common law courts. Although, in England and Australia, equity – Chancery's law – is still, in certain areas, contrasted with common law in this sense, the phrase "common law court" is rarely applied to a subset of the superior courts. In another of its many senses, the term common law now refers to a family of legal systems that trace their origins back to English law; and in this sense, it is contrasted with civil law, which describes systems that identify Roman law as their historical source.

In this latter sense of being a court belonging to a common law system, the High Court is certainly a common law court, although it would not normally be described in that way. On the other hand, the *Oxford Companion to the Supreme Court of the United States*[12] explicitly describes the Supreme Court as a common-law court. In an entry entitled "Common-law Court," Richard Hamm says,

> The Supreme Court is a common-law court. ... Common law is a system of law made not by legislatures but by courts and judges. ... In common law, the substance of the law is to be found in the published reports of court decisions. Two points are critical to the workings of a common law system. First, law emerges only through litigation about actual controversies. Second, precedent guides courts: holdings in a case must follow previous rulings, if the facts are identical. This is the principle of *stare decisis*. But subsequent cases can also change the law. If the facts of a new case are distinguishable, a new rule can emerge. And sometimes, if the grounds of a precedent are seen to be wrong, the holding can be overruled by later courts.

12 K.L. Hall (ed), *The Oxford Companion to the Supreme Court of the United States*, 2nd edn (Oxford, Oxford University Press, 2005).

As far as it goes, no objection can be made to this account. However, from my point of view, and for the purposes of this chapter, it omits reference (explicitly, at least) to what – I would suggest – is (*in theory, anyway*)[13] one of the most fundamental characteristics of a common law system as compared with a civil law system. This characteristic relates to the location of the *foundational* (or *autonomous*) power (and obligation) to make law; and it is the characteristic on which both of the two features of a common law system, identified by Hamm, are founded.

By "the foundational power to make law," I mean the power to answer any legal question that has not previously been answered within the system – or, in other words, to fill gaps in the law and, concomitantly, to work the law, both legislative and judge-made, into a coherent whole. In systems (such as civil law systems of private law) based on a *code*, this power belongs ultimately to the legislature. By contrast, in a common law system, it belongs ultimately to the courts. In this sense, a civil law code is comprehensive,[14] and the inherent role of the courts is to interpret and apply the code. If a litigant asks a civil law court a question to which the code provides no explicit or obvious answer, the court's inherent role is to search for the answer in the code, not to supply an answer of its own.[15]

---

13 A methodological assumption I make here is that even if practice deviates from theory, the theory may be important in understanding the technical significance, as opposed to the actual effect, of the practice. For a very helpful discussion, see C.P. McGrath and H. Koziol, "Is Style of Reasoning a Fundamental Difference between the Common Law and the Civil Law?" (2014) 76 *Rabels Zeitschrift für ausländisches und internationales Privatrecht* 709, esp 714–21. The distinction drawn by Beverley McLachlin in her contribution to this volume (see ch 1) between "top-down" and "bottom-up" styles of reasoning is different from, although it may be related to, the distinction based on the location of the foundational power to make law.

14 On the distinction between a "relatively comprehensive, coherent, self-contained" code and legislation that does not "possess the same degree of conceptual and terminological consistency," and the relevance of this distinction to interpretation, see further M.A. Glendon, "Comment" in A. Gutmann (ed), *A Matter of Interpretation: Federal Courts and the Law* (Princeton, NJ, Princeton University Press, 1997) at 95–114.

15 Of course, in a civil law system, the legislature may empower courts to fill gaps in the code – as in Art 4 of the French Civil Code and Art 1, para 2 of the Swiss Civil Code. However, in my terms, such power is conferred, not inherent. In a common law system, courts do not need statutory authorization to make law.

This explains why individual decisions of civil law courts do not create precedents in the sense identified by Hamm.[16] Civil law courts have no inherent, autonomous power to make law. In this respect, their position is very different from that of a common law court. If a litigant asks a common law court a question of law that has not previously been answered, it is inherently the court's power and obligation to provide an answer to that question. In doing so, it exercises an autonomous, law-making power that gives its answer the "full force of law" – subject, of course, to its consistency with statute and constitutional law.[17]

A corollary of this difference is that answers to previously unanswered questions of law given by civil law courts do not constitute a separate, autonomous source of law. By contrast, answers to previously unanswered questions of law given by common law courts are a source of law autonomous of – albeit subordinate to – statute law. In one of its senses, law made by courts in exercise of their autonomous power to make law *is* "the common law."

Another corollary is that the role of a common law court in interpreting and applying statute law is different from the role of the civil law court in interpreting and applying the code. In this context, it is useful to distinguish what may be called *independent common law* from *dependent common law*. Dependent common law is law made by courts in the process of interpreting and applying a statute or a constitution. Independent common law is law made by courts in contexts other than application and interpretation of a statute or a constitution. Although a common law court is bound by the canonical words of a statute in a way that it is not bound by precedent, nevertheless, when common law courts gloss statutory provisions, they exercise autonomous power in a way that civil law courts do not when they interpret and apply the code.[18] An authoritative interpretation of a statute by a common

16 Once again, of course, the legislature may effectively give court decisions the force of law, as under Art 1, para 3 of the Swiss Civil Code (instructing judges to follow established doctrine and case law). By contrast, in a common law system, judicial decisions possess legal force independently of statute or constitution.

17 Ironically, perhaps, a common law court can decline to change the common law on the ground that doing so is more appropriately a job for the legislature. By contrast, a civil law court cannot refer a matter to the code-maker because the code is, in theory, complete and capable of answering every relevant legal question.

18 For fuller discussion, see L.M. Solan, "Precedent in Statutory Interpretation" (2016) 94 *North Carolina Law Review* 1165.

law court has the full force of law and can be altered only by another court with authority over that court or by the legislature following normal legislative procedure. Similarly, an interpretation of a constitution by a common law court has the full force of (constitutional) law and can be altered only by following the normal process of constitutional amendment.

My claim here is that while the High Court is a common law court in this sense, the Supreme Court cannot be called a common law court in the same sense but only in a somewhat different and modified sense. Let me explain. The US Constitution vests the judicial power of the United States in the Supreme Court. That judicial power extends "to all Cases, in Law and Equity, arising under this Constitution, the Laws of the United States, and Treaties made, or which shall be made, under their Authority" (Art. III, s. 2[1]). This provision echoes the Supremacy Clause (Art. VI [2]), which refers explicitly to three sources of law: the Constitution itself, congressional legislation, and treaties made "under the authority of the United States."

The judicial power also extends to "all cases of admiralty and maritime jurisdiction ... to which the United States shall be a party" (Art. III, s. 2[1]), thereby implying (so it has been held)[19] that decisions of the Supreme Court exercising this jurisdiction may be an autonomous source of law. Beyond that (and a few other exceptional cases), the Supreme Court has held that there is, in general, no federal common law and that common law is state law. It is only in exceptional cases that federal courts can develop a separate body of federal common law.[20] Even so, except in exercise of admiralty and maritime jurisdiction, such federal common law can be made only in the context of regulating the performance of a constitutionally permitted function[21] or of applying a federal statute. It follows that, in general, the Supreme Court (and other US federal courts) lack the power to make independent common law and that their main function is to interpret and apply the Constitution and congressional statutes, as required by the Constitution. Put differently, the Supreme Court's role in the constitutional design was not to make law

19 T.W. Merrill, "The Common Law Powers of Federal Courts" (1985) 52 *University of Chicago Law Review* 1 at 30.

20 See eg ibid. In the nineteenth century, in diversity cases, the Court was prepared to create federal common law in preference to the law of any of the relevant states. It abandoned this position in 1938.

21 *Clearwater Trust Co v United States* 318 US 363 (1943).

(that was to be the job of Congress and the president), but rather to enforce the Constitution and, in so doing, maintain the constitutional balance of power between the other branches (and itself).

By contrast (as we have seen), the High Court is a distant descendant of the English courts, which were, probably until the nineteenth century, the most significant source of law in the English system. By the sixteenth century, anyway, statute law was generally recognized as being superior to judge-made law. At the same time, however, law-making by Parliament was not understood to be qualitatively different from law-making by courts. In different ways, both forms of law gave expression to an underlying "customary," or "community," law. In interpreting statutes, courts began not with the text but with ideas of purpose, informed by concepts such as the common good and "the ancient rights of the English." In this sense, both Parliament and the courts (as well as the monarch) were ultimately under "the rule of law," where *law* was understood, metaphysically, as (in some sense) prior to and separate from law made by institutions of state. By the nineteenth century, this metaphysical interpretation of law-making had given way to positivism, according to which both common law and statute were merely products of institutional activity. In statutory interpretation, the text was now the starting – and often the ending – point, and courts were bound by (or, perhaps, owed their allegiance to) decisions of earlier courts, not metaphysical concepts of the right and the good. Nevertheless, although ideas changed about the nature of judge-made law, courts continued to exercise autonomous, law-making power.

The Australian equivalent of the US Supremacy Clause is (the so-called) Covering Clause 5 of the Commonwealth of Australia Constitution Act 1900.[22] It provides that "all laws made by the Parliament of the Commonwealth under the Constitution, shall be binding on the courts, judges, and people of every State and every part of the Commonwealth." This clause has not been interpreted or understood as altering the foundational status of the common law. On the contrary, s. 80 of the (federal) Judiciary Act 1903 provides that "the common law in Australia as modified by the Constitution and by the statute law in force in the State or Territory in which the Court in which the jurisdiction is exercised is held shall, so far as it is applicable and not inconsistent with

22 The Australian Constitution is contained in s 9 of the 1900 Act, which is an Act of the Westminster Parliament.

the Constitution and the laws of the Commonwealth, govern all Courts exercising federal jurisdiction in the exercise of their jurisdiction in civil and criminal matters."

By contrast, the US Constitution implied a sharp break from this English common law tradition.[23] It spelled out the sources of federal law and declared their supremacy; and court decisions were not (understood to be) among them. To repeat: the constitutional task of the Supreme Court was not to make law (that was to be the job of Congress and the president), but rather to enforce the Constitution and, in so doing, maintain the constitutional balance of power between the other branches (and itself). That task might, coincidentally, give the Court opportunities to make law, but dependently, not independently. Only in exceptional cases would the Court have autonomous power to make law "out of entirely new cloth," as it were. The foundation of US law is not the rule of law but the rule of the Constitution. The Court is guardian of the Constitution, not the law. As a result, (federal) common law came to be understood, first and foremost, as law that could not plausibly be passed off as interpretive of the Constitution or a statute, even though that was its technical status.[24]

23 Confirmed by statute: Merrill, "The Common Law Powers of Federal Courts," above n 19 at 27–32 (discussing the Rule of Decision Act, enacted in 1789).

24 See eg M.A. Field, "Sources of Law: The Scope of Federal Common Law" (1986) 99 *Harvard Law Review* 881. This helps to explain why the nature of interpretation is a much larger issue in US law than in Australian (or English) law and why, for instance, originalism has much greater salience in US constitutional law than in Australian constitutional law. It also helps to explain why the phrase *common law constitution(alism)* has a subtly different connotation in the US context than in the English context (in particular). In English discourse, *common law constitutionalism* describes the theory that the legal foundation of the constitution is the common law, not any particular legislative text or set of texts. In US discourse, by contrast, the common law constitution is a more or less (il)legitimate gloss on the Constitution, and the phrase *common-law statutory interpretation*, when used pejoratively, anyway, conveys an accusation of illegitimate judicial activism. In the famous case of *Vermont Yankee Nuclear Power Corp v Natural Resources Defense Council, Inc* 435 US 519 (1978), the Supreme Court attempted to limit the activism of lower federal courts in interpreting the Administrative Procedure Act: D.A. Strauss, "Foreword: Does the Constitution Mean What It Says?" (2015) 129 *Harvard Law Review* 1 at 26. See also J.M. Beermann, "Common Law and Statute in Administrative Law" (2011) 63 *Administrative Law Review* 1.

The High Court, the Supreme Court, and Federalism

Both Australia and the United States are federations. However, they came into existence in quite different circumstances. In the United States, there was a strong anti-federalist movement. The famous *Federalist Papers* were propaganda designed to neutralize the opposition to federation. The Bill of Rights began life as a set of concessions to anti-federalist sentiment and concerns about creating an overweening federal polity. The checks-and-balances principle underlying the design of the Constitution was meant to weaken the federal government, not only vis-à-vis the citizens but also vis-à-vis the states. In Australia, by contrast, there was no significant anti-federalist faction. The Australian federation was born not out of perceived necessities of security but to encourage trade and development.[25] As a result, although federation necessarily entails a vertical distribution of power, the resulting degree of diffusion in the US system is much greater than in the Australian system, which is much more unitary and centralized. Federalism in Australia is better understood in terms of increasing overall governmental capacity than in terms of dividing power and regulating the relationship between the federal and state governments.[26]

This difference is reflected in the fact that, in the US system (as already noted), common law is generally identified as state law, not federal law. Pockets of independent, federal common law are few and far between. Nevertheless, like the Constitution and federal statute law, federal common law pre-empts (prevails over) state law.[27] In Australia, by contrast, the High Court has held that there is a single, national, Australian common law that subsumes or renders redundant the concept of a federal common law.[28] It follows that the issue of pre-emption of state law by federal law cannot arise in Australia in the same form as in the United States.[29]

---

25 For a significant period after federation, the UK government remained responsible for Australia's defence and foreign relations.

26 J. Stellios, "Federal Jurisdiction" in C. Saunders and A. Stone, *The Oxford Handbook of the Australian Constitution* (Melbourne, Oxford University Press, 2018).

27 Merrill, "The Common Law Powers of Federal Courts," above n 19 at 6.

28 M. Leeming, "Common Law within Three Federations" (2007) 18 *Public Law Review* 186.

29 See more generally J.M. Beermann, "The Supreme Common Law Court of the United States" (2008) 18 *Public Interest Law Journal* 119.

The contrast between Australian and US federalism is also reflected in the design of the court systems in the two countries. Whereas the US Constitution empowers Congress to create federal "inferior courts" (US Constitution, Art. III, s. 1), the Australian Constitution empowers the Commonwealth Parliament not only to create "other federal courts" but also to confer federal jurisdiction on "other courts" – an implicit reference to state courts (Australian Constitution, s. 71). This so-called "autochthonous expedient" (under which federal jurisdiction may be conferred on state courts) expresses a degree of confidence and trust in state courts that certainly does not exist in the US system, where federal and state jurisdiction are separately allocated to two separate sets of courts. Furthermore, unlike the Supreme Court, the High Court has appellate jurisdiction not only over courts (whether federal or state) exercising federal jurisdiction but also over state courts exercising state jurisdiction, reflecting the fact that the (UK) Privy Council remained the ultimate court of appeal for Australia for most of the twentieth century. The result of this constitutional architecture is a distinctively Australian brand of "judicial federalism."[30]

For present purposes, the significance of these differences in the way that power is allocated vertically in the two systems is that they greatly reduce the Supreme Court's scope to operate as a common law court, in the sense of a court that has power to make independent common law. The Supreme Court has very limited opportunities to make independent federal common law. Furthermore, except in the context of diversity suits between citizens of different states, in which the Court must apply the common law of one of the states, it has even fewer opportunities to make independent common law in traditional common law areas such as contract and tort; and when it does, it makes state common law, not federal common law (and its decisions in diversity suits do not bind the relevant state courts). Moreover, the Eleventh Amendment prohibits citizens of one state from suing the government of another state in a federal court.

The High Court, the Supreme Court, and Separation of Powers

As already noted, the Founders of the Australian polity looked to the United States for guidance and inspiration in drafting a foundational constitutional document for a federation. However, as we have also

30 Stellios, "Federal Jurisdiction," above n 26.

noted, they ended up with a quite different federal design than the US Founders. The Australian Founders also settled upon an institutional design for federal government institutions very different from that in the United States. Perhaps most fundamentally, the Founders never intended, and the High Court soon decided that the Constitution had not brought about,[31] diffusion of legislative and executive power. On the contrary, far from being separated or diffused, legislative and executive power were concentrated by virtue of the adoption of the principle of responsible government, under which legislative initiative belongs to the executive and the executive depends, for continuance in office, on its ability to command a majority of votes in the lower house of Parliament. Power is even further concentrated in the Australian system by the operation of strong, cohesive political parties, which makes it much easier for governments to maintain the necessary control over the lower house of Parliament, and by virtue of the inherited power of Australian governments to design and manage the bureaucracy largely without recourse to statute (under "the prerogative"). In fact, in an essentially two-party system of universal suffrage, responsible government "concentrates" executive, legislative, and bureaucratic power in the government of the day.

Contrast the position in the US system, in which legislative power, including power over taxation and appropriation, is diffused among the president, the House of Representatives, and the Senate, and in which the legislative initiative rests with the legislature, not the executive. One result is that Congress possesses the prime power and responsibility to establish and maintain the bureaucracy, while, at the same time, the president has constitutional power over the bureaucracy by virtue of the obligation to ensure that the laws are "faithfully executed."[32] This means that the bureaucracy effectively has two masters, who compete with one another for control. It also means that, in consequence, the bureaucracy can play one off against the other, thus giving it a degree of autonomy from both that is much greater than that enjoyed by the bureaucracy vis-à-vis the executive in a system of concentrated power, such as the Australian system.[33]

31 *Victorian Stevedoring and General Contracting Company Proprietary Ltd v Dignan* (1931) 46 CLR 73.

32 US Constitution, Art II, s 3.

33 P. Cane, *Controlling Administrative Power: An Historical Comparison* (Cambridge, Cambridge University Press, 2016) at 87–94.

Because legislative, executive, and bureaucratic power are much more diffused in the US system than in the Australian system and, conversely, much more concentrated in the Australian system than in the US system, the role of the Supreme Court in the US system in controlling the exercise of power by the legislature, the executive, and the bureaucracy is much different from that of the High Court in the Australian system. In this regard, it is helpful to distinguish between two modes of controlling public power, which I shall call *checks and balances* and *accountability*, respectively.[34] As I have already explained, diffusing power by sharing it among a number of institutions establishes a balance of power among the institutions and enables each to check the other(s). *Checking* has two connotations: one is stopping or delaying, as in "checking someone's progress." The other is supervising, as in "checking up on" someone or "keeping an eye" on them. The characteristic mode of controlling public power in a system of highly diffused (legislative, executive, and bureaucratic) power, such as the US system, is checks and balances. Checks and balances operate prospectively or continuously to weaken government by making the effective exercise of power more costly and time-consuming.

By contrast, accountability is the mode of control characteristic of a system of highly concentrated (legislative, executive, and bureaucratic) power, such as the Australian system. The classic example of this mode of control is ministerial responsibility to Parliament in systems of responsible government. Ministerial responsibility is the price that governments pay in parliamentary systems for the large amounts of concentrated power they enjoy. Whereas diffusion involves sharing one and the same type of power among various institutions, so that they have incentives to bargain and cooperate in the exercise of that power, concentration involves allocating different types of power to different institutions in such a way that each can exercise its characteristic power more or less unilaterally, both to promote its respective policy objectives and to hold other institutions to account for the way they exercise their characteristic powers. Accountability (in this narrow sense)[35] operates retrospectively by requiring power holders to provide

34 See further ibid, esp. ch 1.

35 The word is often used to cover checks and balances as well as accountability in my sense.

reasons and explanations, and possibly amendment and recompense, for abuses and excesses of power. Accountability leaves actors quite free to exercise their powers, subject only to *ex post facto* control.

This difference between the way that power is divided and allocated horizontally in the Australian system compared with the US system, and the associated difference between the ways in which public power is characteristically controlled in the two systems, also affect the respective roles and positions of the High Court and the Supreme Court in the system of government. Furthermore, they inform understandings of the nature of judicial power and the rule of law in the two systems as well as the significance attached to judicial independence.

The Supreme Court and the High Court each play a part in controlling the exercise of public power in their respective systems. The Supreme Court does this as a sort of umpire, maintaining the constitutional balance among the various branches and checking each by defining the limits of their respective powers. Of course, in performing this umpiring function, the Court is itself one of the institutions in the balance. For this reason, the Constitution gives the other institutions means of checking the Court and defending themselves against aggrandizement of judicial power. Nevertheless, the Court is in a conflicted position because it is, to some extent, a self-regulator, a "coordinate participant" in the very interplay of institutions that it has the power and responsibility to monitor.

By contrast, the High Court plays its role in controlling public power by providing opportunities to hold other governmental institutions accountable. Its ability to do this depends crucially on the fact that, in a significant sense, it stands outside government, perched between the state and civil society, and in a position to mediate between the two. Whereas the Supreme Court participates in government as a coordinate institution policing it on behalf of the people, the Australian government is largely left to police itself. The High Court steps in only after the event, if and when self-regulation fails, to provide citizens with avenues of recourse for governmental breaches of the law.

This difference between the respective roles of the two Courts helps us to understand many of their particular features and characteristics. First, it partly explains why, although Supreme Court justices strongly protest their fidelity to the law[36] and their independence from the other

36 Originalism as a mode of constitutional interpretation is one way of avoiding charges of judicial activism.

branches, the Supreme Court is standardly considered to be a political institution in a way that the High Court is not. The Supreme Court is, in a meaningful sense, a participant in the processes of government, whereas the High Court stands and holds itself aloof from those processes in a state of almost monastic isolation.[37]

Second, it helps to explain differences between the processes for appointing justices to the two Courts and why the US appointment process is so public and politicized. Under the US Constitution, the president has power to nominate individuals as justices, and their appointment is subject to confirmation by the Senate. Especially during periods of divided government, when the president's political party does not control the Senate, the selection process can be highly contentious and protracted as the two parties compete to influence, as best they can, the likely ideological complexion of the Court. It is generally agreed that, since the middle of the twentieth century, US politics has become much more polarized along party lines. Observers have also noted increasing political polarization in the Supreme Court.[38] At the extreme, the result may be the decision of a significant proportion of cases by a 5–4 or 6–3 split and concentration of power in one or two "moderate," "swinging voters." This effect is aggravated by the relatively large proportion of cases on the Court's docket – raising, for instance, issues of rights, separation of powers, or federalism – that have high political salience.

In Australia, justices of the High Court are appointed technically by the governor general and in reality by the federal government. The

37 In this context, it is worth noting that when Blackstone, in the *Commentaries*, "domesticated" Montesquieu's account for English consumption, he stressed separation of judicial power and judicial independence; and that A.V. Dicey put the courts at the centre of his theory of the rule of law, expounded in his *Introduction to the Study of the Law of the Constitution*: Cane, *Controlling Administrative Power*, above n 33 at 36.

38 B.L. Bartels, "The Sources and Consequences of Polarization in the US Supreme Court" in J.A. Thurber and A. Yoshinaka (eds), *American Gridlock: The Sources, Character and Impact of Political Polarization* (Cambridge, Cambridge University Press, 2015). On the death of Justice Antonin Scalia in 2016, Senate Republicans refused to consider *any* nomination for a replacement by President Obama. Scalia's death effectively divided the Court evenly between conservatives and liberals, and the Republicans took the position that the political affiliation of the replacement for Scalia should effectively be decided in the presidential election of 2016. Such a situation is inconceivable in England, Australia, or, indeed, any other common law jurisdiction. I am grateful to Colm McGrath for pointing out this example of stalemate caused by political polarization.

process is closed and conducted outside the public gaze. Federal governments obviously have incentives to appoint justices whom they calculate will be sympathetic to their policies. In fact, however, during the Court's life, relatively few appointments have been openly or controversially partisan, and the only formal criterion is merit, qualified by the generally accepted desirability of a measure of diversity, particularly in terms of gender and region. Once appointed, justices are expected to keep their (party-)political allegiances (if any) to themselves. In these ways, the Court maintains an apolitical ethos – or, at least, its appearance. Moreover, because Australia lacks a bill of rights, and because the High Court has general appellate jurisdiction, only a relatively small proportion of its business has high (party-)political salience.

The two Courts also differ in terms of the tenure of the justices: justices of the High Court must retire at the age of seventy,[39] whereas appointments to the Supreme Court are for life. At the margin, life tenure may encourage Supreme Court justices to "[linger] in office longer than they should … because of ideology and party."[40]

Third, the differing roles of the two Courts help to explain why US political scientists are much more interested in the Supreme Court in particular, and in courts more generally, than their Australian counterparts;[41] and why the political party of the president who appoints a particular justice is widely used as a proxy for judicial ideology in empirical research analysing voting patterns in federal courts.

Fourth, the differences of role suggest a reason why Australian constitutional law insists more strongly than US law on protection of judicial power from contamination by legislative and executive power. Australian law requires not only that non-judicial bodies not exercise judicial power (to prevent dilution of the judicial function) but also that judicial bodies not exercise non-judicial power (to prevent its contamination). Moreover (in principle, at least), the anti-contamination principle is subject to fewer qualifications than the anti-dilution principle.

---

39 Life tenure was abolished by constitutional amendment in 1977. The retiring age is statutory.

40 D.N. Atkinson, *Leaving the Bench: Supreme Court Justices at the End* (Lawrence, KS, University of Kansas Press, 1999) at 8.

41 Eg R.L. Pacelle, Jr, B.W. Curry, and B.W. Marshall, *Decision-Making by the Modern Supreme Court* (Cambridge, Cambridge University Press, 2011), which provides an excellent overview of the literature in addition to original research. Re Australia, see R. Turner, "The High Court of Australia and Political Science: A Revised Historiography and New Research Agenda" (2015) 50 *Australian Journal of Political*

Thus, the Australian system draws a categorical distinction between judicial review of administrative action, based on legality, and review on the merits. Review on the merits is classified as a non-judicial function that cannot be performed by federal courts. Instead, it is undertaken by an elaborate system of tribunals, which technically exercise executive power.[42]

Relatedly, Australian law maintains a very strong distinction between law and policy. The role of the courts, and the source of their authority and legitimacy, is to enforce the law and not to get involved in matters of policy. US law, by contrast, distinguishes much less clearly between law and policy. Indeed, the terms law-making and policymaking are often used more or less synonymously, law-making being understood as a species of policymaking. In US law, the famous dictum of Marshall CJ in *Marbury v Madison*, to the effect that it is the role of courts to enforce the law, does not prevent sharing the power to interpret legislation between the courts and the executive in such a way as to allow and require courts to accord a certain degree of deference to administrative interpretations. By contrast, in Australian law, the dictum has been used to justify blanket judicial refusal to defer to administrative statutory interpretations[43] and to insist that statutory interpretation is the sole province of courts.

Fifth, we may also find here an explanation of the fact that whereas, in the Australian system, a judicial monopoly over constitutional interpretation is firmly and uncontroversially entrenched, in the United States there have long been debates between the supporters of judicial supremacy on the one hand, and "departmentalists" on the other.[44]

Science 347. Concerning the Canadian Supreme Court, see C.L. Ostberg and M.E. Wetstein, *Attitudinal Decision Making in the Supreme Court of Canada* (Vancouver, UBC Press, 2007); D.R. Songer, S.W. Johnson, C.L. Ostberg, and M.E. Wetstein, *Law, Ideology, and Collegiality: Judicial Behaviour in the Supreme Court of Canada* (Montreal and Kingston, McGill-Queen's University Press, 2012); E. Macfarlane, *Governing from the Bench: The Supreme Court of Canada and the Judicial Role* (Vancouver, UBC Press, 2012).

42 P. Cane, *Administrative Tribunals and Administration* (Oxford, Hart Publishing, 2009).

43 See generally Cane, *Controlling Administrative Power*, above n 33, ch 6.

44 See M. Tushnet, *The Constitution of the United States of America*, 2nd edn (Oxford, Hart Publishing, 2015) at 134–7; M.-S. Kuo, "In the Shadow of Judicial Supremacy: Putting the Idea of Judicial Dialogue in Its Place" (2016) 29 *Ratio Juris* 83 at 90–5. There might also be an explanation here for the common perception that the High Court is more willing than the Supreme Court to hold legislative provisions unconstitutional. In other words, the Supreme Court is more deferential to the legislature than the High Court.

Departmentalists interpret the Constitution as sharing out the power to interpret the document among the various branches of government, making none supreme in that activity.[45] Although judicial supremacy seems to have won the day,[46] the very fact of the debate underscores the extent to which the Supreme Court may be understood as a coordinate participant in government, not its external controller.

In this sense, the rule of law is a much stronger constitutional principle in the Australian system than in the US system. This, I would argue, can be traced back to the impact on English courts of the Glorious Revolution. Recall that one important consequence of the revolution was that in return for their marginalization from the day-to-day conduct of government, courts were given exclusive power to interpret parliamentary legislation. In Australia, this monopoly also (and, perhaps, even more strongly) applies to interpreting the Constitution. Ironically, judicial supremacy in matters of interpretation is a corollary of the marginalization and subordination of courts in the system of government. On the other hand, the subordinate ("marginal," or "outsider") status of the judiciary finds its clearest expression in the strong distinction drawn by Australian law between law and policy, the relatively strong anti-contamination principle, and the relatively high degree of deference that courts accord to administrative fact-finding and policymaking.

Unsurprisingly, in this light, while US law allows courts to defer to administrative statutory interpretations much more than Australian courts do, it requires (or, at least, allows) them to take a hard look at administrative fact-finding and policymaking. In US law, the power of interpretation is shared between the courts and the executive, and, conversely, the executive's power to find facts and make policy is shared by the courts. The Supreme Court is understood to be integral, not marginal, to the business of government.

More speculatively, it may be suggested that the different positions of the High Court and the Supreme Court in their respective systems of government help to explain certain other differences between them. For instance, the coordinate status of the Supreme Court may be reflected in the fact that, in every case, it publishes a judgment of the Court, whether unanimous or by plurality, whereas each individual justice of

---

45 Judicial deference to administrative statutory interpretations can be understood as a form of departmentalism.

46 L. Alexander and F. Schauer, "Defending Judicial Supremacy: A Reply" (2000) 17 *Constitutional Commentary* 455.

the High Court speaks individually, even in cases where only one, unanimous set of reasons is published. Partly for this reason, the High Court does not have a formal conferencing system such as characterizes the behind-the-scenes proceedings of the Supreme Court. This difference (I would suggest) marks one way in which the Supreme Court is a political institution in a sense that the High Court is not: the Supreme Court *as an institution* has a more distinct identity as a constitutional actor than the High Court.[47] It may also have implications for the authority of the respective courts' judgments. To the extent that judgments of the Supreme Court represent compromises "composed by committee," it may be difficult to find in them a *ratio decidendi*, and it may be quite difficult for individual justices to develop their personal jurisprudence over a period of years (except at the price of dissenting or, at least, concurring rather than joining with the plurality).

By contrast, difficulty in discerning a *ratio* for decisions of the High Court is more likely to arise from the fact that the majority justices may produce more than one judgment among them, and maybe one each. This way of proceeding makes it easier for individual justices to develop a personal jurisprudence over a period of time but is more likely, perhaps, to generate inconsistency or tension between decisions of various, differently composed majorities. The practice of issuing single plurality judgments has certainly increased in recent years, but it is by no means universal, and some justices take the view that they have an obligation to state their own reasons in every case, even when they agree with the result and, essentially, with the reasons given by other justices for that result.

We may hypothesize an association between the role of each Court and the scope of its respective jurisdiction. The jurisdiction of the Supreme Court is (now) almost entirely discretionary and almost completely appellate. The Supreme Court can entertain appeals from state courts only on issues of federal law. The main mechanism by which appeals come to the Court is the writ of *certiorari* (*cert*). In the 2014 term, 7,033 cases were filed (5,488 by indigents, mostly in criminal matters), and 75 cases were argued and disposed of. The High Court has more extensive original jurisdiction than the Supreme Court, although, in practice, most cases that come directly to the Court are remitted for hearing to another court exercising federal jurisdiction – notably, the

47 See eg K.T. McGuire, "The Institutionalization of the US Supreme Court" (2004) 12 *Political Analysis* 128.

Federal Court, established in 1977. However, because the original jurisdiction of the Court is mandatory and constitutionally entrenched, the volume of its business in this jurisdiction is subject to political manipulation. For instance, in the 1990s, the federal Parliament significantly truncated the jurisdiction of the Federal Court in immigration and asylum matters, thus preventing remittal by the High Court and causing a sharp increase of applications in the High Court's original jurisdiction.

One notable area of the Court's original jurisdiction relates to applications for injunctions and writs of *mandamus* and prohibition against officers of the Commonwealth, which can be made under s. 75(v) of the Constitution. This provision was inserted to prevent a repeat in Australia of the decision in *Marbury v Madison*, which held that the Supreme Court lacked original jurisdiction to award a writ of *mandamus* against an officer of the United States. In the year 2014–15, ninety-five writs were filed under this provision, ninety of which were in immigration matters. This provision provides a bulwark against legislative attempts to oust judicial review of executive action by providing a constitutionally entrenched "minimum" of review. In US law, by contrast, the law governing ouster of the jurisdiction of the Supreme Court is relatively unclear, perhaps reflecting the status of "court-curbing" as a "weapon of self-defence," which can be deployed in the ongoing contest among the branches over the balance of power among them.

As already noted, the High Court has appellate jurisdiction not only in relation to decisions of courts exercising federal jurisdiction but also in relation to decisions of courts exercising state jurisdiction. Access to the Court's appellate jurisdiction is rationed by the requirement of "special leave" to appeal. In 2014–15, about 500 applications for special leave were filed. Of these, approximately 250 were filed by litigants in person, and some 175 related to immigration matters. Special leave applications are heard by benches of two, or occasionally three, justices, and they are resolved (as in the United States) on the basis of an extremely abstract and vague criterion of importance.[48] In the year 2014–15, the High Court heard some sixty-five cases and decided about sixty. This figure might seem comparatively high given Australia's small population (about 24 million people). But it must be remembered that the High Court is the final appeal court on all matters of state as well as federal law, and it

48 In the Supreme Court, *cert* applications are considered by all the justices, and at least four must vote in favour if the application is to be granted.

has assumed responsibility for developing a single, national, Australian common law. By contrast, the Supreme Court's docket consists almost entirely of matters arising under the Constitution or a federal statute. Once again, this difference reflects the status of the High Court as a traditional common law court. Enforcing the Constitution and federal statutes, and controlling the federal government, are not its only functions.

We might further hypothesize an association between the differing roles of the two Courts and (1) the much greater opportunity for oral argument provided by the High Court compared with the Supreme Court, (2) the much greater accessibility of Supreme Court proceedings to third parties (submitting "Brandeis briefs") compared with High Court proceedings, and, more fundamentally, (3) different understandings of the nature and purpose of judicial law-making. Regarding the first point, even in public law matters, the High Court is much more oriented towards "doing justice" between the parties than the Supreme Court, which is (or so it seems to me) more oriented towards the other institutions of government and its relationship with them than towards the parties. This orientation towards "the system" may also help us to understand why the Supreme Court is more open to non-litigants than the High Court.

The third point deserves a little more elaboration. It is widely accepted, I think, that, in the course of the nineteenth century, US lawyers and courts developed an essentially "instrumental," or "realist," understanding of the role of courts as lawmakers.[49] As economic activity and government regulation increased, the need for law also increased; and courts came to be seen as providing a necessary additional source of law to supplement the limited capacity of the legislature,[50] a lack further aggravated by the inertia that may result from diffusion of legislative

49 M.J. Horwitz, *The Transformation of American Law 1780–1860* (Cambridge, MA, Harvard University Press, 1977) ch 1; B.Z. Tamanaha, *Law as a Means to an End: Threat to the Rule of Law* (Cambridge, Cambridge University Press, 2006).

50 According to Melvin Eisenberg, courts perform two "paramount" social functions: resolution of disputes and "enrichment of the supply of legal rules": M.A. Eisenberg, *The Nature of the Common Law* (Cambridge, MA, Harvard University Press, 1988). According to Eisenberg (at 6), "Under the enrichment model … the establishment of legal rules to govern social conduct is treated as desirable in itself – although subordinated in a variety of important ways to the function of dispute resolution – so that the courts consciously take on the function of developing certain bodies of law, albeit on a case-by-case basis."

power among the various branches of government. This view of courts has led, for instance, to "restatement" of judge-made law in propositional, "black-letter" form by the American Law Institute and to what has been dubbed "the textualization of precedent."[51] Under such an approach, the most important part of a court's decision – not only for the parties but also more generally – is the outcome, not the reasoning. The reasons provide more a justification for, than a reasoned explanation or elaboration of, the result. Put crudely, for instrumentalists, what the judges do is what counts most, not what they say.[52]

With such an approach we may contrast the traditional, Anglo-Australian view, according to which what really matters, for society and the system as a whole, is the ongoing, always provisional, and never completed dialogue between judges and lawyers, bench and bar, about what the law is and what it ought to be.[53] It is in this sense that judicial law-making is a matter of discovery rather than invention. In this view, law-making by judges is qualitatively different from law-making by legislators, not quantitatively supplementary. The US tendency to think of judicial law-making in instrumental terms may help to explain the US preoccupation with the "counter-majoritarian difficulty" associated with judicial review of legislation, Alexander Bickel's advocacy of the "passive virtues,"[54] and Herbert Wechsler's famous search for "neutral principles"[55] – as well, perhaps, as the attraction of originalism

51 P. Tiersma, "The Textualization of Precedent" (2007) 82 *Notre Dame Law Review* 1187; S. Grossi, *The United States Supreme Court and the Modern Law Approach* (Cambridge, Cambridge University Press, 2015) ch 1; F. Schauer, "Opinions as Rules" (1995) 62 *University of Chicago Law Review* 1455 at 1455: "It is a routine charge against contemporary judicial opinions that they read more like statutes than like opinions of a court."

52 In legal scholarship, such an approach is manifested in extreme form in descriptive ("positive") economic analysis of law.

53 A.W.B. Simpson, "The Common Law and Legal Theory" in A.W.B. Simpson (ed), *Oxford Essays in Jurisprudence, Second Series* (Oxford, Clarendon Press, 1973); G. Postema, "Philosophy of the Common Law" in J. Coleman and S. Shapiro (eds), *The Oxford Handbook of Jurisprudence and Philosophy of Law* (Oxford, Oxford University Press, 2002).

54 A.M. Bickel, "Foreword: The Passive Virtues" (1961) 75 *Harvard Law Review* 40.

55 H. Wechsler, "Toward Neutral Principles of Constitutional Law" (1959) 73 *Harvard Law Review* 1. Concerning the lesser concern with the counter-majoritarian difficulty in Australia, see T. Josev, "The Late Arrival of the Judicial Activism Debate in Australian Public Discourse" (2013) 24 *Public Law Review* 17.

as a mode of constitutional interpretation. It may also throw some light on Ronald Dworkin's theory of judicial reasoning, which starts from the proposition that when judges make law, "they neither should be nor are deputy legislators."[56] In his account, judges are bound by principles and the pre-existing body of legal materials in a way that legislatures are not.

The traditional idea that judicial law-making is qualitatively different from law-making by the legislature informs the understanding of *dependent common law*, not just *independent common law*. In this way of thinking, statutes are conceptualized as interventions in the ongoing stream of the (non-democratic, elitist) legal dialogue between society (represented by lawyers) and courts, the results of which are found in the reasons for the decisions of courts. This explains why there is a large literature in the Anglo-Commonwealth, which has no real US counterpart, about the relationship between "common law and statute"[57] and why judge-made law continues to loom so large in the legal consciousness despite the ever-increasing dominance of legislatures as sources of law, at least since the middle of the nineteenth century.

In a code system, the code is the comprehensive source of law. In a traditional common law system, judge-made law is foundational, and statute law is interstitial and, in a significant sense, rooted in the soil of the common law. In these terms, the US (federal) system is a hybrid: constitutional and statutory law are not comprehensive, either in theory or in practice. However, the role of judges as lawmakers is supplementary, not foundational. The Supreme Court can make law, but only to supplement law-making by the other (democratic) branches. It is true that US courts have a reputation for making a lot of law and for giving that role higher priority than courts elsewhere in the common law world. But I would argue that the best explanation – at least in relation

56 R. Dworkin, *Taking Rights Seriously* (London, Duckworth, 1977) at 82. See also R.A. Posner, *Law and Legal Theory in England and America* (Oxford, Clarendon Press, 1996) ch 1.

57 Eg E. Bant, "Statute and Common Law: Interaction and Influence in the Light of the Principle of Coherence" (2015) 38 *University of New South Wales Law Journal* 367. But see P.L. Strauss, "The Common Law and Statutes" (1999) 70 *University of Colorado Law Review* 225. The so-called principle of legality refers to a presumption of statutory interpretation that the legislature does not intend to infringe "fundamental common law rights": D.C. Pearce and R.S. Geddes, *Statutory Interpretation in Australia*, 8th edn (Chatswood, NSW, LexisNexis Butterworths, 2014) ch 5.

to the Supreme Court – is that diffusion of power, especially in conjunction with ideological polarization, tends to produce legislative gridlock and inertia, encouraging courts to think of themselves as alternate lawmakers.[58]

As a coordinate branch of government in a system where different types of power are shared, courts may be much more inclined to step into the breach when the legislative process is deadlocked or inert. By contrast, in systems where (legislative, executive, and bureaucratic) power is highly concentrated, courts are more likely to leave legal gaps unfilled on the ground that it is properly the job of the legislature to act. This, I would argue, is a symptom of the marginalization of courts from the processes of government.

In the traditional, common law way of thinking, judicial law-making is foundational, not supplementary. In this view, the role of courts is not to assist the legislature, let alone compete with it for a share of the legislative action. Rather, their role as lawmakers is to engage in an ongoing dialectical process, the prime and ultimate aim of which is not to produce more law (even though it may do that), but rather to work all the law into a coherent, systemic whole.[59] This is the way English courts have traditionally understood their role. As soon as legislation became a significant source of law (starting in the fifteenth century, perhaps), English courts took a back seat, as it were, not in the sense that they produced less law, but in their understanding of their relationship to the legislature and the relationship between common law and statute. Now that legislation is, in terms of quantity and significance, the dominant source of law, courts make proportionally much less law – or, perhaps more accurately, much less independent common law relative to their output of dependent common law. But their understanding of the nature of the common law process and of common law reasoning has not changed. This brings us back full circle to our starting point: the High Court and the Supreme Court may both be understood as common law courts, but in very different senses.

58 Judicial activism may also be encouraged by the brevity and difficulty of amending the Constitution.

59 For some interesting reflections on the impact of the development of the US regulatory state on this understanding of the common law, see T.D. Rakoff, "The Shape of the Law in the American Administrative State" (1992) 11 *Tel Aviv University Studies in Law* 9.

Conclusion

In this chapter, I have argued that, despite various obvious similarities, the High Court of Australia and the Supreme Court of the United States are very different institutions. In particular, I have argued that the High Court is a common law court in a sense that does not apply to the Supreme Court. This difference can be explained historically. The High Court is an inheritor of an organic tradition, dating back to 1066, in which courts have autonomous power to make law and in which the common law represents the normative foundation of the legal system on which statutory (and constitutional) law[60] rests. By contrast, the Supreme Court was deliberately established primarily as a guardian of a written constitution and an umpire in disputes about the allocation of public power.[61] In light of this history, we can understand various differences between the two courts, which might otherwise appear fortuitous, as manifestations of two quite different understandings of the role of courts in a system of government.

---

60 In this context, it may be noted that the Australian Constitution (unlike the US Constitution) is better understood as a gloss on the English (common law) constitution than a clean break with it. Currently, the High Court is reinterpreting the relationship between the Constitution and constitutional common law, seeking to interpret (extra-constitutional) common law (constitutional) principles as implicit in the Constitution. For more discussion, see Cane, *Controlling Administrative Power*, above n 33 at 231–4.

61 D.A. Strauss, "Common Law Constitutional Interpretation" (1996) 63 *University of Chicago Law Review* 877 at 878: "the terms of debate in American constitutional law continue to be set by the view that principles of constitutional law must ultimately be traced to the text of the Constitution, and by the allied view that when the text is unclear the original understandings must control. An air of illegitimacy surrounds any alleged departure from the text or the original understandings"; cited in J. Komarek, "Judicial Lawmaking and Precedent in Supreme Courts," http://papers.ssrn.com/sol3/papers.cfm?abstract_id=1793219 at 8.

4 Against All Odds: Numbers Sitting in the UK Supreme Court and Really, Really Important Cases

JAMES LEE*

Introduction

In 2017, the Supreme Court of the United Kingdom decided *R (Miller) v Secretary of State for Exiting the European Union*,[1] which concerned the constitutional route by which the United Kingdom could begin negotiations to leave the European Union (EU) after the outcome of the 2016 referendum on the issue. The case saw "the Supreme Court [find] its way into public consciousness to an unprecedented degree."[2] It was also the first time ever that the Court had sat with a full bench of justices. For the UK Supreme Court (UKSC) is unusual when compared with other common law apex courts as it has had (and will continue

---

* I am grateful to Gabrielle Appleby, John Bell, Andrew Burrows, Robert Chambers, Paul Daly, Brice Dickson, Rosalind Dixon, Matthew Dyson, Matthew Harrington, Simon Lee, Luigi Lonardo, Andrew Lynch, Federico Ortino, Alan Paterson, Natalie Pratt, Eloise Scotford, Findlay Stark, James Turner QC, George Williams, and the anonymous referees for helpful comments. I also greatly benefited from discussions with my colleagues at a staff seminar at the Dickson Poon School of Law at King's College London in March 2016, at the conference giving rise to this collection in Montreal in May 2016, and during a research visit to the Gilbert + Tobin Centre of Public Law, Faculty of Law, University of New South Wales, Sydney, in August 2016. The statistics here aim to be correct up to the end of August 2018. All views, and any errors, are my own.

1 [2017] UKSC 5 (on appeal from [2016] EWHC 2768 (Admin)) ("*Miller*"); see in particular "The First Eleven" below.

2 M. Ormerod, Introduction, *The Supreme Court Annual Report and Accounts* (2016–17) (HC 31) 7.

generally to have) a practice of never sitting *en banc*.[3] Lady Hale, the Court's new president, has explained,

> We in the UK are unusual in sitting in panels [in the top appellate court], usually of five but sometimes of seven or nine. Since moving from the House of Lords, we have sat in larger panels more often than we did there. There are various reasons for this, including our ready access to a larger courtroom, but one is the greater authority it gives to a decision, the greater the number of justices who agree upon it. Another is the (apparently) reduced risk that the composition of the panel will dictate the result. We do not accept that any of us is sufficiently consistent and predictable in his or her approach for this to be a real problem. But we acknowledge that the public may think it so.[4]

It is a point to which Lady Hale returned more recently in an extra-judicial speech as president.[5]

This chapter presents a study of the UKSC's seven-, nine-, and now eleven-justice decisions (*enlarged panel* cases) in its first nine years, from

---

3 The Supreme Court of the United States, the Supreme Court of Canada, and the Supreme Court of New Zealand generally sit *en banc* for substantive appeals. The High Court of Australia generally sits in panels of five, but also in panels of a full bench of seven. I do not here consider any comparative data since I do not wish to trespass on the territory of others in this collection, but eg in 2016, the High Court sat in fifty-three cases, of which fourteen (26.4 per cent) were *en banc*. In 2017, the High Court decided fifty-six cases, of which eighteen were *en banc* (seventeen with seven justices; the other, *Perara-Cathcart v The Queen* [2017] HCA 9, was heard in September 2016, before the appointment of Edelman J): that is 32.14 per cent. These results were obtained using austlii.edu.au. The Supreme Court of Ireland usually has nine justices and follows a similar practice to the UKSC.

4 Lady Hale DPSC, "Appointments to the Supreme Court," conference to mark the tenth anniversary of the Judicial Appointments Commission, University of Birmingham, 6 November 2015, https://www.supremecourt.uk/docs/speech-151106.pdf, 2–3 (reproduced in Baroness Hale of Richmond, "Appointments to the UK Supreme Court" (2016) 7 *UK Supreme Court Yearbook* 41; references here are to the publicly accessible version). Lady Hale was deputy president at the time of that speech and was speaking a year before the decision to sit *en banc* in *Miller*. Note also Lady Hale's "Judges, Power and Accountability: Constitutional Implications of Judicial Selection," Constitutional Law Summer School, Belfast, 11 August 2017.

5 Lady Hale, "Should the Law Lords Have Left the House of Lords?," Michael Ryle Lecture 2018, House of Lords, 14 November 2018, accessed 29 November 2018, https://www.supremecourt.uk/docs/speech-181114.pdf.

October 2009 to August 2018: the period that marked the tenure of the Court's first two presidents, Lord Phillips and Lord Neuberger, and the first year of Lady Hale's presidency. My statistical analysis demonstrates that there was a variation in practice between Lord Phillips's presidency and that of Lord Neuberger in the frequency with which the Court sat in an enlarged panel. Overall, the Court sat in a panel with other than five justices in just under 20 per cent of its 621 decisions in the relevant period. The chapter involves an assessment of the decisions themselves as well as extra-curial observations from the justices on the subject. I argue that the UKSC's difference in practice from other supreme courts raises special challenges for the Court's decision-making.

After the first three years of the Supreme Court, Professor Burrows wrote a valuable and concerned note commenting on the increased use of enlarged panels.[6] Some of Burrows's reasons for alarm are echoed here. However, the early years of the Supreme Court saw an abnormally high number of enlarged panel cases, as the figures in the tables below show. The second half of the period saw a falling off of the rate, which coincided with the arrival of Lord Neuberger as president of the Supreme Court. The percentage of enlarged panel cases between 2009 and 2012 was 25.25 per cent; between 2013 and 2017, it was 14.2 per cent; and in the 2017–18 year, only 5.6 per cent of cases saw an enlarged panel.[7] The substantive examples discussed here will inevitably be somewhat selective: there are over one hundred enlarged panel cases, after all. For ease of reference here, I shall use *EP* to refer to *enlarged panel* and *3JP, 5JP, 7JP, 9JP*, and *11JP* for those cases heard by the respective number of justices. The statistics are from 2009 until the end of the summer in 2018, drawing, in particular, on themes arising out of the cases decided in the last three years.

Overall, the pattern of decision-making leads to several conclusions. Initially, it is clear that the peculiar workload and role of the UKSC, and the continuing role of the Privy Council, mean that the existing practice of generally sitting in panels of five is justifiable.

In terms of significant recommendations for change, I argue that it is necessary to reconsider the criteria for larger panels because the current

6 A. Burrows, "Numbers Sitting in the Supreme Court" (2013) 129 *Law Quarterly Review* 305. Paterson also considers the point briefly in A. Paterson, *Final Judgment* (Oxford, Hart Publishing, 2014) 72; and see further D. Clarry and C. Sargeant, "Judicial Panel Selection in the UK Supreme Court: Bigger Bench, More Authority?" (2016) 7 *UK Supreme Court Yearbook* 1.

7 See tables below. As of 30 November 2018, there were five further 7JP cases with judgment or hearing pending (according to the Supreme Court database of current cases).

approach seems erratic from one case to another, especially as to the concept of *importance* (or possibly various kinds of importance). Is there any answer to Burrows's concern that "it is hardly satisfactory for litigants to be told that, although their case has been given permission to appeal, it only merits being heard by five Supreme Court judges rather than the seven or nine that sit on 'really important cases'"?[8] Surely every litigant thinks their case is important.[9] Dickson has noted the "apparent randomness of when enhanced benches are convened."[10]

More generally, the *reasons* relied upon for sitting in EPs, as outlined by Lady Hale above, are open to question. I argue that the current practice risks perpetuating, rather than challenging, the concern that it matters which justice(s) one gets on a panel. This problem is particularly apparent in the nine-justice cases, where the Court has rarely been unanimous or univocal. A second, related recommendation is that the criteria may need to be revised for the granting of permission to appeal in the first place – the current criteria for seven or nine panels ought arguably to be applicable to any case for which permission should be granted to appeal to the highest court in the jurisdiction.

Some of the EP cases have been false alarms, where the Court has been convened to reconsider a precedent, only then to reaffirm the existing authority in a matter-of-fact way. In other cases, the Court has been perfectly content to depart from a previous authority, sometimes dramatically, with a panel of only five. These contrasting cases perhaps suggest that the Court's approach to precedent needs some re-evaluation.

A final conclusion relates to the role of an apex court, a theme that underlies this chapter and runs through this collection. Some of the cases that the UKSC hears will be principally focused on the resolution of the dispute before the Court, with the Court straightforwardly acting as a final court of appeal. In other cases, the role of the Court will be more ambitious in developing the law, offering guidance to lower courts or departing from a precedent. But this bifurcation does not map onto the present approach with regard to numbers sitting on panels or which cases count as important. And, in any event, whether a case falls

8 Burrows, "Numbers Sitting in the Supreme Court," above n 6 at 309.

9 Indeed, the Supreme Court Annual Report 2016–17 notes (at 30), "Although every appeal heard by the UKSC is of importance, many also attract considerable public interest owing to their impact on wider society, or legal interest because of the scope of the precedent set."

10 B. Dickson, "UK Supreme Court Justices and Human Rights in the 2015–16 Legal Year" (2016) 7 *UK Supreme Court Yearbook* 214 at 219 fn 29.

into the "straightforward" or "more ambitious" category is not a simple question: it will depend upon the arguments of counsel and of the justices.[11] My study here reveals such inconsistencies in the Court's adjudicative structures that the approach ought to be reconsidered, and the arguments are thrown into relief by the decision to sit *en banc* in *Miller*.

Background

Practice and Procedure

The Supreme Court was provided for by the Constitutional Reform Act 2005, Part 3, with s. 23(1) stating, "There is to be a Supreme Court of the United Kingdom"; it replaced the Appellate Committee of the House of Lords.[12] The Court is to consist of the full-time equivalent of twelve justices, pursuant to s. 23(2): there are currently twelve full-time justices.[13] Section 42 provides for when the Court is duly constituted:

(1) The Supreme Court is duly constituted in any proceedings only if all of the following conditions are met –
  (a) the Court consists of an uneven number of judges;
  (b) the Court consists of at least three judges;
  (c) more than half of those judges are permanent judges.
(2) Paragraphs (a) and (b) of subsection (1) are subject to any directions that in specified proceedings the Court is to consist of a specified number of judges that is both uneven and greater than three.
(3) Paragraph (b) of subsection (1) is subject to any directions that in specified descriptions of proceedings the Court is to consist of a specified minimum number of judges that is greater than three.

The Court must always sit in odd numbers to avoid the risk of an evenly split decision. The only exception is provided for by s. 43, where a member of the Court is unable to continue during proceedings. In the

11 See eg *Zurich Insurance PLC UK Branch v International Energy Group Limited* [2015] UKSC 69 at text to n 117 below.

12 On the history, see L. Blom-Cooper QC, B. Dickson, and G. Drewry (eds), *The Judicial House of Lords 1876–2009* (Oxford, Oxford University Press, 2009).

13 As amended by s 20 of the Crime and Courts Act 2013, giving effect to Schedule 13, Part 2, para 2. There has so far been only a maximum of twelve serving justices at any one time, and so for convenience, I shall generally proceed on the basis of there normally being twelve justices in total as well as twelve justices being the full-time equivalent.

event of an evenly split decision in such a case, it would be re-argued with a regularly constituted panel. Where issues can be discretely separated, it might be possible for a justice to be replaced for remaining issues.[14] The Court decided that it would sit in a panel of eleven for the first time in *Miller*,[15] although there must generally be allowance for conflicts that would prevent a judge from sitting.[16] (On a more practical point, the largest courtroom in the Supreme Court's Middlesex Guildhall building, Court 1, was designed for only nine places at which justices might sit; thus, in *Miller*, two extra chairs were added.)[17]

The usual number of judges per appeal is five, out of (usually) twelve members of the Court. This means that the Court can hear two appeals in parallel during the course of a sitting day. The number of five accords with a general principle of appellate review that each time one goes up a level of the court hierarchy, there should be more judges to hear a case than below, and always in odd numbers to avoid a split decision. So, for example, a defamation claim would be heard first by one judge in the Queen's Bench Division of the High Court,[18] then three Lord or Lady Justices of Appeal in the Court of Appeal, and then finally five justices in the Supreme Court. That means, of course, that a case reaching the

---

14 Such an instance occurred in *Al-Waheed v Ministry of Defence* [2017] UKSC 2 ("*Al-Waheed*"), where Lord Toulson retired after the conclusion of oral argument on some of the issues, thereafter being replaced by Lord Hodge for the remainder of the hearing: [2017] UKSC 2 (Lord Sumption), [231] (Lord Toulson), and [232] (Lord Hodge).

15 See "Interaction with the Privy Council" below.

16 Paterson, *Final Judgment*, above n 6 at 69 fn 17: "Justices recently promoted from the Court of Appeal of the Court of Session cannot sit on appeals from cases where they were involved in the lower court. … Nor may Lord Mance sit in a case from the Court of Appeal in which his wife Dame Mary Arden was present." There may be other personal conflicts, or the case where a judge has spoken publicly on a particular point so must be recused: such as Lord Steyn in *A v Home Secretary* [2004] UKHL 56 or Lords Scott and Hoffmann in *Jackson v Attorney General* [2005] UKHL 56: Paterson, *Final Judgment*, above n 6 at 71; and Hale, "Should the Law Lords Have Left the House of Lords?," above n 5 at 4.

17 I am grateful to Gabrielle Appleby for offering the example of the Constitutional Court of South Africa, which sits *en banc* with eleven justices in the cases that it hears. However, it has a much lighter workload than other apex courts (not least because South Africa has the Supreme Court of Appeal as the final court of appeal for non-constitutional matters), and its working practices of having so many judges for so few cases have been criticized; see J. Lewis, "The Constitutional Court of South Africa" (2009) 125 *Law Quarterly Review* 440.

18 S 11 of the Defamation Act 2013 greatly reduced the scope for a jury trial in defamation claims.

Supreme Court will have usually been heard by nine judges in total on its appellate journey. Yet in EP cases, it can be nine (or now eleven) judges hearing the case in the Supreme Court alone.[19]

The Enlarged Panel Criteria

As Lady Hale noted, the Court has developed a practice of sitting more frequently in larger panels,[20] which developed during the later years of the Judicial House of Lords. The practice of sitting in larger panels was reintroduced by Lord Bingham: "a salient feature of [his Lordship's] tenure of the top position was the selection of nine-judge benches, something that had not occurred since 1910 [before Lord Bingham's appointment in 2000]."[21] Figures on the Supreme Court's approach to such sittings are provided in the tables, but, for now, we shall focus on the criteria that the Court has published – hereafter the *EP criteria* – when considering whether to sit with a panel of seven or nine (I have added numbers for ease of identification and subsequent reference):

1. If the Court is being asked to depart, or may decide to depart from a previous decision.
2. A case of high constitutional importance.
3. A case of great public importance.
4. A case where a conflict between decisions in the House of Lords, Judicial Committee of the Privy Council and/or the Supreme Court has to be reconciled.
5. A case raising an important point in relation to the European Convention on Human Rights.[22]

Burrows has noted that the EP criteria, especially the third and fifth, are "very wide-ranging."[23] Lord Neuberger has said extra-judicially

---

19 For more detail on the working practices of the Supreme Court, see J. Lee, "The United Kingdom Supreme Court: A Study in Judicial Reform" in E. Guinchard and M.-P. Granger (eds), *The New EU Judiciary: An Analysis of Current Judicial Reforms* (The Netherlands, Kluwer, 2017).

20 See also Burrows, "Numbers Sitting in the Supreme Court," above n 6 at 306–7.

21 B. Dickson, "A Hard Act to Follow: The Bingham Court, 2000–8" in L. Blom-Cooper QC, B. Dickson, and G. Drewry (eds), *The Judicial House of Lords 1876–2009* (Oxford, Oxford University Press, 2009).

22 https://www.supremecourt.uk/procedures/panel-numbers-criteria.html.

23 Burrows, "Numbers Sitting in the Supreme Court," above n 6 at 307.

that "no more than a third of the diet of the Supreme Court consists of cases involving human rights under the Convention, and even those cases involving human rights frequently raise, and even ultimately turn on, points which have nothing to do with the Convention."[24] Although that was in the context of emphasizing the breadth of the Supreme Court's work, it also highlights the fact that many of the Court's cases fall within a single EP criterion.

These criteria are only those "to be used when considering whether more than five Justices should sit on a panel."[25] The mere presence of one or more of these criteria is not in itself sufficient – as we shall see below, there are various 5JP cases that met at least one of those criteria. The weight to be accorded to each is not indicated. Even when applying the published criteria, then, there are issues of transparency – it is not clear why one decision merits such status and another does not. There are some potentially relevant factors that are not adverted to in the criteria. For example, in the context of the House of Lords and Supreme Court's doctrine of precedent, it has often been observed that how recently decided a challenged authority is will be relevant.[26] Nor is there any guidance on the difference in the application of the criteria between deciding to convene a panel of seven as opposed to nine or the eleven in *Miller*.

The EP criteria are partly reflected in the procedural requirements for applications for permission to appeal. Practice Direction 3.1.3 provides:

If an application for permission to appeal

a. asks the Supreme Court to depart from one of its own decisions or from one made by the House of Lords;
b. seeks a declaration of incompatibility under the Human Rights Act 1998; or
c. seeks a reference to the Court of Justice of the European Union, this should be stated clearly in the application and full details must be given.

---

24 Lord Neuberger, "The Supreme Court and the Rule of Law," Lecture 2014, Liverpool Law Society, 9 October 2014, https://www.supremecourt.uk/docs/speech-141009-lord-neuberger.pdf, para 12.

25 https://www.supremecourt.uk/procedures/panel-numbers-criteria.html.

26 See eg Lord Bingham in *Rees v Darlington Memorial Hospital NHS Trust* [2003] UKHL 52, at [7]: "it would be wholly contrary to the practice of the House to disturb its unanimous decision in *McFarlane* [*v Tayside Health Board* [2000] 2 AC 59] given as recently as 4 years ago, even if a differently constituted committee were to conclude that a different solution should have been adopted. It would reflect

Notably, the EP criteria do not refer expressly to questions of European law. These may be subsumed within the "cases of high constitutional importance" criterion, but then so might the express criterion on the European Convention on Human Rights (ECHR).

There are other consequences to sitting in a Court of nine or eleven that need to be weighed in the balance. Most obviously, it would leave only three justices (or one) not sitting on the case. That means that the Supreme Court could hear the one appeal only for the duration of the 9JP/11JP case (although, admittedly, in a 9JP case, the Privy Council could sit, either with only three justices or, more likely, with two non-UKSC Privy Counsellors in addition).[27]

In what follows below, I shall argue that the EP criteria pose difficulties when measured against the practice of the Court. However, the publication of the criteria does at least represent an attempt to introduce transparency into an aspect of the Court's process. There are no such criteria with respect to the allocation of justices to a panel, whether in a regular 5JP case or one with an EP. This is consistent with an approach adopted by the Appellate Committee of the House of Lords: in Paterson's study, the key conclusion is that "the senior Justices have the most say in which appeals are admitted and in whether they get to participate in the hearing."[28] More recently, Lord Neuberger and Lady Hale have spoken of the considerations involved in panel selection and the conscious desire to achieve a balance of expertise and generalist engagement[29] and to avoid accusations of stacking the Court in favour of a particular outcome.

---

no credit on the administration of the law if a line of English authority were to be disapproved in 1999 and reinstated in 2003 with no reason for the change beyond a change in the balance of judicial opinion."

27 See "Interaction with the Privy Council" below. In *Bannerman Town, Millars and John Millars Eleuthera Association v Eleuthera Properties Ltd (Bahamas)* [2018] UKPC 27, the Privy Council sat in a panel of five with only two serving UKSC justices: Lords Sumption and Briggs. The other three Privy Counsellors were Sir Rupert Jackson (recently retired from the Court of Appeal of England and Wales), Lord Menzies (of the Inner House of the Court of Session), and Sir Ben Stephens (of the Northern Ireland Court of Appeal).

28 Paterson, *Final Judgment*, above n 6 at 73, with more detail at 70–3. See also B. Dickson, "The Processing of Appeals in the House of Lords" (2007) 123 *Law Quarterly Review* 571 at 589–91.

29 See Lord Neuberger, "Twenty Years a Judge: Reflections and Refractions," Neill Lecture 2017, Oxford Law Faculty, 10 February 2017 at para 30; Hale, "Judges, Power and Accountability," above n 4 at 17–18; and Hale, "Should the Law Lords Have Left the House of Lords?," above n 5 at 11.

We can contrast the Supreme Court's approach with approaches taken in civilian jurisdictions: for example, the Conseil d'État in France has published the procedure for which judges should sit on L'Assemblée du contentieux, a convening of the court for cases of "remarkable" or "exceptional" importance.[30] Thus, the Conseil d'État has criteria not just for when a special panel should be convened but also for who should sit. The UKSC retains flexibility, but with the concomitant risk that its processes may seem to lack rigour.

Statistics

Of the 621 decisions of the Supreme Court handed down in the assessment period, the vast majority had five justices sitting on the panel: 513 decisions, or 82.61 per cent. Of the remaining 108, four[31] were 3JP cases – all of which concerned procedural or costs issues, including the Court's very first decision, in a procedural application concerning costs ahead of the substantive decision in the *JFS* case.[32] Eighty-four were 7JP decisions, nineteen were 9JP decisions, and *Miller* is the only 11JP. The arguments in the remainder of the chapter will be informed by the analysis of these cases.

The statistics are arranged by calendar year rather than by Court year (which runs from October to, usually, July); see tables 4.1 and 4.2. The reason for this is to take account of the time that it takes to deliver judgment after hearing a case. In the Court's first term in 2009, ten out of the seventeen decisions were heard as cases in the House of Lords, before the Court's inauguration. Similarly, in terms of observing change, Lord Neuberger succeeded Lord Phillips in October 2012, and so any change in practice is better reflected from the start of 2013. Lord Neuberger's tenure as president concluded at the end of the 2016–17 legal year, with Lady Hale being sworn in as president on

---

30 "L'Assemblée du contentieux," http://www.conseil-etat.fr/Conseil-d-Etat/Missions/Juger-l-administration/Les-formations-de-jugement/L-Assemblee-du-contentieux. I am very grateful to John Bell for this example.

31 *R (on the application of E) v Governing Body of JFS* [2009] UKSC 1 ("*JFS*"); *Stanford International Bank Ltd v Director of The Serious Fraud Office* [2012] UKSC 3; *Apollo Engineering Ltd v James Scott Ltd (Scotland)* [2013] UKSC 37; and *McGraddie v McGraddie* [2015] UKSC 1.

32 *JFS*, above n 31.

Table 4.1. 7JP Cases, 2009–18

Year	2009	2010	2011	2012	2013	2014	2015	2016	2017	2018	Total
No. of 7JP cases	2	10	15	11	7	7	13	7	9	3	84
Total cases in year	17	58	60	63	81	68	79	65	82	48	621
Percentage	11.76	17.24	25.00	17.46	8.64	10.29	16.46	10.76	10.98	6.25	13.53

Table 4.2. 9JP Cases, 2009–18[33]

Year	2009	2010	2011	2012	2013	2014	2015	2016	2017	2018	Total
No of 9JP cases	1	5	4[34]	2	2	1	0	3	1	0	19
Total cases in year	17	58	60	63	81	68	79	65	82	48	621
Percentage	5.88	8.62	6.67	3.17	2.47	1.47	N/A	4.62	1.21	N/A	3.06

2 October 2017. The figures, therefore, cover Lady Hale's first legal year as president.

In 2014 and 2015, the Court decided only one case with nine justices (*R (on the application of Nicklinson) v Ministry of Justice*),[35] and, indeed, it went from June 2014 to July 2016 without deciding any. There have been nineteen 9JP cases overall, including the Court's first 9JP decision in the *Jewish Free School* case.[36]

33 Lord Neuberger has noted, "Nine judge panels rarely occur more than twice in any year": Lord Neuberger, "The Jewish History of the Supreme Court," 17 May 2017, https://www.supremecourt.uk/docs/speech-170517.pdf.

34 I have excluded from this classification the costs decision in *Manchester City Council v Pinnock* [2011] UKSC 6 since it was consequential upon the decision in the original substantive appeal in the case of the same name at [2010] UKSC 45. There was no suggestion that this issue merited a 9JP by itself (unlike *Willers v Joyce*, considered below). I therefore treat the two decisions as one case. "The issue relating to the terms of the order gives rise to a point of a little difficulty and potentially more general application. It therefore seems right to set out our conclusions and reasons on the two issues in this short further judgment."

35 [2014] UKSC 38 ("*Nicklinson*").

36 *JFS*, above n 31.

Table 4.3. All Enlarged Panel Cases, 2009–18

Year	2009	2010	2011	2012	2013	2014	2015	2016	2017	2018	Total
No of EP cases	3	15	19	13	9	8	13	10	11	3	104
Total cases in year	17	58	60	63	81	68	79	65	82	48	621
Percentage	17.65	25.86	31.67	20.63	11.11	11.76	16.46	15.38	13.41	6.25	16.75

All Enlarged Panel Cases

For all EP cases, the figures are shown in Table 4.3 (which includes the sole instance of eleven justices sitting in *Miller* in the figures for 2017).

Taking the data altogether, we can express it in this chart:

Figure 4.1. Supreme Court Enlarged Panel Decisions, 2009–18

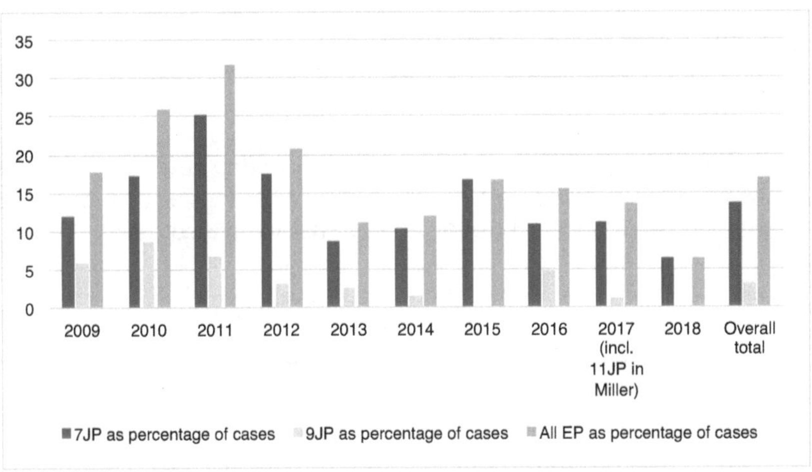

Detailed analysis of these statistics is developed below, but some initial points can be made. First, as noted in the introduction, Professor Burrows's concerns about the increasing frequency of sitting in EPs have been somewhat allayed by the reduction since he wrote his piece – 2011 being a high point. With Lord Neuberger succeeding Lord Phillips as president in the autumn of 2012, the figures from 2013 onwards represent a marked shift away from the trend of increasing use of EPs, culminating in the sharp reduction in the first year of Lady Hale's presidency.

Second, there has been considerable variation in the Court's workload over the first nine years of decisions: the lowest full year was 2010, with fifty-eight decisions, and then eighty-two in 2017 (a variation of 41.37 per cent). The trend has been for the Court to hear more cases overall than it did in its early years. There is an obvious connection between the number of cases to be heard and the ability of the Court to sit in EPs: the more cases that are to be heard, the less it is possible for it to sit in panels of seven or nine. Lord Neuberger has estimated that the usual practice of sitting with five justices enables the Court "to get through around twice as many cases as we otherwise would. And hearings with five judges are normally more manageable both for the judges and for the advocates."[37] Lady Hale has similarly noted that sitting with more judges more often "would reduce the number of cases we could take."[38]

The Importance of Being Important

Importance and the Criteria

Given these statistics, how are we meant to understand the Supreme Court's view of what counts as important and the various apparent degrees of importance?[39] Lord Neuberger has explained that

> [the] role of the UK Supreme Court is to take an appeal only if it raises one or more points of general public importance. In that connection I think that our functions can be summarised in six words, namely "to clarify, correct, declare and develop."[40]

37 Neuberger, "Twenty Years a Judge," above n 29.

38 Hale, "Should the Law Lords Have Left the House of Lords?," above n 5 at 11.

39 Compare P. Keyzer, "When Is an Issue of 'Vital Constitutional Importance'? Principles Which Guide the Reconsideration of Constitutional Decisions in the High Court of Australia" (1999) 2 *Constitutional Law and Policy Review* 13. I am grateful to Andrew Lynch for this reference.

40 "UK Supreme Court Decisions on Private and Commercial Law: The Role of Public Policy and Public Interest," Centre for Commercial Law Studies Conference 2015, https://www.supremecourt.uk/docs/speech-151204.pdf, para 15. Lord Neuberger

When invited by *The Independent* newspaper in 2014, Lord Neuberger nominated five key cases from the first five years of the Supreme Court.[41] All five were 7JP or 9JP cases. For her part, Lady Hale has added that a case to be heard by the Supreme Court will be "of general public importance"

> because it matters to a great many more people than the parties to the case, often to the public as a whole, whose interests need to be protected. And the case is a suitable vehicle for the Supreme Court to decide it. These are the hard cases which matter to us all. They are also the cases where the judges have a choice.[42]

Thus, any case that reaches the Supreme Court ought to be of "general public importance," but the EP criteria, as seen above, refer to "high constitutional importance," "great public importance," and "a case raising an important point in relation to the European Convention on Human Rights." The assessment of *importance* is nowhere explained beyond occasional observations from the justices extra-judicially. We can infer that "general public importance" is somewhere below "great public importance" on the scale, but how "great" compares to "high" cannot be readily calculated. (It may be that one is a metric and the other an imperial measurement.)

In applying the criteria, a pair of cases may be compared.[43] *AXA General Insurance Ltd v Lord Advocate*[44] concerned public law and human

---

continued in parentheses, "(Or if you are a stickler for not splitting infinitives, nine words, namely 'to clarify, to correct, to declare and to develop')."

41 The five cases were "*Nicklinson,*" above n 35 (nine justices), *Prest v Petrodel Resources Ltd* [2013] UKSC 34 (seven), *R v Horncastle* [2009] UKSC 14 (seven), *Al Rawi v The Security Service* [2011] UKSC 34 (nine), and *R (on the application of HS2 Action Alliance) v Secretary of State for Transport* [2014] UKSC 3 (seven): "Lord Neuberger on the Supreme Court: Five Key Cases from Its First Five Years," *Independent on Sunday*, 12 October 2014, http://www.independent.co.uk/news/people/lord-neuberger-on-the-supreme-court-five-key-cases-from-its-first-five-years-9789269.html.

42 Hale, "Judges, Power and Accountability," above n 4 at 1. See the unusual and careful reasons given for refusing permission to appeal in the case of *R (on the application of Conway) v Secretary of State for Justice* on 27 November 2018, https://www.supremecourt.uk/docs/r-on-the-application-of-conway-v-secretary-of-state-for-justice-court-order.pdf.

43 Lady Hale has compared the cases from a constitutional perspective: "The Supreme Court: Guardian of the Constitution?," Sultan Azlan Shah Lecture, Kuala Lumpur, 9 November 2016, https://www.supremecourt.uk/docs/speech-161109.pdf, 5–6.

44 [2011] UKSC 46.

rights challenges to the Damages (Asbestos-Related Conditions) (Scotland) Act 2009, and it examined the limits of legislative competence of devolved legislatures under the various 1998 settlements. The Supreme Court, in a panel of seven, upheld the legislation as falling within the legislative competence of the Scottish Parliament, but various dicta set the parameters of future review.

In the case of Recovery of Medical Costs for Asbestos Diseases (Wales) Bill,[45] the Court then explored further questions, drawing on *AXA* and, for the first time,[46] held that a piece of legislation of the Welsh Assembly was outside its legislative competence. In that case, the Court sat in a panel of five (with Lord Thomas LCJ sitting, albeit seemingly in his coincidental capacity as a Welsh judge rather than as Lord Chief Justice).[47] One may assume that the fact that one case was Welsh and the other Scottish is not relevant to their relative importance. Both cases may, though, raise the same questions of great public importance – in similar areas of compensation for alleged industrial diseases, of high constitutional importance, and, indeed, involving an important point concerning the ECHR as a limitation on legislative competence. The Court sat in a panel of seven for the first case referred to it by Law Officers in Scotland, on the UK Withdrawal from the European Union (Legal Continuity) (Scotland) Bill.[48]

We can find instances of the Court expressly engaging with the criteria in the judgment from recent EP cases. Lord Wilson described the 7JP case of *Ali v Secretary of State for the Home Department*[49] as "an important

45 *Recovery of Medical Costs for Asbestos Diseases (Wales) Bill (Reference By The Counsel General For Wales)* [2015] UKSC 3.

46 Two previous references saw the Court find the relevant legislation valid: *Local Government Byelaws (Wales) Bill 2012* [2012] UKSC 5 and *Agricultural Sector (Wales) Bill* [2014] UKSC 43.

47 Lord Neuberger, "The UK Constitutional Settlement and the Role of the UK Supreme Court," Legal Wales Conference 2014, 10 October 2014, https://www.supremecourt.uk/docs/speech-141010.pdf, para 28: noting that, in the case of the Lord Chief Justice, "it is one thing to identify him as the Judge, but another thing to find a couple of free days in his diary." In October 2017, Lord Lloyd Jones JSC became the first justice to take his oath in both English and Welsh.

48 *The UK Withdrawal from the European Union (Legal Continuity) (Scotland) Bill – A Reference by the Attorney General and the Advocate General for Scotland* [2018] UKSC 64. Then see further Hale, "Should the Law Lords Have Left the House of Lords?," above n 5 at 9.

49 [2016] UKSC 60.

day in the life of our court"[50] as it was the first opportunity to consider the relationship between the state's power to deport a foreign criminal and the criminal's right to family or private life.[51] The Court has also considered the "constitutionally important, if rarely invoked" doctrine of Crown act of state in *Mohammed (Serdar) v Ministry of Defence (No 1)*,[52] the defences of state immunity and foreign act of state in *Belhaj v* Straw,[53] and the relationship between UN Security Council resolutions and European human rights law in the 9JP case of *Al-Waheed v Ministry of Defence*.[54] One of the Court's highest-profile recent decisions was *R (on the application of Unison) v Lord Chancellor*,[55] which ruled that a scheme[56] imposing employment tribunal fees before a claim could be brought was unlawful. Lord Reed's judgment emphasizes the importance of the issues at stake: "the constitutional right of access to the courts is inherent in the rule of law."[57]

But not all cases necessarily involve high questions of principle: the Supreme Court also has a role in offering guidance to lower courts and the wider public. One such example is the disability discrimination case of *Paulley v Firstgroup plc*:[58] Mr Paulley was a wheelchair user who had been unable to board a bus because the space for a wheelchair was occupied by a pram whose owner refused to move it when politely asked by the driver. The bus company's policy did not require the driver to do anything more in such a situation. The claimant argued that this engaged various accessibility requirements and equality duties under the relevant legislation,[59] and the failure to have a more prescriptive policy amounted to discrimination. Seven justices heard the appeal, and the Court found in Mr Paulley's favour, although, on the basis of

50 Ibid at [65].

51 By virtue of Art 8 of the European Convention on Human Rights.

52 [2017] UKSC 1 at [102] (Lord Neuberger PSC).

53 [2017] UKSC 3.

54 [2017] UKSC 2.

55 [2017] UKSC 51. See A. Bogg, "The Common Law Constitution at Work: *R (on the application of UNISON) v Lord Chancellor*" (2018) 81 *Modern Law Review* 509.

56 Employment Tribunals and the Employment Appeal Tribunal Fees Order 2013, Arts 3 and 4.

57 Ibid at [66].

58 [2017] UKSC 4.

59 The Public Service Vehicles (Conduct of Drivers, Inspectors, Conductors and Passengers) Regulations 1990, as amended by the Public Service Vehicles (Conduct of Drivers, Inspectors, Conductors and Passengers) (Amendment) Regulations 2002.

the judge's findings, a majority held that he was not entitled to damages (since he may not have been able to board the bus even if a more stringent policy had been adopted).

The judgments of the justices are marked by not only an awareness of the difficulties of working out what the position should be but also consciousness of the need for the Supreme Court "to provide as much guidance as possible in this important field":[60] Lord Neuberger argued that "one of the principal functions of this court is to clarify the law, and therefore to keep the grey areas as few and as small as possible."[61] Bus companies, wheelchair users, passengers, and lower courts needed assistance in knowing the kind of policy required by the law. The Court divided over what the policy should be, but at least a majority thought that the driver should be expected to do more than simply make a single request to the non–wheelchair user to vacate the space.[62] Several justices also called for renewed legislative consideration of the area.[63] *Paulley* is thus an example of another function of an apex court: to offer practicable guidance on the application of the law.[64]

Communication, Public Confidence, and Public Importance

How else might we approach *public importance*? We might take as an analogy the trite law that "what interests the public is not necessarily [that which is] in the public interest."[65] As Baroness Hale (as she then was, in a decision of the House of Lords) said in the context of the former defence of *Reynolds* privilege to a claim in defamation,

> The public only have a right to be told if two conditions are fulfilled. First, there must be a real public interest in communicating and receiving the information. This is, as we all know, very different from saying that it is information which interests the public – the most vapid tittle-tattle about the activities of footballers' wives and girlfriends interests large sections

60 Ibid at [61] (Lord Neuberger PSC).

61 Ibid at [71]. See also Lord Toulson at [81]: "the case has raised points on which those who are affected need a clear ruling from this court."

62 Ibid at [66] (Lord Neuberger).

63 Ibid at [70] (Lord Neuberger) and [87] (Lord Toulson).

64 Another recent 7JP example is *Ilott v The Blue Cross* [2017] UKSC 17: see Lord Hughes at [48].

65 [2006] EWCA Civ 1714, Buxton LJ at [66].

of the public but no one could claim any real public interest in our being told all about it.[66]

When it comes to *public importance*, the same point presumably applies. What is of public importance is not necessarily what is of importance to the public. This point may be illustrated by the Court's own approach to publicizing permission decisions, which seems to involve some judgment as to cases that are of importance to the public. The Court publishes, roughly monthly, a list of cases for which permission has been granted or refused and has, since March 2012, provided brief reasons for refusal.[67] Normally, these reasons are somewhat formulaic, such as "Permission to appeal be refused because the application does not raise an arguable point of law of general public importance,"[68] but they still provide some information on why appeals have been refused. No reasons are provided as to why a permission to appeal has been granted.

Two recommendations can be made here in respect of communication relating to permission-to-appeal decisions. The first recommendation concerns the Court's current practice of issuing standard lists of decisions, by month, but then, in some cases, issuing a specific press release in respect of the appeal. Some of those are refusals and offer substantial information on the reasons ahead of the publication of the tabulated list.[69] There have been such press releases for various cases. But only some of those cases saw a panel of more than five: for example, both *Assange v The Swedish Prosecution Authority*[70] and the announcement about the *Bedroom Tax* cases[71] had seven justices. This means that there were several cases where the Court saw fit to publicize the permission to appeal because it was important to the public, but not of sufficient public importance to have an EP. This feature may be taken in

66 *Jameel (Mohammed) v Wall Street Journal Europe Sprl* [2007] 1 AC 359 at [147].

67 At https://www.supremecourt.uk/docs/permission-to-appeal-2012-03.pdf.

68 The reasons given for refusal in *The Charity Commission for Northern Ireland v Bangor Provident Trust Limited (Northern Ireland)* Case No: UKSC 2015/0131, https://www.supremecourt.uk/docs/permission-to-appeal-2015-12.pdf.

69 See eg the announcement regarding *R (British American Tobacco UK Ltd and others) v Secretary of State for Health* UKSC 2017/0012, https://www.supremecourt.uk/news/permission-to-appeal-decision-12-april-2017.html.

70 [2012] UKSC 22.

71 [2016] UKSC 58. The advance announcement can be found here: https://www.supremecourt.uk/news/rutherford-v-dwp.html.

several ways. On one level, why publicize certain permissions to appeal over others at all? Surely the general list is enough. It risks reinforcing the concern above about different tiers of litigants: "your case is quite important, but neither of sufficient public importance for a larger panel to hear it nor of sufficient importance to the public for us to tell people about it."

The practice also perhaps suggests that there is a limit to the public confidence factor in deciding to hear a case with a larger panel: the Court clearly (and commendably) seeks to engage with the public. But there may be a disconnect between raising public interest in a case and then not being seen to decide it with as many judges as possible (especially now that the Court has decided that it can and will sit *en banc*). The practice of selective press releases should be reconsidered. Since 2009, the Court has commendably sought to engage the public using communication strategies and enhanced transparency,[72] but the limits and inconsistencies in practice potentially detract from the value of such engagement.

Another, separate point arises out of the press releases. In the *Assange* case, the Court not only publicized that permission to appeal had been granted but also announced that seven justices would hear the case "given the great public importance of the issue raised, which is whether a prosecutor is a judicial authority."[73] *Assange* is the only occasion in any of the press releases when *reasons* for permission *being granted* have been published, and it is also the only case (whether mentioned in a special press release or not) in which the Court has given reasons why an EP was to hear it (other than subsequently explaining in a judgment).

Admittedly, the reason, "the great public importance of the issue raised," is not unduly revelatory, although the Court must be careful not to queer the pitch by giving too much away ahead of the argument in the case. But publishing the reasons for an EP is still a step towards greater transparency and potential for consistency in the size of panels. I would therefore argue that the Court should give brief reasons for recommending the number of judges to hear the case. Even when announcing in *Miller* the decision to sit with eleven justices for the first time, the Court did not explain why it was doing so (although the

72 Dominic Grieve QC, "Topsy-Turvydom: The UK Supreme Court in an Uncertain Political World" (2016) 7 *UK Supreme Court Yearbook* 195 at 201.

73 At https://www.supremecourt.uk/news/application-for-pta-julian-assange.html.

judgments and extra-curial speeches from Lord Neuberger and Lady Hale have since done so).[74] If reasons were always given, it would perhaps alleviate the issue of selective press releases and also reduce concerns about the application of the EP criteria.[75]

Judging in Enlarged Panels

Unanimity, Univocality, and Differences of Opinion

One of the justifications provided for EPs is that it matters which judge one gets. But a split decision is still a split decision, whether 3–2, 4–3, or 5–4. And a lone dissent may be as powerful as those dissenting in a 5–4 split.[76] In the more complicated cases with several points, there may be different splits, risking confusion and incoherence, like a game of musical chairs. It is instructive, therefore, to look at the decision-making when the judges sit as panels of nine (and the eleven in *Miller*). Decisions may raise more than one ground of appeal, and it can be controversial to identify dissents. I have therefore taken, as a guide to each decision, my classification from the official press summaries[77] that are produced by the Court. The twenty such cases are shown in table 4.4.

An immediate point is that there are very few 9JP cases in which the Court was both unanimous and univocal: indeed, in only five of the cases were the justices unanimous on each point in the case, and even then, there were differences as to reasoning in *Patel*, as we see below. Of course, with more judges, it perhaps follows that it is more likely that one will disagree, and if the 9JP cases are particularly difficult cases, it may be expected that the arguments will result in differences of opinion. It is noticeable, for example, that although in *Miller* there was an

74 At https://www.supremecourt.uk/news/permission-to-appeal-decision-08-november-2016.htm. See "The First Eleven" below.

75 For more on the Court's communications strategy, see J. Lee, "The United Kingdom Supreme Court," above n 19 at 4.06; and A. Blackham and G. Williams, "Social Media and Court Communication" [2015] *Public Law* 403.

76 See J. Alder, "Dissents in Courts of Last Resort: Tragic Choices?" (2000) 20 *Oxford Journal of Legal Studies* 221; A. Lynch, "Introduction: What Makes a Dissent 'Great?'" in A. Lynch (ed), *Great Australian Dissents* (Cambridge, Cambridge University Press, 2016); and A. Lynch, "Dissent: The Rewards and Risks of Judicial Disagreement in the High Court of Australia" (2003) 27(3) *Melbourne University Law Review* 724.

77 Note that these summaries are not "press releases"; see text to above n 67ff.

Table 4.4. Decisions in Twenty 9JP Cases (Including One 11JP Case), 2009–18

Case	Outcome
R (on the application of E) v Governing Body of JFS [2009] UKSC 15	5–4; unanimous on costs
Norris v Government of United States of America [2010] UKSC 9	Unanimous
R (on the application of Smith) v Secretary of State for Defence [2010] UKSC 29	6–3 on jurisdiction issue and unanimous on inquest
Radmacher v Granatino [2010] UKSC 42	8–1 (Lady Hale dissenting)
Manchester City Council v Pinnock [2010] UKSC 45; [2011] UKSC 6	Unanimous; also on costs
R v Chaytor & Ors [2010] UKSC 52	Unanimous
Lumba v Secretary of State for the Home Department [2011] UKSC 12	6–3 on liability; different 6–3 on damages
R (on the application of Adams) v Secretary of State for Justice [2011] UKSC 18	Unanimous on Mr Adams; 5–4 on MacDermott and McCartney
Al Rawi & Ors v The Security Service [2011] UKSC 34	6–3 (Lord Phillips was a part of the majority but for different reasons from Lord Dyson; Lord Rodger died before judgment was given but had indicated that he would have been in the majority)
Home Office v Tariq [2011] UKSC 35	8–1 allowed the appeal (Lord Kerr dissenting)
Perry & Ors v Serious Organised Crime Agency [2012] UKSC 35	Unanimous on disclosure order; 7–2 on property freezing order
R v Waya [2012] UKSC 51	Unanimous on allowing appeal, but Lord Phillips and Lord Reed partially dissented on extent of order quashing
Bank Mellat v Her Majesty's Treasury (No. 1) [2013] UKSC 38	6–3 on closed material procedure; 5–4 to adopt one in this appeal
Bank Mellat v Her Majesty's Treasury (No. 2) [2013] UKSC 39	6–3 on procedural ground; 5–4 on substantive grounds
R (on the application of Nicklinson) v Ministry of Justice [2014] UKSC 38	7–2 dismissed the appeal; 5–4 split on whether the Court had constitutional authority to decide issue; unanimous on second appeal in the *Martin* case
Patel v Mirza [2016] UKSC 42	Unanimous as to the outcome of the appeal, but Lord Toulson offered one approach (commanding the support of four other justices), while Lords Neuberger, Mance, Clarke, and Sumption offered different (and in the case of the latter three diametrically opposed) reasons

Case	Outcome
Willers v Joyce (No 1) [2016] UKSC 43	5–4 split on whether the tort of malicious prosecution extended to civil proceedings (the majority held that it did)
Willers v Joyce (No 2) [2016] UKSC 44	Unanimous
Al-Waheed v Ministry of Defence [2017] UKSC 2[78]	7–2 dismissed the appeal (Lords Reed and Kerr dissenting)
R (Miller) v Secretary of State for Exiting the European Union [2017] UKSC 5	8–3 dismissed the appeal (Lords Reed, Carnwath, and Hughes dissenting)

8–3 split, the majority judgment was published as a judgment of all eight majority justices, without the identification of a particular author with others agreeing.[79]

A final illustration of the challenge of close calls is the important case involving Northern Irish abortion law decided by the Court in 2018,[80] which "proved an unusually difficult case to resolve."[81] The seven-justice panel of the Supreme Court had to consider two issues: the first was whether the Northern Ireland Human Rights Commission had standing to bring a challenge to the compatibility of relevant legislation in respect of abortion in Northern Ireland with human rights; and, if it did have standing, the second issue was the substantive consideration of whether the legislation was compatible. The Court divided 4–3 in holding that the commission did not have standing, and so the challenge failed as the Court had no jurisdiction to make a declaration of incompatibility. A different majority would have held that the current law was

78 In *Al-Waheed*, Lord Toulson was replaced by Lord Hodge for the hearing of some of the issues: see above n 14.

79 In this respect, the UKSC differs in practice from the general approach of the High Court of Australia, where the practice of joining in judgments is more the norm: Justice Bell AC, "Examining the Judge," speech given at the launch of vol 40 of the *University of New South Wales Law Journal*, 29 May 2017, http://www.hcourt.gov.au/assets/publications/speeches/current-justices/bellj/bellj29May2017.pdf.pdf [*sic*].

80 *In the matter of an application by the Northern Ireland Human Rights Commission for Judicial Review; Reference by the Court of Appeal in Northern Ireland pursuant to Paragraph 33 of Schedule 10 to the Northern Ireland Act 1998 (Abortion) (Northern Ireland)* [2018] UKSC 27.

81 Ibid at [1].

incompatible with certain human rights.[82] Unusually, therefore, it was decided that judgments would be printed in order of seniority, rather than leading with a judgment representing the majority in favour of the resolution of the appeal.

While I have written before in defence of the right to issue concurring opinions,[83] a proliferation of judgments is not always to be welcomed, not least because of the potential consequences for clarity of reasoning.[84] As an example, we can compare the 9JP figures with the general figures as to the decisions in the Court's 2015–16 year: the Court handed down seventy-five decisions,[85] of which only thirteen saw a dissent (which is 17.33 per cent). By contrast, the rate of dissents in 9JP or 11JP decisions is fifteen out of twenty: 75 per cent. As Clarry and Sargeant have argued, "a larger panel size may only serve to entrench the division and instability in the law, if a larger plurality of Justices disagree on the essential reasoning for the disposition of an appeal."[86]

Long-Running Disagreements

Lord Neuberger has recognized that the nature of a dispute before the Court determines whether it is more likely that justices will issue

---

82 Lady Hale, Lord Mance, Lord Kerr, and Lord Wilson would have held that the law was incompatible with Article 8 in cases of rape, incest, and fatal foetal abnormality; Lady Black agreed with that view in respect of fatal fetal abnormality; Lords Kerr and Wilson would have gone further and held that the law was also incompatible with Article 3.

83 J. Lee, "A Defence of Concurring Speeches" [2009] *Public Law* 305; J. Lee, "A Comment on Collegiality and Collectivity in Common Law Courts" in B. Häcker and W. Ernst, *Collective Judging in Comparative Perspective: Counting Votes and Weighing Opinions* (Cambridge, Intersentia, 2019). See also Lewis, "Constitutional Court of South Africa," above n 17.

84 "A decision of an appellate court sitting with three or more judges may see different combinations of judges joining in agreement on the various propositions of law. Such a possibility is enhanced in cases in the Supreme Court sitting with seven or nine justices who then produce more than one majority and minority judgment." Burnett LJ in *R (on the application of Nealon) v Secretary of State for Justice* [2015] EWHC 1565 (Admin) at [24]. Lee, "A Defence of Concurring Speeches," above n 83 at 312: see further Lord Neuberger's views in favour of limiting the number of separate opinions, "Some Thoughts on Judicial Reasoning across Jurisdictions," Mitchell Lecture, Edinburgh, 11 November 2016, https://www.supremecourt.uk/docs/speech-161111.pdf.

85 More fully considered in Lee, "The United Kingdom Supreme Court," above n 19 at 4.05.

86 Clarry and Sargeant, "Judicial Panel Selection in the UK Supreme Court," above n 6 at 8.

separate opinions: "it is a matter of horses for courses: some appeals are more apt for concurring judgments than others."[87] Those that are primarily focused on the resolution of the matter before the Court are less suitable than those with controversial questions of principle or policy in the development of the law. In the latter type of case,

> the judgments, even if they agree, can involve different approaches or emphases, and can therefore lead to a useful discussion with academics, and indeed other judges, as to how the law on the topic should be taken forward.[88]

A noticeable feature of some of the 9JP cases is that the panels in those cases have been convened to address topics that have been the subject of intractable disagreement among the present justices, and they fall into Lord Neuberger's second category. Two 9JP decisions of the Court from July 2016 illustrate the point. *Patel v Mirza*[89] considered the proper approach to the defence of illegality, which has been the subject of what Lord Sumption has called a "judicial schism":[90] the justices felt the need to consider the defence with a 9JP Court because several recent cases had led to mutually inconsistent judgments (examined below). Lord Toulson delivered the speech for the majority.[91] Lord Kerr offered an additional speech concurring with Lord Toulson's approach. Lord Neuberger PSC concurred, for different reasons. Lords Mance, Clarke, and Sumption issued separate judgments, which concurred in the dismissal of the appeal, but for reasons that were tantamount to dissents.

In *Willers v Joyce (No 1)*,[92] the Supreme Court had to consider whether the tort of malicious prosecution of civil proceedings existed. This required resolving the tension between the decision of the House of Lords in *Gregory v Portsmouth City Council*,[93] which had suggested that the tort did not extend to civil proceedings, and the Privy Council's

87 Neuberger, "Some Thoughts on Judicial Reasoning," above n 84 at 38.

88 Ibid.

89 [2016] UKSC 42 ("*Patel*").

90 Ibid at [265] (Lord Sumption).

91 Lady Hale, Lord Kerr, Lord Wilson, and Lord Hodge agreed with Lord Toulson.

92 [2016] UKSC 43. *Willers (No 2)* is assessed in when discussing the role of the Privy Council below.

93 [2000] 1 AC 419.

more recent decision in *Crawford Adjusters v Sagicor General Insurance (Cayman) Limited*,[94] which held that the tort did extend that far.

In *Crawford Adjusters*, Lord Wilson, Lady Hale, and Lord Kerr were in the majority, while Lord Sumption and Lord Neuberger dissented. All five of those justices sat on the 9JP in *Willers (No 1)*.[95] The four additional justices divided evenly, with Lords Toulson and Clarke joining the majority (and issuing the majority opinions), while Lords Mance and Reed separately dissented. The majority of the Supreme Court confirmed the approach in *Crawford*, with Lord Toulson observing that the "appeal to justice is both obvious and compelling"[96] in favour of allowing a claimant to sue. Lord Toulson noted that his reasons "largely replicate[d] the judgments of the majority in *Crawford*."[97] Lords Mance and Sumption wrote particularly strongly worded dissents, accusing the majority of creating a new cause of action out of a tort that was nearly moribund (which Lord Mance described as "close to necromancy")[98] and of ignoring the history and coherence of the matter.[99]

The effect of the split decision in *Willers (No 1)* was certainly to resolve the point as a matter of English law, but it also served to magnify the disagreements among the justices.[100]

Brice Dickson, in his definitive study of "close calls" in the House of Lords,[101] argued for the Court to sit as a bench of nine more often

94 [2013] UKPC 17.

95 Joined by Lord Mance, Lord Clarke, Lord Reed, and Lord Toulson.

96 *Willers (No 1)* at [43].

97 Ibid at [59].

98 Ibid at [131].

99 See eg Lord Sumption, ibid at [177]–[9].

100 One could contrast it with a previous nine-justice case, *Lumba v Home Secretary* [2011] UKSC 12, on false imprisonment. The Supreme Court in that case divided 6–3 on liability. A similar case, *Kambadzi* [2011] UKSC 23, which was heard before Lumba but decided afterwards, saw the 5JP divide 3–2, with three of the Lumba majority in the majority and two of the *Lumba* minority in the minority [*sic*]. Burnett J has since described the complications of *Lumba* (in *R (on the application of EO) v Secretary of State for the Home Department* [2013] EWHC 1236 (Admin) at [21]): "Eight judgments were delivered (Lords Brown of Eaton-under-Heywood and Rodger of Earlsferry gave a joint judgment). Their Lordships aligned themselves in many different combinations on the various issues." See also "*Lumba* was a decision of nine Justices of the Supreme Court and is very long," *Parker v The Chief Constable of Essex Police* [2017] EWHC 2140 (QB) [47] (Stuart-Smith J).

101 B. Dickson, "Close Calls in the House of Lords" in J. Lee (ed), *From House of Lords to Supreme Court: Judges, Jurists and the Process of Judging* (Oxford, Hart Publishing, 2011).

because "the suspicion that the appeal system has a distinctly aleatory aspect to it, with the outcome depending on which judges happen to be selected to hear the case, will only grow and fester."[102] But I would argue that even though the majority of the 9JP cases are not close calls, we risk underestimating the interaction of the justices. As long as there is, as there inevitably will be, one justice on the substitutes' rather than the judicial bench,[103] there could still be a concern that any one judge would have made a difference, and not only in terms of a swing vote in a 5–4 case. For one judge's intellectual charisma and force of argument may have won other justices over to their side so that even an original 6–3 or 7–2 or 8–1 split might have seen a different outcome, rather than just more judges dissenting.[104]

Further Implications

What is more, accepting the idea that the public can or should have more confidence in a decision of a larger bench – which Lady Hale's speeches, quoted above, suggest is a key factor[105] explaining the present practice – and that convening such panels more often would lend further credence to it, risks undermining the status of "ordinary" cases where there are "only" five judges.

---

102 Ibid at 302.

103 In a 2008 Chancery Bar Association Lecture, Lord Neuberger referred to a "case [that] went to the House of Lords, and they decided to have a committee of nine to hear it. As they pick from the top, and I am the baby Law Lord, I was not wanted on the journey. So, rather than skulking around, I made a nuisance of myself in the Court of Appeal": Lord Neuberger, "The Conspirators, the Tax Man, the Bill of Rights and a Bit about the Lovers," 10 March 2008, http://www.chba.org.uk/for-members/library/annual-lectures/the-conspirators-the-taxman-the-bill-of-rights.pdf. The case in which His Lordship "made a nuisance of himself" was *Laskar v Laskar* [2008] EWCA Civ 347 (the law on the specific point has been developed by the Privy Council in *Marr v Collie* [2017] UKPC 17; see M. George and B. Sloan, "Presuming Too Little about Resulting and Constructive Trusts?" [2017] *Conveyancer* 303).

104 For fascinating detail on the dynamics among the justices, see Paterson's *Final Judgment*, above n 6 (generally but especially at 158ff). See also an article by Justice Gageler of the High Court of Australia, "Why Write Judgments?" (2014) 36 *Sydney Law Review* 189 especially at 197–201.

105 Hale, "Judges, Power and Accountability," above n 4.

Examining judicial and extra-judicial references to EPs is helpful because it speaks to the justices' attitudes (and those of judges in the lower courts). Lord Neuberger PSC has said,

> A court consisting of more than one judge has a collegiate character. It is true that ... the common law perception seems to be more like a number of judges, who happen to be sitting in one court, hearing the same case. But the common law view does not alter the fact that there is a single court and it does not justify rejecting collegiality, and by that I do not merely mean mutual respect and friendliness.[106]

Lady Hale stated that an EP lent a decision "greater authority."[107] We appear to see EP cases attracting a currency of their own as it is often subsequently mentioned that a given case involved a larger panel.[108] There would appear to be an assumption that, although relatively rare, 7JP or 9JP cases are more likely to achieve the right answer: "[if] all or most of the top judges in the country have given the case their best shot then perhaps it is the best that can be done."[109] So in *Ramdeen v The State (Trinidad and Tobago)*,[110] a case on the Privy Council's jurisdiction to commute a death sentence, Lord Toulson sought, and was able to find, "an alternative explanation to the possibility that ... nine Homers nodded"[111] in *Matthew*,[112] an earlier 9JP case from the Privy Council.

Yet the authority of a Supreme Court decision comes from the fact that it is a decision of the Supreme Court, not the number of justices who sat on the case. It may be that, rather than greater "authority" in a strict sense, her Ladyship means "greater legitimacy in the eyes of the public." However, I would argue, with respect, that encouraging that view is not satisfactory, either. The increase in

---

106 Lord Neuberger, "Sausages and the Judicial Process: The Limits of Transparency," presented at the annual conference of the Supreme Court of New South Wales, Sydney, 1 August 2014, para 25. For an Australian perspective, see also Justice Bell AC, "Examining the Judge," above n 79.

107 Hale, "Judges, Power and Accountability," above n 4; and Hale, "Should the Law Lords Have Left the House of Lords?," above n 5 at 11.

108 Eg *Re J (Children)* [2013] UKSC 9 at [18]: "the question did arise in *In re S-B* [2010] 1 AC 678, a judgment of this court to which seven Justices subscribed" (Lady Hale).

109 Hale, "Should the Law Lords Have Left the House of Lords?," above n 5 at 11.

110 [2014] UKPC 7.

111 Ibid at [55].

112 *Matthew v The State (Trinidad and Tobago)* [2004] UKPC 33.

the use[113] of EPs, and in pointing out when a case was decided by such a panel, seems to diminish regular cases – the vast majority of the Court's diet – which are heard by "only" five justices. Sitting for the first time as a (temporarily) full panel[114] in *Miller* simply exacerbates this problem further. We would appear to be developing a jurisprudence borrowed from an old advert for the British department store Marks & Spencer: "This is not *just* a United Kingdom Supreme Court decision; this is an *eleven-justice* United Kingdom Supreme Court decision."[115]

Judicial Numbers as a Constraint on Decision-Making

EP cases may, then, have their own rhetorical force, but they also appear to act as a constraint on aspects of decision-making in the Supreme Court. Another notable – if relatively rare – feature of the Court's approach is that the justices are willing to consider pausing argument in a case and re-arguing it before a 7JP or 9JP. Two such examples will suffice. *R v Waya*,[116] a case on Part 2 of the Proceeds of Crime Act 2002, was heard by seven justices – thus, already judged as "really important" – but then re-argued in front of nine – when it had become clear that it was, presumably, "really, really important." In *Zurich Insurance PLC UK Branch v International Energy Group*,[117] a case on exceptional tests for causation in tort and the consequences for insurance liability – the case was initially heard by five justices, after which the Court raised further questions, which were re-argued before a panel of seven.[118] The Court then split 4–3 on the relevant re-argued points (although Zurich continued to decline the invitation to withdraw a concession in respect of its contractual liability for the whole loss).

In late 2015, the Court gave judgment in *Keyu v Secretary of State for Foreign and Commonwealth Affairs*,[119] which saw a challenge to the British

113 By which I mean since the transition from the House of Lords.

114 See "Interaction with the Privy Council" below.

115 I appreciate that this may be a somewhat Anglocentric reference for an international audience – a version of the relevant advertising campaign can be found here: https://www.youtube.com/watch?v=EHFKE6PD_6U.

116 [2012] UKSC 51.

117 [2015] UKSC 33.

118 Ibid, Lord Sumption dissenting at [147].

119 [2015] UKSC 69 ("*Keyu*"). Clarry and Sargeant, "Judicial Panel Selection in the UK Supreme Court," above n 6 at 9–12.

government's refusal to hold an enquiry into the 1948 killing of unarmed civilians in Batang Kali, in what was then the Federation of Malaysia. Lord Neuberger gave the lead judgment on the grounds of appeal,[120] which included a challenge from the appellants that the Court should adopt a generalized proportionality test "in place of rationality in all domestic judicial review cases."[121] Lord Neuberger rejected this invitation, both substantively but also because of the composition of the Court:

> It would not be appropriate for a five-Justice panel of this court to accept, or indeed to reject, this argument, which potentially has implications which are profound in constitutional terms and very wide in applicable scope. Accordingly, if a proportionality challenge to the refusal to hold an inquiry would succeed, then it would be necessary to have this appeal (or at any rate this aspect of this appeal) re-argued before a panel of nine Justices.[122]

His Lordship held that it would be unnecessary to do so here because the appellants' challenge would fail even if proportionality were to be adopted. Lord Neuberger said that the "move from rationality to proportionality, as urged by the appellants, would appear to have potentially profound and far-reaching consequences."[123] But it is interesting to note the implication that even when the Court has already assessed that a case raises questions of sufficient importance for permission to appeal to be granted, the case may develop in such a way as to take it beyond the authoritative competence of the panel. (That is so even where, as in *Keyu*, we have the four most senior justices sitting in the panel of five.) The view that such an argument is not for merely five judges would appear to be the judicial equivalent of Sherlock Holmes's "three-pipe problem."[124]

---

120 Lord Mance gave the main judgment on a jurisdiction point raised by the Secretary of State, but which is not relevant for present purposes.

121 *Keyu*, Lord Neuberger at [131].

122 Ibid, Lord Neuberger at [132].

123 Ibid, Lord Neuberger at [133]. See more recently *Youssef v Secretary of State for Foreign and Commonwealth Affairs* [2016] UKSC 3 [55]–[61] (Lord Carnwath); and *Poshteh v Royal Borough of Kensington and Chelsea* [2017] UKSC 36 at [42] (Lord Carnwath).

124 "It is quite a three-pipe problem, and I beg that you won't speak to me for fifty minutes." A. Conan Doyle, "The Red-Headed League" in *The Adventures of Sherlock Holmes*.

The situation becomes more incongruous in the case of the defence of illegality. The law of illegality as a defence to private law claims has been a mess since, arguably, the decision of the House of Lords in *Tinsley v Milligan*,[125] and it is an excellent example of the unsatisfactory approach to EPs. I have traced the history more fully elsewhere,[126] but, briefly, the Supreme Court considered aspects of the doctrine in two cases in 2014 – *Hounga v Allen*[127] and *Les Laboratoires Servier v Apotex Inc.*[128] Those two cases revealed some tension as to the relevant principles to be applied: principally over whether there is, or should be, any public policy or discretionary aspect to the Court's judgment over whether the defence operates to defeat the claim.

In October 2014, the Supreme Court heard a third case on illegality, *Jetivia SA v Bilta (UK) Ltd*,[129] this time convening in a panel of seven. But when judgment was given in April 2015, the Court did not resolve the uncertainty in this area in the light of the recent differences of opinion. Rather, in four separate opinions, the judges continued to differ as to the reasoning (although the outcome was unanimous). Lord Neuberger, with whom Lords Clarke and Carnwath agreed, gave an introductory plurality opinion:

> In my view, while the proper approach to the defence of illegality needs to be addressed by this court (certainly with a panel of seven and conceivably with a panel of nine Justices) as soon as appropriately possible, *this is not the case in which it should be decided.*[130]

---

125 [1993] 3 WLR 126.

126 J. Lee, "The Etiquette of Law Reform" in M. Dyson, J. Lee, and S. Wilson Stark (eds), *Fifty Years of the Law Commissions: The Dynamics of Law Reform* (Oxford, Hart Publishing, 2016) at 286–92; and J. Lee, "Illegality, Familiarity and the Law Commission" in S. Green and A. Bogg (eds), *Illegality after Patel v Mirza* (Oxford, Hart Publishing, 2018).

127 *Hounga v Allen* [2014] UKSC 47.

128 [2014] UKSC 55.

129 [2015] UKSC 23.

130 *Jetivia* at [15]; emphasis added. For similar reticence, see *Doherty v Birmingham City Council* [2008] UKHL 57, Lord Hope at [19]. See also Lord Sumption in *Rock Advertising Ltd v MWB Business Exchange Centres Ltd* [2018] UKSC 24 at [18]: "The reality is that any decision on this point [of contract law] is likely to involve a re-examination of the decision in *Foakes v Beer* [(1883–84) LR 9 App Cas 605]. It is probably ripe for re-examination. But if it is to be overruled or its effect substantially modified, it should be before an enlarged panel of the court and in a case where the decision would be more than obiter dictum."

So in *Jetivia*, a 7JP case, the Court demurred from deciding an issue because it would be appropriate for *another* 7JP or 9JP to consider the problems. But that calls into the question the point of making *Jetivia* a case for seven justices in the first place.[131] Lord Neuberger went on to note that the argument in *Jetivia*[132] had focused mainly on attribution and not the broader issues. The Court could, however, have sought argument on the wider issues, as it did in *Zurich*.

The promised 9JP case on illegality was decided in July 2016. *Patel v Mirza*[133] was a case on illegality and the doctrine of *locus poenitentiae* (essentially, withdrawal from the illegal act before it is carried out). It would have been perfectly possible in that case (as in *Jetivia* and perhaps virtually every appeal) for argument to be narrowly focused. But, if so, one might not have needed an EP to hear it. Lord Neuberger flirted with the possibility of deciding the case on narrower grounds,[134] but concluded that the wider considerations should be determined because he "feared that the different approaches adopted by members of this court in the … [three recent cases] … have left the law on the topic in some disarray."[135]

The majority departed from the key House of Lords authority in *Tinsley*.[136] Lord Toulson held that the "essential rationale of the illegality doctrine is that it would be contrary to the public interest to enforce a claim if to do so would be harmful to the integrity of the legal system"[137] and that judges should take into account the underlying purpose of the relevant law that had been broken, public policy, and the proportionality of denying the claim given the illegality in question.[138] Lord Sumption was among the dissentients, and he dissented stridently, viewing the majority approach as "far too vague and potentially far too wide" and converting "a legal principle into an exercise of judicial

131 Sir Terence Etherton C (as he then was) endorsed the urgency of the matter after *Jetivia*: "the proper approach to the defence of illegality needs to be addressed by the Supreme Court (conceivably with a panel of nine justices) as soon as appropriately possible": *Sharma v Top Brands Ltd* [2015] EWCA Civ 1140 at [38]. See also *Molton Street Capital LLP v Shooters Hill Capital Partners LLP* [2015] EWHC 3419 (Comm), Popplewell J at [178].

132 *Jetivia* at [15].

133 [2016] UKSC 42.

134 *Patel*, above n 89 at [164].

135 Ibid.

136 *Tinsley v Milligan* [1994] 1 AC 340.

137 *Patel*, above n 89 at [120].

138 Ibid at [120].

discretion."[139] Although we thus now have an answer as to how courts should apply the defence of illegality in respect of private law cases, should it really have taken the Supreme Court to engage four times in two years with the same issue before resolving it?[140]

There are also dicta that the number of judges in a precedent is relevant to whether and how a case may be departed from. So, in one of the UKSC 9JP cases, *Pinnock*,[141] on adverse possession and human rights, Lord Neuberger gave judgment for the Court. The main issue was the development of the applicable principles by the ECHR since the decision by seven Law Lords in *Kay v Lambeth* had been handed down.[142] Lord Neuberger said,

> Although *McCann v UK* had been decided by the time of *Doherty v Birmingham, it would have been inappropriate for a five-judge court, at least in the particular circumstances, to depart substantially from the decision of the seven-judge court in Kay*. Importantly, the judgments in *Cosic v Croatia, Zehentner v Austria, Paulic v Croatia* and *Kay v UK* were all given after the last of the three House of Lords decisions.[143]

Lord Neuberger did not say there that it would never be appropriate for a five-judge Court to depart from a decision of a larger panel, but the number on the panel is clearly an important factor. And, if so, then any increased frequency of sitting in EPs will act as a significant check on the future review of such decisions.

False Alarms

So far, I have argued that reform is necessary to the Court's criteria for assigning the number of judges in two main ways. First, the utility of sitting in EPs, and the reasons for doing so, need to

139 Ibid at [265]. See J. Lee, "The Judicial Individuality of Lord Sumption" (2017) 40(2) *University of New South Wales Law Journal* 862 at 874–80.

140 For remaining uncertainties relating to the defence, even after *Patel*, see S. Green and A. Bogg (eds), *Illegality after Patel v Mirza* (Oxford, Hart Publishing, 2018).

141 [2010] UKSC 45.

142 [2006] 2 AC 465.

143 *Pinnock* at [47]; emphasis added, case citations omitted. See also *Doran v Liverpool City Council* & Ors [2009] EWCA Civ 146, Toulson LJ at [19]: "*Kay* had been decided by a seven judge panel and it would have [been] unprecedented for its decision to be departed from shortly afterwards by a five judge panel." See more generally eg *Jones v Kernott* [2011] UKSC 53, Lord Collins at [58].

be reconsidered. One simply cannot be sure what is a five-, seven-, nine-, or eleven-judge-worthy case. Second, revising those criteria, particularly in terms of what is and is not really, really important, may lead to reconsideration of the granting of permission to appeal in the first place.[144] Currently, as I have endeavoured to establish, the authority of 5JP cases (the vast majority of the Court's output) risks being undermined.

The Supreme Court departed from previous decisions relatively rarely in its early years of hearing cases, as I have demonstrated in a previous article.[145] Of those outside the fields of human rights and European law (where the interventions of courts in Luxembourg and Strasbourg complicate matters in terms of judicial hierarchy), the Court unquestionably[146] departed from an authority for the first time in *R (Barkas) v North Yorkshire County Council*.[147] The Court held that *R (Beresford) v Sunderland City Council*[148] had been wrongly decided on the relevant points,[149] but was sufficiently confident to do so with a panel of "only" five justices. The next two such cases to depart from a precedent did, admittedly, have a panel of seven: *Montgomery v Lanarkshire Health Board*[150] and *FHR European Ventures v Cedar Capital Partners*.[151] But there is no apparent metric for when the first EP criterion (which may often overlap with the fourth criterion) – "If the Court is being asked to depart, or may decide to depart from a previous decision" – requires an EP and when it does not.

---

144 It should be noted that occasionally the Court of Appeal grants permission to appeal by certifying that a case raises a question of law of general public importance: the 7JP case of *R v Golds* [2016] UKSC 61 is one such example, on the partial defence of diminished responsibility under s 2 of the Homicide Act 1957: see *R v Golds* [2015] 1 WLR 1030 at 1045.

145 J. Lee, "Fides et Ratio: Precedent in the Early Jurisprudence of the United Kingdom Supreme Court" (2015) 21(1) *European Journal of Current Legal Issues*.

146 I take this as where the Court agreed that it was departing from an authority. Controversy may rage on about whether in other cases there was a departure from precedent: see eg the dissents of Lord Hope DPSC and Lady Hale in *Jones v Kaney* [2011] UKSC 13 on the majority's approach to *Waston v M'Ewan* [1905] AC 480, considered in Lee, ibid at section 4.

147 [2014] UKSC 31.

148 [2004] 1 AC 889.

149 See eg Lord Neuberger in *Barkas* at [48]–[9].

150 [2015] UKSC 11.

151 [2014] UKSC 45.

In terms of the precedent-related criteria, some of the EP cases have been false alarms. *R (on the application of KM) v Cambridgeshire County Council*[152] is one such case. A 7JP had been convened to hear the case, which concerned a local authority's assessment of the support it should provide for the disabled claimant's needs under the Chronically Sick and Disabled Persons Act 1970. The case was thought to be going to involve a challenge to a previous House of Lords decision, *R v Gloucestershire County Council, ex p Barry*,[153] which Lady Hale had criticized in dissent in *R (McDonald) v Kensington and Chelsea Royal London Borough Council*.[154]

But *Barry* was a case involving resource allocation, and it transpired in *KM* that the Council's decision had not been based on resource constraints at all, simply on a decision to meet the claimant's needs at lower cost. Lord Wilson, giving the lead judgment for the Court, apologized,[155] and Lady Hale lamented, that the case did not engage *Barry* as had been thought (and in some cases hoped).[156] *KM* also shows that it is not only the Court's resources that might be tested by convening a larger panel – interveners might be encouraged to engage in the litigation in the expectation that the case would turn out to be more significant.

One or two swallows do not make a summer, but another short example may be helpful as it reinforces my argument that there is uncertainty over which cases are important and which are really, really important. *Sims v Dacorum Borough Council*[157] saw the Court invited to depart from the decision of the House of Lords in *Hammersmith and Fulham LBC v Monk*[158] in light of the enactment of the Human Rights Act 1998. Lord Neuberger, who is not only the Court's president but also its expert on landlord and tenant law, took just twenty-six paragraphs to reaffirm the existing rule. *Monk* had established that the common law rule was that a joint periodic tenancy might be terminated if any of the co-tenants served the landlord with a notice to quit. Mrs Sims had left Mr Sims after incidents of domestic violence against her, and she had given their landlord notice to quit. Mr Sims had argued on appeal that the common

152 [2012] UKSC 23.
153 [1997] AC 584.
154 [2011] UKSC 33.
155 *KM* at [7] (Lord Wilson).
156 Ibid at [40].
157 [2014] UKSC 63 ("*Sims*").
158 [1992] AC 478.

law rule was incompatible with his rights under Article 8 and Article 1 Protocol 1 (A1P1) ECHR. The Court of Appeal dismissed his appeal. It is a point that has been much considered by the academic literature.[159]

On A1P1, Lord Neuberger held that the first-instance judge had been not only entitled to find in favour of the landlord, but indeed, "she reached the only appropriate conclusion she could have reached."[160] On Article 8, Lord Neuberger considered that a point on proportionality "[got] Mr Sims nowhere"[161] as the judge's decision was "plainly correct."[162] And one other argument, that Mr Sims's rights had been infringed by the very service of the notice to quit, could not succeed because "no judgment of the Strasbourg court begins to justify such a proposition."[163]

One might, therefore, be forgiven for thinking that not much was added to the law by the Court's perfunctory resolution of the appeal. Would it not have been simpler not to grant permission to appeal in the first place, stating that the case did not raise an arguable point of law? Even if the appeal should have been heard, the way in which Mr Sims's case was determined calls into question the need for seven justices. A justification for hearing the appeal with seven justices, and unanimously reaffirming *Monk*, would be reasoned engagement with the arguments to the contrary. But that was not offered in what turned out to be one of the briefest Supreme Court judgments in its short history, and the case does not seem to live up to Lord Neuberger's expectation

159 Eg I. Loveland, "Tackling the Rule in *Hammersmith v Monk*: In Theory and in Practice" (2012) *European Human Rights Law Review* 629; I. Loveland, "Tackling the Rule in *Hammersmith v Monk*: In Theory and in Practice" (2013) *European Human Rights Law Review* 28; S. Nield, "Human Rights and the Rule in *Hammersmith and Fulham LBC v Monk*" [2013] *Conveyancer* 326; "After Qazi: 1 – Sole Tenant Termination of Joint Tenancies" [2005] *Conveyancer* 12; M. Davis and D. Hughes, "Gateways or Barriers? Joint Tenants, Possession Claims and Article 8" [2010] *Conveyancer* 57; T. Gallivan and D. Cowan, "The Rule in *Hammersmith and Fulham LBC v Monk* Reconsidered" (2010) 13 *Journal of Housing Law* 107; M. Davis and D. Hughes, "An End of the Affair: Social Housing, Relationship Breakdown, and the Human Rights Act 1998" [2004] *Conveyancer* 19; S. Pascoe, "Can a Joint Tenant Remain in Possession after the Other Joint Tenant Has Given Notice to Quit?" [2004] *Conveyancer* 370; and I. Loveland, "The Impact of the Human Rights Act on Security of Tenure in Public Housing" [2004] *Public Law* 594.

160 *Sims*, above n 157 at [19].

161 Ibid at [21].

162 Ibid.

163 Ibid at [22].

that appeals to the Supreme Court should be necessary to "clarify, correct, declare [or] develop"[164] the law.

Equally crisp, although not exactly a false alarm, was *Knauer v Ministry of Justice*,[165] in which the Supreme Court (Lord Neuberger and Lady Hale giving the judgment for the Court) took just twenty-seven paragraphs to briskly depart from two House of Lords decisions[166] on the date for assessing the damages for future loss under the Fatal Accidents Act 1976. The matter-of-fact disposal of these two decisions suggests, perhaps, that it did not require seven justices to resolve the issue.

To be clear, I am not suggesting that reaffirming a precedent rather than departing from it retrospectively undermines the choice to have an EP in the first place. The justices, after full argument, can reach only that conclusion that appears appropriate in a given case. However, the *manner* in which the Court has resolved the appeals in some EP cases does give reason to doubt why it was necessary to have an EP or even (in the case of false alarms) to hear the appeals at all.

Interaction with the Privy Council

The opportunity to sit on the Judicial Committee of the Privy Council (JCPC) is valued by the judges on the Supreme Court, both out of constitutional duty and as informing their more regular diet: as Lord Mance has noted, "The Privy Council retains an unexpectedly active jurisdiction – 30% or more of our total workload. And it offers a great variety of work, which broadens our horizons."[167] And although other Privy Counsellors – whether judges from the English Court of Appeal or from a court of the home jurisdiction – may sit on the Privy Council, Supreme Court justices continue to make up 95 per cent of all those sitting on JCPC cases.[168]

164 Neuberger, "UK Supreme Court Decisions on Private and Commercial Law," above n 40.

165 [2016] UKSC 9.

166 *Cookson v Knowles* [1979] AC 556; and *Graham v Dodds* [1983] 1 WLR 808.

167 Lord Mance, "Jurisdiction and Justiciability," Fifth Annual Judicial Distinguished Guest Lecture, Cayman Islands, 31 March 2015, https://www.supremecourt.uk/docs/speech-150331.pdf, 2.

168 Lord Neuberger, "The Judicial Committee of the Privy Council in the 21st Century," Annual Caroline Weatherill Memorial Lecture, Isle of Man (2014) 3 *Cambridge Journal of International and Comparative Law* 30 at 31.

The JCPC requires at least three judges to be quorate,[169] and the Court generally sits in five. It has not sat in a board of nine members[170] since the inauguration of the Supreme Court and, indeed, not since the controversial decision in *Attorney General for Jersey v Holley*[171] in 2005, considered below. An important 9JP[172] UKSC decision of July 2016 is appropriate to consider here. *Willers v Joyce (No 2)*[173] was a companion decision to *Willers (No 1)*, which, as we have seen, decided that the tort of malicious prosecution of civil proceedings existed. The case also raised the broader issue considered in the separate judgment, which was

> whether the Courts of England and Wales should continue to treat decisions of the Privy Council, made by a board comprising solely of serving Supreme Court Justices who have heard full argument and made their decision on the basis of English law, as having no status as legal precedent in England and Wales.[174]

Lord Neuberger delivered the single judgment for the 9JP Court, on an issue that is clearly an important one of precedent: that is, the Court is not just resolving the status of *Crawford Adjusters* as against *Gregory v Portsmouth* but also trying to provide more general guidance to lower courts and, indeed, the Privy Council for the future.

The Court noted that, in the absence of an English decision to the contrary, the courts of England and Wales can normally be expected to follow a relevant Privy Council decision.[175] Where there is a conflict with a decision of a superior court, the Supreme Court confirmed that "a court should not, at least normally, follow a decision of the JCPC, if

---

169 S 5A of the Judicial Committee Act 1833, as inserted by Statute Law (Repeals) Act 2004 (c 14), s 1(2) at sch 2 para 2.

170 Taking the figures up to August 2018, the Privy Council has decided only one case with a panel of more than five since the start of 2016, when seven judges sat in *Re Baronetcy of Pringle of Stichill* [2016] UKPC 16.

171 [2005] UKPC 23; [2005] 2 AC 580.

172 I continue to use the terminology of *XJP* for "X Justice Panels" in this section for consistency's sake, notwithstanding the fact that the judges are not acting as justices of the Supreme Court when sitting in the Privy Council.

173 [2016] UKSC 44.

174 UKSC 2015/0154, https://www.supremecourt.uk/cases/uksc-2015-0154.html.

175 *Willers (No 2)*, above n 173 at [16].

it is inconsistent with the decision of a court which is binding" in the English hierarchy.[176] Lord Neuberger went further and disapproved of the suggestion that a lower court could follow a Privy Council decision in preference to a Court of Appeal or Supreme Court, where it was thought to be "a foregone conclusion" that the higher court would accept the view of the JCPC. This idea had some support in Court of Appeal decisions,[177] but Lord Neuberger held that, instead, the rule of precedent should be absolute,[178] although subject to an important qualification. The qualification was that

> it seems to me to be not only convenient but also sensible that the JCPC, which normally consists of the same judges as the Supreme Court, should, when applying English law, be capable of departing from an earlier decision of the Supreme Court or House of Lords to the same extent and with the same effect as the Supreme Court.[179]

A full consideration of the implications of this conclusion is beyond my present scope.[180] But I can make several brief observations. The first is that the Court reaffirmed the basic principles of precedent and also deprecated the potential exceptional doctrine of the foregone conclusion. Second, in recognizing the exception, Lord Neuberger limited it to cases where the JCPC is applying English law only. Third, Lord Neuberger also set out practical steps that the JCPC could take in a decision where an authority of the Court of Appeal, House of Lords, or Supreme Court was being challenged.[181] The burden would thus appear to be on the Privy Council to take appropriate steps to indicate that it was intending to depart from previous authority: it was recognized that the Board was only "*capable* of departing from an earlier decision."[182] The difficulty with this aspect is that it is not clear whether the decision in *Willers* confers retrospective authority on the JCPC to have departed

176 Ibid at [16].

177 *R v James* [2006] EWCA Crim 14 at [43]. Lord Neuberger stated that he was not doubting the status of *James* on the point of law.

178 *Willers (No 2)*, above n 173 at [17].

179 Ibid at [21].

180 See P. Mirfield, "A Novel Theory of Privy Council Precedent" (2017) 133 *Law Quarterly Review* 1.

181 *Willers (No 2)*, above n 173 at [19]–[21].

182 Ibid at [21].

from previous decisions or whether it applies only from now on, where Lord Neuberger's practical guidelines are followed.

A final point is that the Supreme Court in *Willers (No 2)* did not, with respect, directly answer the question set (or that it had set itself). That issue, as originally framed, was limited to Privy Council decisions of a panel of Supreme Court justices only. In Lord Neuberger's formulation, however, His Lordship referred to the JCPC as "normally consist[ing] of the same judges as the Supreme Court."[183] But would a case in which the Lord Chief Justice or the Master of the Rolls sat as a member of the Board really be any different? Last, Lord Neuberger noted in passing that the president of the JCPC can take into account the challenge in precedent in deciding "the constitution and size of the panel which is to hear the appeal": there is no express requirement that there be seven or nine justices, for example.

The 9JP convened in the *Willers v Joyce* litigation might be contrasted with the decision with regard to the panel in *R v Jogee*,[184] which concerned questions of precedent and (relatively narrow) aspects of the doctrine of joint enterprise in criminal law. It was also the first time in history[185] that the Supreme Court (or House of Lords) had sat in a case alongside an appeal to the JCPC. It required an assessment of whether the law "took a wrong turn"[186] in the JCPC decision in *Chan Wing-Siu v The Queen*[187] and later developed by the House of Lords in *R v Powell and R v English*.[188] The Court/Board unanimously decided to depart from those decisions so that "the correction of the error in *Chan Wing-Siu* [would bring] the common law back into recognition of the difference between foresight and intent."[189] What is more, the Court/Board took the view that the only reason for hesitation was the fact that it would involve reversing thirty years of practice:

> We do not consider that the *Chan Wing-Siu* principle can be supported, except on the basis that it has been decided and followed at the highest

183 Ibid.

184 *R v Jogee and Ruddock* [2016] UKSC 8 ("*Jogee*"). See further, from the perspective of precedent, L. Blom-Cooper and G. Drewry, "Correcting Wrong Turns: The 50th Birthday of the 1966 House of Lords Practice Statement on Precedent" [2016] *Public Law* 381.

185 At least as far as my best research efforts have been able to determine.

186 *Jogee*, above n 184 at [3].

187 [1985] AC 168.

188 [1999] AC 1.

189 *Jogee*, above n 184 at [86].

> level. In plain terms, our analysis leads us to the conclusion that the introduction of the principle was based on an incomplete, and in some respects erroneous, reading of the previous case law, coupled with generalised and questionable policy arguments. We recognise the significance of reversing a statement of principle which has been made and followed by the Privy Council and the House of Lords on a number of occasions. We consider that it is right to do so for several reasons.[190]

The Court went on to "restate" the law and to address the potential impact on past convictions.

Thus, as important cases go, *Jogee* would seem to be pretty, really, very important. The case satisfies at least two ("great public importance" and invitation to depart from previous decisions) and arguably three (resolving a conflict in authority) of the EP criteria. As mentioned, it is also a historic case in that the JCPC had never before sat alongside the Supreme Court in a single joined appeal. And yet, the case had a panel of *only* five justices (albeit including the president and deputy president of the Supreme Court and the Lord Chief Justice). Perhaps, in addition to the mere numbers on the Court, one needs to assess who the judges on any given appeal are, with bonus points for the Lord Chief Justice or Master of the Rolls.[191] *Jogee* is further evidence that the current practice is unsatisfactory and inconsistent.[192]

---

190 Ibid at [79] (Lord Hughes and Lord Toulson). See also "It would not be satisfactory for this court simply to disapprove the *Chan Wing-Siu* principle. Those who are concerned with criminal justice, including members of the public, are entitled to expect from this court a clear statement of the relevant principles. We consider that the proper course for this court is to re-state, as nearly and clearly as we may, the principles which had been established over many years before the law took a wrong turn" (at [87]).

191 In *R v Harvey* [2013] EWCA Crim 1104, Jackson LJ noted of *R v Waya* [2012] UKSC 51, "A panel of nine judges, including the Lord Chief Justice, heard this appeal" (at [55]).

192 And the decision in *Jogee* has been criticized substantively: by F. Stark, "The Demise of 'Parasitic Accessorial Liability'" (2016) 75 *Cambridge Law Journal* 550; F. Stark, "The Taming of Jogee" (2017) 76 *Cambridge Law Journal* 4; and A.P. Simester, "Accessory Liability and Common Unlawful Purposes" (2017) 133 *Cambridge Law Journal* 73. Compare M. Dyson, "Ever Working in Practice, but Never in Theory? The New English Law of Criminal Complicity" [2017] *Zeitschrift für die gesamte Strafrechtswissenschaft* 232.

The First Eleven

This chapter has primarily been a study of the cases in the first nine years of Supreme Court decisions and has demonstrated the difficulties with the present practice in respect of EP cases. Before stating some conclusions, a brief cadenza may be added in respect of the seminal *Miller* case.[193] As noted, it was decided that, for the first time,[194] all serving justices would sit on the appeal in *Miller*. Interestingly, the announcement did not refer to the EP criteria (the *Assange* case remains the only instance of the Court indicating in advance why an EP was sitting). But it would seem that the case satisfies the second criterion – "A case of high constitutional importance" – and the third – "A case of great public importance." Lady Hale has extra-curially explained that it was "a case of such fundamental constitutional importance that ... we plan[ned] that all eleven of the current serving Justices [should] sit on it."[195] Lord Neuberger has also observed that

> bearing in mind the intense public interest in the case and also in the Supreme Court itself, it seemed to me appropriate that all the Justices sat on Miller. Sitting a full panel was important to ensure that there was public confidence in the legitimacy of the decision, particularly in the event of a close decision.[196]

The eight-justice majority judgment also referred to the significance of the case in raising some "of the most important issues which

---

193 This chapter is not the place for reflection on the judgments in *Miller*, although its institutional implications are addressed where appropriate. For consideration of the substantive constitutional principles, see D. Feldman, "Pulling a Trigger or Starting a Journey?" (2017) 76 *Cambridge Law Journal* 217; M. Elliott, "The Supreme Court's Judgment in *Miller*: In Search of Constitutional Principle" (2017) 76 *Cambridge Law Journal* 257; R. Ekins, "Constitutional Practice and Principle in the Article 50 Litigation" (2017) 133 *Cambridge Law Journal* 347; and the special section of *Modern Law Review* (July 2017) 80(4) at 685–745, which features articles by J. Murkens, T. Poole, K. Ewing, and N. Aroney.

194 At https://www.supremecourt.uk/news/permission-to-appeal-decision-08-november-2016.htm.

195 Lady Hale, "The Supreme Court: Guardian of the Constitution?," Sultan Azlan Shah Lecture, Kuala Lumpur, 9 November 2016, https://www.supremecourt.uk/docs/speech-161109.pdf, 12.

196 Neuberger, "Twenty Years a Judge," above n 29 at para 31.

judges have to decide concern[ing] questions relating to the constitutional arrangements of the United Kingdom."[197] But it is noteworthy that *Miller* satisfies only two of the five EP criteria at best (whereas other cases considered here have raised more). Building upon my criticisms so far, there are several points that may be made about the decision to sit *en banc* in *Miller*. First, once the Court has decided that it is possible to sit in a panel of eleven, there will be pressure to do so again and uncertainty caused by not doing so in the future. If the facts of the physical confines of the largest courtroom and the workload of the Court are not barriers to sitting in eleven in *Miller*, then why not do so more often? A fourth category of really, *really*, *Really* important case has been recognized.

It might be argued that *Miller* presented a unique situation. The occasion of the United Kingdom preparing to leave the EU, and the political sensitivities and public attention trained on the courts as a result, might be thought to be a one-off. At the same time, we had the relatively unusual situation that the Court had only eleven serving justices in the 2016–17 legal year because of the decision to make three appointments in one round in the summer of 2017. But we should be sceptical about such an argument. The case raised many questions of constitutional law, some basic and some sophisticated. It may not be the last time that the Court is invited to consider a legal question related to the process of the United Kingdom leaving the EU or the consequences of it. Will it always be that the Court will seek to sit with eleven when there is a politically controversial case to be decided? *Politically controversial* is, of course, not one of the published EP criteria, and both the majority and minority recognized that the boundary between law and politics must be closely monitored.[198]

---

197 *Miller*, above n 1 at [4] (Lord Neuberger of Abbotsbury PSC, Baroness Hale of Richmond DPSC, Lord Mance, Lord Kerr of Tonaghmore, Lord Clarke of Stone-Cum-Ebony, Lord Wilson, Lord Sumption, Lord Hodge JJSC).

198 Ibid at [3] (Majority): "Those are all political issues which are matters for ministers and Parliament to resolve. They are not issues which are appropriate for resolution by judges, whose duty is to decide issues of law which are brought before them by individuals and entities exercising their rights of access to the courts in a democratic society." Lord Reed, dissenting at [240]: "It is important for courts to understand that the legalisation of political issues is not always constitutionally appropriate, and may be fraught with risk, not least for the judiciary."

The fact that the Court currently happened to have eleven serving justices is also a difficult point as there have been, and will be, several occasions where it may have only eleven serving, or perhaps available, justices, whether because a justice has retired, or dies in office, or is unavailable for another reason.[199] And yet the Supreme Court has, for most of its existence, had twelve justices and will continue to do so. Allowing for eleven justices merely highlights the concern that one justice could have made the difference, rather than addressing it. Lady Hale also speculated in a recent lecture that if the Supreme Court always sat *en banc*, politicians would likely take more of an interest in appointments to the Court.[200]

Second, why did *only* eleven justices sit in *Miller*? As noted above, Lord Toulson and Lord Dyson were serving on the Supplementary Panel in 2016–17. They were joined by two former Lord Presidents, Lord Gill and Lord Hamilton, who could assist with Scots law. With the Court having only eleven full-time justices, the judges on the Supplementary Panel would be called to sit with a certain frequency. It might, therefore, be thought that the Court could have sat in thirteen or fifteen so that every available judge who heard UKSC cases would be seen to be involved. We have seen that the Lord Chief Justice and the Master of the Rolls may, and do, also sit as acting judges, but they sat in the Divisional Court in *Miller* and so would have been ineligible on this occasion.[201]

Furthermore, the possibility[202] under recent reforms of justices being appointed on a part-time basis, so that two serving justices amounted to the full-time equivalent of one justice, would complicate matters

199 Exceptionally, Lord Saville was unavailable to sit because he was chairing the Bloody Sunday Inquiry, which reported in June 2010, http://webarchive.nationalarchives.gov.uk/20101103103930/http://www.bloody-sunday-inquiry.org/.

200 Hale, "Judges, Power and Accountability," above n 4 at 18.

201 I leave aside the possibility of other acting judges from any of the relevant appeal courts in the jurisdictions of the United Kingdom: see s 38 of the 2005 Act.

202 The first round of appointments under that scheme in 2017 saw the appointment of three full-time justices – Lady Black, Lord Briggs, and Lord Lloyd Jones – to the three full-time equivalent vacancies. A second round in 2018 saw the appointments announced of Lady Arden, Lord Kitchin (who were both sworn in, in October 2018), and Lord Sales (who was sworn in, in January 2019 after the retirement of Lord Sumption in December 2018).

further. If, in the future, two justices were appointed on a job-share arrangement, then the Court would have a total of thirteen justices. Different configurations of justices might be appointed on this flexible basis, but a requirement or practice of sitting *en banc* would potentially undermine the purpose of the reforms. Once the working cap of nine justices has been lifted, then it will be hard for the logic of sitting with all justices not to be followed through in other cases.

I am certainly not advocating such numbers hearing cases, merely highlighting yet further difficulties of the *Miller* arrangement beyond those already discussed. Is it conceivable that we now take *Miller* as the yardstick by which we judge how many judges should sit in a case? For example, "This case is 45 per cent as important as *Miller*, so it needs only five justices." The political and tactical reasons for sitting *en banc* in *Miller* were understandable at the time, but it may have underestimated and undesirable implications.

Conclusions

This study of the EP cases heard by the UKSC has led to argument for reform in several key respects. There is at least perceived to be some value in convening a larger bench to hear really important cases. But it is not clear that the justifications for the practice stand up to scrutiny. I have argued that the present practice calls into question the ill-defined concept of *importance*, and, if anything, it risks perpetuating the perceptions about judging that the approach is meant to challenge.[203] The statistics here show that just under 17 per cent of the cases heard by the Court have had an EP: is it right that all cases that go to the Supreme Court are important, but that one in five (or latterly around one in seven) are deemed to be more important than others? And why is *Miller* deemed to be the most important of all? As we have seen, with the possible exception of the "false alarm" cases, one may well agree that the EP cases meet the criteria, but the trouble is that many of the other 80 per cent appear to do so too.

203 If "we accept the argument that two separate groups of five judges may differ in their treatment of any case, then it follows that they should sit in sevens or nines as often as possible": P Darbyshire, *Sitting in Judgment: The Working Lives of Judges* (Oxford, Hart Publishing, 2011) 137.

I have, therefore, argued that reforms are necessary – both to the approach to EP cases and to "run-of-the-mill," five-judge cases. This includes the Court's public communications regarding permission to appeal in the first place. A preferable solution may be to remove the criteria altogether and instead to give reasons why, in each case, it has been determined that a larger panel should sit. Although removing criteria might, at first sight, seem less transparent, it would be replaced by observable, rationalized practice from now onward. At present, the inconsistency as to what *importance* means renders the criteria almost meaningless. It also invites scrutiny as to which judges are allocated to sit on a case in a way that is not seemingly intended, and it poses questions that the Court, at present, cannot answer.

There should be continuity, I have argued, in the practice of not usually sitting *en banc*, principally on the grounds of the necessary caseload for the Court, in both the Supreme Court and the Privy Council. There are other reasons that suggest that the decision to sit with eleven justices in *Miller* sets a difficult and regrettable precedent for the practice of the Court. Also, as we have seen, the Court must sit in odd numbers, and so any shift to sitting *en banc* would require a statutory amendment, presumably to change the total number of justices to either eleven or thirteen. Such numbers generally sitting in one case would be unwieldy for the UKSC given the workload of the justices. It may be for this reason that Lady Hale, who, we have seen, has expressed support in principle for sitting in enlarged panels more often, has nonetheless overseen a significant reduction in such cases in the first year of her presidency.

In his 2015 F.A. Mann Lecture, Lord Neuberger noted that with an increase in judicial power comes an increase in responsibility.[204] I have argued that it does not follow that, with an increase in responsibility, one necessarily needs serial increases in the size of panels sitting on appeals. The reforms recommended here would resolve some of the problematic aspects of decisions about EP decision-making and retain public confidence in the Court. The start of a new era under Lord Neuberger's successor, Lady Hale, represents a good opportunity to

204 "'Judge Not, That Ye Be Not Judged': Judging Judicial Decision-Making," F.A. Mann Lecture, 2015, https://www.supremecourt.uk/docs/speech-150129.pdf. See also J. Lee and S. Lee, "Humility in the Supreme Court" (2015) 26 *King's Law Journal* 165 at 174.

reconsider the practice, and we have seen that the number of EP cases has fallen. A final implication of the uncertainties identified here is that, whatever the size of the panel, the Supreme Court's approach to precedent may require some re-evaluation. Judging in the Supreme Court is really, really important and should not be a question of making up the numbers.

5 The Reference Jurisdiction of the Supreme Court of Canada

CARISSIMA MATHEN

Since the founding, in 1875, of the Supreme Court of Canada,[1] the federal executive has enjoyed the power to refer questions to the Court in the absence of a live case.[2] (Provincial governments exercise a similar power in their respective jurisdictions.)[3] References – also known as advisory opinions – have been extremely significant to the development of Canadian constitutional jurisprudence. Yet, as a distinct phenomenon, they remain largely unexplored. This chapter considers their role in Supreme Court[4] decision making.

1 The Court was originally established by ordinary federal law, enacted under the authority of s 101 of the Constitution Act, 1867, 30 & 31 Victoria, c 3 (UK): Supreme and Exchequer Court Act SC, 1875, c 11 [Supreme and Exchequer Court Act]. In 2014, the Supreme Court ruled that its composition and "essential features" had, over time, acquired protected status under the Constitution such that they could not be changed through simple legislation: *Reference re ss 5 and 6 of the Supreme Court Act* 2014 SCC 21, [2014] 1 SCR 433 [*Supreme Court Act Reference*]. The implications of this opinion are discussed, below n 120 and surrounding text.

2 Supreme Court Act, RSC 1985, c S-26, s 53. When a federal reference concerns the validity of provincial legislation, the relevant attorney general is to be advised: s 53(5). S 54 provides a power for either chamber of the House of Commons to refer "private bills" for report by any two judges. It has not been used in over a century and is clearly of a different character than the reference opinions sought and issued under s 53.

3 Provinces enjoy a right of appeal to the Supreme Court for references issuing from their respective courts of appeal: ibid at s 36. There have been very dramatic provincial references, such as the reference on polygamy issued by the BC Supreme Court in 2011; see C. Mathen, "Reflecting Culture: The Charter and Polygamy" in B.L. Berger and J. Stribopoulos (eds), *Unsettled Legacy: Thirty Years of Criminal Justice under the Charter* (Toronto, LexisNexis, 2013) 391.

4 At the time of Confederation, the Judicial Committee of the Privy Council (JCPC) was the final court of appeal for Canada and, in that role, heard appeals of advisory

A Brief History

The reference jurisdiction has been a constant, and distinguishing, feature of the Supreme Court. It is, for example, a key difference between the Court and its US counterpart. Because the United States Constitution permits the judiciary to decide only "cases and controversies,"[5] federal courts, including that country's Supreme Court, do not issue advisory opinions.[6] By contrast, Canadian law appears to view the judiciary as having the ability to act as "the official adviser of the executive."[7]

The Canadian reference power can be traced to s. 4 of the Judicial Committee Act 1833, which authorized the Crown to refer for consideration to the committee "any such matters whatsoever as His Majesty shall think fit."[8] The section was almost certainly the model for the following clause in Canada's Supreme and Exchequer Court Act:

> 52. It shall be lawful for the Governor in Council to refer to the Supreme Court for hearing or consideration, any matters whatsoever as he may think fit; and the Court shall thereupon hear and consider the same and certify their opinion thereon to the Governor in Council: Provided that any Judge or Judges of the said Court who may differ from the opinion of the majority may in like manner certify his or their opinion or opinions to the Governor in Council.[9]

---

opinions issued by the Supreme Court. Over time, the JCPC's jurisdiction was curtailed until it finally vanished in 1949. The focus in this chapter is the Supreme Court of Canada – the country's current apex court. During the period that the Supreme Court did not occupy that position, relevant JCPC advisory opinions will be discussed.

5 US Constitution, Art III.

6 *Muskrat v United States* 219 US 346 at 362 (1911). Some state constitutions do allow for advisory opinions, but their courts describe them as "extrajudicial" and possessed of "dramatically limited *stare decisis* effect." L. Tribe, *American Constitutional Law* (Mineola, NY, Foundation Press, 1988) at 73 fn 4. See generally L. Tribe, "Note: Advisory Opinions on the Constitutionality of Statutes" (1956) 69 *Harvard Law Review* 1302; A. Bickel, "The Supreme Court 1960 Term Foreword: The Passive Virtues" (1961) 75 *Harvard Law Review* 40 at 42.

7 *In re References by the Governor-General in Council* (1910) 43 SCR 536 at 547, aff'd [1912] AC 571 (PC). [*Reference re References*]. The Judicial Committee refers to the "4th section of the Act of William IV" (at 7).

8 3 & 4 Wm IV, c 41. As discussed in Barry L. Strayer, *The Canadian Constitution and the Courts* (Toronto, Butterworths, 1988) at 311.

9 Supreme and Exchequer Court Act, above n 1.

For several reasons, s. 52 proved to be problematic. For one thing, it did not require the Court to explain its answers with reasons.[10] Nor did it prescribe a real framework to guide the reference process. It also provoked concerns from the provinces that it granted a structural bias to the federal government.

In 1891, the Supreme and Exchequer Court Act was amended. The Court was required to "hear and consider [a reference], and to answer each question so referred" and to certify "its opinion upon each such question, with the reasons for each such answer."[11] An opinion was to be "pronounced in like manner as in the case of a judgment upon an appeal to the Court"; and any dissenting opinions were to be recorded.[12] References could include "important questions of law or fact" as well as "any other matter" that the Governor in Council saw fit to refer.[13] This, in effect, granted the federal Cabinet unlimited discretion to set reference questions. A separate clause, subsequently abandoned for reasons that remain obscure, deemed such opinions to be "advisory only."[14] But, for all purposes of appeal, a reference was to be treated as a final judgment.[15] The Act further required that notice be given to affected provinces when questions touched on their respective jurisdictions or laws, and it provided an automatic right of appeal to the Court for advisory opinions rendered by provincial courts of appeal.[16]

Provincial concerns did not abate and were formally considered in *In Re References by the Governor-General in Council*.[17] The so-called *Reference*

---

10 In early references, the Supreme Court was content to state a bare answer without reasons: Strayer, *Canadian Constitution and the Courts*, above n 8 at 312. In fairness, the JCPC apparently agreed, a mysterious conclusion given the history of references in England. Depending on the question's specificity, this could obviously fail to provide suitable guidance. See eg the *McCarthy Act Reference*: *Sess Papers* no 85a, 1885 (Can) at 12–13.

11 Supreme and Exchequer Court Act, SC 1891, c 25, s 4.

12 Ibid.

13 Ibid. The Act permitted "Important questions of law or fact touching (a) the interpretation of the British North America Acts, 1867 to 1886; or (b) The constitutionality or interpretation of any Dominion or provincial legislation; or … (d) The powers of the Parliament of Canada, or of the legislatures of the provinces, or of the respective governments thereof, whether or not the particular power in question has been or is proposed to be executed; or, (e) Any other matter … with reference to which the Governor in Council sees fit to submit any such question."

14 Ibid.

15 Ibid.

16 Most of these changes have survived.

17 *Reference re References*, above n 7 (SCC).

re References arose out of a federal question concerning the provincial power to incorporate companies. Six provinces contested the hearing on the basis that it offended the division of powers for the federal government to refer questions of law concerning provincial matters and that the entire advisory function was incompatible with the "general court of appeal" contemplated by s. 101 of the Constitution Act, 1867.[18]

A majority of the Supreme Court held that the phrase "a general court of appeal"[19] was broad enough to encompass a reference jurisdiction. In addition, it said, nothing in the Constitution Act, 1867 suggested that the jurisdiction of such a court must be limited to questions of federal law. An appeal to the Judicial Committee of the Privy Council (JCPC) was unsuccessful.[20] The JCPC stated, "[W]hatever belongs to self-government in Canada belongs either to the Dominion or the Provinces."[21] While the Canadian Constitution did not expressly mention an advisory function for courts, s. 101 described one such court capable of rendering such opinions, and it granted to the federal government the power to establish that court. The JCPC dismissed the objection that a reference function was incompatible with the judicial role. It noted that such a power was established (if infrequently used) within British constitutional tradition; and numerous references had already been appealed without objection to the Privy Council.[22]

As a result, Canadian courts accepted the reference function as part of their duties. As opposed to providing a check on executive power, the advisory function drew the executive and judiciary into a different sort of relationship.[23] Between 1867 and 1986, references accounted for one-quarter of the Supreme Court's constitutional law docket.[24] Since

---

18 Constitution Act, 1867 30 & 31 Vict, c 3 S 101 provides, "The Parliament of Canada may, notwithstanding anything in this Act, from Time to Time provide for the Constitution, Maintenance, and Organization of a General Court of Appeal for Canada, and for the Establishment of any additional Courts for the better Administration of the Laws of Canada."

19 Ibid.

20 *Reference re References*, above n 7 (PC).

21 Ibid at 5.

22 Ibid at 10.

23 This continues to the present day as the Supreme Court has noted that the American understanding of separation of powers does not find an exact corollary in Canada. *Reference Re Secession of Quebec* [1998] 2 SCR 217 at para 15.

24 Strayer, *Canadian Constitution and the Courts*, above note 8 at 331.

the expansion of the Constitution of Canada to include a bill of rights, references have not arisen as frequently. No doubt, that is partially explained by the expanded scope for constitutional litigation entailed by the Canadian Charter of Rights and Freedoms and other provisions adopted in the constitutional reforms of 1982.[25] But references have continued to play an important role in the development of jurisprudence post-1982, touching on such consequential topics as criminal responsibility,[26] prostitution,[27] and same-sex marriage.[28]

An important difference between references and live cases is that references fail to engage a court's remedial powers. From the outset, some viewed this feature as inconsistent with the Supreme Court's role. As discussed above, the JCPC rejected such a truncated view of the judicial branch. Yet it did not explain precisely what a court does when it issues a reference opinion and, in particular, how Supreme Court references would coexist with its many appellate decisions.

In *Reference re Criminal Code*,[29] an early answer emerged. Again, certain provinces objected to the proceeding itself, this time on the grounds that the reference was a disguised criminal appeal. Although sympathetic to that concern, Supreme Court Justice Girouard articulated what he considered to be an important difference. He wrote, "[A]s our advice has no legal effect, does not affect the rights of parties, nor the provincial decisions, and is not even binding upon us,"[30] he saw no objection to answering the questions. Justice Davies made the same point in *Reference re References:* "Being advisory only and not binding upon the body to whom they are given or upon the judges who give them [, such opinions] cannot be said to be in any way binding upon the judges of any of the provincial courts."[31]

Thus, Canadian courts expressed early confidence in being able to maintain a feasible distinction between references and cases. In 1910,

25 These would include the rights of "aboriginal peoples," which are affirmed in s 35 of the Constitution Act, 1982.

26 *Reference Re s 94(2) of Motor Vehicle Act (British Columbia)* [1985] 2 SCR 486 [*Motor Vehicle Reference*].

27 *Reference re ss 193 and 195.1(1)(C) of the criminal code (Man)* [1990] 1 SCR 1123 [*Prostitution Reference*].

28 *Reference re Same-Sex Marriage* 2004 SCC 79, [2004] 3 SCR 698 [*Same-Sex Marriage*].

29 *Reference Re Criminal Code (Canada), s 873(A)* (1910) 43 SCR 434 [*Reference Re Criminal Code*].

30 Ibid at 426.

31 *Reference re References*, above n 7 at 561; emphasis added.

the Chief Justice of Canada said that it was not "to be supposed for one moment" that the court would consider itself bound by its reference opinions.[32] In truth, it did not take long for the unthinkable to occur. In one scholar's acid words, the Supreme Court began to follow reference opinions with "undiscriminating zeal."[33] It was not until 1957 that the Court clarified that a reference opinion failed to trigger *res judicata* with respect to future litigation in respect of the same subject.[34] Of course, the absence of *res judicata* simply means that a case can proceed. It does not decide the persuasive value of a prior opinion on the same subject. Indeed, in that 1957 case, the Court followed a prior rule laid down, by the JCPC, in a reference.

In view of how the reference function evolved, it was probably inevitable that opinions would receive a measure of respect and deference from all, including the Court itself. The 1891 amendments to the Supreme Court and Exchequer Act[35] rendered references and cases similar in terms of important points of process. Notice was required, pleadings were made, and reasons were expected. As a result, advisory opinions in structure and reasoning presented as largely identical to ordinary decisions.[36]

Two key moments in Charter jurisprudence, the *Motor Vehicle Reference*[37] (which struck down most absolute liability offences) and *R. v Vaillancourt*[38] (which struck down the "felony murder"[39] rule) illustrate the above point. Consider the following paragraphs taken from the *Motor Vehicle Reference*:

> The issue in this case raises fundamental questions of constitutional theory, including the nature and the very legitimacy of constitutional

---

32 Ibid at 550.

33 G. Rubin, "The Nature, Use and Effect of Reference Cases in Canadian Constitutional Law" (1959) 6 *McGill Law Journal* 168 at 175–9; Strayer, *Canadian Constitution and the Courts*, above n 8 at 331.

34 *CPR v Town of Estevan* [1957] SCR 365.

35 Supreme Court and Exchequer Act, above n 11 and surrounding text.

36 Even style of cause is not consistently observed. A number of early references are styled as division of powers cases – eg *AG Canada v AG Ontario* – and do not use the *Ref re* convention.

37 *Motor Vehicle Reference*, above n 26.

38 *R v Vaillancourt* [1987] 2 SCR 636 [*Vaillancourt*].

39 I borrow this term, which no longer has purchase in Canada, to describe an offence by which a homicide arising in the circumstances of another criminal offence

> adjudication under the Charter as well as the appropriateness of various techniques of constitutional interpretation. ...
>
> A law enacting an absolute liability offence will violate s. 7 of the Charter only if and to the extent that it has the potential of depriving of life, liberty, or security of the person. ... Obviously, imprisonment (including probation orders) deprives persons of their liberty. An offence has that potential as of the moment it is open to the judge to impose imprisonment. ...
>
> I am therefore of the view that the combination of imprisonment and of absolute liability violates s. 7 of the Charter and can only be salvaged if the authorities demonstrate under s. 1 that such a deprivation of liberty in breach of those principles of fundamental justice is, in a free and democratic society, under the circumstances, a justified reasonable limit to one's rights under s. 7.[40]

This led to the following conclusion:

> In the result, I would dismiss the appeal and answer the question in the negative ... and declare s. 94(2) of the Motor Vehicle Act, R.S.B.C. 1979, as amended by the Motor Vehicle Amendment Act, 1982, inconsistent with s. 7 of the Canadian Charter of Rights and Freedoms.[41]

Now, contrast those passages with the following taken from *Vaillancourt*:

> Prior to the enactment of the *Charter*, Parliament had full legislative power with respect to "The Criminal Law," including the determination of the essential elements of any given crime. ... Once the legislation was found to have met this test, the courts had very little power to review the substance of the legislation.
>
> However, federal and provincial legislatures have chosen to restrict through the *Charter* this power. ... As a result, while Parliament retains the power to define the elements of a crime, the courts now have the jurisdiction and, more important, the duty, when called upon to do so, to review

---

may rise to the level of "murder" regardless of the defendant's intent to kill or his subjective foresight of death.

40 *Motor Vehicle Reference*, above n 26.

41 Ibid. The reference was an appeal of an advisory opinion issued by the British Columbia Court of Appeal.

> that definition to ensure that it is in accordance with the principles of fundamental justice.
>
> This Court's decision in *Re B.C. Motor Vehicle Act* stands for the proposition that absolute liability infringes the principles of fundamental justice, such that the combination of absolute liability and a deprivation of [liberty] is a restriction on one's rights under s. 7. … [The decision] thus elevated *mens rea* from a presumed element [to a constitutionally required one]. …
>
> [W]hatever the minimum *mens rea* for the act or the result may be, there are, though very few in number, certain crimes where, because of the special nature of the stigma attached to a conviction therefor or the available penalties, the principles of fundamental justice require a *mens rea* reflecting the particular nature of that crime. … Murder is [one] such offence. … [T]here must be some special mental element with respect to the death before a culpable homicide can be treated as a murder. …
>
> As a result of the foregoing, I would answer the first constitutional question in the affirmative, as s. 213 (*d*) violates both s. 7 and s. 11 (*d*) of the *Charter*, and I would declare s. 213 (*d*) of the *Criminal Code* to be of no force or effect.[42]

In the two sets of passages, the Court appears to perform the same function. It identifies broad principles, and it applies those principles to produce a legal rule capable of future application. Note that the Court's decision in *Vaillancourt* cites the *Motor Vehicle Reference*. And, in the latter opinion, the Court goes so far as to "declare" the subject law to be invalid. This (possibly inadvertent) slip[43] raises questions about classifying a reference outcome in terms of its "binding-ness." It seems a reasonable argument that, in a system bound by the rule of law, the government is presumed to act with constitutionally compliant motives and, therefore, will not wish to maintain an unconstitutional

---

42 *Vaillancourt*, above n 38 at paras 25–28, 43.

43 There have been other such "slips," such as in the *Supreme Court Act Reference*, above n 1 at para 6, where the Court said,

> The practical effect is that the appointment of Justice Nadon and his swearing-in as a judge of the Court were void *ab initio*. He remains a supernumerary judge of the Federal Court of Appeal.

The above declaration followed the Court's summary answers to the questions.

law.[44] If that is correct, then once an apex court has identified the relevant constitutional norms and determined that a particular law falls short of them, the specific provenance of its answer will count for less than the content of that answer.

The latter observation is borne out by the fact that, in Canada, advisory opinions are invariably regarded as having the force of law.[45] No government has treated a Supreme Court reference as simple "advice."[46] As will be discussed in the second part of this chapter, the idea, then, that references are "merely" advisory is probably incomplete.

Canadian references are intriguing. Because they put to courts a question or questions selected by the executive, references have implications for the separation of powers among the branches of the state (at least, in terms of how that separation is commonly understood).[47] References draw the executive and judicial branches into a relationship of some interdependence, into which the legislative branch intrudes – if at all – not as an equal, but as an object for discussion. In addition, because references are untethered to a concrete, live dispute between parties, it can be difficult to constrain their scope (a constraint that, at the Supreme Court, was previously provided for by the Court's power to set constitutional questions).[48]

In *Reference re References*, the JCPC noted "the mischief and inconvenience which might arise from an indiscriminate and injudicious use of the Act."[49] Over the years, the Supreme Court has articulated a variety

---

44 I leave aside a possible override of the Constitution. In the Canadian context, this is provided by s 33 of the Charter, which states, *inter alia*,

> (1) Parliament or the legislature of a province may expressly declare in an Act of Parliament or of the legislature, as the case may be, that the Act or a provision thereof shall operate notwithstanding a provision included in s 2 or ss. 7 to 15.

45 See eg the discussion about *Canada v Bedford*, below n 62 and surrounding text.

46 The Supreme Court has described reference holdings as being "persuasive": *Manitoba v Canada* [1981] 1 SCR 753 (*per* Martland J referring to the *Reference Re Legislative Authority of the Parliament of Canada in Relation to the Upper House* [1980] 1 SCR 54 [*Upper House Reference*]. Indeed, the fact that the Supreme Court Act no longer refers to such opinions as "advisory" might cast doubt upon the above assertion.

47 Admittedly, as a Westminster-style democracy, Canada does not have a rigid separation of powers; for an excellent discussion, see D. Baker, *Not Quite Supreme: The Courts and Coordinate Constitutional Interpretation* (Kingston and Montreal, McGill-Queen's University Press, 2010).

48 *Rules of the Supreme Court of Canada*, Rules 60–1. Note that these were repealed in 2016. The current process relating to stating a constitutional question is set out in Rule 33.

49 *Reference re References*, above n 7 at para 16.

of circumstances in which it can qualify or refuse to answer a reference question. Those circumstances include insufficient factual context,[50] mootness,[51] lack of specificity,[52] vagueness,[53] and the risk that the opinion will produce legal uncertainty.[54] The discretion is rarely exercised. But, given that the Supreme Court Act uses mandatory and not permissive language in framing the reference function, claiming that such a discretion exists is extraordinary. In asserting the freedom to *decline to answer*, the Court most likely is relying upon principles, such as judicial independence, derived from the separation of powers.[55]

While it is axiomatic that a reference does not directly engage a dispute *inter partes*, current controversies frequently inform an executive decision to initiate one. For example, the famous *Secession Reference*[56] took place in the light of some two decades of debate, referenda, and federal elections spurred by the fact that a significant portion of Quebeckers had expressed a desire to separate from Canada. References are most often initiated in relation to laws currently or anticipated to be under democratic review[57] or as a way to secure speedier resolution of a case that is already before the courts.[58]

With the foregoing history in mind, the next section delves in more detail into how a robust advisory function has shaped the Court's decision making and, through it, Canadian constitutional law.

References and Supreme Court Decision Making

The reference function is accurately described as an important, arguably essential, component of the Supreme Court's decision making. Advisory opinions have produced exceptional moments in Canadian jurisprudence.[59] Yet the nature of the function has received only

---

50 *Attorney General (Ontario) v Attorney General (Canada)* [1896] AC 348.

51 *Re Objection by Quebec to a Resolution to Amend the Constitution* [1982] 2 SCR 793 at 806 [*Quebec Veto*].

52 *Upper House Reference*, above n 46.

53 *McEvoy v Attorney General (New Brunswick)* [1983] 1 SCR 704.

54 *Same-Sex Marriage*, above n 28.

55 One can only speculate here, since the Court has not precisely articulated the basis for the discretion.

56 *Secession Reference*, above at n 23.

57 *Reference re Assisted Human Reproduction Act* 2010 SCC 61, [2010] 3 SCR 457 [*Human Reproduction*]; *Reference re Securities Act 2011 SCC* 66, [2011] 3 SCR 837.

58 *Supreme Court Act Reference*, above n 1.

59 As discussed in the next section.

sporadic attention. Initially, the function was imposed on the Court. Its role today is the product of history, politics, and constitutional change. It has both informed and influenced the Supreme Court's evolution into arguably the nation's most powerful constitutional actor.

The advisory function provokes a number of issues and questions. These include the imprecise authority of a reference opinion, whether the function should be used more regularly, and the degree to which recent Supreme Court jurisprudence has rendered reform largely unachievable. Below, those issues are considered in turn.

Authority

An intriguing aspect of reference opinions is the way in which they compel compliance from other actors. As a purely descriptive matter, there is no doubt that the references issued by the Supreme Court generate significant authority of this kind.

First, advisory opinions have played a formative role in Canadian jurisprudence, featuring in what I call "constitutional moments." One of the best examples is the 1929 Persons Case. The reference concerned the interpretation of s. 24 of the Constitution Act, 1867, which provides for the appointment of "qualified persons" to the Senate of Canada. Asked whether *qualified persons* includes females, the Supreme Court advised that it did not. The JCPC decided that it did. Among other things, the committee endorsed what has become known as the *living tree doctrine*:

> The British North America Act planted in Canada a living tree capable of growth and expansion within its natural limits. The object of the Act was to grant a Constitution to Canada. Like all written constitutions it has been subject to development through usage and convention. …
>
> Their Lordships do not conceive it to be the duty of this Board – it is certainly not their desire – to cut down the provisions of the Act by a narrow and technical construction, but rather to give it a large and liberal interpretation so that the Dominion to a great extent, but within certain fixed limits, may be mistress in her own house, as the provinces to a great extent, but within certain fixed limits, are mistresses in theirs.[60]

---

60 *Edwards v Canada (AG)* [1930] AC 123 at 136, 1 DLR 98 (PC). Although see the analysis in B.W. Miller, "Origin Myth: The Persons Case, the Living Tree, and the New Originalism" in G. Huscroft and B.W. Miller (eds), *The Challenge of Originalism:*

Faced with a relatively narrow interpretative question, the JCPC articulated what can fairly be described as a defining principle of Canadian constitutional law: that the Constitution is akin to a living tree and its meaning is not frozen to the time of initial enactment. It is possible to contest the soundness of a "living" approach to constitutional interpretation. It is not possible to contest its impact on Canadian jurisprudence. Briefly stated, the living tree approach has greatly diminished the scope for alternative interpretative approaches that rely on original meaning or intent.[61] In the post-Charter era, especially, the doctrine has enabled a malleable, expansive, and values-guided approach to constitutional law.[62]

A different but equally important constitutional moment occurred in the *Patriation Reference*.[63] The matter arose after Prime Minister Pierre E. Trudeau sought approval from the UK Parliament for the Constitution Act, 1982 without provincial consent.[64] Three provinces decided to initiate references in their respective courts of appeal, which eventually were heard by the Supreme Court. A majority of the judges advised that while the federal government was legally entitled to seek constitutional change on its own, the specific nature of the amendments triggered a constitutional convention requiring a substantial degree of provincial consent.[65] For the federal government to proceed unilaterally, in other

Theories of Constitutional Interpretation (Cambridge, Cambridge University Press, 2011), which suggests that the case is best understood as a conventional application of well-accepted principles of statutory interpretation.

61 I do not deny that "original approaches" can be found in Canadian jurisprudence; or that such terms are highly contested. For an illuminating recent discussion, see B. Oliphant and L. Sirota, "Has the Supreme Court of Canada Rejected 'Originalism?'" (2016) 42 *Queen's Law Journal* 107.

62 *R v Big M Drug Mart Ltd* [1985] 1 SCR 295; *R v Therens* [1985] 1 SCR 613; *R v Oakes* [1986] 1 SCR 103; *Canada (Attorney General) v Bedford* 2013 SCC 72, [2013] 3 SCR 1101 [*Bedford*]. For criticism, see Baker, *Not Quite Supreme,* above n 47; J.L. Hiebert, *Charter Conflicts: What Is Parliament's Role?* (Montreal and Kingston, McGill-Queen's University Press, 2002); C.P. Manfredi, *Judicial Power and the Charter: Canada and the Paradox of Liberal Constitutionalism,* 2nd edn (Toronto, Oxford University Press, 2001).

63 *Reference re Resolution to Amend the Constitution,* [1981] 1 SCR 753.

64 Constitution Act, 1982, enacted as Schedule B to the Canada Act 1982, (UK) 1982, c 11 [CA 1982]. Until the Canada Act 1982, changes to the Constitution of Canada required an Act of the UK Parliament: Statute of Westminster, 1931, 22 Geo V, c 4 (UK) s 7.

65 For further discussion of conventions, see A. Dodek, "Courting Constitutional Danger: Constitutional Conventions and the Legacy of the *Patriation Reference*" (2011)

words, was constitutional in the legal sense but unconstitutional in the conventional sense.

The *Patriation Reference* had a profound political effect. The prime minister resumed negotiations with the provinces, and the resolution ultimately forwarded to Westminster reflected the consent of the federal Parliament and nine provincial legislatures.[66] The Reference had a powerful jurisprudential effect as well. As I have discussed elsewhere,[67] it cemented certain trends, and foreshadowed others, that have come to define Canadian constitutionalism. Those trends include the lack of a "political questions" doctrine, under which the Court might decline systematically to decide cases that it deemed to be political, and the embrace of a progressive approach to interpreting the Constitution. Equally important, at the dawn of a new constitutional era, the Reference thrust the Supreme Court to the centre of constitutional enquiry, a position it has occupied ever since.

The notion that Supreme Court references wield a significant degree of authority is evident, first, in their treatment by non-judicial actors. The authority is observed as a constant, even when an actor obviously finds the result objectionable. For example, in the *Senate Reform Reference*,[68] the Court considered a number of proposed avenues for reform of the Upper House. The federal government of the day had long advocated for a Senate that was "equal, elected and effective."[69] The prime

54 *Supreme Court Law Review* 117; E.A. Forsey, "The Courts and the Conventions of the Constitution" (1984) 33 *University of New Brunswick Law Journal* 11; G. Marshall, *Constitutional Conventions: The Rules and Forms of Political Accountability* (Oxford, Clarendon Press, 1984).

66 The province of Quebec did not consent. One year later, the Supreme Court of Canada advised that Quebec did not enjoy a veto over constitutional change: *Quebec Veto*, above n 51 at 806.

67 C. Mathen, "'The Question Calls for an Answer, and I Propose to Answer It': The *Patriation Reference* as Constitutional Method" (2011) 143 *Supreme Court Law Review* at 163–6.

68 *Reference re Senate Reform* 2014 SCC 32, [2014] 1 SCR 704 [*Senate Reform Reference*]. The Court was asked whether, under Part V of the Constitution Act, 1982 (the amending framework), Parliament enjoyed the unilateral power to implement a framework for consultative elections to guide Senate appointments, set fixed senatorial terms, and remove the property and net worth requirements for appointees. The Court also considered the degree of provincial consent that would be required to abolish the Senate entirely.

69 "The Reform Party of Canada," *Canadian Encyclopedia* online, accessed 21 September 2016, http://www.thecanadianencyclopedia.ca/en/article/reform-party-of-canada/. The Senate of Canada is appointed, not elected, and does not represent provinces equally. It also rarely impedes the passage of legislation.

minister, Stephen Harper, urged the Court to confirm that most of the government's proposed changes could be achieved through ordinary law and executive decision making. A number of provinces objected.[70] Arguing that the Senate was a fundamental feature of Canadian federalism and integral to the original Confederation bargain, those provinces urged the Court to find that the proposed changes required formal amendment of the Constitution, which included provincial consent.[71] The Court agreed.

Harper called the reference result "a decision for the status quo ... that is supported by virtually no Canadian."[72] Indeed, he later announced that he would refuse to appoint additional senators until the provinces themselves were prepared to discuss reform.[73] Yet he did not contest the notion that Senate reform would have to proceed in accordance with the principles set forth in the advisory opinion.[74]

In the 2014 *Supreme Court Act Reference*,[75] the Court delivered another blow to the Harper government when it declared that the most recent appointment to the Court was void *ab initio*. The government was caught utterly off guard. The opinion has been heavily criticized.[76] But,

---

70 The strongest opponents of the federal plan were Ontario, Quebec, Nova Scotia, New Brunswick, Prince Edward Island, Manitoba, and Newfoundland and Labrador. Other provinces, particularly Alberta and British Columbia, supported the federal government's position. See written submissions of attorneys general at http://www.scc-csc.ca/case-dossier/info/af-ma-eng.aspx?cas=35203.

71 Some of the proposed changes would require the "7/50 rule," found in s 38(1) of the CA 1982, above n 64, while others would trigger the unanimity formula in s 41(d). *Senate Reform Reference*, above n 68.

72 Cite: http://www.cbc.ca/news/politics/stephen-harper-says-senate-reform-is-off-the-table-1.2622053.

73 See https://www.thestar.com/news/canada/2015/07/24/stephen-harper-imposes-moratorium-on-senate-appointments.html. See also C. Mathen, "Gaming the Constitution," *Ottawa Citizen*, 30 July 2015, http://ottawacitizen.com/news/politics/carissima-mathen-gaming-the-constitution.

74 It is certainly arguable that Stephen Harper's refusal to continue to appoint senators was unconstitutional: Mathen, ibid. But, on its face, the announcement did not contradict the specific "advice" received from the Supreme Court.

75 *Supreme Court Act Reference*, above n 1.

76 J. Press, "Harper Government 'Genuinely Surprised' by Supreme Court's Decision to Reject Marc Nadon," *National Post*, 21 March 2014, http://news.nationalpost.com/news/canada/canadian-politics/marc-nadon-not-allowed-to-sit-on-supreme-court-of-canada-top-court-rules. For criticism of the opinion, see G. Huscroft, "The Supreme Court's Faulty Logic on Nadon," *National Post*, 25 March 2014, http://news.nationalpost.com/full-comment/grant-huscroft-the-supreme-courts-faulty-logic-on-nadon; A. Coyne, "Flaky Supreme Court Ruling Meets

in the end, the prime minister appointed another judge in accordance with the Court's interpretation of the law. And, to date, no one has seriously questioned that future appointments must also follow those parameters.

The authoritative nature of references likely derives from the Court's general approach to constitutional law. Since 1982, the Court has largely accepted the idea that when it interprets the Constitution, it may both generate and rely on norms of general application. To borrow a term used by the former chief justice of Canada in her contribution to this volume, the Court may be characterized as engaging, at least sometimes, in "top-down reasoning."[77] The Court clearly views the identification of broad principles as fundamental to its judicial craft.

The Court's embrace of a values-imparting role has led it to shed some of the normal constraints on a court operating in a common law system.[78] It is rare for the Court to refuse to hear a constitutional case on the ground that the issues are not properly before it. There is little reliance on such limiting doctrines as mootness[79] and political

---

Dubious Appointment," *National Post*, 24 March 2014, http://news.nationalpost.com/full-comment/andrew-coyne-on-marc-nadon-flaky-supreme-court-ruling-meets-dubious-appointment; Leonid Sirota, "What You Wish For," *Double Aspect* (blog), 22 March 2014, https://doubleaspectblog.wordpress.com/2014/03/22/what-you-wish-for/. More positive commentary included Paul Daly, quoted in S. Fine, "Supreme Court's Rejection of Nadon Is a Legal Marker and a Political Blow," *Globe and Mail*, 21 March 2014, http://www.theglobeandmail.com/news/politics/supreme-courts-rejection-of-nadon-is-a-legal-marker-and-a-political-blow/article17625541/; Adam Dodek quoted in J. Geddes, "Q & A: Supreme Court of Canada Rejects Harper Appointment," *Maclean's*, 21 March 2014, http://www.macleans.ca/politics/ottawa/q-a-supreme-court-of-canadas-rejects-a-harper-appointment/; C. Mathen, "Nadon Ruling Hits Like an Earthquake," *Ottawa Citizen*, 21 March 2014, A8.

77 McLachlin (see ch 1).

78 In this way, the Supreme Court of Canada can be contrasted with both the Australian High Court and United States Supreme Court, which are discussed by Peter Cane in his contribution to this volume (see ch 3). Like the Australian High Court, the Canadian Supreme Court considers appeals on legal issues relating to sub-national jurisdictions, and it routinely develops common law. But like the US Supreme Court, it functions as a political actor providing a check on other branches of the state. Due to its apex position in a unified legal system that partakes in both common law and "constitutional code" reasoning, the Canadian Court may well be more powerful than either its Australian or its US counterpart.

79 *Canada (Minister of Justice) v Borowski* [1981] 2 SCR 575.

questions,[80] and a decidedly relaxed approach to standing.[81] The Court also has largely abandoned any distinction between *obiter dicta* and *ratio decidendi.*[82] To the extent that the Court's live cases are not constrained by such factors, they are not far removed from advisory opinions.[83] Consider, too, that to the extent that advisory opinions involve an aspect of the declaratory function of law (in that they elucidate, or "declare," certain rules and norms), they become difficult to distinguish from the Court's declaratory power by which, under s. 52 of the Constitution Act, 1982, it deems laws to be of no force or effect.[84] It would be foolhardy for any government to disregard a declaration of law contained in a reference opinion, because it could not expect to achieve a different result in "live" litigation.

One reason why a government would be foolish to expect a different result in subsequent litigation is that references are captured under the doctrine of *stare decisis*. That fact has been demonstrated in numerous cases, including *Canada v Bedford*.[85] *Bedford* was a 2013 constitutional challenge to three prostitution-related offences alleged to violate certain provisions of the Canadian Charter of Rights and

---

80 *Operation Dismantle v The Queen* [1985] 1 SCR 441 at paras 52–4 (no political questions doctrine in Canada, although see also *Canada (Prime Minister) v Khadr* 2010 SCC 3, [2010] 1 SCR 44 and the discussion of the restrained judicial approach to prerogative powers in P. Daly, "Royal Treatment: The Special Status of the Crown in Administrative Law" (2017) 22 *Review of Constitutional Studies* 81 at 98–100).

81 *R v Big M Drug Mart* [1985] 1 SCR 295 at 313; Canada *(Attorney General) v Downtown Eastside Sex Workers United Against Violence Society* 2012 SCC 45, [2012] 2 SCR 524.

82 *R v Henry* 2005 SCC 76 [2005] 3 SCR 609. But see *R v Prokofiew* 2012 SCC 49, [2012] 2 SCR 639 for an example of where an *obiter* statement is treated as such. Thanks to Paul Daly for pressing this point.

83 See eg *M v H* [1999] 2 SCR 3 (statute prohibiting access to spousal support for same-sex common law couples unconstitutional; neither spouse appealed provincial court of appeal ruling, but leave granted to provincial attorney general); *New Brunswick (Minister of Health and Community Services) v G (J)* [1999] 3 SCR 46 (lack of counsel for indigent parent facing state guardianship application unconstitutional; children returned to applicant's care before appeal reached Supreme Court; although dispute "moot," decision appropriate).

84 S 52, the "supremacy clause," states, *inter alia*, "The Constitution of Canada is the supreme law of Canada, and any law that is inconsistent with the provisions of the Constitution is, to the extent of the inconsistency, of no force or effect." CA 1982.

85 *Bedford*, above n 62. Note that this was a constitutional challenge initiated by private litigants.

Freedoms.[86] In a previous reference, issued in 1990, a majority of the Court had concluded that two of those laws were consistent with the Charter.[87] The lower courts in *Bedford* accepted that they were, in principle, bound to follow that earlier opinion.[88]

Because of the way that it had decided the Charter claims in *Bedford*, the Supreme Court found it unnecessary to determine whether the precise *ratio* articulated in the earlier *Prostitution Reference* should be followed.[89] But it obviously accepted that the doctrine of *stare decisis* applied, regardless of the fact that the prior rule had arisen in a reference:

> Certainty in the law requires that courts follow and apply authoritative precedents. Indeed, this is the foundational principle upon which the common law relies. ...
>
> In this case, the precedent in question is the Supreme Court of Canada's 1990 advisory opinion in the *Prostitution Reference*. ... While reference opinions may not be legally binding, in practice they have been followed. ...
>
> In my view, a trial judge can consider and decide arguments based on *Charter* provisions that were not raised in the earlier case; this constitutes a new legal issue. Similarly, the matter may be revisited if new legal issues are raised as a consequence of significant developments in the law, or if

86 The offences were keeping a common bawdy house; soliciting in a public place, for the purpose of prostitution; and living on the avails of a prostitute. Criminal Code, ss 210, 212(1)(f), and 213(1)(c). S 7 of the Charter states, "Everyone has the right to life, liberty and security of the person, and the right not to be deprived thereof except in accordance with the principles of fundamental justice."

87 *Prostitution Reference*, above n 27. The reference considered whether the bawdy house and solicitation laws violated s 2(b) (freedom of expression) and s 7 of the Charter. The Court found that the laws were inconsistent with s 2(b) but saved under s 1; and that the laws were not inconsistent with s 7.

88 I have added the words "in principle" because both lower courts accepted that the obligation is not absolute and that past precedents may occasionally be departed from. That finding, though, had nothing to do with the distinction between references and cases. *Bedford*, above n 62 at paras 31, 41.

89 The Supreme Court concluded that while the *Prostitution Reference* focused on s 7's "liberty" interest, *Bedford* was argued on the basis of the section's guarantee of "security of the person." The Court also held that, since 1991, s 7's "principles of fundamental justice" had evolved to include new principles – in particular, overbreadth and gross disproportionality: *Bedford*, above n 62 at paras 45, 47. Because the Court found that all the impugned laws violated s 7's guarantee of security of the person, it deemed it unnecessary to revisit whether the laws ran afoul of s 2(b) of the Charter – the section supporting the key *ratio* from the *Prostitution Reference*.

> there is a change in the circumstances or evidence that fundamentally shifts the parameters of the debate. …
>
> These considerations do not apply to the question of whether the communication provision is a justified limit on freedom of expression. That issue was decided in the *Prostitution Reference*.[90]

The Court clearly regarded the *Prostitution Reference* as entitled to consideration and deference under *stare decisis* – a key element in the judicial hierarchy and in common law reasoning. Note that the Court did so even as it repeated the refrain that references were not "legally binding."

In the modern era, the *Same-Sex Marriage Reference*[91] contains the most detailed consideration of the implications of the difference between an advisory opinion and a decision. The Reference was initiated after several provincial courts of appeal had ruled that the common-law definition of marriage violated the Charter equality rights of gays and lesbians.[92] At the time, the political and legal landscape in Canada was just starting to accommodate full marriage equality.[93] Instead of appealing those judicial rulings to the Supreme Court, the federal government referred to it draft legislation, the Civil Marriage Act,[94] that would, in

90 *Prostitution Reference*, above n 27 at paras 38, 40 per McLachlin CJC.

91 *Same-Sex Marriage*, above n 28.

92 *Hendricks c Québec (PG)* [2004] RJQ.851 (CA); *Halpern v Toronto (City)* (2003) 65 OR (3d) 161 (CA); *EGALE Canada v Canada (AG)* (2003) 13 BCLR (4th) 1, 2003 BCCA 251. At common law, marriage was defined as "the union of one man and one woman for life, to the exclusion of all others": *Hyde v Hyde* (1866), LR 1 P & D 130 at 133.

93 The court proceedings began in 2002. As late as 1999, though, the federal government had voted in favour of a motion affirming "that marriage is and should remain the union of one man and one woman to the exclusion of all others, and that Parliament will take all necessary steps to preserve this definition of marriage in Canada": Hansard (8 June 1999) 15960. Prior Supreme Court rulings had contained minority and dissenting opinions sympathetic to an opposite-sex-only definition of marriage: *Miron v Trudel* [1995] 2 SCR 418 at 448–52, Gonthier J dissenting; *Egan v Canada* [1995] 2 SCR 513 at 535–9, La Forest J. Even in *M v H* – a near-unanimous judgment for a same-sex, common law spouse – the majority specified that it was not dealing with "marriage": [1999] 2 SCR 3 at para 134, Cory and Iacobucci JJ.

94 Bill C-38, *An Act respecting certain aspects of legal capacity for marriage for civil purposes*, 1st Sess, 38th Parl, 2005. The draft legislation provided:

> 1. Marriage, for civil purposes, is the lawful union of two persons to the exclusion of all others.
> 2. Nothing in this Act affects the freedom of officials of religious groups to refuse to perform marriages that are not in accordance with their religious beliefs.

effect, confirm those lower court rulings by enacting a gender-neutral definition of *marriage*.[95] But the government did not ask whether the existing common law definition of marriage was itself consistent with the Charter – a curious omission since that issue was the basis of the originating Charter challenges. Only after significant criticism and political pressure did the government pose that question.[96] It refused to take a position on it during the proceeding.

Unexpectedly, the Supreme Court declined to answer the fourth question. Its reasons merit consideration in full:

> A unique set of circumstances is raised by Question 4, the combined effect of which persuades the Court that it would be unwise and inappropriate to answer the question.
>
> The first consideration ... is the government's stated position that it will proceed by way of legislative enactment, regardless of what answer we give to this question. ... Given the government's stated commitment to this course of action, an opinion on the constitutionality of an opposite-sex requirement for marriage serves no legal purpose. On the other hand, answering this question may have serious deleterious effects. ...
>
> The second consideration is that the parties to previous litigation have now relied upon the finality of the judgments they obtained through the court process. In the circumstances, their vested rights outweigh any benefit accruing from an answer to Question 4. ...

---

95 The bill ultimately became law: SC 2005, c 33.

96 The four questions were:

1. Is the annexed *Proposal for an Act respecting certain aspects of legal capacity for marriage for civil purposes* within the exclusive legislative authority of the Parliament of Canada? If not, in what particular or particulars, and to what extent?
2. If the answer to question 1 is yes, is section 1 of the proposal, which extends capacity to marry to persons of the same sex, consistent with the *Canadian Charter of Rights and Freedoms*? If not, in what particular or particulars, and to what extent?
3. Does the freedom of religion guaranteed by paragraph 2 (*a*) of the *Canadian Charter of Rights and Freedoms* protect religious officials from being compelled to perform a marriage between two persons of the same sex that is contrary to their religious beliefs?
4. Is the opposite-sex requirement for marriage for civil purposes, as established by the common law and set out for Quebec in section 5 of the *Federal Law–Civil Law Harmonization Act, No. 1*, consistent with the *Canadian Charter of Rights and Freedoms*? If not, in what particular or particulars and to what extent?

> … [Finally,] consideration of the fourth question has the potential to undermine the uniformity that would be achieved by the adoption of the proposed legislation. The uniformity argument succeeds only if the answer to Question 4 is "no." By contrast, a "yes" answer would throw the law into confusion. The decisions of the lower courts in the matters giving rise to this reference are binding in their respective provinces. They would be cast into doubt by an advisory opinion which expressed a contrary view, even though it could not overturn them. The result would be confusion, not uniformity.[97]

Citing a "unique set of circumstances," the Court concluded that it would be unwise to answer question 4.[98] Were it to hold that the Charter did *not* compel the inclusion of same-sex couples within the state institution of marriage, the Court said, "confusion" might result. The confusion would spring from the uncertain status of a reference opinion issued by an apex court that conflicted with a "final judgment," on the same issue, in a lower one. The Court may also have been referring to the confusion that would result because of the force that such an advisory opinion would exert on those same courts in future cases.[99] While the reference opinion would not affect the law in the provinces in which final judgments had been issued, it would nonetheless create an anomaly. In my view, that argument holds only if the Court's answer, in the Reference, is deemed to be an authoritative statement of the law.

Finally, it is a marker of authority that the weight of advisory opinions is independent of judicial consensus. References issuing from a divided panel compel compliance just as much as a unanimous one. In the *Patriation Reference*, the Court split along not one but *two* issues.[100] The *Supreme Court Act Reference* was decided 6–1, and the dissent was vigorous.[101] There have even been 5–4 splits, such as in the *Reference*

97 *Same-Sex Marriage*, above n 28 at paras 65–9.

98 I have never been persuaded by this analysis: C. Mathen, "Mutability and Method in the *Marriage Reference*" (2005) 55 *University of New Brunswick Law Journal* 43 at 53–4.

99 I thank Paul Daly for raising this point with me.

100 The splits, one 7–2 and the other 6–3, were over whether (a) it was *legal* for Parliament to seek constitutional change on its own and (b) there was nonetheless a *convention* requiring "substantial provincial consent" for constitutional change affecting provincial powers.

101 See the discussion in C. Mathen, "The Shadow of Absurdity and the Challenge of Easy Cases: Looking Back on the *Supreme Court Act Reference*" (2015) 71 *Supreme*

re Assisted Human Reproduction Act.[102] If advisory opinions were truly exercises in seeking "advice," one might expect it to matter that a particular opinion did not attract unanimity. Yet it does not. One can, of course, dispute whether *any* split judicial decision ought to carry the same weight as a unanimous one.[103] The point is that to the extent that such authority is unaffected by lack of unanimity, that holds for references just as surely as it does for cases.

Politics

Advisory opinions occur against a broad narrative of law and politics. Politics are always present in constitutional law, but, in the Charter era, the debate over judicial politicization in Canada has become especially pointed.[104] The Supreme Court's power to overturn the decisions of democratic majorities remains controversial, making it a frequent target for criticism.[105] While references do not technically invoke the Court's broad panoply of remedies, they are, clearly, highly politicized. In many reference proceedings, the relevant actors have looked to the Court as much for political as for legal vindication.

The politics of advisory opinions give rise to numerous issues. This section will focus on calls to use the advisory function pre-emptively – to put highly contested questions to the Supreme Court in advance of a legislative decision. To date, Canadian federal and provincial governments have been largely content to wait for constitutional challenges to arise in the ordinary course. Sometimes, though, governments have

---

Court Law Review 161 at 184–5. To be sure, there was some reliance by government ministers on the dissenting opinion, but that was offered more as a defence of undertaking the reference at all.

102 Human Reproduction, above n 57.

103 For related discussion of this point, see Jeremy Waldron, *Political Political Theory: Essays on Institutions* (Cambridge, MA, Harvard University Press, 2016) ch 10.

104 For a discussion of politics as an essential aspect of constitutional adjudication, see E. Macfarlane, *Governing from the Bench: The Supreme Court of Canada and the Judicial Role* (Vancouver, UBC Press, 2013); L. Hausegger et al, *Canadian Courts: Law, Politics, and Process*, 2nd edn (Don Mills, ON, Oxford University Press, 2014). For a sampling of claims that courts have become highly political and politicized actors, see Baker, *Not Quite Supreme*, above n 47; Hiebert, *Charter Conflicts*, above n 62; A.C. Hutchinson, *Waiting for Coraf: A Critique of Law and Rights* (Toronto, University of Toronto Press, 1995).

105 P. MacKay, "Respect the Rule of Law," *National Post*, 25 April 2016.

used references to pre-empt or supersede litigation, as in the references dealing with securities regulation,[106] assisted human reproduction,[107] Senate reform,[108] and same-sex marriage.[109] In recent years, there have been more, and higher-profile, calls to refer controversial legislation to the Court.[110]

Would greater recourse to reference opinions before law-making be a good thing? Certainly, there are reasonable arguments supporting that view. Reference opinions have been integral to, and can facilitate, the development of constitutional law. Given that the Constitution empowers judges to lay down rules obligating members of the legislative and executive branches, it might be sensible to have them to do so pre-emptively. By enabling the government to obtain an authoritative pronouncement, in advance, references might be seen to promote judicial economy and, indeed, by inviting an authoritative statement on the legality of proposed regulatory structures before funds are allocated to develop them, the efficient use of public resources. Their pre-emptive use could also contribute to certainty and coordination – values that hold particular force in a federal system that can produce multiple competing rules.

Against the above argument lie several objections of varying persuasiveness. First, one might argue that since references do not provide a proper factual context for adjudication, it would be a mistake to expand their scope.[111] That objection has weight if a reference involves a new social problem or very broad questions. Most references, though, do not. A reference concerning a law that has been in force for some time, or draft legislation that builds on or responds to an existing regime, or a question that has already been the subject of considerable study would not be as problematic. The Supreme Court enjoys the power to structure a hearing to address any gaps, including appointing *amicus curiae* or third party interveners. In any event, if a question remains

106 *Reference re Securities Act 2011* SCC 66, [2011] 3 SCR 837.

107 *Human Reproduction*, above n 57.

108 *Senate Reform Reference*, above n 68.

109 *Same-Sex Marriage*, above n 28.

110 At http://www.macleans.ca/politics/ottawa/mulcair-urges-supreme-court-reference-to-test-assisted-dying-law/.

111 Tribe, *American Constitutional Law*, above n 6; Tribe, Note, "Advisory Opinions on the Constitutionality of Statutes," above n 6.

unacceptably vague or outside the Court's sense of propriety, it can refuse to answer it.

Another risk of greater recourse to references is their discretionary nature. In Canada, the executive enjoys the exclusive authority to both initiate them and frame the questions put to the Court. To be sure, a move to greater pre-emptive use of references might be twinned with either legal or political changes that bring the legislative branch into the reference-framing process.[112] Nonetheless, political considerations will factor into any decision. Such considerations may be unavoidable, but it means that greater use of references will further draw the judiciary into political disputes. Admittedly, the Supreme Court's position at the pinnacle of the constitutional hierarchy renders it impossible to shield it from politics. But initiatives that would further entrench that fact, or heighten that perception, may lead to negative consequences that offset any benefit.

In my view, the most serious objection is the risk of further encouraging democratic malaise. By this, I mean that pre-emptive use of references could add to the already considerable temptation for political actors to avoid difficult issues by tossing them to the courts. That would lessen the incentive for deliberative assemblies to do the hard but necessary work of debating difficult questions that go to the heart of a nation's values and core political agreements.

Of course, Canadian legislatures no longer enjoy supremacy in the way that they once did.[113] But, within the broad parameters of the Constitution, and the Charter in particular, there are a variety of ways to achieve legislative objectives. A court might be able to rule out one or more alternatives from the outset, and, in limited circumstances, that could be helpful. But, in such cases, the relevant information would likely emerge during democratic deliberation. Parliament would then face a choice: jettison those alternatives altogether or press ahead, believing that it could yet offer sufficient arguments for validity. Pressing ahead might reflect a calculated risk that legislation would ultimately be found constitutionally deficient. But it is far from evident that taking such a risk would be so intolerable that we should routinely remove the ability to do it. If the trade-off for obtaining more constitutional clarity is decreased enthusiasm for constitutional debate in non-judicial fora, then, in my view, the cost is too high.

---

112 But see the next section for some possible constitutional barriers.

113 *Vriend v Alberta* [1998] 1 SCR 493 at para 131.

Reform

The foregoing discussion has tried to show the ways in which references have been critical both to Supreme Court decision making and to Canadian constitutional law. Accepting that characterization, there remain reasonable questions about whether and how the function might be improved. In this final section, I will address one change relating to the relationship among the various branches of government.

As described earlier, the executive's complete discretion over how and when references are triggered arguably creates an imbalance in the relationship among it, the judiciary, and the legislature. That can be especially important when a government holds only a minority of seats.[114] While the roots of the advisory jurisdiction presume that a court can act as an "adviser" to the "sovereign," that concept has little purchase today. In a system where the Supreme Court routinely reviews legislation for constitutional compliance, and its directives and enquiries are invariably directed at Parliament, it seems odd that that body should be so captive to executive discretion vis-à-vis when it receives that advice.

Notwithstanding my hesitation to use the reference function more frequently, there is some merit to the idea of redressing that imbalance. One possible reform would be to amend the Supreme Court Act so that a reference could be initiated not only by the Governor in Council but also by some process within the control of the legislature. For example, the Speaker of the House of Commons might be empowered to initiate a proceeding on a majority resolution of members.[115] Other possibilities include giving that power to either a standing committee of Parliament or an independent parliamentary officer, or providing for legislative input into reference questions.

To be sure, a change of that kind would raise issues. A ministry might regard a legislative reference launched against its wishes as a vote of non-confidence. Such an expanded function would also make more sense if Parliament were able to maintain independent carriage of the subsequent litigation – currently, such litigation is undertaken by government lawyers subject to the direction of the minister of justice

114 This was the case during the *Same-Sex Marriage Reference*, when the Liberal Party held a minority of seats in Parliament.

115 One could extend this to the Senate.

(an executive actor).[116] In a parliamentary system, there may well be limits to the degree of separation that is feasible.

A more general complicating issue, which would apply to all attempts at reform, is whether such changes could be enacted through ordinary legislation. That is because of the uncertain implications of the 2014 *Supreme Court Act Reference*.[117] That reference considered, *inter alia*, s. 6 of the Supreme Court Act, which requires that three of the Court's nine judges be appointed "from among the judges of the Court of Appeal or of the Superior Court of the Province of Quebec or from among the advocates of that province."[118] Controversy arose when Prime Minister Harper nominated a Federal Court of Appeal judge, Marc Nadon, who was neither sitting on a Quebec court nor a current member of the Quebec bar. After Justice Nadon had been sworn in, an individual launched a judicial review of the prime minister's decision.

The federal government responded with a "two-track" approach. It initiated a reference to the Court, while simultaneously passing declaratory legislation so that s. 6 would read as having always permitted the appointment of someone in Nadon's circumstances.[119] The Supreme Court advised that Justice Nadon was ineligible under s. 6 as originally enacted. It then found the new declaratory legislation *ultra vires*. The Court rested the latter conclusion on a novel principle: the Court's composition and "essential features" have, over time, come to be protected under Part V of the Constitution Act, 1982 and therefore could not be changed by ordinary law.[120] To the extent that such rules are found in the Supreme Court Act, that legislation is no longer subject to change by Parliament alone.

The *Supreme Court Act Reference* has created considerable ambiguity about the prospect of future changes to the Court. Already, a debate has sprung up over whether and how to ensure that future appointments to the court are "functionally bilingual."[121] Should the reference function

---

116 I am grateful to Aniz Alani for raising these points.

117 *Supreme Court Act Reference*, above n 1.

118 Ibid s 6. The reason for the reserve of three seats is because Quebec is the sole jurisdiction within Canada to follow a civilian legal tradition.

119 Economic Action Plan 2013 Act, No. 2 (Bill C-4), SC 2013, c 40, ss 471, 472.

120 *Supreme Court Act Reference*, above n 1. Part V contains the amending formulae.

121 Minister of Justice Mandate Letter, http://pm.gc.ca/eng/minister-justice-and-attorney-general-canada-mandate-letter. See also a lawsuit launched by a trial lawyers' association objecting to the Trudeau government's apparent willingness to

be found to be one of the Court's "essential features," then some types of reform to it would require the consent not just of Parliament but also of at least seven of Canada's ten provinces.[122] It is almost certainly the case, for example, that a move to abolish references altogether would require formal constitutional amendment.[123] Now, it could be that the essence of the reference function is not how or by whom it is initiated, but what it does. Still, the uncertainty may be enough to dissuade other actors from seriously contemplating reform, unless, of course, they are prepared to initiate a reference on that issue.[124]

~

The foregoing discussion offers an entry point into an important yet often overlooked aspect of the Supreme Court's decision making: its reference jurisdiction. Borrowed from centuries-old English constitutionalism, references have evolved into a distinctly Canadian phenomenon and an integral component of the nation's constitutional jurisprudence. In different ways, the function has foreshadowed and enabled the robust posture of Canada's apex court. Both constitutive and exemplar, the reference function holds rich potential to tell us about the nature of law as such. Certainly, it tells us much about the Supreme Court.[125]

---

abandon the tradition of regional representation on the Court, which some describe as a constitutional convention. "Atlantic Canada Lawyers Challenge Trudeau on Changes to Supreme Court Appointment Process," *Canadian Press,* 19 September 2016, http://www.cbc.ca/news/politics/atlantic-lawyers-supreme-court-1.3769108. In light of the October 2016 appointment of a Newfoundlander, Malcolm Rowe, the lawyers' association has indicated that it will abandon the suit. The issue of regional representation, though, is likely to continue to percolate.

122 CA 1982, above n 64 at s 41(1)(d).

123 See eg Bill S-34, An Act to amend the Department of Justice Act and the Supreme Court Act to remove certain doubts with respect to the constitutional role of the Attorney General of Canada and to clarify the constitutional relationship between the Attorney General of Canada and Parliament, 1st Sess, 38th Parl, 2005.

124 This does not preclude informal change, such as a statement of principles whereby the executive agrees to consult with Parliament on the framing of reference questions.

125 For additional discussion, see C. Mathen, *Courts without Cases: The Law and Politics of Advisory Opinions* (Oxford, Hart Publishing, forthcoming).

PART II

Public Law Issues

6 Judicial Review in the American States

ROBERT F. WILLIAMS

Most people's understanding of the topic of judicial review in the United States is based on the United States Supreme Court's and lower federal courts' exercise of judicial review. Like many aspects of constitutional law in America, this view is only partly accurate. The fifty state constitutions operate, in many important ways, differently from the United States Constitution, even though they share the name *constitution*.[1] Naturally, the differing federal and state constitutions themselves have direct implications for the functions of judicial review. Extremely important exercises of judicial review are performed by the fifty state supreme courts.[2] In fact, judicial review in the American

1 E.J. Zackin and M. Versteeg, "American Constitutional Exceptionalism Revisited" (2014) 81 *University of Chicago Law Review* 1641. See also M. Versteeg and E. Zackin, "Constitutions Unentrenched: Toward an Alternative Theory of Constitutional Design" (2016) 110 *American Political Science Review* 657 (further analysis of the differences between the United States Constitution and state constitutions).

2 For an exhaustive review of the evolution of state supreme courts and the nature of their workload and opinions, see R.A. Kagan, B. Cartwright, L.M. Friedman, and S. Wheeler, "The Evolution of State Supreme Courts" (1978) 76 *Michigan Law Review* 961; R.A. Kagan, B. Cartwright, L.M. Friedman, and S. Wheeler, "The Business of State Supreme Courts, 1870–1970" (1977) 30 *Stanford Law Review* 121; R.A. Kagan, B. Cartwright, L.M. Friedman, and S. Wheeler, "State Supreme Courts: A Century of Style and Citation" (1981) 33 *Stanford Law Review* 773; and R.A. Kagan, B. Cartwright, L.M. Friedman, and S. Wheeler, "Do the 'Haves' Come Out Ahead? Winning and Losing in State Supreme Courts, 1870–1970" (1987) 21 *Law & Society Review* 403. Books concerning a range of issues on state supreme courts include G.A. Tarr and M.C.A. Porter, *State Supreme Courts in State and Nation* (New Haven, CT, Yale University Press, 1988); M.C. Porter and G.A. Tarr (eds), *State Supreme Courts: Policymakers in the Federal System* (Westport, CT, Greenwood Press, 1982). One of these studies concluded that,

states differs in a number of very important respects, and it needs to be acknowledged and understood to gain a complete picture of American judicial review.

The state courts are *apex* courts, but they sit atop differently constructed and smaller bases. The United States Supreme Court is quite independent of the other branches of the federal government, or, according to Peter Cane, it fits the model of "concentration." The state courts, by contrast, interact by design more with the other branches of government – in particular, given their common law powers, together with the others – and therefore fit Cane's model of "diffusion."[3]

This chapter will proceed to describe a number of the important differences in the nature of state constitutions as well as the impact of these differences on the function of state judicial review. State constitutions are real constitutions, but they differ in important ways from the federal Constitution. I have said,

> Legal scholars, political scientists, and the media have contributed to ignorance about state constitutions by their preoccupation with federal constitutional matters as defined by the United States Supreme Court. However, the federal Constitution is "incomplete" in the sense that it relies extensively on mechanisms established in, and pursuant to, state constitutions and leaves nearly all matters within the sphere of state power to be regulated by state constitutions and laws. ...
>
> State constitutions are *sui generis*, differing from the federal Constitution in their origin, function, form, and quality. State constitutions are not miniature versions of the federal Constitution, nor are they clones of it. They originate from a very different process from that leading to the federal Constitution. State constitutions perform functions that are different from the federal Constitution. They do not look or work like the federal Constitution. They are longer, more detailed, and cover many more topics: taxation and finance, local government, education, and corporations. The

---

by 1977, state supreme court justices "have come to view their role less conservatively. They seem to be less concerned with the stabilization and protection of property rights, more concerned with the individual and the downtrodden, and more willing to consider rulings that promote social change"; see Kagan et al, "The Business of State Supreme Courts" at 155. For a detailed review of colonial judicial development in each of the original states, see S.D. Gerber, *A Distinct Judicial Power: The Origins of an Independent Judiciary, 1606–1787* (2011).

3 P. Cane, ch 3 in this volume.

constitutional conversation at the state level is considerably different from the federal constitutional conversation.[4]

American state constitutions predated the federal Constitution and provided positive and negative models for the drafters at the federal Constitutional Convention. As many as twenty state constitutions were adopted in the newly independent colonies before, and after, Independence. Most of the Founding Fathers had direct experience debating or serving under state constitutions.[5]

Two Regimes of American Common Law and Judicial Review

The American state courts have remained, since 1938, the primary common law courts. That year, in the landmark case of *Erie Railroad v Tompkins*, the United States Supreme Court overturned over a century of precedent and declared that "there is no federal general common law."[6] Before 1938, federal courts hearing cases under their jurisdiction over matters between citizens (including corporations) of different states were free to apply their own view of general common law, regardless of that established in the relevant state.[7] *Erie* ended this and left virtually all common law development to the states.[8] As a consequence, the American federal courts, including the United States Supreme Court, have very little role in shaping the common law.

In the past century, the common law, primarily developed in the states since 1938, has undergone what has been referred to as

---

4 R.F. Williams, *The Law of American State Constitutions* (Oxford, Oxford University Press, 2009) at 2, 20 citing Donald S. Lutz, "The Purposes of American State Constitutions" (1982) 12 *Publius: The Journal of Federalism* 27 at 38–42. See also Donald S. Lutz, "The United States Constitution as an Incomplete Document" (1988) 496 *Annals of the American Academy of Political and Social Science* 23. In addition, J. Kincaid, "State Constitutions in the Federal System" (1988) 496 *Annals of the American Academy of Political and Social Science* 12 at 13:

> Although the term "American Constitution" is often used synonymously with "Constitution of the United States," the operational American constitution consists of the federal Constitution and the 50 state constitutions. Together, these 51 documents comprise a complex system of constitutional rule for a republic of republics.

5 Williams, above n 4 at 38–9.

6 304 US 64 at 78 (1938).

7 Ibid.

8 J. Hart Ely, "The Irrepressible Myth of Erie" (1974) 87 *Harvard Law Review* 693.

"statutorification."[9] Extensive statutory codes and uniform laws such as the Uniform Commercial Code, the Uniform Probate Code, etc. have been enacted in the states to revise, codify, and supplant common law doctrines. Therefore, there is a rise in "top-down" judicial reasoning in the states in many of the fields that used to be dominated by classic "bottom-up," judge-made common law. But this change is not judge-made but rather legislature-mandated. Now much of the law in those fields is dominated by statutory interpretation by state judges.

Further contributing to this revolution in judicial roles is the rise of "programmatic legislation," whereby a legislature identifies a problem, sets basic rules, and then creates a government agency to implement and enforce the Act.[10] These developments have led to a similar, but not judge-made, transition to that common law analysed by former chief justice McLachlin in this volume.[11] Common law flexibility is greatly reduced in the states. There is some evidence of judge-made reference to top-down principles in common law, but it is difficult to generalize for the fifty states.

Further, *state* judicial review under state constitutions is separate and independent from *federal* judicial review under the federal Constitution. Although the two court systems basically have concurrent jurisdiction to interpret the other's constitution, an interpretation of a state's constitution that is separate from, or "adequate and independent" of, any federal constitutional analysis is not reviewable by the United States Supreme Court.[12] Notably, however, because of the dominance of federal constitutional law, and the tendency of lawyers and judges to intermix federal and state constitutional doctrine in their arguments and opinions, respectively, the Supreme Court has had difficulty determining whether cases submitted to its discretionary jurisdiction are really based on federal constitutional law. After spending a number of years

---

9 G. Calabresi, *A Common Law for the Age of Statutes* (New Haven, CT, Yale University Press, 1982); M.D. Rosen, "What Has Happened to the Common Law? Recent American Codifications and Their Impact on Judicial Practice and the Law's Subsequent Development" (1994) 1994 *Wisconsin Law Review* 1119.

10 F.P. Grad, "The Ascendency of Legislation: Legal Problem Solving in Our Time" (1985) 9 *Dalhousie Law Journal* 228.

11 B. McLachlin, ch 1 in this volume.

12 Williams, above n 4 at 122–5, 229–31; *Michigan v Long* 463 US 1032 (1983).

wrestling with this problem of assessing its own jurisdiction, the Court, in 1983, established the bright-line test:

> Accordingly, when, as in this case, a state court decision fairly appears to rest primarily on federal law, or to be interwoven with the federal law, and when the adequacy and independence of any possible state law ground is not clear from the face of the opinion, we will accept as the most reasonable explanation that the state court decided the case the way it did because it believed that federal law required it to do so. If a state court chooses merely to rely on federal precedents as it would on the precedents of all other jurisdictions, then it need only make clear by a *plain statement* in its judgment or opinion that the federal cases are being used only for the purpose of guidance, and do not themselves compel the result that the court has reached. In this way, both justice and judicial administration will be greatly improved. If the state court decision indicates clearly and expressly that it is alternatively based on bona fide separate, adequate, and independent grounds, we, of course, will not undertake to review the decision.[13]

As a result, the two regimes of American judicial review operate separately from each other, with the United States Supreme Court having no say over the interpretations of state constitutions if they are independent of federal constitutional law. The *Michigan v Long* rule is controversial on the Supreme Court and not followed as often as one would think by state courts.[14]

An important development in state judicial review in the past three or four decades is the New Judicial Federalism.[15] I have said,

> The term describes the fact that state judges in numerous cases have interpreted their state constitutional rights provisions to provide *more* protection than the national minimum standard guaranteed by the federal Constitution. In the American system of constitutional federalism, we have "dual enforcement of constitutional norms." Of course, state constitutions may also be interpreted to provide *less* protection than the federal Constitution, but the national minimum standards must still be enforced.[16]

---

13 *Michigan v Long*, above n 12 at 1040–1; emphasis added.

14 *Arizona v Evans* 514 US 1 at 24, 30–2 (1995) (Ginsburg J dissenting).

15 Williams, above n 4 at ch 5.

16 Ibid at 114; emphasis in original.

This is an extremely important development in American constitutionalism and has stimulated much of the interest in state judicial review. It is also a possibility in other federal systems with sub-national rights protections.

Differences in the American Federal and State Constitutions

Constitutional Origins

State constitutions originate from a different source than the United States Constitution. There was no public referendum on the United States Constitution or any of its amendments. Rather, the original Constitution was ratified by the state legislatures, as all the amendments have been.[17] By contrast, after some early experiments with techniques, the public referendum on adopting new state constitutions and amendments thereto has been settled in forty-nine of the fifty states.[18] I have claimed,

> In fact, state constitutions are more democratic than the Federal Constitution in that they involve the citizenry in approving their amendment and revision, voting to approve borrowing, and in some states, approving new forms of gambling. In many states, like Iowa, for better or worse there is popular participation through electing or retaining judges. Further, because of the many waves of revision of state constitutions over the years, they reflect the input of the alternative voices of African Americans, Hispanics, Native Americans and women – voices that had little impact on the Federal Constitution.[19]

The records and content of these public debates has led to the concept of interpreting state constitutions (judicial review) as a quest for the

---

17 Williams, above n 4 at 38–9.

18 Delaware provides for legislative adoption of amendments, with passage through two sessions. Randy J. Holland, *The Delaware State Constitution: A Reference Guide* (New York, Oxford University Press, 2002) 229.

19 R.F. Williams, "Response: Why State Constitutions Matter" (2011) 45 *New England Law Review* 901 at 905. See also G.A. Tarr, "Popular Constitutionalism in State and Nation" (2016) 77 *Ohio State Law Journal* 237.

"voice of the people."[20] Even newspaper reports and editorials concerning state constitutional change are considered relevant by state courts.[21] These differing materials can lead to a different type of judicial review at the state level.

Function

The political and legal function of state constitutions is, in many ways, the opposite of the federal Constitution. It is well known that, other than guaranteeing *negative* rights, the American federal Constitution *enumerates* powers to the federal government. The important questions of interpretation and judicial review at the federal level are whether the Constitution *authorizes* the actions taken by the federal government. Most of the difficult questions concern, therefore, implied *powers*. After the federal Constitution was adopted, and the states delegated, or enumerated, certain powers to the national government, all other powers were reserved to the states. Therefore, the great questions of interpretation or judicial review at the state level, other than negative and *positive* rights guarantees, concern *limitations* on state governmental power and implied *limits* on state governmental power.[22]

The State Constitutions Are Much More Malleable

Dr Alan Tarr has stated,

> Perhaps the most striking contrast with federal constitutional practice is the states' reliance on the formal mechanisms of revision (replacement of one constitution by another) and amendment (the alteration of an existing

---

20 *Vreeland v Byrne* 370 A 2d 825, 830 (NJ 1977); J. Gray Pope, "An Approach to State Constitutional Interpretation" (1993) 24 *Rutgers Law Journal* 985 (1993); Williams, above n 4 at 315.

21 For a discussion of compilations of newspaper reports on state constitutional conventions and commissions, for which there were no official proceedings, see P.J. Mazzei and R.F. Williams, "'Traces of Its Labors': The Constitutional Commission, the Legislature, and Their Influence on the New Jersey State Constitution, 1873–1875" (2002) 33 *Rutgers Law Journal* 1059 at 1071–5.

22 Walter F. Dodd, "Implied Powers and Implied Limitations in Constitutional Law" (1919) 29 *Yale Law Journal* 137 at 160.

constitution by the addition or subtraction of material) to promote constitutional change.[23]

The states have had hundreds of constitutional conventions, and there are thousands of state constitutional amendments. This more flexible state constitutional structure was quite intentional and is common in other federal countries that use "sub-national" constitutions.[24] From our earliest experience with state constitutions, before the adoption of the federal document, their mechanisms for amendment or revision has been, until very recently, steadily liberalized.[25] Consequentially, the current text of any state constitution may represent significant changes or additions over the years. Many state constitutional provisions are "layered." Questions of interpreting these provisions in judicial review, therefore, may need to take account of significant changes in the text,

---

23 G.A. Tarr, *Understanding State Constitutions* (Princeton, NJ, Princeton University Press, 1998) at 23. Although it has been assumed that frequent textual amendment of state constitutions results in less "informal" amendment through judicial review, recent empirical research indicates that may not be the case. See generally Jonathan L. Marshfield, "The Amendment Effect" (2018) 98 *Boston University Law Review* 55.

24 See J. Dinan, "Patterns of Subnational Constitutionalism in Federal Countries" (2008) 39 *Rutgers Law Journal* 837 at 841–4; T. Ginsburg and E.A. Posner, "Subconstitutionalism" (2010) 62 *Stanford Law Review* 1583 at 1600, 1618–19; J.L. Marshfield, "Dimensions of Constitutional Change" (2013) 43 *Rutgers Law Journal* 593 at 598. Marshfield explains (at 608–9), referring to Ginsburg and Posner's analysis, that agency costs of constitutional change are much less at the sub-national than national level:

> Because agency costs are reduced at the subnational level, Posner and Ginsburg observe that there is an inevitable disparity in constitutional stability between "states" and "substates." High agency costs mean that national constitutional constraints must be relatively strong, static, and difficult to change. Subnational constitutions, however, can be relatively more fluid and responsive to public input because agency costs are lower. The basic intuition is that there are strong incentives for a national constitution to be stable in its creation of core government institutions and protection of essential individual liberties. And, a stable national constitution creates a safe place for subnational units to engage in constitutional experimentation because inappropriate experiments will be corrected by enforcement of the national constitution's overarching rules.

25 J. Dinan, "21st Century Debates and Developments Regarding the Design of State Amendment Processes" (2016) 69 *Arkansas Law Review* 283. See also J. Dinan, State Constitutional Politics: Governing by Amendment in the American States (Chicago: University of Chicago Press, 2018).

and the debates surrounding such changes, over time. This is quite rare in American federal constitutional judicial review.

States Have More Constitutional Materials

As a consequence of the more flexible and changeable characteristics of state constitutions, there is simply much more in the way of constitutional history materials available for the interpreter. Many of these materials are of more recent origin than the federal Constitution or even the original state constitutions. Professor Steven Gottlieb observed,

> Constitutional history is valuable whether or not one subscribes to a jurisprudence of original intent. For those who do, history becomes controlling – important because it does, or should, determine constitutional interpretation. For those who reject a jurisprudence of original intent, constitutional history nevertheless helps us to preserve the lessons embodied in the drafting of the provisions at issue and to explore the consequences of the language chosen. State constitutional history has become more important as the United States Supreme Court has become less protective of individual rights.[26]

Because there are several avenues for state constitutional change (not the same in every state), this availability of constitutional ("legislative") history of state constitutional provisions can emanate from a variety of sources: the state legislature, constitutional conventions, the initiative process in states that authorize this for constitutional change, and constitutional commissions. The availability of these materials lends itself to a slightly more "originalist" focus, joined with references to what the voting public thought they were accomplishing when they voted for revised constitutions or amendments thereto ("voice of the people").[27]

Positive Rights

By contrast with the federal Constitution, which is famous for including only negative, rather than positive, rights, the American state

26 S.E. Gottlieb, "Foreword: Symposium on State Constitutional History: In Search of a Usable Past" (1989) 53 *Albany Law Review* 255 at 258.

27 G.A. Tarr, "Constitutional Theory and State Constitutional Interpretation" (1991) 22 *Rutgers Law Journal* 841 at 850–6. See above nn 20–21 and accompanying text.

constitutions do contain a number of positive, or "third-generation," rights. According to political scientist Emily Zackin,

> The texts of state constitutions force us to question the ubiquitous assertions that America lacks positive constitutional rights. ... Throughout the nineteenth and twentieth centuries and across the United States, activists, interest groups, and social movements championed positive rights, and built support for their inclusion in state constitutions. As a result of these political campaigns, state constitutions have long mandated active government intervention in social and economic life, and have delineated a wide array of situations in which government is not only authorized, but actually obligated to intervene. State constitutions contain many different kinds of mandates for interventionist and protective government, not only with respect to laborers, but also with respect to government's obligations to care for the poor, aged, and mentally ill, preserve the natural environment, provide free education, and protect debtors' homes and dignity.[28]

Interpreting state-constitutional, positive rights provisions in judicial review can be different from interpreting and applying negative rights, as in the federal Constitution.[29] Professor Helen Hirshkoff has, therefore, argued for a "very different framework" for judicial review of state-constitutional, positive rights claims.[30] Many state courts "import"

---

28 E.J. Zackin, *Looking for Rights in All the Wrong Places: Why State Constitutions Contain America's Positive Rights* (Princeton, NJ, Princeton University Press, 2012) at 2–3; Zackin and Versteeg, above n 1; A. Bridges, *Democratic Beginnings: Founding the Western States* (Lawrence, KS, University Press of Kansas, 2015) at 88–99, 120–4.

29 B. Neuborne, "Foreword: State Constitutions and the Evolution of State Constitutional Rights" (1989) 20 *Rutgers Law Journal* 881 (arguing that state courts are better situated than federal courts to enforce positive rights). For other considerations of the positive rights possibilities of state constitutions, see D. Braveman, "Children, Poverty and State Constitutions" (1989) 38 *Emory Law Journal* 577; B.B. Lockwood, Jr, R. Collins Owens, III, and G.A. Severyn, "Litigating State Constitutional Rights to Happiness and Safety: A Strategy for Ensuring the Provision of Basic Needs to the Poor" (1993) 2 *William & Mary Bill of Rights Journal* 1. See also H. Gugel, "Note: Remaking the Mold: Pursuing Failure-to-Protect Claims under State Constitutions via Analogous Bivens Actions" (2010) 110 *Columbia Law Review* 1294. For a treatment of mandates in a state constitution, see L. Hargrave, "Ruminations: Mandates in the Louisiana Constitution of 1974: How Did They Fare?" (1998) 58 *Louisiana Law Review* 389. See also J.R. Grodin, "Rediscovering the State Constitutional Right to Happiness and Safety" (1997) 25 *Hastings Constitutional Law Quarterly* 1.

30 H. Hershkoff, "Positive Rights and State Constitutions: The Limits of Federal Rationality Review" (1999) 112 *Harvard Law Review* 1131.

the deferential federal constitutional "rational basis" test for evaluating states' compliance with their state constitution's positive rights.[31] Rather, she argues, such courts should apply "rigorous scrutiny to determine whether the provision is likely to effectuate the constitutional goal."[32]

Quality

State constitutions are much longer and more detailed than the more familiar American federal Constitution. According to Justice Hans Linde of Oregon,

> Most state constitutions are dusty stuff – too much detail, too much diversity, too much debris of old tempests in local teapots, too much preoccupation with offices, their composition and administration, and forever with money, money, money. In short, no grand vision, no overarching theory, nothing to tempt a scholar aspiring to national recognition. Serious theorists understandably care about methods, principles, and outcomes that have nationwide importance. They are willing to let the states pursue their local peculiarities by statutes, by common law, or by interpreting or amending state constitutions; and who can blame them?
>
> Yet I think this is a loss to theory.[33]

State constitutions need to cover more territory because the reserved plenary powers of the states are much broader than the enumerated powers of the federal government. In addition, because of the relative ease of state constitutional change, a very large proportion of state constitutions, averaging around 40 per cent, concerns policy matters that could be treated by ordinary legislation.[34] Alan Tarr observed,

> During the nineteenth century, state constitutions became more polished and professional, as their framers built upon the constitutional experience of their own states and developments in sister states. The shape of the

31 Ibid at 1136.

32 Ibid at 1184.

33 H.A. Linde, "E Pluribus – Constitutional Theory and State Courts" (1984) 18 *Georgia Law Review* 165 at 196–7.

34 C.W. Hammons, "State Constitutional Reform: Is It Necessary?" (2001) 64 *Albany Law Review* 1327 at 1333. See also C.W. Hammons, "Was James Madison Wrong? Rethinking the American Preference for Short, Framework-Oriented Constitutions" (1999) 93 *American Political Science Review* 837 at 840.

documents and their contents also changed. Over the course of the century, state constitutions increasingly became instruments of government rather than merely frameworks for government.[35]

There are a variety of motivations leading to the entrenchment of policy matters in state constitutions. Constitutional provisions, of course, are relatively more permanent and difficult to change than ordinary statutes. Policy matters can be included in state constitutions to "overturn" judicial decisions or eliminate doubt ahead of time concerning the constitutionality of the particular policy.[36] In states where legislatively proposed constitutional amendments do not have to submitted to the governor, they may be pursued to avoid an executive veto of an ordinary statute purporting to establish the policy.

Judicial Review under These Different Constitutions

American Judicial Review Originated in the States

Judicial review actually originated in the states, under their constitutions, as early as 1780. The famous United States Supreme Court decision in *Marbury v Madison*,[37] of course, did not occur until 1803. Further, Chief Justice John Marshall's famous opinion in *Marbury* did not even mention the earlier state cases. It is difficult to know why he chose not to rely on those cases, of which he must have been aware. In modern times, federal judges are deferential to state common law decisions[38] as well as instances of state constitutional judicial review.[39] As noted later, federal and state judges often apply different (states more relaxed) prudential doctrines such as standing, ripeness, and mootness to their approach to judicial review.[40]

It is widely acknowledged that the first American instance of judicial review took place in New Jersey in 1780.[41] The jury trial provision of

35 Tarr, above n 23 at 132. See also Tarr, above n 23 at 20–1.

36 J. Dinan, "Foreword: Court-Constraining Amendments and the State Constitutional Tradition" (2007) 38 *Rutgers Law Journal* 983.

37 5 US 137 (1803).

38 See above nn 6–8 and accompanying text.

39 See above nn 13–15 and accompanying text.

40 See below nn 55–6 and accompanying text.

41 R.F. Williams, *The New Jersey State Constitution*, 2nd edn (Oxford, Oxford University Press, 2012) at 10–1.

the 1776 Constitution gave rise to one of the few, and likely the earliest, of the pre–*Marbury v Madison* examples of judicial review in *Holmes v Walton* (1780).[42] This New Jersey case involved a successful challenge to a six-man jury provision contained in a statute concerning trade with the British. The legislature acquiesced and amended the Act to include the twelve-man jury required by common law. Edward S. Corwin stated that the *Holmes* case was the initial American example of judicial review after Independence,[43] and this conclusion has been confirmed by Scott Gerber.[44] Also, there are a number of other instances of judicial review in the states before *Marbury v Madison*.[45] Some states experimented with supermajority requirements for a judicial declaration of a statute's unconstitutionality. For example, the North Dakota Constitution, Art. VI, s. 4 provides,

> A majority of the supreme court [consisting of five justices] shall be necessary to constitute a quorum or to pronounce a decision, provided that the supreme court shall not declare a legislative enactment unconstitutional unless at least four of the members of the court so decide.[46]

---

42 This case is not available in the law reports but is discussed in Austin Scott, "Holmes v Walton: The New Jersey Precedent" (1898–99) 4 *American Historical Review* 456; and Gerber, above n 2 at 243–5.

43 Edward S. Corwin, "The Progress of Constitutional Theory between the Declaration of Independence and the Meeting of the Philadelphia Convention" (1925) 30 *American Historical Review* 521. See also Edward S. Corwin, "The Establishment of Judicial Review" (1910) 9 *Michigan Law Review* 102 at 110–2.

44 Gerber, above n 2 at 243–5.

45 For studies of the early development of judicial review under state constitutions, see J.B. Thayer, "The Origin and Scope of the American Doctrine of Constitutional Law" (1983) 7 *Harvard Law Review* 129; W.E. Nelson, "The Eighteenth Century Background of John Marshall's Constitutional Jurisprudence" (1978) 76 *Michigan Law Review* 893; W.E. Nelson, "Changing Conceptions of Judicial Review: The Evolution of Constitutional Theory in the States, 1790–1800" (1972) 120 *University of Pennsylvania Law Review* 1166; W.M. Treanor, "The Case of the Prisoners and the Origins of Judicial Review" (1994) 143 *University of Pennsylvania Law Review* 491. See also H. Jefferson Powell, "The Uses of State Constitutional History: A Case Note" (1989) 53 *Albany Law Review* 283 (1989); T.W. Ruger, "'A Question Which Convulses a Nation': The Early Republic's Greatest Debate about the Judicial Review Power" (2004) 117 *Harvard Law Review* 826; E. Zackin, "Kentucky's Constitutional Crisis and the Many Meanings of Judicial Independence" (2012) 58 *Studies in Law, Politics, and Society* 73; J. Handelsman Shugerman, "Economic Crisis and the Rise of Judicial Elections and Judicial Review" (2010) 123 *Harvard Law Review* 1061.

46 This provision limits judicial review by requiring a supermajority of the court to declare a statute unconstitutional. See also Neb Const art V s 2. This approach to

Advisory Opinions

One of the major doctrines of federal judicial review is that the United States Supreme Court does not issue *advisory opinions*.[47] A number of state constitutions (eight), by contrast, specifically authorize the state high courts to issue advisory opinions.[48] Although these advisory opinions are not supposed to be "precedential," in most states, in fact, they are treated by lawyers and judges in almost the same way as ordinary judicial precedents are treated.[49] Therefore, they become extremely important in the process of state judicial review.

I have observed that "when state supreme courts issue advisory opinions, they act more like European constitutional courts than the United States Supreme Court."[50] The procedure also resembles the Supreme Court of Canada's reference jurisdiction, as analysed for the first time in detail by Professor Carissima Mathen in this volume.[51] She notes that this authority, "borrowed from nineteenth-century English constitutionalism," differs from that of the United States Supreme Court,[52] and "Canadian law appears to view the judiciary as having the ability to act as the official adviser of the executive."[53] Many of the same issues arising, and remaining unresolved, in the American state courts arise in Canada and vice versa. The advisability and utility of advisory

---

judicial review was a product of the progressive movement. See J. Dinan, "Framing a 'People's Government': State Constitution-Making in the Progressive Era" (1999) 30 *Rutgers Law Journal* 933 at 949–57. For an excellent analysis of Ohio's supermajority provision, see J.L. Entin, "Judicial Supermajorities and the Validity of Statutes: How Mapp Became a Fourth Amendment Landmark Instead of a First Amendment Footnote" (2001) 52 *Case Western Reserve Law Review* 441.

47 F. Frankfurter, "A Note on Advisory Opinions" (1924) 37 *Harvard Law Review* 1008.

48 See generally H. Hershkoff, "State Courts and the 'Passive Virtues': Rethinking the Judicial Function" (2001) 114 *Harvard Law Review* 1834 at 1844–52; Comment: "The State Advisory Opinion in Perspective" (1975) 44 *Fordham Law Review* 81; J.D. Persky, "Note: 'Ghosts That Slay': A Contemporary Look at State Advisory Opinions" (2005) 37 *Connecticut Law Review* 1155; Williams, above n 4 at 296–8.

49 M.A. Topf, *Doubtful and Perilous Experiment: Advisory Opinions, State Constitutions, and Judicial Supremacy* (Oxford University Press, Oxford, 2011) (critical of state advisory opinions on this and other grounds).

50 Williams, above n 4 at 296.

51 See ch 5.

52 Ibid. She also notes the authority of some American states.

53 Ibid.

opinions, therefore, remains an important issue throughout supreme courts and constitutional courts.

Justiciability Doctrines

The United States Supreme Court is well known as applying fairly rigid prudential requirements for justiciability, including standing, mootness, ripeness, etc. These doctrines are rooted in the federal Constitution's requirement of a "case or controversy."[54] State constitutions, however, do not contain the case-or-controversy requirement, and it is very common for state high courts to apply relaxed attitudes towards these justiciability requirements for the exercise of judicial review.[55] Brice Dickson has identified this pattern in other common law supreme courts.[56]

State Constitutional Amendments Overturning Judicial Interpretations

While it is extremely difficult to amend the federal Constitution to overturn a decision of the United States Supreme Court, it is much more common for this phenomenon to take place in the states.[57] Further, state

54 US Const art III, s 2, cl 1.

55 Hershkoff, above n 48 at 1886–8.

56 B. Dickson, ch 2 in this volume. Dickson also noted that common law supreme courts are increasingly adjudicating disputes concerning the actions of public bodies. In the United States, this is true of both state and federal courts. But in the states, the constitutions often create independent government bodies and structures that differ from those in the federal Constitution. As a consequence, American state courts are often called upon to adjudicate constitutional disputes among state officials and agencies, and even among such officials and agencies and local officials and agencies: H.A. Linde, "The State and Federal Courts in Governance: Vive la Différence!" (2005) 46 *William & Mary Law Review* 1273; C.M. Durham, "The Judicial Branch in State Government: Parables of Law, Politics and Power" (2001) 76 *New York University Law Review* 1601.

57 Dinan, above n 36. In *State v Pena-Reyes* 962 P 2d 1040 at 1041 (Idaho 1998), the Idaho Supreme Court noted,

> The Idaho Supreme Court, in *State v McCoy*, 94 Idaho 236, 486 P.2d 247 (1971), held the judiciary had the inherent right to suspend sentences. In 1978, in response to McCoy, the legislature proposed and the people adopted an amendment to Article 5, Section 13, of the Idaho Constitution, which added the following language; "provided, however, that the legislature can provide mandatory minimum sentences for any crimes, and any sentence imposed

constitutional amendments are adopted sometimes to eliminate doubt about the applicability of some limit in a state constitution and to eliminate, ahead of time, the possibility of judicial review.[58] State constitutional amendments can overrule a specific exercise of judicial review by a state's courts, such as in Massachusetts and California when those states amended their constitutions to overturn decisions declaring the death penalty unconstitutional. Notably, such amendments may leave room for further exercises of judicial review, as happened in both California and Massachusetts after amendments reinstated the death penalty.[59]

Other types of state constitutional amendments require the state high courts to interpret their state constitutional provisions in "lockstep," or in conformity, with future decisions of the United States Supreme Court exercising judicial review under identical or similar clauses of the federal Constitution. For example, the Florida constitution was amended twice to require "forced linkage" of the state constitutional search-and-seizure clause to the United States Supreme Court's interpretation of the Fourth Amendment.[60] The same type of amendment was adopted concerning Florida's "cruel and unusual" clause.[61] California did the same with its equal protection clause in the area of school bussing.[62] These types of provisions, of course, limit state courts' independent interpretation of their constitutions.

Finally, instances of judicial review under state constitutions, enforcing limitations on government powers in addition to rights guarantees,

---

shall be not less than the mandatory minimum sentence so provided. Any mandatory minimum sentence so imposed shall not be reduced." Idaho Const. art. V, § 13. This amendment effectively circumscribes the power of our courts to suspend a mandatory minimum sentence contained in a statute enacted pursuant to the authority of our constitution. Thus, we find that I.C. § 37-2732B(a)(7) does not violate Article 5, Section 13, of the Idaho Constitution.

58 Dinan, above n 36 at 995 ("court-preempting amendments").

59 *Commonwealth v Colon-Cruz* 470 NE 2d 116 (Mass 1984); *People v Superior Court of Santa Clara Co* 647 P 2d 76 (Cal 1982).

60 Fla Const art I s 12. See generally C. Slobogin, "State Adoption of Federal Law: Exploring the Limits of Florida's 'Forced Linkage' Amendment" (1987) 39 *University of Florida Law Review* 653; T.C. Marks, Jr, "Federalism and the Florida Constitution: The Self-Inflicted Wounds of Thrown-Away Independence from the Control of the US Supreme Court" (2003) 66 *Albany Law Review* 701.

61 Fla Const art I s 17.

62 Cal Const art I s 7.

can be overturned by constitutional amendment. For example, when the Supreme Court of North Dakota ruled that local governments could not exercise an expedited form of eminent domain, the state constitution was amended to permit such powers.[63] In New Jersey, when the state Supreme Court ruled that the legislature could not cancel administrative regulations by the passage of a resolution, rather than an actual law, the constitution was amended to permit "legislative veto."[64]

Stare Decisis

American judges apply different doctrines of precedent, depending on whether they are dealing with common law, statutory interpretation, or constitutional law.[65] In common law, precedent is important, especially in areas where vested rights or reliance interests are involved, such as property and contracts. In areas such as torts, the doctrine is important but gives way to necessary improvements in the law. In statutory interpretation, on the other hand, because it involves judges interpreting the product of a coequal branch, the legislature, there are different issues at play. There is an argument that once a statute has received an authoritative judicial interpretation and the legislature does not change the statute to overrule the decision, it has "acquiesced" in the interpretation, and the precedent should not be overruled. This is seen as a matter of legislative supremacy.[66] This view has strong adherents but is not followed as a rigid rule by either state or federal judges.[67] Constitutional law is still different.

The United States Supreme Court applies a slightly relaxed doctrine of *stare decisis* to its constitutional decisions because it is quite difficult to amend the federal Constitution to "correct errors." Justice Brandeis explained this point in his dissent in *Burnet v Coronado Oil & Gas Co.*, adding this important point:

> The policy of *stare decisis* may be more appropriately applied to constitutional questions arising under the fundamental laws of those States

63 *Johnson v Wells Co Water Resource Bd* 410 NW 2d 525 (ND 1987).

64 Williams, above n 41 at 95, 142.

65 E. Maltz, "The Nature of Precedent" (1988) 66 *North Carolina Law Review* 367.

66 Ibid at 389.

67 *Patterson v McLean Credit Union* 491 US 164 (1989); W. Eskridge, Jr, "Overruling Supreme Court Statutory Interpretation Decisions" (1991) 101 *Yale Law Journal* 331.

> whose constitution may be easily amended. The action following the decision in *Ives v South Buffalo* Ry. Co., 201 N.Y. 271, 94 N.E. 431 shows how promptly a state constitution may be amended to correct an important decision deemed wrong. See Frankfurter and Landis. "The Business of the Supreme Court," pp. 193–198. In only two instances – the Eleventh and the Sixteenth Amendments – has the process of constitutional amendment been successfully resorted to, to nullify decisions of this Court. See *Chisholm v Georgia …; Pollock v Farmers' Loan & Trust Co., 158 U.S. 601*. It required eighteen years of agitation after the decision in the *Pollock* case to secure the Sixteenth Amendment.[68]

Based on the view that the difficulty of amending the *federal* Constitution justifies a slightly relaxed doctrine of precedent, then the relative ease of *state* constitutional amendment, and the reality of such amendments overturning instances of state judicial review, might be seen, as Justice Brandeis indicated, to justify a more rigid doctrine of precedent. This argument has not taken hold in state courts, but it has been noted in academic literature.[69] On the other hand, state constitutions are not *that* easy to amend, and I have said,

> Regardless of the relative ease of amending state constitutions when compared with the federal Constitution, the fact remains that, in an absolute sense, state constitutions are the highest source of law in any given state, and they are much harder to change than common law or statutory law.[70]

Horizontal Federalism

When state courts engage in judicial review, interpreting their state constitutions, they can also (unlike federal constitutional law) look to the

68 285 US 393 at 409 fn 5 (1932) (Brandeis J dissenting); citation omitted.

69 See J.C. Rehnquist, "The Power That Shall Be Vested in a Precedent: Stare Decisis, the Constitution and the Supreme Court" (1986) 66 *Boston University Law Review* 345 at 351–2 (1986); *Chase Securities v Donaldson* 325 US 304 at 312–13 (1945).

70 Williams, above n 4 at 351. See also Jack L. Landau, "Do Precedents Take Precedence? Stare Decisis and Oregon Constitutionalism" (2013–14) 77 *Albany Law Review* 1347; Jack L. Landau, "Some Thoughts about State Constitutional Interpretation" (2011) 115 *Penn State Law Review* 837 at 867–71.

decisions of other state courts interpreting identical or similar state constitutional provisions. This is referred to as *horizontal federalism*:

> Many state courts will examine, in comparison to the state constitutional issue before it, the constitutional texts and judicial interpretations of other states. This approach, referred to by the term "horizontal federalism," describes state courts looking for guidance to other state courts interpreting similar or identical state constitutional provisions, rather than looking vertically to the United States Supreme Court decisions interpreting similar federal constitutional provisions. This is a very common approach and can also be used effectively to *contrast* a state's constitutional provisions with others.[71]

In addition, state courts have exhibited a more flexible, common law–oriented form of judicial review. In the words of the former chief judge of the New York Court of Appeals, "while federal constitutional law is cabined by the text of the Constitution, state courts move seamlessly between the common law and state constitutional law, the shifting ground at times barely perceptible."[72] Professor Hershkoff notes that state courts (which have general common law powers that federal courts do not have) may look to their state constitutions as sources of public policy, which may inform their common law decisions. In this way, state constitutions may be applied "indirectly" to situations that they would not govern directly, such as where the behaviour of non-governmental actors would not be subject to constitutional constraint, such as contract enforcement, where the contract is for an illegal purpose, or termination of private employment for reasons that violate public policy.

> Viewing this accepted judicial practice through the lens of indirect constitutional effect carries analytic bite that goes beyond mere redescription:

---

71 Williams, above n 4 at 352. Contrast the sceptical approach the United States Supreme Court has taken to reliance on decisions of foreign courts: "Symposium, International Law and the Constitution: Terms of Engagement" (2008) 77 *Fordham Law Review* 399.

72 J.S. Kaye, "State Courts and the Dawn of a New Century: Common Law Courts Reading Statutes and Constitutions" (1995) 70 *New York University Law Review* 1 at 15. See also E.A. Peters, "Book Review: State Constitutional Law: Federalism in the Common Law Tradition" (1986) 84 *Michigan Law Review* 583; H. Hershkoff, "'Just Words': Common Law and the Enforcement of State Constitutional Social and Economic Rights" (2010) 62 *Stanford Law Review* 1521.

acknowledging that state constitutions provide the source of the policy affects the legitimacy of the court's interpretive process as well as the nature of the court's justifications. On a policy model, the claimant asks the court to review a common law rule in light of values that the judge thinks important or that a legislature might consider. On an indirect effect model, the claimant asks the court to protect a right that already exists under a state constitution and that the common law is being asked to weigh in resolving a particular claim. The existence of a positive right may affect the court's judgment in a number of different ways: I previously have written that such rights may form a part of the background "interpretive regime" for common law decision making; they may constitute a piece of the "implicit dimension" of private law and enlarge the focus of factors to be considered; or they may establish, or change, an interpretive "default rule" that pushes the court in one direction rather than another.

The practice of indirect constitutional effect assumes that a court can marshal interpretive resources in uncovering the constitution's meaning and in discerning its influence.

> The common law court need not commit itself to a particular interpretive approach. But what it may not do is ignore the constitutional provision or refuse to take its range of meanings into account. The constitutional provision thus constrains the court's decision making and does not provide merely a policy perspective that is unmoored from positive law. … The principle of indirect effect thus can be expected to contribute to a state constitutional interpretive process in which all legal actors may participate and to which all may contribute.
>
> Some state courts currently apply and extend state constitutional provisions even where a lack of state action would bar constitutional enforcement of the right. In these cases, the court explicitly looks to the state constitution as a source of public policy to inform its common law decision making – whether to support the creation of a cause of action in tort; to interpret or imply a contract term, such as reasonableness or good faith; or to raise an affirmative defense.[73]

73 Hershkoff, above n 72 at 1556–8. See also H. Hershkoff, "State Common Law and the Dual Enforcement of Constitutional Norms" in J. Gardner and J. Rossi (eds), *Dual Enforcement of Constitutional Norms: New Frontiers in State Constitutional Law* (New York, Oxford University Press, 2010).

Finally, state judges engaged in judicial review under their state constitutions may have a very different perspective on the intra-state and interstate consequences of their decisions than those considered by the justices of the United States Supreme Court.[74] These consequences can include such things as concern over a judge's reappointment or re-election; possible state constitutional amendments overruling the decision; a backlash in other states, such as happened with the same-sex marriage cases, etc.[75] Again, these are consequences about which the life-tenure justices of the United States Supreme Court need not worry.

The sub-national distinctions in institutional circumstances and positions of state and federal judges, despite the fact that they emerge from the same group of lawyers, can thus result in different approaches to judicial review depending on the court system in which they serve. For example, United States Supreme Court justices must assess the fifty-state consequences of their process of judicial review, while state judges need concern themselves only with in-state consequences. They may apply different "strategies" to their constitutional rulings.[76] Professor Lawrence Sager explained,

> State judges confront institutional environments and histories that vary dramatically from state to state, and that differ, in any one state, from the homogenized, abstracted, national vision from which the Supreme Court is forced to operate. It is natural and appropriate that in fashioning constitutional rules the state judges' instrumental impulses and judgments differ.
>
> ...
>
> In light of the substantial strategic element in the composition of constitutional rules, the sensitivity of strategic concerns to variations in the social and political climate, the differences in the regulatory scope of the federal and state judiciaries, the diversity of state institutions, and the special familiarity of state judges with the actual working of those institutions, variations among state and federal constitutional rules ought to be both expected and welcomed.[77]

74 N. Devins, "How State Supreme Courts Take Consequences into Account: Toward a State-Centered Understanding of State Constitutionalism" (2010) 62 *Stanford Law Review* 1629.

75 Ibid.

76 L.G. Sager, "Foreword: State Courts and the Strategic Space between the Norms and Rules of Constitutional Law" (1985) 63 *Texas Law Review* 959.

77 Ibid at 975–6.

Sager also noted that United States Supreme Court justices might "under-enforce" federal constitutional norms against the states because of concerns about respecting federalism.[78]

The well-known United States Supreme Court Justice William J. Brennan, Jr, who had earlier served on the New Jersey Supreme Court, experienced these different perspectives. In 1966, Justice Brennan made the following observation:

> [A] comment recently made to me by one of my former law partners suggested what I think is a wholly appropriate subject. He said he thought some recent opinions of mine indicated that I had changed some views I had expressed when a member of the New Jersey Supreme Court. In reply, I suggested to my old friend that perhaps what to him seems to reflect a changed viewpoint, may with greater accuracy be said to reflect a change of function. For unmistakably, a high state court judge and a United States Supreme Court Justice must often look at the same case with different eyeglasses.[79]

Two years earlier, he had noted the change of "climate" between a state high court and the United States Supreme Court:

> These substantive differences between the functions of the two courts are accompanied by a difference in climate; the winds of criticism and controversy that swirl around the Court in Washington are generally of a higher velocity than those blowing in state capitals – and the temperature is hotter.[80]

Of course, in current times, as noted by Professor Devins,[81] the temperature for state Supreme Court justices can get pretty hot!

---

78 L.G. Sager, "Fair Measure: The Legal Status of Underenforced Constitutional Norms" (1978) 91 *Harvard Law Review* 1212.

79 W.J. Brennan, Jr, "State Supreme Court Judge versus United States Supreme Court Justice: A Change in Function and Perspective" (1966) 19 *University of Florida Law Review* 225 at 227.

80 W.J. Brennan, Jr, "Some Aspects of Federalism" (1964) 39 *New York University Law Review* 945 at 949.

81 Devins, above n 74.

Conclusion

This short sketch of some of the major differences in judicial review under the American federal and state constitutions will, hopefully, introduce these distinctions to a wide audience of those interested in comparative constitutional law. Further, an understanding of American state constitutions, and state judicial review under them, can contribute to the understanding of American constitutionalism as a whole in comparison to other countries' constitutionalism. Possibly, as a result, American constitutionalism will not seem so "exceptional."[82]

82 Zackin and Versteeg, above n 1.

7 The Common Law, the Constitution, and the Alien

AUDREY MACKLIN

The courts have consistently held that immigration is a privilege, and not a right. … I do not think this kind of analysis is acceptable in relation to the *Charter*.

– *Singh v Canada (Minister of Employment and Immigration)*, [1985] 1 SCR 177 at paras 49–51.[1]

The most fundamental principle of immigration law is that non-citizens do not have an unqualified right to enter or remain in the country. At common law an alien has no right to enter or remain in the country.

– *Canada (Minister of Employment and Immigration) v Chiarelli*, [1992] 1 SCR 711 at 733.[2]

The quotations from *Singh* and *Chiarelli* that open this chapter speak to the relationship between the common law and the Canadian Charter of Rights and Freedoms. In the first, the Supreme Court declines to import a common law axiom as a guide to Charter interpretation. In the second, the Court swallows it whole.

Singh and *Chiarelli* are two of the earliest Supreme Court of Canada Charter judgments concerning immigration. *Singh*'s afterlife has transpired mainly outside immigration law, and it radiates openness: s. 7 protects everyone and not just citizens. Life, liberty, and security of the person should be interpreted broadly rather than narrowly. Fundamental justice requires that decisions imperilling a s. 7 interest emerge from a fair process.

1 [1985] 1 SCR 177 [*Singh*].
2 [1992] 1 SCR 711 [*Chiarelli*].

Chiarelli's sphere of influence is mainly confined to immigration law, and it signifies closure: since non-citizens have no unqualified right to enter or remain in Canada, deportation for breach of a condition on entry or residence need not comport with fundamental justice in substance or in process. *Chiarelli*'s impact on subsequent immigration jurisprudence has been wide and deep and, in absolute terms, easily surpasses that of *Singh*.

My objective is to subject these early engagements between common law and constitutional adjudication to scrutiny as a matter of jurisprudential technique. I contend that *Singh* and *Chiarelli* are, at best, in tension and, at worst, in conflict. The claim that immigration is a privilege and not a right springs from the same common law source as the principle that non-citizens do not have an unqualified right to enter or remain,[3] revealing incongruity between rejection of the former proposition and embrace of the latter.

This may seem to demonstrate no more than an anomaly peculiar to immigration law that holds no theoretical import outside the subject area. I think there is more to it. Immigration law is liminal in the literal and figurative sense. It is concerned with stabilizing and managing political borders (between inside and out), but also hierarchies of status (between insiders and outsiders) and the boundary between the juridical and political (between subject of law and object of power).[4] To the extent that states insist that border control is the intrinsic measure of sovereignty, the liminality of the non-citizen is definitive and unalterable.

In my contribution to this volume, I provide an account of how, in the context of immigration, the Court has internalized a rights-annihilating common law principle into the nucleus of a rights-generative bill of rights, with necrotizing effect.[5] I suggest that it is a mistake to reflexively privilege a common law norm as a tool of Charter interpretation; in the specific case of immigration, the Court has adopted a tacit conception of immigration regulation as akin to (but not a literal) common law prerogative power. Ironically, this may immunize the exercise of the deportation power from rights claims more effectively than would

3 I will variously refer to the claim that non-citizens do not have an unqualified right to enter as the *common law axiom, maxim*, or *principle*.

4 Or, to invoke the more popular phrase, "norm versus exception."

5 See R.M. Cover, "The Supreme Court, 1982 Term – Foreword: Nomos and Narrative" (1983) 97 *Harvard Law Review* 4 for an account of legal judgment as variously jurispathic and jurisgenerative.

an actual prerogative power. As Paul Daly explains in the Introduction, one strand of the relationship between apex courts and the common law that other authors are addressing is "the influence, if any, of constitutionalism and bills of rights on apex courts' relationships to the common law."[6] In this chapter, I reverse direction and enquire into the influence of common law on apex courts' relationships to constitutionalism and bills of rights.

The common scenario animating my intervention concerns a long-term permanent resident who arrives in Canada as a child and grows up without obtaining citizenship. To the extent that an individual is formed by the society and circumstances in which he or she grows up, these individuals – criminal offenders included – are products of Canada. The individual's familial and other attachments are all in Canada, yet he or she faces automatic deportation to the country of citizenship due to a criminal conviction with a sentence of six months or more. The individual typically never left Canada (lacking citizenship and therefore a Canadian passport), may or may not speak the language of the country of origin, and has few if any meaningful connections to that country. Nevertheless, whatever risks the individual might face upon deportation to the country of nationality do not amount to a basis for refugee protection. The harm subsists in the expulsion of the individual from the place that is, in all but the legal sense, home. I refer to the harm of deportation in such cases as "deracination." Deracination does not register as an infringement of life, liberty, or security of the person under s. 7 of the Charter, ostensibly because the common law, as articulated in *Chiarelli*, does not register it.

The analysis offered in this chapter sets the stage for a normative challenge to the unrestricted power of the state to deport non-citizens. Implicitly, it also cautions against an overly romanticized account of the common law as a resource for rights-enhancing norms applicable to the contemporary adjudication of human rights claims.

The *Singh* Decision

In 1969, Canada ratified the Protocol Relating to the Status of Refugees.[7] In so doing, it bound itself under international law to the provisions of the Convention Relating to the Status of Refugees,[8] with neither

6 Daly, this volume.

7 31 January 1967, 606 UNTS 267 (entered into force on 4 October 1967, ratified by Canada on 4 June 1969).

8 28 July 1951, 189 UNTS 137 (entered into force on 22 April 1954).

temporal nor geographical limitation. The Immigration Act incorporated into domestic law the international definition of a refugee, the right of refugees against *refoulement*,[9] and provisions that excluded certain people from refugee protection.[10] Mr Singh was an unsuccessful refugee claimant who challenged the process of refugee determination laid out in the Immigration Act. Wilson J wrote for three of six judges who heard the case and decided that s. 7 of the Charter applied and that the process did not comport with fundamental justice. The other three judges ruled that the process violated the Canadian Bill of Rights, but all judges agreed that it was unlawful. Today, the Charter decision is generally regarded as the controlling precedent.

It is tempting but inaccurate to interpret *Singh* as guaranteeing a Charter right to refugee protection. Elements of the judgment could support a future claim of that nature, but the actual decision is more circumspect or, as Cass Sunstein would have it, minimalist:[11] the Immigration Act already granted to refugees a statutory right not to be *refouled* to a country where they would face a well-founded fear of persecution, a permit entitling them to remain in Canada, and the right to appeal a deportation order.[12]

Wilson J acknowledges at the outset of her judgment that s. 6 of the Charter guarantees mobility rights only to citizens, and then adds that "at common law an alien has no right to enter or remain in Canada except by leave of the Crown."[13] But her observation about the common law is of no constitutional moment because statute supersedes common law, and the statute created a right to remain in the form of protection against *refoulement*. Wilson J did not need to consider what the Charter would require had the Immigration Act made no provision for refugee protection, nor did she confront the situation of those who could meet the refugee definition but whom the statute siphoned off at the front end as ineligible to access refugee determination or excluded from its protection at the back end. All the Court needed to address was the process for determining access to the extant statutory right, and this enabled Wilson J to caution that it was "unnecessary for the Court to

9 *Refoulement* means expulsion to the country of nationality or former habitual residence.

10 Immigration Act, 1976, SC 1976–77 c 52 at s 2(1), s 55, s 4(2)(b).

11 C.R. Sunstein, *One Case at a Time: Judicial Minimalism on the Supreme Court* (Cambridge, MA, Harvard University Press, 1999).

12 Immigration Act, 1976, above n 10 at s 2(1), s 37, s 70(1).

13 *Singh*, above n 1 at para 13.

consider what it would do if it were asked to engage in a larger inquiry into the substantive rights conferred in the Act."[14]

Having delimited the bounds of the enquiry, Wilson J addresses the two elements of a s. 7 analysis: was Singh's life, liberty, or security of the person imperilled by the process of refugee determination? Did the actual process comport with fundamental justice?

Wilson fends off the attempt to limit s. 7 to citizens and affirms that "everyone" under s. 7 "includes every human being who is physically present in Canada and by virtue of such presence amenable to Canadian law."[15] (The application of the Charter to persons outside Canadian territory but amenable to Canadian law remains ambiguous to the present day.)

Wilson J finds that *security of the person* is engaged by refugee determination, even if *refoulement* presents only a risk rather than a certainty of persecution and even though the proximate agent of persecution is the state of nationality, not Canada:

> "[S]ecurity of the person" must encompass freedom from the threat of physical punishment or suffering as well as freedom from such punishment itself. I note particularly that a Convention refugee has the right under s. 55 of the Act not to "... be removed from Canada to a country where his life or freedom would be threatened." In my view, the denial of such a right must amount to a deprivation of security of the person within the meaning of s. 7.[16]

Wilson J addresses the assertion that "immigration is a *privilege*, and not a *right*" near the end of her analysis of life, liberty, and security of the person.[17] It is asserted as an impediment to Mr Singh's claim of a *right* to security of the person. Its location in the analysis invites speculation that the Court was invited to endorse the following chain of reasoning: refugee protection is a subset of immigration; immigration is a privilege and not a right; therefore, removal to a country where the person may be persecuted does not infringe a *right* to security of the person because the non-citizen possesses no right in relation to immigration. The implication for principles of fundamental justice is that one

14 Ibid at para 55.
15 Ibid at para 35.
16 Ibid at para 47.
17 Ibid at para 49; italics added.

has no constitutional *right* to a process that may culminate in a result that affords only the *privilege* of remaining in Canada.

The precedent advanced by the government in support of the right/privilege dichotomy is *Mitchell v The Queen*,[18] a case decided under s. 2(3) of the Canadian Bill of Rights, in which an inmate challenged the parole revocation process as a denial of his right to a "fair hearing in accordance with the principles of fundamental justice."[19] The majority of the Supreme Court of Canada rejected his appeal:

> The appellant had no right to parole. He was granted parole as a matter of discretion by the Parole Board. He had no right to remain on parole. His parole was subject to the revocation at the absolute discretion of the Board.[20]

Wilson J both distinguishes and rejects *Mitchell*. She narrowly distinguishes *Mitchell* on the basis that parole is granted as a matter of statutory discretion, whereas a person who meets the definition of *refugee* is "entitled as a matter of law to the incidents of that status."[21] In other words, refugee protection is a statutory right for those who meet the definition. So, if *privilege* is read as the positive outcome of discretion, then refugee protection is not a privilege in this sense.

Wilson J also rejects *Mitchell* by impugning the right/privilege dichotomy as such:

> I do not think this kind of analysis is acceptable in relation to the Charter. It seems to me rather that the recent adoption of the Charter by Parliament and nine of the ten provinces as part of the Canadian constitutional framework has sent a clear message to the courts that the restrictive attitude which at times characterized their approach to the Canadian Bill of Rights ought to be re-examined. I am accordingly of the view that the approach taken by Laskin C.J. dissenting in Mitchell is to be preferred to that of the

18 [1976] 2 SCR 570, [1976] 1 WWR 577 [*Mitchell*], cited in *Singh*, above n 1 at para 50. The contemporary approach of the Supreme Court to parole under the Charter proceeds from the understanding that denial of parole breaches the s 7 right to liberty, triggering access to principles of fundamental justice. See eg *Cunningham v Canada* [1993] 2 SCR 143, [1993] SCJ no 47.

19 SC 1960, c 44.

20 *Mitchell*, above n 18.

21 *Singh*, above n 1 at para 52.

> majority as we examine the question whether the Charter has any application to the adjudication of rights granted to an individual by statute.[22]

Rather than rely on a formal designation of the interest as right versus privilege to determine access to fundamental justice, Wilson J looks to the consequences of state action for the person concerned. The potential impact of *refoulement* for a refugee makes this an easy case in her estimation:

> [I]f the appellants had been found to be Convention refugees as defined in s. 2(1) of the Immigration Act, 1976 they would have been entitled as a matter of law to the incidents of that status provided for in the Act. Given the potential consequences for the appellants of a denial of that status if they are in fact persons with a "well-founded fear of persecution," it seems to me unthinkable that the Charter would not apply to entitle them to fundamental justice in the adjudication of their status.[23]

This conclusion, then, grounds the Court's assessment of why the existing determination process failed to accord with fundamental justice, and the imposition of a minimum set of required procedures, such as disclosure of the evidence upon which the minister relies and an oral hearing to test credibility.

The Court in *Singh* does advert to the principle that would subsequently figure prominently in *Chiarelli* – namely, that "at common law an alien has no right to enter and remain in Canada except by leave of the Crown."[24] However, Wilson J simply mentions it at the outset of the judgment, alongside the observation that the appellants do not claim the citizen's right under s. 6 of the Charter to enter and remain.[25] She quickly moves to a description and analysis of the supervening provisions of the Immigration Act relating to refugee status, and her analysis remains tied to s. 7 of the Charter in light of the statutory right of refugee protection.

The US corollary of the common law principle resurfaces later in the judgment, however. Wilson J adumbrates the US plenary power

---

22 Ibid at para 50.

23 Ibid at para 52.

24 *Prata v Minister of Manpower and Immigration* [1976] 1 SCR 376, 52 DLR (3d) 383, [*Prata*], cited in *Singh*, above n 1 at para 13.

25 *Singh*, above n 1 at para 13.

doctrine, whereby aliens seeking entry to the United States are excluded from the ambit of constitutional protection. The rationale for the doctrine turns on a conception of immigration law as embedded in the conduct of foreign relations and thus "a fundamental sovereign attribute exercised by the Government's political departments largely immune from judicial control."[26] As such, plenary power is a species of the political questions doctrine, which holds certain issues essentially political and non-justiciable. Wilson J does not engage deeply with US doctrine, except to note that the "political" question of whom to admit is already spelled out in the Immigration Act respecting refugees and that the Court in the instant case was addressing only the procedural entailments.[27]

Wilson J thus leaves dangling the important question of whether the Charter guarantees a s. 7 right to refugee protection independent of the contingent existence of the statutory rights set out in the Immigration Act. In other words, if a government repealed the statutory regime of refugee protection in Canada, could a refugee claimant standing at (or inside) the border claim a Charter right against *refoulement*? Wilson J's earlier emphasis on the consequences of a denial of refugee status, and how those consequences make it "unthinkable" to deprive a claimant of fundamental justice in the determination of that status, might incline some to impute an affirmative answer.[28] After all, the same concern about the consequences of *refoulement* that animates her insistence that principles of fundamental justice apply to refugee determination militates towards a finding that *refoulement* violates a right to security of the person. But, as noted earlier, the Court does not venture down that path, leaving an unresolved tension in the judgment.[29] This minimalist approach is not necessarily or always objectionable. Indeed, incrementalism is a feature of common law method. Perhaps it is unsurprising that constitutional jurisprudence would follow the same path, especially in the early days of Charter interpretation.

---

26 *Shaughnessy v Mezei* 345 US 206 at 210 (1953), cited in *Singh*, above n 1 at para 54. See generally D.A. Martin, "Why Immigration's Plenary Power Doctrine Endures" (2015) 68 *Oklahoma Law Review* 29.

27 *Singh*, above n 1 at para 55.

28 Ibid at para 52.

29 C. Grey, "Thinkable: The Charter and Refugee Law after *Appulonappa* and *B010*" (2016) 76 *Supreme Court Law Review* (2d) 87.

So, in the end, *Singh* adverts to the common law prerogative to exclude the alien but assigns it no analytical weight, engages security of the person through the portal of a statutory right to refugee protection, rejects the common law right/privilege distinction in favour of consequences as the basis for determining the reach of fundamental justice, and declines to pronounce on a free-standing Charter right against return to persecution.

The *Chiarelli* Decision

Mr Singh challenged the process leading to recognition of refugee status, which confers a statutory right to remain in Canada on a non-citizen who otherwise has no legal basis for entering or remaining in Canada. Mr Chiarelli challenged the process leading to deportation from Canada of a permanent resident. Permanent residents are entitled to enter and remain in Canada indefinitely (and to eventually apply for citizenship) subject to certain conditions. Breach of those conditions may lead to loss of status and expulsion. In contrast to Singh, Chiarelli did not allege a risk of persecution if deported, and, unlike Singh, he enjoyed a relatively secure immigration status in Canada for about a dozen years before that status was revoked.

Joseph (Giuseppe) Chiarelli immigrated to Canada from Italy at age 15. At age 24, he was convicted of uttering threats and possessing a narcotic for purposes of trafficking. He received a sentence of six months' imprisonment. Criminality is a ground of inadmissibility for permanent residents, and so Chiarelli was subject to loss of status and deportation because of his criminal convictions and subsequent sentence. Under the ordinary operation of the Immigration Act, Chiarelli could appeal the loss of status and removal order to the Immigration Appeal Board (IAB), which was the predecessor to the current Immigration Appeal Division (IAD). Before the IAB, he could, *inter alia*, seek a reversal of the decision on "all the circumstances of the case," meaning humanitarian and compassionate (H&C) considerations.[30]

In broad terms, the exercise of H&C discretion assesses the consequences to an individual of removal from Canada, and of return to the country of nationality, as well as the likely impact to Canada of his or her continued presence in Canada. Relevant factors include the length

30 Immigration Act, 1976, above n 10 at s 72(1)(b).

of residence in Canada; the range and depth of familial and other personal relationships; social and economic integration; severity of actual offences and prospects for rehabilitation (where criminality is at issue); and personal, linguistic, cultural, and other connections to the country of citizenship.[31] It is worth noting here that it is not uncommon for some non-citizens to immigrate to Canada as children, acquire permanent resident status, yet never obtain citizenship (or even travel outside Canada), and then face removal as adults on grounds of serious criminality.

Chiarelli was statute-barred from asking the IAB to exercise humanitarian and compassionate discretion in his case. The reason was that the government believed that Chiarelli was not merely an "ordinary" criminal but also someone engaged in organized crime (a separate ground of inadmissibility).[32] Therefore, the Minister of Employment and Immigration and the Solicitor General exercised their option to issue a security certificate against Chiarelli, thereby shunting him into a separate process.[33] For purposes of the judgment, the most important consequence of the security certificate regime (as it then existed) was that Chiarelli could no longer appeal his deportation order on H&C grounds.

Chiarelli challenged the regime as a violation of ss. 7, 12, and 15 of the Charter. With respect to the s. 7 claim, Chiarelli contended that deportation infringed his liberty through coercive, permanent, physical expulsion from Canada and transfer to another state. Doing so without regard to his personal circumstances was arbitrary and disproportionate, and it failed to accord with a substantive conception of fundamental justice.[34]

The Court's approach to assessing Chiarelli's s. 7 right finds no support in prior or subsequent s. 7 jurisprudence outside the domain of immigration. The Court leapfrogs over the question of whether deportation violates life, liberty, or security of the person, and it finds that it does not matter anyway because there could be no breach of

31 See *Ribic, Marida v MEI* (IAB T84–9623), D Davey, Benedetti, Petryshyn, 20 August 1985.

32 Ibid at s 19(1)(d)(ii).

33 A subsequent iteration of the security certificate regime was found unconstitutional in *Charkaoui v Canada (Citizenship and Immigration)* 2007 SCC 9 [*Charkaoui*]. Its successor was upheld in *Canada (Citizenship and Immigration) v Harkat* 2014 SCC 37.

34 The procedural deficiencies concerned the process for issuing a security certificate in existence at the time (which differed significantly from the process that was successfully challenged in 2007 in *Charkaoui*).

fundamental justice in deporting a permanent resident for breach of the conditions upon which status was contingent:

> The appellant correctly points out that the threshold question is whether deportation per se engages s. 7, that is, whether it amounts to a deprivation of life, liberty or security of the person. ... I do not find it necessary to answer this question, however, since I am of the view that there is no breach of fundamental justice.[35]

The Court does cite earlier jurisprudence in support of the proposition that the "principles of fundamental justice are to be found in the basic tenets of our legal system."[36] Sopinka J repeatedly invokes the centrality of "context" and a "contextual approach" in determining the scope of fundamental justice, which leads him to the view that the relevant context consists of the principles and policies underlying immigration law:

> Thus in determining the scope of principles of fundamental justice as they apply to this case, the Court must look to the principles and policies underlying immigration law. The most fundamental principle of immigration law is that non-citizens do not have an unqualified right to enter or remain in the country. At common law an alien has no right to enter or remain in the country: R. v Governor of Pentonville Prison, [1973] 2 All E.R. 741; Prata v Minister of Manpower and Immigration, [1976] 1 S.C.R. 376.[37]

The Court offers extradition jurisprudence as an example of the same principle in action:

> La Forest J. recently reiterated this principle in Kindler v Canada (Minister of Justice), supra, at p. 834:
>
>> The Government has the right and duty to keep out and to expel aliens from this country if it considers it advisable to do so. This right, of course, exists independently of extradition. If an alien known to have

35 *Chiarelli*, above n 2 at 731–2.
36 Ibid at 732.
37 Ibid at 732–3.

> a serious criminal record attempted to enter into Canada, he could be refused admission. And by the same token, he could be deported once he entered Canada. …
>
> If it were otherwise, Canada could become a haven for criminals and others whom we legitimately do not wish to have among us.[38]

Sopinka J then presents s. 6 of the Charter, which guarantees only to citizens the right to enter and remain, as the constitutional instantiation of the common law principle.

Viewed against this legal landscape, the Immigration Act simply specifies in statutory form those qualifications on the right of non-citizens to enter and remain. One of those conditions is that the permanent resident not be convicted of a crime punishable by more than five years' imprisonment:

> This condition represents a legitimate, non-arbitrary choice by Parliament of a situation in which it is not in the public interest to allow a non-citizen to remain in the country. … It is true that the personal circumstances of individuals who breach this condition may vary widely. … However there is one element common to all persons who fall within the class of permanent residents described [as inadmissible on grounds of criminality]. They have all deliberately violated an essential condition under which they were permitted to remain in Canada. In such a situation, there is no breach of fundamental justice in giving practical effect to the termination of their right to remain in Canada. In the case of a permanent resident, deportation is the only way in which to accomplish this. There is nothing inherently unjust about a mandatory order. The fact of a deliberate violation of the condition imposed by [the criminal inadmissibility provision] is sufficient to justify a deportation order. It is not necessary, in order to comply with fundamental justice, to look beyond this fact to other aggravating or mitigating circumstances.[39]

Later in the judgment, Sopinka J reiterates the same conclusion, this time focusing on an appeal as the vehicle for injecting individualized factors into the adjudicative process.

It is useful to contrast his genealogy of the conditions on the statutory right to enter and remain with his genealogy of constraints on the

38 Ibid at 733.
39 Ibid at 734.

power to deport. According to the Court, the former derives from a timeless principle immanent in the common law. The latter lacks any such normative anchor in the tenets of the legal system and simply reflects the vagaries of legislative choice by successive parliaments. Thus, attention to individualized considerations as a component of a deportation decision is merely a contingent feature of the legislation in its various iterations. And, as Sopinka J notes, "there has never been a universally available right of appeal from a deportation order on 'all the circumstances of the case.'"[40]

Before 1967, only the minister possessed broad discretion to provide relief from deportation. Thereafter, the independent, quasi-judicial IAB had jurisdiction to quash a deportation order on the basis of "all the circumstances of the case," but this discretion could be overridden by the minister of immigration and the solicitor general if it would be "contrary to the national interest to provide such relief."[41] The Court cites with approval the depiction of this residual ministerial authority by Martland J in *Prata*:

> The effect of s. 21 is to reserve to the Crown, notwithstanding the powers conferred upon the Board by the Act, the right, similar to the prerogative right which existed at common law, to determine that the continued presence in Canada of an alien, subject to a deportation order, would not be conducive to the public good.[42]

I return below to querying how much normative distance the word *similar* actually puts between the prerogative power under common law and the statutory discretion afforded the ministers under the immigration statute.

For present purposes, *Chiarelli* can be distilled to the following propositions: access to fundamental justice can be determined independently of whether, how, or to what extent a right to life, liberty, or security of the person has been breached. Indeed, the Court's dicta cast doubt on how much fundamental justice constrains deportation at all. The paramount common law principle relevant to non-citizens subject to immigration

40 Ibid at 741. This focus on a "right" to an appeal is an unfortunate distraction. The central issue is whether deportation of a long-term permanent resident potentially violates s 7 and thus requires consideration by a decision maker, not whether that consideration happens by way of appeal or other procedure.

41 Immigration Appeal Board Act, SC 1966–67, c 90 at s 15, s 21.

42 *Prata*, above n 24 at 381, cited in *Chiarelli*, above n 2 at 740.

law is that aliens have no unqualified right to enter and remain. In light of this principle, a legitimate, non-arbitrary qualification on the right of aliens to remain cannot violate a principle of fundamental justice. Inadmissibility based on criminality is a legitimate and non-arbitrary qualification. The power to deport non-citizens on that basis must be co-extensive with the power to deny initial entry on that basis. Consideration of individual circumstances is a policy choice of legislators, not a legal principle rooted in basic tenets of the legal system.

Although the Court is not explicit on this point, a necessary inference is that it is not arbitrary to deport a permanent resident without regard to personal circumstances. It should be noted that *Chiarelli* was decided when non-arbitrariness as a principle of fundamental justice was relatively undeveloped, and whether the same inference would flow today is debatable.[43] Moreover, the common law generally extends greater protection to those who already enjoy a benefit or entitlement than to those who are seeking it. By stating that the power to deport must be co-extensive with the power to deny entry, the Court erases that distinction to the disadvantage of permanent residents.

Chiarelli's s. 12 and s. 15 challenges were cursorily dismissed. While the Court affirmed pre-Charter jurisprudence insisting that deportation was not punishment, it granted that deportation constituted "treatment" for purposes of s. 12. Nevertheless, automatic deportability of a permanent resident convicted of a criminal offence punishable by five years' imprisonment was not "grossly disproportionate."[44] Indeed, Sopinka J opined that it would outrage standards of decency if "individuals granted conditional entry into Canada were permitted, without consequence, to violate those conditions deliberately."[45] As with *arbitrariness*, the meaning of *gross disproportionality* under s. 7 and s. 12 of the Charter has evolved since *Chiarelli* was decided.[46]

---

43 See eg *Carter v Canada (Attorney General)* 2015 SCC 5 [*Carter*] and *Canada (Attorney General) v Bedford* 2013 SCC 72 [*Bedford*]. In the former, the Court explained that "arbitrariness targets the situation where there is no rational connection between the object of the law and the limit it imposes on life, liberty or security of the person" (at para 83).

44 *R v Smith* [1987] 1 SCR 1045 at 1072, [1987] SCJ no 36, cited in *Chiarelli*, above n 2 at 735–6.

45 *Chiarelli*, above n 2 at 736.

46 See eg *Carter*, above n 43; *Bedford*, above n 43. In the former, the Court explained, "gross disproportionality compares the law's purpose, 'taken at face value,' with its negative effects on the rights of the claimant, and asks if this impact is completely out of sync with the object of the law" (at para 89).

The Charter after *Singh* and *Chiarelli*

I offer here a truncated tour of Charter-related immigration jurisprudence after *Singh* and *Chiarelli*. Although it wanders astray from the common law principle that launched the enquiry, these cases enable us to assay its effects.

Neither *Singh* nor *Chiarelli* directly resolves the question whether an otherwise lawful deportation breaches liberty or security of person. The Court in *Singh* did not need to because the Immigration Act provided refugees with a statutory right against removal anyway and the issue concerned the procedures for determination of that statutory right. *Chiarelli* did not need to since, as the Court saw it, aliens had no unqualified right to enter and remain and so fundamental justice was not implicated in the content of "legitimate and non-arbitrary" conditions on the statutory right to remain.[47]

In *Medovarski v Canada (MCI)*,[48] the Supreme Court directly answered the question. The appellants were permanent residents ordered deported for serious criminality, having received custodial sentences of more than six months.[49] They were caught in a transition between a system that permitted them to appeal the deportation to the IAD (the successor to the IAB) on "all the circumstances of the case" and amendments that excluded them from an equitable appeal.[50] The Charter arguments took up four short paragraphs in the judgment. Ms Medovarski argued that deportation "removes her liberty to make fundamental decisions that affect her personal life, including her choice to remain with her partner."[51] Security of the person was engaged because of the "state-imposed psychological stress of being deported."[52]

The Court disposes of the s. 7 claim by returning to the common law principle:

> The most fundamental principle of immigration law is that non-citizens do not have an unqualified right to enter or remain in Canada: *Chiarelli v Canada (Minister of Employment and Immigration)*, [1992] 1 S.C.R. 711,

47 *Chiarelli*, above n 2 at 734.
48 2005 SCC 51 [*Medovarski*].
49 Immigration and Refugee Protection Act, SC 2001, c 27, s 64.
50 Ibid at s 196.
51 *Medovarski*, above n 48 at para 45.
52 Ibid.

> at p. 733. Thus the deportation of a non-citizen in itself cannot implicate the liberty and security interests protected by s. 7 of the *Canadian Charter of Rights and Freedoms*.[53]

Recall that, in *Chiarelli*, the Court did not find it necessary to determine whether deportation breached the s. 7 right to liberty and security of the person because the common law principle meant that fundamental justice was not engaged anyway. Now, the same common law principle is the reason that deportation does not implicate liberty or security of the person. If this is the case, it is unclear why the Court did not simply say so in *Chiarelli*. If nothing else, it is analytically more coherent to deny that a s. 7 interest is engaged than to proceed on the basis that even if deportation breaches a s. 7 right – no matter how egregious and profound the infringement (which cannot be known absent the precluded enquiry) – no principle of fundamental justice constrains the process or substance of that rights deprivation.

In later jurisprudence, the Supreme Court presses on the qualifier contained in *Medovarski* – namely, that deportation does not *in itself* implicate liberty or security of the person. The Court leaves open the possibility that even if forcibly transferring a person from one country to another does not implicate liberty or security of the person, incidental or consequential features of deportation may do so.

So, in *Charkaoui*, the Court ruled that the process of adjudicating the reasonableness of a security certificate engaged s. 7 in two ways: first, because the automatic detention that was incidental to the security certificate regime engaged the liberty interest under s. 7, and second, because upholding the security certificate could lead to removal to a country where the named person faced a substantial risk of torture.[54]

This second basis for engaging s. 7 derives from the notorious "*Suresh* exception." In *Suresh v Canada*,[55] the Court attended to torture as a possible consequence of deportation. Here the Court conceded that s. 7 was engaged by deportation where it exposed a non-citizen to a substantial risk of torture in the destination country.[56] Recognition that return to torture breaches s. 7 rights initially looks like a simple variation on the

53 Ibid at para 46.

54 *Charkaoui*, above n 33 at paras 13–14.

55 2002 SCC 1 [*Suresh*].

56 Ibid at para 77.

reasoning in *Singh*, where the Court found that returning a refugee to the risk of persecution engaged security of the person. The important difference is that, in *Singh*, the statute created the right to refugee protection to a person in Singh's situation provided that he came within the refugee definition. In *Suresh*, the Court finds that deportation to a substantial risk of torture engages s. 7 even though the statute authorizes the minister to deport a refugee to face torture if the minister deems the refugee to pose a threat to national security. The Court in *Suresh* concludes that there is a free-standing Charter right not to be returned to torture unless there are "exceptional circumstances."[57]

Because persecution encompasses more than torture, *Suresh* did not resolve whether *refoulement* to persecution short of torture violates s. 7 or, put in other terms, whether the Charter guarantees a right to refugee protection. In *Febles v Canada (MCI)*, however, the Court declared that removal may be prevented "where Charter-protected rights may be in jeopardy."[58] At the same time, the Court declared that "the Charter does not give a positive right to refugee protection."[59] Thus, the Charter is engaged in a more limited, negative sense as a brake on removal, but it does not necessarily put an individual on a path to secure residence.

In the years since *Singh*, successive governments have eroded the scope of legislated refugee protection through expanded ineligibility to claim refugee status, expanded exclusion from refugee protection, differentiated procedures among refugee claimants, and selective access to post-decision recourse.[60] One consequence is that some people who may be refugees are denied access to an oral hearing before an independent, quasi-judicial tribunal (Immigration and Refugee Board) to determine whether they meet the refugee definition and are instead confined to a paper review by a ministerial delegate.[61] This Pre-Removal Risk Assessment (PRRA) is intended as the penultimate step before deportation; it is described by the Supreme Court as a "stay of removal."[62] Unlike

57 Ibid at para 78.

58 2014 SCC 68 at para 67 [*Febles*].

59 Ibid at para 68.

60 For a critique of recent developments, see Idil Atak, Graham Hudson, and Delphine Nakache, "The Securitisation of Canada's Refugee System: Reviewing the Unintended Consequences of the 2012 Reform" (2018) 1 *Refugee Survey Quarterly* 37, 1–24.

61 Immigration and Refugee Protection Act, above n 49 at s 101, s 103, s 112.

62 See eg *Febles*, above n 58 at para 67; *B010 v Canada (Citizenship and Immigration)* 2015 SCC 58 at para 75 [*B010*].

an application for leave to seek judicial review of an adverse refugee decision by the IRB, an application for leave to seek judicial review of a negative PRRA decision does not automatically halt removal. A person may be deported pending the outcome of the application for leave to seek judicial review of the PRRA.[63]

In *B010*, the Supreme Court of Canada issued a terse *obiter dicta* indicating that the Charter is not typically engaged in relation to those asserting a need for refugee protection until the PRRA stage.[64] The PRRA is not affirmative refugee protection, but only a stay of removal. So without overruling or distinguishing *Singh*, the Court shifts s. 7 downstream to the penultimate, pre-removal stage of the deportation process, where the procedural protections are thinner than those guaranteed by *Singh* and fall far short of the procedures for refugee determination before the quasi-judicial, independent IRB. The implication is that the consequence of *refouling* refugees – persecution – may no longer warrant compliance with the principles of fundamental justice enumerated in *Singh*.

Back to the Common Law

Seeing Like a State, Feeling Like a Person

In *Singh*, Wilson J rejects the traditional common law characterization of immigration as a privilege for purposes of discharging the state from the procedural obligations of fundamental justice. Her narrow justification is that refugee protection is a statutory right, in contrast to a discretionary benefit like parole. The more expansive claim is that the formal, *ex ante* classification of an interest as right or privilege, from the state's perspective, is the wrong methodological pathway into evaluating an infringement on life, liberty, or security of the person. Wilson J insists that the enquiry must focus on the impact of state action on the life, liberty, or security of the person in functional terms. This means that

63 Immigration and Refugee Protection Act, above n 49 at s 49(2).

64 *B010*, above n 62, citing *Febles*, above n 58. As Gerald Heckman and Colin Grey each explain, the Court in *B010* appears to attribute to *Febles* a dictum that departs from (or perhaps revises) the actual reasoning in *Febles* about the engagement of s 7 in refugee determination. See Grey, "Thinkable," above n 28; G Heckman, "Rethinking the Application of Section 7 of the Charter in Canadian Immigration and Refugee Law" (2017) 68 *University of New Brunswick Law Journal* 312.

infringement of a legal right (e.g., property ownership) will not necessarily engage life, liberty, or security of the person, while infringement of an interest falling short of a legal right may do so, depending on the effect on the rights-bearer. So, describing an interest in formal terms as a privilege does not foreclose the s. 7 enquiry, nor does describing it as a right dictate the result of a s. 7 enquiry.

This impact-based approach is consistent with prior and subsequent common law trends in administrative law, such as *Baker v Canada (MCI)*.[65] Mavis Baker had no lawful status in Canada, not even a claim to refugee protection. All she could request was a favourable exercise of humanitarian and compassionate discretion to exempt her from deportation to Jamaica, based on the impact that deporting her from Canada would have on her and her children. Insofar as H&C is a discretionary exemption from the negative application of immigration law, Mavis Baker was seeking a privilege from the minister, not claiming a right. Yet administrative law jurisprudence had long conceded that the duty of fairness applied to H&C decisions because, as the Court notes, it is a decision of "exceptional importance to the lives of those with an interest in the result – the claimant and his or her close family members."[66]

Indeed, this attention to the substantive impact of a discretionary decision as against its formal character as privilege can be traced back to *Roncarelli v Duplessis*.[67] The formal approach is driven by the character of the relationship between state and legal subject, as viewed from the perspective of the state. It asks how the state sees the individual who is the object of the decision. The legal category to which the state assigns the legal subject (rights-bearer, benefit-seeker, licence-holder, etc.) is comprehensive, exhaustive, and determinative. The substantive approach adopts the perspective of the legal subject. It asks how the individual experiences the decision to which he or she is subject.[68]

In *Chiarelli* and then *Medovarski*, the work performed by the assertion that an alien has no unqualified right to enter and remain is to

65 [1999] 2 SCR 817, [1999] SCJ 39 [*Baker*].

66 Ibid at para 31.

67 [1959] SCR 121, [1959] SCJ no 1. See generally D. Dyzenhaus, "The Deep Structure of *Roncarelli v Duplessis*" (2004) 53 *University of New Brunswick Law Journal* 111.

68 Compare *Chieu v Canada (Minister of Citizenship and Immigration)* 2002 SCC 3 (at para 57), where the Court quotes approvingly from *Prata*, above n 24, the assertion that a person appealing a lawful removal order "does not, therefore, attempt to assert a right, but, rather, attempts to obtain a discretionary privilege" (at 380).

preclude access to fundamental justice in the first instance and to life, liberty, and security of the person in the second. That is the same work done historically by the common law right-versus-privilege dichotomy in blocking procedural fairness and unfettering the exercise of discretion. As deployed by the Supreme Court, the principle that an alien has no unqualified right to enter or remain simply restates the claim that immigration is a privilege, not a right, and restores to that dichotomy the juridical force that *Singh* sought to divest from it.[69]

One might object that I am mixing apples and oranges here. After all, in both *Singh* and *Baker*, the statute created a mechanism (refugee status and H&C discretion, respectively) for enabling the petitioners to remain in Canada. The Court's attention to the consequences of removal was oriented solely towards how those decisions would be made, both procedurally and substantively, not towards whether the individuals were entitled to such a mechanism in the first place. At the heart of the appellants' claims in *Chiarelli* and *Medovarski*, however, is a claim that the Charter mandates individualized assessment of the impact of removal in the course of the decision.[70] Neither *Singh* nor *Baker* endorses the relevance of impact for that broader purpose. And so *Chiarelli* and *Medovarski* are superficially reconcilable with *Singh* and *Baker* on the rationale that the human impact of deportation is legally relevant to the lawful exercise of the power to deport if and only if Parliament has already decided to qualify the power to deport on that basis.

The hazard with this containment strategy is normative spillover – or perhaps the cognitive dissonance required to repel leakage. Once a court recognizes that deportation as such can "[affect] in a fundamental

---

69 S 6 of the Charter, which guarantees only to citizens the right to enter and remain, only bolsters the argument if one reads all citizens' right to remain under s 6 as defeating any non-citizen's claim to a right to remain under s 7. This would be akin to arguing that since s 10(b) guarantees all criminal accused a right to legal counsel, no person who is not a criminal defendant has a right to counsel. Yet the Supreme Court of Canada rejected this logic when it found that, in certain circumstances, s 7 mandates the provision of state-funded legal counsel in child apprehension proceedings: *New Brunswick (Minister of Health and Community Services) v G(J)* [1999] 3 SCR 46, [1999] SCJ no 47.

70 The Court in *Chiarelli*, above n 2, submerges this issue beneath an enquiry into whether Chiarelli had a Charter right to a particular institutional vehicle for addressing the consequences – namely, an equitable appeal examining "all the circumstances of the case" (at 741).

manner the future of individuals' lives"[71] and that exposing a person to certain risks consequent to deportation – persecution, torture – may impair life, liberty, or security of the person,[72] switching off that awareness using the common law principle in relation to the same or other potential harms of deportation strains against the integrity of judicial reasoning.

One way of illustrating this is to notice how the Court toggles unselfconsciously between status and personhood in conceptualizing the non-citizen. The non-citizen is a rights-bearer under s. 7, yet she can lay no claim as rights-bearer when it comes to state action in the form of deportation. Why? Because she is a non-citizen. She has been reassigned from legal subject on the basis of personhood ("everyone" in s. 7) to the object of governance-through-status ("alien" under the common law). Note that this disengagement from s. 7 is not the same as concluding that the harms of deportation in a given case do not rise to the level of a s. 7 infringement. Nor is it tantamount to concluding that fundamental justice is not breached by deportation because of countervailing concerns. To engage in a balancing exercise, one must first recognize a rights infringement, assess the nature and intensity of the infringement, and then weigh it against the state interest.

What *Chiarelli* does instead is short-circuit the analysis by refusing to enquire into the circumstances that may reveal a rights infringement:

> This condition [criminal inadmissibility based solely on length/severity of crime] represents a legitimate, non-arbitrary choice by Parliament of a situation in which it is not in the public interest to allow a non-citizen to remain in the country. All persons falling within the class of permanent residents described [as inadmissible for serious criminality] have deliberately violated an essential condition under which they were permitted to remain in Canada. Fundamental justice is not breached by deportation: it is the only way to give practical effect to the termination of a permanent resident's right to remain in Canada. Compliance with fundamental justice does not require that other aggravating or mitigating circumstances be considered.[73]

71 *Baker*, above n 65 at para 15.
72 *Singh*, above n 1 at para 44.
73 *Chiarelli*, above n 2 at 715.

It is undeniable that the common law recognizes and attaches considerable weight to interests that do not count under the Charter. Property rights spring to mind as an example. But it is more difficult to explain how the impact of deportation could count for so much in *Baker* and for nothing in *Chiarelli*.[74]

Another objection might be that s. 6 of the Charter, which guarantees only to citizens the right to enter and remain, elevates the common law principle to constitutional norm. But this only bolsters the argument if one reads every citizen's right to remain under s. 6 as authorizing the state to deport every non-citizen. In one of the Court's earliest dicta, Dickson CJ remarked that the Charter "is intended to constrain governmental action inconsistent with those rights and freedoms; it is not in itself an authorization for governmental action."[75] In the same spirit, s. 6 exists to protect the rights of citizens, not to deny rights protection to non-citizens. It does not follow from the fact that s. 6 guarantees to all citizens the right to enter and remain that no non-citizen could ever have a right to remain. This would be akin to arguing that since s. 10(b) guarantees a right to counsel to those who are arrested or detained, no one who is not arrested or detained can claim a constitutional right to legal counsel under s. 7. The Supreme Court of Canada rejected this logic when it found that, in certain circumstances, in principle, a "right to counsel under s. 7 may apply in other cases besides those which are encompassed by s. 10 (*b*)."[76]

If I am correct that the common law principle and the right/privilege binary are corollaries that perform equivalent doctrinal work, it is unsurprising that the embrace of the former by the Court in *Chiarelli*

74 This differential treatment is distinguishable from the solicitude towards property rights in administrative law and their exclusion from the Charter: the common law exerts influence in administrative law but does not control how the Charter regards property. In the case of deportation, the common law does not control how administrative law regards the impact of deportation, but it seems to control how the Charter regards the impact of deportation.

75 *Hunter v Southam* [1984] 2 SCR 145 at 156, [1984] SCJ no 36. Dickson CJ explained that s 8's prohibition on unreasonable search and seizure "acts as a limitation on whatever powers of search and seizure the federal or provincial governments already and otherwise possess. It does not in itself confer any powers, even of 'reasonable' search and seizure, on these governments" (at 156–7).

76 *Dehghani v Canada (Minister of Employment and Immigration)* [1993] 1 SCR 1053 at 1077. The case concerned a refugee claimant questioned without counsel at a port of entry. On the facts of the case, the Court determined that no breach of fundamental justice had occurred because the secondary examination was for "routine information gathering purposes."

and its progeny, and the rejection of the latter by the Court in *Singh* and *Baker*, have generated two strands of jurisprudence that pull in different directions. The Court's scepticism about whether there is a freestanding right to refugee protection gestures towards the ascendance of *Chiarelli* and *Medovarski*, and the tensile strength of the common law principle. A refugee claimant with a well-founded fear of persecution cannot rely confidently on the Charter to guarantee Canada's international legal obligation not to *refoule* her.

At the limit, the Court in *Suresh* concedes that deportation to torture – inflicted by another state – *prima facie* violates s. 7, albeit subject to justification in "exceptional circumstances."[77] But the Court is reluctant to extend Charter protection to those who face persecution short of torture. Leaving aside the obvious use of force to effectuate expulsion, the potential injury inflicted by the Canadian state through deportation – the harm of deracination – remains legally invisible. Severing an individual's connection to Canada, even where that person is deeply embedded in a web of familial, personal, linguistic, cultural, social, political, and economic relationships, does not sound as a possible infringement of liberty or security of the person because the Court has covered its ears. Importantly, this harm has been recognized by the United Nations Human Rights Committee as a violation of the right to enter and remain in one's "own country" and, arguably, by the European Court of Human Rights jurisprudence on the protection of family life.[78]

In the next section, I examine more closely the role of the common law principle in curtailing the Charter. The doctrinal puzzle is this: how does a common law declaration of the state's unbridled power over certain individuals come to circumscribe a Charter right instead of vice versa?

The Origins of the Common Law Principle

Chiarelli's articulation of the common law principle is an abbreviated version of a dictum from the English Court of Appeal in *R v Governor*

77 *Suresh*, above n 55 at para 78.

78 *Warsame v Canada* Communication no 1959/2010, CCPR/C/102/D/1959/2010 (21 July 2011); *Nystrom v Australia* Communications no 1557/2007 UN Doc CCPR/C/102/D/1557/2007 (18 July 2011); *Moustaquim v Belgium* Application no 12313/86, 18 February 1991 (ECtHR). The Human Rights Committee receives communications (complaints) about breaches of the International Covenant on Civil and Political Rights by States Party.

of Pentonville Prison, ex parte Azam,[79] which the Court in *Chiarelli* cites. The Court of Appeal in *Azam* was concerned with three non-status migrants, citizens of India and Pakistan, who had entered the United Kingdom clandestinely and remained and worked unlawfully for up to three years before coming to the attention of authorities. Lord Denning noted that, until 1962, a Commonwealth citizen "could come as of right into this country [and] could not be deported, not even if he was an habitual criminal, nor even if his presence here was very obnoxious to the rest of the people."[80] He contrasted the situation of the Commonwealth citizen with that of the alien at common law:

> At common law no alien has any right to enter this country except by leave of the Crown; and the Crown can refuse leave without giving any reason. If he comes by leave, the Crown can impose such conditions as it thinks fit, as to his length of stay, or otherwise. He has no right whatever to remain here. He is liable to be sent home to his own country at any time if, in the opinion of the Crown, his presence here is not conducive to the public good.[81]

In *Azam*, the common law status of the alien is introduced, along with the pre-1962 legal position of Commonwealth citizens, to situate the appellants' own legal position after 1968 reforms to UK law had significantly restricted rights of entry and residence of Commonwealth citizens. It is a historical reference inserted for comparative purposes. Importantly, however, it does illustrate that the obverse of the alien's rightlessness at common law is the absolute power of the sovereign. Restated, the common law principle asserts the unqualified power of the Crown to exclude or expel the alien.

In *Chiarelli*, this common law principle is invoked to supply "context" for the interpretation of s. 7.[82] And for this purpose, it matters

79 [1974] AC 18, [1973] 2 All ER 741 [*Azam*], cited in *Chiarelli*, above n 2 at 733. *Chiarelli* does not mention another oft cited case about the power to exclude and expel aliens – namely, *Attorney General for the Dominion of Canada v Cain* [1906] UKPC 55. That case stands for the proposition that the power to make laws governing entry, exclusion, and expulsion is a "supreme power in every State," which the Imperial Government could, and did, delegate to the Dominion Government of Canada (at 3).

80 *Azam*, above n 78 at 27, aff'd *Azam v Secretary of State for the Home Department* [1973] UKHL 7.

81 Ibid; citations omitted.

82 *Chiarelli*, above n 2 at 732–3.

that neither Lord Denning nor Sopinka J affixed the Crown's authority at common law with a label. For what they describe is, in essence, a royal prerogative over immigration. The precise definition of a *royal* (or Crown or executive) *prerogative power* remains disputed thanks to differing interpretations by Blackstone and Dicey, but contemporary consensus inclines towards Dicey's description of it as "the residue of discretionary or arbitrary authority which at any time is left in the hands of the Crown."[83] Dicey's definition encompasses any powers the Crown could exercise free of parliamentary authority, whereas Blackstone would confine it to those powers unique to the Crown *qua* public actor. Matching Dicey's general definition against Lord Denning's account of the Crown's authority over aliens under common law reveals a close fit. In the absence of immigration law, it is not the case that borders are open; rather, the Crown allegedly possesses plenary and unfettered power to admit, exclude, or expel the alien.

Exercised in the past by the monarch, today prerogative powers are usually held by the Governor in Council's ministers – the executive. The persistence of prerogative powers raises obvious democratic and rule of law concerns about the accountability of the Crown to the legislature and the courts for the exercise of the prerogative. The insulation of the prerogative from judicial review has diminished but not disappeared over time. Because prerogative powers are rooted in the common law, the courts adjudicate the existence and ambit of a given prerogative. The actual exercise of a prerogative, however, has been largely insulated from judicial review until relatively recently.

Canadian courts' unease with prerogative powers is reflected in techniques that shrink and curtail them. One is the doctrine of displacement. A prerogative power may be extinguished by statute, and "once a statute has occupied the field formerly occupied by the prerogative, the Crown must comply with the statute."[84] A displaced prerogative cannot be revived by repeal of the statute.

Assuming that Lord Denning (among others) accurately described the common law prerogative in relation to aliens, the next question is – so what? Once displaced by successive immigration statutes, the

---

83 P.W. Hogg, P.J. Monahan, and W.K. Wright, *Liability of the Crown*, 4th edn (Toronto, Carswell, 2011) 19, citing A.V. Dicey, *The Law of the Constitution*, 10th edn (London, Macmillan, 1959).

84 Ibid at 21.

prerogative has no enduring legal force. So what is it doing in *Chiarelli*? The common law principle is not merely a source of context in *Chiarelli*, it is the only source of context for thinking about fundamental justice in relation to non-citizens under immigration law.

To press the point further, the common law contains other resources that are apposite to contemporary immigration law. For example, *domicile* is a common law concept that links an individual to a jurisdiction through a combination of residence and the subjective intention of the individual to make that place the centre of his or her existence. It is not formally bestowed by the state in the form of permanent resident status. Rather, it is legal recognition of the de facto functional and intentional attachment by the individual to the jurisdiction. The common law declares domicile to come into existence when the "facts on the ground" support it, and state recognition is neither an element nor prerequisite of domicile.

Importantly, for most of the twentieth century, immigrants who were domiciled in Canada for at least five years were virtually non-deportable, even though they were not naturalized as British subjects of Canada or (after 1947) as Canadian citizens.[85] The lesson is that the common law of domicile was incorporated into immigration law and tacitly recognized the sociological "fact of attachment"[86] between individual and jurisdiction that comes into existence independently of status; up until the 1976 Immigration Act, Canadian immigration law regarded those with domicile as entitled to greater protection from removal than those immigrants or even naturalized Canadians who had either not acquired or had relinquished Canadian domicile.[87]

I am sceptical that the statement that "non-citizens have no unqualified right to enter and remain" is really there to provide context for the interpretation of s. 7. Were that its function, it should have been accompanied by other contextually relevant features of the common

85 The criminal grounds for deportation of domiciled immigrants fluctuated over the years; the law that the Immigration Act, 1976, above n 10, replaced restricted deportation to subversion, disloyalty, and certain narcotics offences (s 19). Non-domiciled immigrants were deportable for any offence for which the actual sentence was six months.

86 *Nottebohm Case (Liechtenstein v Guatemala)* [1955] ICJ Rep 4 at 23.

87 See eg *R v Hall* (1983) 3 DLR (4th) 135; 44 OR (2d) 45 (domiciled non-citizen immune from deportation for crime committed before Immigration Act, 1976, but deportable as permanent resident for same offence committed after Immigration Act in force).

law, such as domicile. More importantly, it would have been followed by an acknowledgment that qualifications on the non-citizen's right to enter and remain are still subject to the Charter. That non-citizens, and only non-citizens, can be deported does not address whether the actual laws governing deportation violate life, liberty, or security of the person or whether, if they do, they comport with fundamental justice. After all, even the exercise of an actual prerogative power is reviewable under the Charter.[88]

Evidently, the common law principle is doing important normative work: that non-citizens do not enjoy an unqualified right to enter and remain is asserted as a free-standing normative claim that pre-empts the s. 7 enquiry first (in *Chiarelli*) in respect of fundamental justice and subsequently (in *Medovarski)* in relation to the s. 7 right. Upon mere declaration, it obviates Charter accountability for direct effects caused by the state's exercise of the deportation power.[89]

The problem with this sequence of reasoning is that the common law is supposed to be subject to the Charter, not vice versa. To the extent that a common law principle may inform interpretation of the Charter, it is not by dint of its mere existence, but rather because it embodies or expresses deeper principles and values animating the Charter. In *Re BC Motor Vehicle Act*, Lamer J cautioned that contenders for s. 7 principles of fundamental justice must be "recognized as elements of a system for the administration of justice which is founded upon a belief in the human dignity and worth of the human person ... and on the rule of law."[90] In *R v Oakes*, Dickson CJ summarized the values underpinning the Charter as "respect for the inherent dignity of the human person, commitment to social justice and equality, accommodation of a wide variety of beliefs, respect for cultural and group identity, and faith in social and political institutions which enhance the participation of individuals and groups in society."[91] The pertinence of the common law to the project of rights interpretation must depend on the extent to which a given norm furthers the values underlying the Charter.

88 See eg *Operation Dismantle v The Queen* [1985] 1 SCR 441, [1985] SCJ no 22; *Canada (Prime Minister) v Khadr* 2010 SCC 3.

89 The qualification *direct* acknowledges that at least one indirect consequence (torture) engages s 7; it remains unclear whether persecution does.

90 [1985] 2 SCR 486 at para 30, [1985] SCJ no 73.

91 [1986] 1 SCR 103 at para 64, [1986] SCJ no 7.

While the common law is a valuable source of guidance in interpreting the Charter, it is important not to romanticize the common law in its entirety. As the former chief justice notes in her keynote address delivered at the "Supreme Courts and the Common Law" international symposium, women were not persons under the common law when the Person's Case was litigated, but the Judicial Committee of the Privy Council did not regard that as definitive for purposes of constitutional interpretation.[92]

Clearly, not all common law principles qualify according to that metric. Perhaps that explains why Wilson J disqualified the right/privilege distinction as an unacceptable tool for Charter interpretation. (As noted earlier, judicial review seems to have moved beyond relying on the formal character of the interest at stake or the formal status of the individual towards a focus on the nature or intensity of the harm experienced by that individual.) Where the Court asserts with no elaboration that the mere existence of a common law principle suffices to pre-empt enquiry into whether, for example, the harm of deracination breaches security of the person, the Court subverts the Charter's supremacy from within. It is a self-inflicted wound.

The Crown prerogative over immigration was literally extinguished over a century ago, with the advent of successive immigration statutes, but maybe it has been undead all along. It sporadically resurrects itself in Supreme Court of Canada jurisprudence. Recall that *Chiarelli* quotes with approval the following passage from the Court's 1976 judgment in *Prata*:

> The effect of s. 21 is to reserve to the Crown, notwithstanding the powers conferred upon the Board by the Act, the right, similar to the prerogative right which existed at common law, to determine that the continued presence in Canada of an alien, subject to a deportation order, would not be conducive to the public good.[93]

So despite the rule that statute displaces prerogative, the prerogative seems to haunt us, lurking in the interstitial spaces of immigration law.

Consider as well the *Suresh* exception. The Court had before it a discretion akin to s. 21 in *Prata*. Section 53(1)(b) of the Immigration Act

92 B. McLachlin, ch 1 in this volume.

93 *Prata*, above n 24 at 381, cited in *Chiarelli*, above n 2 at 740.

permitted the *refoulement* of a refugee where the minister was "of the opinion that the person constitutes a danger to the security of Canada."[94] Suresh was a refugee found inadmissible on national security grounds. He faced a substantial risk of torture if deported to Sri Lanka. Confronted with the question of whether deportation to torture violates s. 7 of the Charter, the Court could have said yes or no. Instead, it said "yes, unless there are exceptional circumstances."[95]

Elsewhere, I have speculated on what exceptional circumstances the Court could possibly have contemplated as justifying a ministerial decision to deport someone to face a substantial risk of torture.[96] The classic excuse for torture, the "ticking bomb" scenario, clearly has no relevance to a decision to expel a non-citizen. If evidence showed that the person was extremely dangerous, the expansive powers of Canadian anti-terrorism law could confine him. My powers of imagination failed to conjure up any scenario where the benefits to national security of deporting a person exceeded the harm of torturing that person, no matter how heinous the individual. Indeed, the more demonstrably heinous the individual, the more certain the availability of alternative means of containment – including criminal prosecution.

I eventually arrived at the opinion that the *Suresh* exception does not exist because the Court seriously contemplated a hypothetical case where deportation to torture could be justified according to any rational calculus. Rather, I suspect that the Court simply could not bring itself to impose an absolute judicial limit on the executive's power to deport, no matter the gravity of the rights violation, even if it meant flouting international law, and despite precedents from the European Court of Human Rights and elsewhere.[97]

One way of depicting this apparent judicial diffidence is as follows: The Supreme Court sits at the apex of the judicial hierarchy, yet it subordinates its authority to a power that presents itself as the pinnacle of sovereignty – namely, the absolute power to admit or exclude

94 RSC 1985, c I-2.

95 *Suresh*, above n 55 at para 78.

96 A. Macklin, "Still Stuck at the Border" in C. Forcese and. F Crépeau (eds), *Terrorism, Law & Democracy: 10 Years after 9/11* (Ottawa, Canadian Institute for the Administration of Justice, 2012) 261 at 274–85.

97 See eg *Chahal v United Kingdom* (1996) 25 EHRR 33; *Saadi v Italy* (2008) 47 EHRR 17; *Attorney General v Zaoui* [2005] NZSC 38.

non-citizens. And the juridical technique that accomplishes this move mimics a common law prerogative power. For what the Court does with its *Suresh* exception is fabricate and deliver to the executive a new prerogative, the power to deport a non-citizen to torture in exceptional circumstances.

This authority resembles a prerogative more than a type of ordinary discretion in two respects. First, it is a judicial creation in the tradition of the common law's authority to identify and delimit the prerogative. It is not a statutory discretion legislated by Parliament. Second, it is impervious to the discipline of legality. No technique of judicial review, not even under the rubric of deference, could furnish a principled account of a decision to deport to torture as a "reasonable" (much less "correct") rights violation.[98] A conventional narrative of common law constitutionalism recites how judges have used rights-regarding common law principles as interpretive resources to thwart statutory incursions on individual liberty.[99] The twist here is that the common law is being creatively deployed to deflect constitutional rights protection.

This new pseudo-prerogative also has the pernicious knock-on effect of propagating further distortions of legality upstream in the process: In *Belmarsh*, the UK House of Lords ruled, *inter alia*, that the impossibility of deportation to torture discredited the government's argument that confinement of non-citizens deemed security threats did not constitute indefinite detention. Detention in the service of facilitating deportation lost its rationale if detention was not foreseeably practicable, and it became indefinite and arbitrary. In *Charkaoui*, the Court found that the hypothetical possibility of lawful deportation to torture meant that detention of persons named in security certificates was not detached from the ultimate purpose of deportation. So the Canadian Supreme Court tolerates a species of indefinite detention that the UK court does not because the former clings to the possibility that the detention may be a prelude to a lawful deportation to torture, whereas the UK court has foreclosed that possibility.[100]

98 Macklin, "Still Stuck at the Border," above n 95.

99 See generally Varuhas, ch 8 in this volume; and Zhou, ch 9.

100 See R. Thwaites, "Discriminating against Non-Citizens under the *Charter*: *Charkaoui* and Section 15" (2009) 34 *Queen's Law Journal* 669.

This judicial inability to "just say no" to the executive's will to expel tracks extradition jurisprudence.[101] In the 1991 *Ng* and *Kindler* judgments,[102] the Court ruled that the Charter did not require the Canadian government to request assurances from the United States that extradited individuals would be spared the death penalty. In *Chiarelli*, Sopinka J quotes from *Kindler* in support of the "right and duty of the state to keep out and expel aliens from this country if it considers it advisable to do so."[103] A decade later, the Supreme Court of Canada reversed itself in *Burns and Rafay*.[104] Henceforth, the Canadian government was "constitutionally required in all but exceptional cases" to seek assurances that the extradited person would not be subject to the death penalty.[105] Here again, the Court narrows but does not eliminate the range of executive discretion. As with torture, one struggles to conjure up a scenario that would justify a refusal to request assurances.[106] One surmises that, as with torture, the Court gambled on never being called on to judicially review the unreasonableness of the undecidable.

Conclusion

I conclude with a claim I am not making. I do not contend, *contra* the common law principle, that non-citizens do have an unqualified right to enter or remain. In fact, I do not know of a single constitutional challenge to any facet of immigration law predicated on that claim. The present critique is relatively modest and directed at expulsion. It shows how and why the common law principle is the wrong starting point within a framework of constitutional rights to evaluate the legality of

---

101 See C. Dauvergne, "How the *Charter* Has Failed Non-citizens in Canada: Reviewing Thirty Years of Supreme Court of Canada Jurisprudence" (2013) 58:3 *McGill Law Journal* 663. In her survey of thirty years of Supreme Court jurisprudence on the Charter and non-citizens, Dauvergne makes the more general observation that the Court prefers to create a "'constitutionalized' space for discretionary decision-making, rather than make a hard rights-based response" (at 722).

102 *Kindler v Canada (Minister of Justice)* [1991] 2 SCR 779, [1991] SCJ no 63 [*Kindler*]; *Reference re Ng Extradition (Canada)* [1991] 2 SCR 858, [1991] SCJ no 64.

103 *Kindler*, *above* note 101 at 834, cited in *Chiarelli*, above n 2 at 733.

104 *United States v Burns* 2001 SCC 7 [*Burns and Rafay*].

105 Ibid at para 8.

106 It is noteworthy that the Court in *Burns and Rafay*, above n 104, did not rely on the appellant's Canadian citizenship as a distinguishing factor. The ruling applies equally to citizens and non-citizens.

deportation. Simply put, the proper question from a rights perspective is not whether a non-citizen has an unqualified right to remain in Canada, but whether deportation in the particular legislative and factual circumstances of the individual violates a constitutional right. My focus is on s. 7, although one might also raise s. 12 or even s. 2(d) (freedom of association) as contenders. The reasons why a state might legitimately deport a non-citizen already within its borders belong in the realm of justifications for state action, in the same way as other justifications for state coercion that rise to the level of infringing life, liberty, or security of the person, or cruel and unusual treatment.

I suspect that the main impediment to recognizing the rights of non-citizens in the context of deportation is the impulse to suppress the flagrantly coercive mechanics of deportation. Seizing an individual and forcibly expelling him or her epitomizes state interference with liberty. But, realistically, no court will open up every act of deportation to s. 7 scrutiny because it is regarded as intrinsic to border control. Given that, the most generous reading of the dictum in *Medovarski* would be that the liberty-infringing coercion that accompanies every act of deportation does not *in itself* violate s. 7 (or is justified under s. 1); this does not, however, predetermine whether the effects of deportation (deracination or persecution) violate s. 7, depending on the evidence.

Where deportation also breaches life or security of the person (or another Charter right), as measured against the usual metrics of impact on a vital interest of an individual, one expects the countervailing state interest to be tested against the severity of the violation. This is how Charter adjudication normally works. If deracination or persecution were cognizable s. 7 infringements, then considerations of fair procedures, arbitrariness, overbreadth, and gross disproportionality would enter the calculus as principles of fundamental justice potentially constraining deportation.[107] But this normal process is derailed by the assertion that the state's power to deport precludes enquiry into whether the state violated the right in the first place. From *Chiarelli* to *Suresh* to *Medovarski*, the Charter is subordinated to what is, on its face, an extinguished common law prerogative.

The problem does not lie with reliance on the common law as a source of constitutional interpretation, but rather with the absence of

107 See *Carter* and *Bedford*, above n 43; *Canadian Doctors for Refugee Care v Canada (Attorney General)*, 2014 FC 651.

a critical apparatus for discerning whether the common law principle recruited to the task is normatively congruent with the values animating a twenty-first century bill of rights. And even if it is, one must also determine whether it pertains to identifying a rights infringement, a principle of fundamental justice, or a justification for limiting a right. Stipulating criteria and methodology for that classification exercise exceeds the remit of this chapter. But this much seems clear: a common law principle that confers state power is ill suited to the task of defining the content of a right whose purpose is, *inter alia,* to restrain the exercise of state power. The question of whether the state has infringed the constitutional right of a legal subject cannot be answered by invoking the common law's assertion of unrestrained state power over the legal subject.

8 Administrative Law and Rights in the UK House of Lords and Supreme Court

JASON N.E. VARUHAS*

Introduction

Over the last three years, the UK Supreme Court has undertaken renewed efforts to forge a jurisprudence of rights within the common law of judicial review. Much has been written of these developments from a contemporary perspective, with a great deal of commentary dedicated to analysing individual cases. The contribution of this chapter is to place these developments in the context of the development of the modern system of judicial review and to offer a "long view" of the role that the House of Lords and Supreme Court have attributed to *rights* within administrative law doctrine. The chapter charts the place of rights within administrative law over four decades, from 1977 to 2017.

The chapter identifies and analyses four episodes in the interrelationship between administrative law and ideas of rights within the House of Lords and Supreme Court. First, from the late 1970s and through

* My thanks to Laureate Professor Emeritus Cheryl Saunders and Professor Rick Rawlings, as well as the book reviewers, for very helpful comments. Earlier versions of this chapter were presented at the international symposium "Supreme Courts and the Common Law" at the University of Montreal, 27 May 2016, and at the Constitutional Theory Scholars' Workshop at Melbourne Law School on 20 July 2017. I am grateful to the participants at both events for stimulating discussions. Aspects of this chapter were also presented at a "Judges and the Academy" seminar on the principle of legality, held on 13 April 2018 and hosted by the Supreme Court of Victoria. I wish to thank the participants for a valuable discussion and, in particular, Justice Chris Maxwell, President of the Victoria Court of Appeal, and my fellow panellists, Justice John Basten, Justice Debbie Mortimer, and Professor Rick Rawlings. The usual disclaimer applies.

the 1980s, the House of Lords actively sought to forge an integrated, unified, and coherent field of public law and, in doing so, constructed the basic superstructure of contemporary judicial review. This new system was based in a public interest conception of public law, which held that public law's principal function was to ensure the proper exercise of public power in the public interest. The corollary of this focus on the protection of the public interest was that the courts marginalized the role of rights within judicial review.

Second, through the 1990s, the House of Lords came under pressure, due to the United Kingdom's commitments under the European Convention on Human Rights (Convention), to give greater recognition and protection to basic rights within administrative law doctrine. The House of Lords duly took a number of steps to afford basic interests greater protection through the common law of review, albeit the courts were constrained in how far they could develop the common law by the public interest framework that had only recently been erected.

Third, the 2000s saw the entry into force of the Human Rights Act 1998 (HRA), which created a field of law specifically constituted to afford strong protection to basic rights and which bestowed English courts with the tools to ensure compliance with Convention obligations. With the emergence of this new field, the pressure that had built up during the 1990s to develop the common law of review along rights-based lines fell away. With this pressure release, the common law continued to develop broadly in line with the public interest framework put in place during the 1980s.

Fourth, from around 2014 onward, the new Supreme Court has shown renewed interest in developing a rights jurisprudence at common law and "synthesizing" the common law of review and the law under the HRA, albeit there are divisions among the justices as to how precisely the two fields ought to interrelate. The result has been that the common law of review, and human rights law, have been pushed into a state of flux. The new jurisprudence is characterized by a core tension. On the one hand, the Justices have been moved to introduce a new discourse of rights into common law review by extra-legal drivers, including Brexit and government threats to repeal the HRA. On the other hand, responding to these "external" concerns is liable to undermine the "internal" coherence of the common law of review.

Thus, in line with this book's subject, this chapter tells a story of an apex court steering a significant field of common law doctrine over time, with a view to contextualizing and analysing contemporary trends. In doing so, the chapter illustrates the different forces that operate to shape an apex court's development of the common law. These drivers range from more orthodox legal phenomena, such as concerns for coherence and statutory interventions, to external drivers beyond law, such as judicial pride in the common law, a new Supreme Court's concern to establish itself in the constitutional order, domestic politics, international pressures, individual judicial ideologies, and concerns for the courts' perceived legitimacy.

At times, as in the 1970s and 1980s, external and internal drivers may pull in broadly similar directions. On the other hand, in other time periods, such as the present, difficulties arise where the Supreme Court seeks to respond to external drivers, but in doing so risks disruption of the law's internal coherence. Importantly, the range of drivers, their variation over time, and their unpredictability tell against any neat, linear narrative of legal change or development. So too does the common law method, its case-by-case nature meaning that legal development is liable to ebb and flow. It is also important to emphasize that many of the drivers of legal change are quintessentially local and jurisdiction-specific. In turn, this suggests that one should be highly sceptical of any teleological narrative of a single legal trend sweeping common law jurisdictions or of "global" models of rights or administrative law. Even if a particular idea such as *rights* or *proportionality* increasingly arises across jurisdictions, a closer look is likely to reveal significant complexity in given systems and stark contrasts among jurisdictions. In this regard, it is a helpful discipline to set legal developments in their local context and, therefore, their historical context.

The Emergence of a New Orthodoxy (Late 1970s and 1980s)

With the rise of the modern administrative state in the post–Second World War era, the 1950s and 1960s witnessed a series of legal developments that established foundational principles of what would become the modern field of administrative law. These developments included landmark cases such as *Ridge* on natural justice,[1] *Anisminic* on error of law,[2] and *Padfield* on improper purposes.[3] From the 1970s and

1 *Ridge v Baldwin* [1964] AC 40.

2 *Anisminic Ltd v Foreign Compensation Commission* [1969] 2 AC 147.

3 *Padfield v Minister of Agriculture, Fisheries and Food* [1968] AC 997.

through the 1980s, the higher judiciary undertook the next step in the development of modern English administrative law, and this is where our narrative begins. This step was to forge emergent rules and principles into an integrated, unified, and coherent *system of public law*.[4] In doing so, the courts, in this time period, fashioned the superstructure of modern judicial review, core aspects of this basic framework continuing to characterize common law review to this day.

This judicial project, in turn, had significant ramifications for the place of rights in English administrative law. To develop an integrated, comprehensive public law system, the courts premised legal development on a unifying conceptual framework. This framework was one focused on the performance of public duties and preservation of the public interest rather than personal rights and individual interests. The protection of rights was principally a task for private law, and public law was developed in contradistinction to rights-based fields such as tort. To the extent that English law recognized ideas of fundamental or constitutional rights, these were associated with rights in tort, which protected interests such as liberty, property, and physical integrity – *and were the province of private law*.[5] Thus, a core feature of the emergence of the contemporary English system of public law was the marginalization of the idea of individual rights.

The opportunity to forge this new public law system was presented by reforms in 1977 (taking effect in 1978), which introduced a new procedure, the application for judicial review.[6] This procedure provided a single route for claiming *certiorari*, prohibition, and *mandamus*. Previously, each remedy had been associated with distinct procedures and substantive law. This connection among remedy, procedure, and substantive law militated against a unified system of public law norms. Further telling against the recognition of a distinct field of administrative or public law had been the continued influence of Dicey's opposition

4 See generally J.N.E. Varuhas, "The Public Interest Conception of Public Law: Its Procedural Origins and Substantive Implications" in J. Bell, M. Elliott, J.N.E. Varuhas, and P. Murray (eds), *Public Law Adjudication in Common Law Systems: Process and Substance* (Oxford, Hart Publishing, 2016).

5 See eg *Morris v Beardmore* [1981] AC 446.

6 Rules of the Supreme Court (Amendment no 3) (SI 1977/1955), r 5, followed later by: Rules of the Supreme Court (Amendment no 4) (SI 1980/2000), rr 2–7; Supreme Court Act 1981, ss 29–31; see now Civil Procedure Rules (SI 1998/3132), pt 54; Senior Courts Act 1981, ss 29–31A.

to a discrete body of public law rules, especially within the profession;[7] as such, administrative law suffered "arrested development."[8] As late as 1964 Lord Reid observed, "We do not have a developed system of administrative law."[9] However, the procedural reforms, by bringing claims for the prerogative remedies under one roof, provided an opportunity for the generalization of principles across different remedies. At the same time, a dedicated procedural forum for review challenges, separate from private law claims, offered a natural break from an older order and an opportunity for the courts to experiment with the idea of a field of public law both procedurally and substantively distinct from private law.

These opportunities were taken. As Wade observed in 1968, "a special administrative jurisdiction would be likely to produce a livelier recognition of the subject as such and therefore greater consistency."[10] The Law Lords, led by Lord Diplock, who clearly viewed the development of a recognized field of administrative law as a personal mission,[11] set about distilling a body of general principles and thus fostering coherence and consistency. In doing so, the law lords were following the lead of academics such as De Smith and Wade, who had sought to demonstrate that decisions on licensing, tax, public housing, etc. were not a wilderness of single instances, but could be shown to make up a discrete field of administrative law.[12]

---

7 See eg Lord Diplock, "Administrative Law: Judicial Review Reviewed" (1974) 33 *Cambridge Law Journal* 233 at 234–6; H.W.R. Wade, "Crossroads in Administrative Law" [1968] *Current Legal Problems* 75 at 79, 84ff; J.D.B. Mitchell, "The Causes and Effects of the Absence of a System of Public Law in the United Kingdom" [1965] *Public Law* 95; S.A. De Smith, *The Lawyers and the Constitution* (London, G. Bell and Sons, 1960) 22–3; Lord Hewart, *The New Despotism* (London, Ernest Benn, 1929).

8 De Smith, above n 7 at 17.

9 *Ridge*, above n 1 at 72.

10 Wade, above n 7 at 89. See also De Smith, above n 7 at 24–5.

11 See eg Diplock, above n 7; and see Lord Diplock's statement in *R v IRC, ex parte National Federation of Self-Employed and Small Businesses Ltd* [1982] AC 617 at 641 that he regarded the progress made "towards a comprehensive system of administrative law" "as having been the greatest achievement of the English courts in my judicial lifetime."

12 Diplock, above n 7 at 234–6, recognizing the contribution of academic lawyers; and see Wade, above n 7 ("Virtually all the constructive work which has been done on the subject, as a subject, has been done in the universities" (at 85)) and the two pioneering doctrinal works on administrative law: S.A. De Smith, *Judicial Review of Administrative Action* (London, Stevens and Sons, 1959); and

The most iconic example of this move towards systemization and generalization was Lord Diplock's distillation of three general grounds of review.[13] The prospect of such generalized principles stood in contrast with the position prior, when "the subject [of administrative law] could barely be said to exist, except as a raw mass of cases"[14] spread across disparate procedures. Importantly, there was an opportunity not only to systemize principles but also to base them in a *common set of normative concerns* and, thus, to forge an integrated *field* or *system* of public law.

Thus, it is in the time period following the procedural reforms that the senior judiciary, led by Lord Diplock, "discovered" the normative distinction between public and private law. This was a radical change in a system in which the Diceyan equality principle was an organizing idea. This new public law was associated with the common law of judicial review, which formed the basis of the vast majority of claims streamed through the new procedure. Within this dichotomy, private law was individual-regarding and concerned with personal rights. In contrast, public law was public-regarding. Its concern was to ensure that public power was exercised properly, according to basic ideas of good decision-practice, and for the public interests set by Parliament. Resting legal development on this idea of public law, therefore, led to common law review being decoupled from a concern for rights and individual protection more generally. Public law was not concerned with remedying private wrongs – breach of individual rights – but rather public wrongs: breach of duties owed by authorities to the public as a collective.[15] Thus, when a court intervenes on judicial review, it

---

H.W.R. Wade, *Administrative Law* (Oxford, Clarendon Press, 1961). And see the earlier important contributions by scholars such as Robson and Jennings pushing for recognition of a field of administrative law: eg W.A. Robson, *Justice and Administrative Law*, 3rd edn (London, Stevens, 1951); and W.I. Jennings, "Courts and Administrative Law: The Experience of English Housing Law" (1936) 49 *Harvard Law Review* 426.

13 *Council of Civil Service Unions v Minister for the Civil Service* [1985] AC 374 at 410–1.

14 P. Birks, *An Introduction to the Law of Restitution* (Oxford, Clarendon Press, 1985) 2–3 (holding out the hope that the incredible progress made towards recognition of the distinct field of administrative law within a short time period was a model of legal development that the law of restitution could follow).

15 H. Woolf, "Public Law–Private Law: Why the Divide? A Personal View" [1986] *Public Law* 220 at 221.

does not do so on behalf of an individual, but "on behalf of the public"[16] or "in defence of the citizenry."[17]

The public interest view unmistakably reflects the distinction from Roman law between *jus publicum*, concerned with the organization of the state, and *jus privatum*, concerned with the well-being of individuals.[18] Indeed, Lord Diplock, in *Hoffmann La Roche*, explicitly drew on this distinction, equating *jus privatum* with "proprietary or contractual rights" and *jus publicum* with protection against harm "to the public or some section of it."[19] This division also reflects the organization of modern civilian systems, of which Lord Diplock had familiarity. Not long ago had continental systems and *droit administratif* been derided; administrative law was "an exotic brand of un-English anti-law."[20] But now the judges were concerned to demonstrate that the new English "Droit Public"[21] was in no way inferior to other systems.[22] This concern for the standing of the common law in comparison to other systems is, as we shall see, a recurring theme. Practically, framing the goals of common law review as being concerned with the public interest may have been attractive because it attributes to that field a distinctive and valuable function not performed by other major fields. The decoupling of public law from ideas of rights was also viewed as a progressive one in that it enabled courts to police administrative unlawfulness, even where no specific individual's rights were prejudiced; a focus on rights protection would constrain the development and effectiveness of the new public law system.[23]

One may also understand judicial attraction to the public interest conception – as opposed to individualistic conceptions – given wider political trends.[24] At a time when public services were, pursuant to

16 *R v Panel on Take-Overs and Mergers, ex parte Guinness Plc* [1990] 1 QB 146 at 193.

17 *R v Panel on Take-Overs and Mergers, ex parte Datafin Plc* [1987] 1 QB 815 at 839.

18 Eg Justinian's Institutes 1.1.4.

19 *F Hoffmann La Roche & Co AG v Secretary of State for Trade and Industry* [1975] AC 295 at 363–4.

20 De Smith, above n 7 at 23.

21 Lord Woolf, "Droit Public – English Style" [1995] *Public Law* 57.

22 See eg Diplock, above n 7 at 241–4; see also Wade, above n 7; De Smith, above n 7 at 17–18; Mitchell, above n 7; C.J. Hamson, *Executive Discretion and Judicial Control: An Aspect of the French Conseil d'Etat* (London, Stevens and Sons, 1954).

23 In particular see the discussion of standing below.

24 See eg P. McAuslan, "Public Law and Public Choice" (1988) 51 *Modern Law Review* 681. More generally a number of factors pushed the courts, whether they welcomed

Prime Minister Thatcher's policies, being privatized and otherwise being inculcated with neo-liberal economic ideas premised on an ideology of self-interest and efficiency, it seems more than coincidental that public law was oriented towards ensuring that powers were exercised for the public good.[25] On the public interest view, the skewing of public power for special individual or corporate interests was one of the very things that public law was concerned to prevent.

All the chief struts of the doctrinal superstructure of the new system of public law were built upon this public interest conception of public law. Let us consider a few, each of which reinforces that administrative law's focus was upon the public interest, not individual rights.

Standing

In the *Fleet Street Casuals* case, Lords Diplock and Scarman articulated what would emerge as the modern approach to standing within judicial review.[26] Whereas, in the pre-reform era, an applicant for a prerogative remedy may have been required to demonstrate that administrative action directly affected his or her private individual rights, or caused personal prejudice, Lords Diplock and Scarman held that an individual or group not personally affected by administrative action could, in principle, launch review proceedings if they demonstrated *prima facie* unlawfulness. Whereas a rights-based approach was appropriate for private law, to so limit access to remedies in public law would be to

---

it or not, into the position of a core accountability mechanism, including an increasingly powerful government lurching ever further to the right, led by a Prime Minister who was operating on a presidential model of government, an Opposition moving further to the left and increasingly marginalized, and a Parliament viewed as ineffective in holding government to account: R. Stevens, *The English Judges* (Oxford, Hart Publishing, 2002) ch 4.

25 This concern was particularly evident in judicial efforts to expand the scope of review to institutions formally outside government, but which were intended to operate in the public interest, in an effort to prevent government escaping public law regulation by outsourcing public functions: *Datafin*, above n 17 at 821F. We also see this concern to plug potential gaps in the coverage of the new public law in the landmark decision in *CCSU*, above n 13, in which the House of Lords held that prerogative powers were in principle reviewable. Of course, another perspective is that the courts were simply reacting defensively to maintain their jurisdiction.

26 *IRC*, above n 11.

rob a remedy such as *mandamus* of "its public law character"; it would become "no more than a remedy for a private wrong."[27] For Lord Scarman, the duties of fairness owed by public entities such as the Revenue were public duties, owed to taxpayers as a collectivity, breach of which constituted a public wrong.[28] It followed that any individual, as a member of the public, who could show a *prima facie* case of public wrongdoing ought to be accorded standing. Similarly, underpinning Lord Diplock's speech is a view that what is at stake in public law is something that we all have a legitimate interest in: the proper exercise of public power in the pursuit of public goals. Narrow standing rules, which limited claims to cases of personal prejudice, would prevent the courts from ensuring the proper performance of public duties – for example, where there was serious illegality, but no one was especially affected. This would leave a "grave lacuna in our system of public law."[29]

While the bases of standing expanded radically, prejudice to private law rights[30] did remain *one* basis for grant of standing and one trigger for public law duties to arise – specifically, procedural fairness. However, in the context of fairness, it was established that something less than a right, such as a legitimate expectation or mere interest, could suffice as a trigger for procedural fairness;[31] in turn, these developments enlarged the scope of public law duties and – along with the recognition of public interest standing – diminished the role of rights. The continued, diminished role of rights in decisions over standing was a remnant of the older law governing the writs, and it was increasingly a conceptual outlier, given the new public interest ethos of public law. Beyond standing, rights had an even more marginal role.

Substantive Law

Turning to substantive law, the judicial starting point on review was non-intervention. Judicial review was a long-stop, secondary, and

27 Ibid at 653.
28 Ibid at 647–55.
29 Ibid at 644.
30 *CCSU*, above n 13 at 408.
31 *Attorney-General of Hong Kong v Ng Yuen Shiu* [1983] 2 AC 629; ibid at 408–9; *McInnes v Onslow-Fane* [1978] 1 WLR 1520; J.N.E. Varuhas, "In Search of a Doctrine: Mapping the Law of Legitimate Expectations" in M. Groves and G. Weeks (eds), *Legitimate Expectations in the Common Law World* (Oxford, Hart Publishing, 2017) 34–40.

supervisory jurisdiction. Administrative action was presumed lawful, and the applicant had to prove otherwise.[32] The reasons for this approach are explicable within a public interest conception. One central goal of review was to ensure that public power was exercised genuinely for public purposes. But what action best serves the common good is principally for repositories of public power. Another central goal was to ensure that administrators adhered to basic expectations of good administrative practice in exercise of their powers, but professional administrators know much more about administration than courts. Furthermore, the courts would risk impeding the proper exercise of power and fulfilment of public goals, the very ends public law served, if they intervened too readily. Thus, the courts adopted a posture of restraint, intervening only where a decision maker had clearly gone off track, deviating from the mandate set by Parliament or very basic principles of good administration. The "public law jurisdiction of the courts [being] supervisory and not appellate in character," the courts would consider intervention only if "something has gone wrong of a nature and extent which might call for the exercise of the judicial review jurisdiction."[33]

The adoption of such an approach, and at times a deferential approach that was extreme even within a supervisory jurisdiction,[34] is also explicable by reference to the wider context. The new public law system was in its formative stages, and an overly aggressive approach could jeopardize its legitimacy and result in the curtailment of judicial power, thereby undermining the public law project.[35] Further, ordinary politics was fractious: the Government was moving ever further to the right, the Opposition ever further to the left, and there were significant tensions between central and local governments. With many high-profile

32 *Hoffmann*, above n 19 at 366; *R v Lancashire County Council, ex parte Huddleston* [1986] 2 All ER 941 at 945.

33 *R v Civil Service Board of Appeal, ex parte Cunningham* [1992] ICR 816 at 823.

34 See eg *R v Hillingdon London Borough Council, ex parte Puhlhofer* [1986] AC 484, not coincidentally concerning the highly contentious issue of public housing (and see the subsequent loosening of approach in *Poshteh v Royal Borough of Kensington and Chelsea* [2017] UKSC 36). On the Law Lords' deferential approach during this era more generally see D. Feldman, "Public Law Values in the House of Lords" (1990) 106 *Law Quarterly Review* 246, explaining the approach as based in a political theory of democratic elitism.

35 A concern explicitly voiced by Lord Scarman in *Duport Steels Ltd v Sirs* [1980] 1 WLR 142 at 169.

political disputes[36] ending up in review litigation, the courts were concerned to ensure that they did not jeopardize their perceived independence by commenting on the substance of policies or decisions or intervening too readily.[37] As will be returned to below, this supervisory approach contrasts with the approach to private law adjudication, in which courts exercise a primary power of decision.

The grounds of review and the way they developed through the late 1970s and 1980s thus reflected two basic concerns: (1) to ensure that primary decision makers stayed "on track," genuinely pursuing public goals; and (2) to uphold basic principles of good administration. Rights and individual interests found reflection in doctrine only to the extent that they formed an aspect of, and were consonant with, the two principal goals.[38]

Turning to (1), what course best serves the common good is for the delegate upon whom Parliament has conferred the power. It is not, therefore, for courts to review administrative decisions by asking what action they consider best serves the common good and then compare this to the actual decision. Rather, the courts rule out certain actions that manifestly do not serve the common good or represent a clear deviation from that course. Within these parameters, the decision is for the decision maker. This goal of keeping decision makers from going off track was capable of rationalizing central grounds of review. The improper purposes doctrine requires administrators not to act other than for statutory purposes. The relevant considerations doctrine requires decision makers to exclude extraneous considerations. To fetter one's power is potentially to rule out action that may best serve the public interest. To act inconsistently with statute is to deviate from one's mandate. To act with bias is to act other than for the common good.

---

36 It was in the context of clashes between central and local governments over financial policy that the courts fashioned their most deferential approach to substantive review: *R v Secretary of State for the Environment, ex parte Nottinghamshire CC* [1986] AC 240.

37 See the strong statements counselling adherence to the separation of powers lest judicial independence be put at risk in *Duport Steels*, above n 35 at 157, 168–9, 171–2.

38 See eg *R v Monopolies and Mergers Commission, ex parte Argyll* [1986] 1 WLR 763 at 774 ("Good public administration requires a proper consideration of the legitimate interests of individual citizens, however rich and powerful they may be and whether they are natural or Juridical persons. But in judging the relevance of an interest, however legitimate, regard has to be had to the purpose of the administrative process concerned").

Rather than individual protection being the focus of review, the special interests of individuals were often seen as a potentially corrupting force: there should be "no favourites."[39] As Lord Diplock explained of the Law Society and its Council, "In exercising its statutory functions the duty of the Council is to act in what it believes to be the best interests of that section of the public [that may be in need of legal advice, assistance or representation], even in the event ... that those public interests should conflict with the special interests of members of the Society or of members of the solicitors' profession as a whole."[40]

Given the starting point that calculations as to the public interest were for the primary decision maker, there was exceptionally limited scope for courts to intervene on the basis of the quality of the administrator's decision.[41] Furthermore, the courts lacked any objective standard by which they could judge one view of what the public interest required better than another: decisions "as to the public interest are not such as courts are fitted or equipped to make."[42] Thus, under the *Wednesbury* standard courts could intervene only on the basis of the substance of the decision where the decision was manifestly absurd.[43] A manifestly absurd outcome is one that no reasonable person could consider a genuine exercise of power for the common good. Given this high threshold, *Wednesbury* was a marginal ground, operating as a safety net for the rare bad case not caught by other grounds.

As Woolf observed during this time period, this judicial approach to substantive legal questions differed from that within private law proceedings, which are based in individual private rights.[44] For example, in negligence, the courts judge the reasonableness simpliciter of a defendant's actions; courts are not limited to enquiring into whether the defendant's actions were perverse. The principal reason why the courts determine questions of reasonableness simpliciter for themselves in tort but not on review is that judicial review

39 *IRC*, above n 11 at 651.

40 *Swain v Law Society* [1983] 1 AC 598 at 608; *Bromley LBC v Greater London Council* [1983] 1 AC 768 at 828.

41 Although there were, as there always have been, the odd inexplicable departures from such a reticent approach, which in turn would prompt criticism that their Lordships were driven or at least coloured by ideology. *Bromley*, above n 40, offers a good example.

42 *Gouriet v Union of Post Office Workers* [1978] AC 435 at 482.

43 *CCSU*, above n 13 at 410 ("a decision which is so outrageous in its defiance of logic or of accepted moral standards that no sensible person who had applied his mind to the question to be decided could have arrived at it").

44 Woolf, above n 15 at 225.

is a supervisory jurisdiction; one in which the courts are checking the decision-making power that Parliament has bestowed on another – the executive official. In tort, a court is itself the primary decision maker – adjudication of legal rights is the constitutional responsibility of the courts within the separation of powers. This difference of approach again marks out and distinguishes judicial review claims from claims based in individual rights.

Turning to (2), the courts conceptualized their relationship with the administration as one of "partnership based on a common aim, namely the maintenance of the highest standards of public administration. … The courts, for their part, must and do respect the fact that it is not for them to intervene in the administrative field, unless there is a reason to inquire whether a particular authority has been successful in its endeavours."[45] Thus, courts were concerned to uphold standards of administration but, given their respect for the professional judgment of administrators, they would intervene only where administrators had clearly failed to adhere to basic standards.

Many existing grounds could be rationalized on this basis. For example, good decision-making practice requires taking into account relevant considerations, exclusion of extraneous considerations, consulting and affording notice to those who will be affected by a decision, and making decisions without bias. New grounds and changes to existing grounds reflected concerns for sound administrative practice. For example, the courts articulated basic procedural requirements for public consultations[46] and increasingly recognized reason-giving requirements, which were justified on the basis of good administrative practice.[47] The courts held that decision makers must take "reasonable steps to acquaint [themselves] with the relevant information to enable [them] to answer [the question] correctly" and that all relevant facts must have been considered.[48] Courts increasingly recognized legitimate expectations, which were justified on the basis of good administration.[49]

45 *Huddleston*, above n 32 at 945.

46 *R v Brent London Borough Council, ex parte Gunning* (1986) 84 LGR 168.

47 *Cunningham*, above n 33 at 822–3.

48 *Secretary of State for Education and Science v Tameside Metropolitan Borough Council* [1977] AC 1014 at 1065.

49 *Ng Yuen Shiu*, above n 31 at 637–8; *CCSU*, above n 13 at 401.

All of these requirements were explained by the courts as being procedural, reflecting the courts' view of their proper judicial role on review.[50] The corollary was that the norms of judicial review did not include substantive legal rights, such as individual entitlements to particular outcomes or goods. The outcomes of decision processes were, subject to *Wednesbury*, for the primary decision maker.

It is important to make one final observation in respect of substantive law. As Feldman observed in 1990, reflecting on the public law decisions of the House of Lords through the 1980s, "human rights have as yet had little real impact on English public law."[51] Thus, cases that could have been analysed on human rights grounds, and had been analysed on this basis by lower court judges or dissentients, were disposed of on orthodox grounds by majorities in the House of Lords with little or no mention of human or fundamental rights.[52]

In this regard, the case of *Harman*,[53] concerning the legality of a solicitor's decision to release documents obtained through discovery, is a striking example. Whereas the minority Law Lords considered that the case clearly engaged the "constitutional right" to freedom of expression, invoking European Court of Human Rights (ECtHR) and United States Supreme Court jurisprudence, Lord Diplock, in the opening paragraph of his leading speech, was at pains to stress that the case did not call for consideration of human rights or the Convention.[54] This resistance is unsurprising. Within a normative framework concerned with maintenance of the common good and promotion of good administrative process, human rights were a conceptual outlier, being associated with an individualist ideology, directing focus to the interests of those affected by a decision rather than the propriety of the process

50 *R v Chief Constable of North Wales, ex parte Evans* [1982] 1 WLR 1155 at 1173.

51 Feldman, above n 34 at 261.

52 See eg *Wheeler v Leicester City Council* [1985] AC 1054 (contrast the approach of the House of Lords and majority in the Court of Appeal with Browne-Wilkinson LJ's dissent in the Court of Appeal, stressing the constitutional importance of free expression); *Re an Inquiry under the Company Securities (Insider Dealing) Act 1985* [1988] AC 660 (contrast the first-instance decision of Hoffmann J, which used the proportionality principle: [1987] BCLC 506); see also *Malone v Metropolitan Police Commissioner* [1979] Ch 344.

53 *Harman v Secretary of State for the Home Department* [1983] AC 280. *Harman* is not a review case, but Lord Diplock's approach is suggestive of the level of resistance to human rights reasoning.

54 Ibid at 299.

leading to the decision, and suggesting entitlements to particular goods or outcomes. In addition, reliance on the Convention threatened dualist orthodoxy (discussed further below), while – in a fractious political environment in which a cautious approach had been taken to review more generally – adjudication of human rights would risk drawing the Law Lords into ordinary politics and compromising the legitimacy of the freshly minted public law system. Indeed, the prompt for Lord Diplock's strong statement in *Harman* eschewing human rights analysis was that the case had already garnered significant publicity.

Reinforcing an aversion to rights reasoning was that English law favoured a negative, civil liberties approach to protection of certain basic freedoms, such as free expression, rather than a positive, rights-based approach.[55] Such liberties are simply aspects of the residue of personal freedom left when one subtracts all the action that the law forbids; as Jennings observed, liberties are the obverse of the rules of criminal law, civil law, etc.[56] Thus, in the English tradition, one had the freedom to express oneself to the extent that one did not contravene a law, but there was no positive legal entitlement to freely express oneself and no duty on others to avoid interfering with one's exercise of free expression.[57] Furthermore, traditionally, there was considered to be nothing special or normatively weighty about these liberties, as reflected in Jennings's observation that "[t]here is no more a 'right to free speech' than there is a 'right to tie up my shoe-lace.'"[58]

Remedies and Procedure

The remedial approach that emerged during the 1980s reflects the core tenets of the public interest model. The courts had wide discretion whether to grant remedies, and which remedies, allowing them the flexibility to protect wider public interests and, specifically, those in effective administration.[59] This marked out public law from rights-based

55 See D. Feldman, "Civil Liberties" in V. Bogdanor (ed), *The British Constitution in the Twentieth Century* (Oxford, Oxford University Press, 2003).

56 W.I. Jennings, *The Law and the Constitution*, 5th edn (London, University of London Press, 1959) 262–3.

57 See *Duncan v Jones* [1936] 1 KB 218; *R (Laporte) v Chief Constable of Gloucestershire* [2007] 2 AC 105 at [34].

58 Jennings, above n 56 at 262–3.

59 *IRC*, above n 11 at 647; *Datafin*, above n 17 at 840–1; *Argyll*, above n 38 at 774–5.

fields such as tort, where the claimant elects his or her remedy; claimant autonomy reflects that such claims relate to the claimant's personal right. Furthermore, it is a core feature of English law that where there is a right, there is a remedy; that review remedies could readily be refused in the public interest reflected the idea that review claims were not based in rights, but rather public duties. Relief was limited to the prerogative orders, declarations, and injunctions. The focus on such specific-type relief reflects the law's concern with keeping administrators on track. Damages were unavailable. Damages would be out of place because damages, in the common law tradition, respond to breaches of individual rights and reverse personal setbacks.[60]

Last, the procedural treatment of judicial review claims bore the hallmarks of the public interest model, again marking out review from rights-based fields. The Law Lords mandated that "public law" claims must be brought through review procedure.[61] Ensuring that such claims were corralled into a dedicated procedural forum, separate from private law claims, was key to the courts' public law system-building project. Furthermore, this exclusivity principle ensured that those bringing claims "in the field of public law" could not evade safeguards within the review procedure, such as short limitation periods and a leave stage, "imposed in the *public interest* against groundless, unmeritorious or tardy attacks upon the validity of decisions made by public authorities."[62] Tort and contract claims were treated differently: "[w]hen individual rights are claimed, there should not be a need for leave or a special time limit, nor should the relief be discretionary."[63] In review proceedings, there were also severe restrictions on discovery and cross-examination to protect authorities from costs and lengthy proceedings, and because fact-finding was principally for the administrative decision maker. In contrast, in rights-based claims, a court conducts fact-finding itself, given that it is exercising a primary jurisdiction, while such claims, being individualistic, require close analysis of the individual case.

60 *Bourgoin SA v Ministry of Agriculture, Fisheries and Food* [1986] QB 716 at 761, 767; *Garden Cottage Foods Ltd v Milk Marketing Board* [1984] AC 130 at 141.

61 *O'Reilly v Mackman* [1983] 2 AC 237.

62 Ibid at 282; emphasis added; *IRC*, above n 11 at 643; and see 630.

63 *Roy v Kensington and Chelsea and Westminster Family Practitioner Committee* [1992] 1 AC 624 at 654.

The Shadow of Europe (1990s)

Thus, a defining feature of the new field of *public law*, which developed from the late 1970s and through the 1980s, was its concern with public duties and the public interest as opposed to individual rights and individual interests, which were considered the proper province of private law fields.

However, from the late 1980s onward, the courts came under pressure to afford greater priority to protection of individual interests within judicial review due to increasing pressure to ensure UK compliance with the Convention.[64] During the late 1980s and in the 1990s, claimants disappointed by the outcome of domestic proceedings were, with increasing frequency, filing applications against the United Kingdom with the ECtHR, with success. Practitioners would increasingly cite Strasbourg judgments before domestic courts, and emphasize the importance of compliance with the United Kingdom's supranational commitments, in the knowledge that the courts were aware that an ECtHR application would follow if the claimants were left disappointed.

Thus, in *Smith* (discussed below), Thorpe LJ admitted, perhaps with a tinge of resignation, that the issue of human rights compliance "will no doubt ultimately be decided in Strasbourg."[65] Practitioners also appealed, often subtly, to a "pride" argument: that it would be surprising if the protection afforded to basic interests by the common law, with its proud history, were inferior to Convention standards. At the same time, there was growing academic support for the development of judicial review to embrace European human rights doctrines such as proportionality.[66] This influence was evident in *Brind*, where Lord Roskill, in leaving open the possibility of adopting proportionality,

---

64 See generally M. Hunt, *Using Human Rights Law in English Courts* (Oxford, Hart Publishing, 1997).

65 *R v Ministry of Defence, ex parte Smith* [1996] QB 517 at 565. Indeed, the issue was ultimately settled at Strasbourg: *Smith and Grady v UK* (2000) 29 EHRR 493.

66 See the classics, J. Jowell and A. Lester, "Beyond *Wednesbury*: Substantive Principles of Administrative Law" [1987] *Public Law* 368; J. Jowell and A. Lester, "Proportionality: Neither Novel nor Dangerous" in J. Jowell and D. Oliver (eds), *New Directions in Judicial Review* (London, Stevens, 1988). And see now the part-retrospective: J. Jowell, "Proportionality and Unreasonableness: Neither Merger nor Takeover" in H. Wilberg and M. Elliott (eds), *The Scope and Intensity of Substantive Review* (Oxford, Hart Publishing, 2015).

observed that this possibility "has already been canvassed in some academic writings."[67] This line of thinking overlapped and intermingled with a wave of "common law constitutionalist" thought, influenced by the contemporary work of Dworkin, which supported a role for the courts in articulating constitutional fundamentals, including fundamental rights.[68] Judicial dissatisfaction with the lack of direct rights protection was reflected in the extra-judicial opinions of several judges, who called for the adoption of a bill of rights and/or incorporation of the Convention.[69]

Simultaneously, the ECtHR was itself becoming increasingly assertive. With its legitimacy and the goodwill of member states, built up over several decades, it was now increasingly willing to develop its own jurisprudence and expand human rights protection under the Convention, tighten the margin of appreciation that it was willing to afford member states, and more willing to find violations. The United Kingdom was particularly susceptible in this regard given that, unusually for a European nation, it had no dedicated rights charter.

However, it is important to note that pre-existing fields of English law, including those outside judicial review, did afford protection, albeit not always perfect protection, to Convention rights. For example, torts had long protected fundamental rights, as had the criminal law.[70] While review doctrines, although premised on a public interest rationale, ensured a measure of protection for basic interests. For example, procedural fairness would often ensure compliance with Article 6. Axiomatic doctrines such as relevant considerations and improper purpose, through their

---

67 *R v Secretary of State for the Home Department, ex parte Brind* [1991] 1 AC 696 at 750.

68 For an analysis of these theories, see eg T. Poole, "Back to the Future? Unearthing the Theory of Common Law Constitutionalism" (2003) 23 *Oxford Journal of Legal Studies* 435. This school of thinking counted some judges among its protagonists: eg J. Laws, "Is the High Court the Guardian of Fundamental Constitutional Rights?" [1993] *Public Law* 59; J. Laws, "Law and Democracy" [1995] *Public Law* 72.

69 Eg T. Bingham, "The European Convention on Human Rights: Time to Incorporate" (1993) 109 *Law Quarterly Review* 390; S. Sedley, "Human Rights: A Twenty-First Century Agenda" [1995] *Public Law* 386.

70 That other fields, apart from review, afforded Convention rights protection ensured that review did not bear the full weight of ensuring Convention compliance, and nor was review the sole site of interaction between domestic law and Convention requirements. For example, breach of confidence has been a core site of activity: *Attorney General v Guardian Newspapers Ltd (no 2)* [1990] 1 AC 109; *Campbell v MGN Ltd* [2004] 2 AC 457.

operation, could protect basic interests, even if individual protection was not their focus.[71]

Lastly, albeit the Convention is typically identified as the key driver of "rights"-based developments in this era, one must not overlook European Union (EU) law. In adjudicating EU claims, English courts exercised extraordinary power, including the capacity to "disapply" legislation, stretch the meaning of statutes, and assess the proportionality of administrative action. Through the application of EU laws that protected basic individual rights (or domestic legislation implementing such norms), such as anti-discrimination laws, and exposure to the European Court of Justice's newly discovered general principles of fundamental rights, English courts gained direct knowledge of adjudicating human rights norms and associated methods. Invariably, this experience "bled through" and shaped, indirectly or directly, domestic judicial review.[72]

Pressure Points

A key point of tension concerned the proportionality method applied in European human rights law. Under the Convention, interferences with certain rights, such as freedom of expression or privacy, can be justified only if proportionate. *Proportionality* here has a specialized meaning, involving a multi-stage analysis: where administrative action breaches rights, to be lawful such action must pursue legitimate ends, there must be a rational connection between means and ends, the intrusion must be the minimum necessary to pursue relevant ends, and the

---

71 See eg *Wheeler*, above n 52 (application of improper purposes to protect free expression). And see *R v Secretary of State for Foreign and Commonwealth Affairs, ex parte World Development Movement Ltd* [1995] 1 WLR 386, which, albeit not a "rights" case, illustrates how the improper purposes doctrine can be deployed as a potent tool to restrict executive discretion.

72 Perhaps the clearest example, albeit concerning remedies, was the case of *M v Home Office* [1994] 1 AC 377, where the House of Lords recognized a jurisdiction at common law to issue an injunction against a minister of the Crown, having only recently issued such a remedy against the Crown in the context of EU law: *R v Secretary of State for Transport, ex parte Factortame (no 2)* [1991] 1 AC 603. Another example of remedial development influenced by EU law was the recognition of a restitutionary claim against the Revenue for recovery of unlawfully demanded tax: *Woolwich Equitable Building Society v Inland Revenue Commissioners* [1993] AC 70.

rights infringement must be proportionate to the ends pursued. The difficulty for English courts was that *Wednesbury* was the standard of substantive review in domestic law. In principle, this test sets the bar for judicial intervention far higher than proportionality, allowing intervention only where a decision is perverse. For example, under *Wednesbury*, a court could not interrogate whether the executive had adopted the least intrusive means possible or intervene on the basis that the court would have struck the balance between individual and public interests differently.

As we have seen, the *Wednesbury* test reflects that, under the public interest model, and within a supervisory jurisdiction, how balances should be struck between competing interests is first and foremost for the primary decision maker. Furthermore, the general concern of the recently constructed public law system was to ensure that decision makers stayed on track in pursuit of public goals, so that public purposes, rather than the interests of individuals who may be affected by public power, were review's focus. As such, English judicial review under the public interest model did not afford the courts the tools necessary to ensure that executive action did not disproportionately infringe rights, while individual rights were not even the starting point under substantive review, the starting point rather being non-intervention. Further, and crucially, the law of judicial review lacked a set of rights to which the proportionality method could be applied. The human rights proportionality method depends on a rights driver – but the rights did not exist. If English law recognized a set of fundamental rights, it was the basic rights protected by tort, which were the province of private law.

Because courts could not, in domestic law, interrogate the proportionality of executive action, there was an ongoing, serious risk that the United Kingdom would be found in breach of the Convention, and the United Kingdom was not infrequently found in breach. In turn, this situation placed pressure on courts to bring domestic law into compliance.

The English courts responded to these pressures in two main ways: by developing (1) substantive review and (2) principles of statutory interpretation. This emergent rights dimension posed a challenge to the public interest model. Albeit one must not overstate the pervasiveness and influence of rights thinking.[73] This influence was largely limited to two pockets of review. Core features of the public interest model, such

73 See further J.N.E. Varuhas, "The Reformation of English Administrative Law? 'Rights,' Rhetoric and Reality" (2013) 72 *Cambridge Law Journal* 369.

as public interest standing, the general approach to remedies and procedure, and most review doctrines, were relatively insulated from rights thinking, so that, even at the height of this rights movement, review continued to bear the hallmarks of the public interest model. That model had, after all, only just been put in place, it was the product of concerted judicial efforts, and many factors motivating adoption of that model remained relevant, such as inculcation of public administration with free market values.

Furthermore, the number of cases that made up this rights trend, while relatively high profile and such as to excite commentators, were in fact relatively few. These cases were typically ones where the interest the claimant sought to protect was not one traditionally protected through positive rights in English law, such as freedom of expression and privacy.[74] If one wished to protect interests in property or liberty, then one could have direct recourse to dedicated actions such as trespass, which provided strong remedies, such as damages, and generally ensured Convention compliance.

Let us turn to consider the major developments during this time period.

Baby Steps: Substantive Review

The Law Lords, faced with submissions emphasizing the importance of Convention compliance, stood firm in their view that the courts could not import the Convention through the back door. For example, Lord Bridge, in the 1991 case of *Brind*, rejected a submission that Parliament ought to be assumed to have intended statutory discretions to be exercised in conformity with Convention requirements:[75]

> When Parliament has been content for so long to leave those who complain that their Convention rights have been infringed to seek their remedy in

74 Freedom of expression: *Brind*, above n 67; see also *Wheeler*, above n 52 at 1064–5; privacy: *Smith*, above n 65; *Marcel v Commissioner of Police of Metropolis* [1991] 2 WLR 1118 at 1124. One also sees the Convention and the jurisprudence under it invoked outside judicial review, especially to reinforce freedom of expression as an important value or principle (contrast the idea of a positive right to free expression) that ought to factor into judicial decision making: eg *Attorney General v Guardian Newspapers Ltd (no 1)* [1987] 1 WLR 1248 at 1286; *Attorney General (no 2)*, above n 70 at 283–4; *Derbyshire County Council v Times Newspapers Ltd* [1993] AC 534.

75 *Brind*, above n 67 at 748.

> Strasbourg, it would be surprising suddenly to find that the judiciary had, without Parliament's aid, the means to incorporate the Convention into such an important area of domestic law and I cannot escape the conclusion that this would be a judicial usurpation of the judicial function.

While the Convention could be used as an interpretive tool to resolve a statutory ambiguity, it could not be implied as a legal limit on every statutory discretion. As Lord Ackner concluded, "The treaty, not having been incorporated into English law, cannot be a source of rights and obligations and the question 'Did the Secretary of State act in breach of article 10?' does not therefore arise."[76] No doubt Lord Diplock's earlier, emphatic warning in *Duport* still echoed strongly: that the courts must not, under the guise of interpretation, effect their preferred amendments to legislation lest they undermine public confidence in the judiciary.[77] Subsequently, in the 1996 case of *Smith*, it was "common ground that the United Kingdom's obligation, binding in international law, to respect and secure compliance with [Article 8] is not one that is enforceable by domestic courts;"[78] that a decision maker had failed to consider Convention requirements was not a ground for impugning its decision.[79]

Thus, the courts would not import the Convention through the back door, consistent with dualist orthodoxy. Nor did they consider the development of common law tests of substantive review, to match European proportionality method, could be justified given the conceptual framework of review. Proportionality would involve the courts trespassing upon the role of the decision maker: it "would be for the court to substitute its own judgment of what was needed to achieve a particular objective for the judgment of the Secretary of State upon whom the duty has been laid by Parliament."[80] Simon Brown LJ echoed this view in the Divisional Court in *Smith*, observing that proportionality would take review beyond a supervisory jurisdiction: if the court "were entitled to ask whether the [challenged] policy answers a pressing social need and whether the restriction on

76 Ibid at 762.

77 *Duport Steels*, above n 35 at 157.

78 *Smith*, above n 65 at 558.

79 Ibid. Contrast comparative developments: *Tavita v Minister of Immigration* [1994] 2 NZLR 257.

80 *Brind*, above n 67 at 750.

human rights involved can be shown to be proportionate to its benefits, then clearly the primary judgment (subject only to a limited 'margin of appreciation') would be for us and not others."[81] He reiterated orthodoxy: courts must approach questions of substance with "some reticence," and the court's approach must "reflect, and not overlook, where responsibility ultimately lies for the defence of the realm."[82]

Lord Lowry's speech in *Brind* most clearly entails a reassertion of the public interest model in the face of counsel's submissions seeking to move substantive review towards a rights model. Affirming a starting point of non-intervention, he observed that it was not the "court's duty to interfere with a discretion which Parliament has entrusted to a statutory body or an individual."[83] Rather, the judicial role on review was limited to maintaining "a check on excesses in the exercise of discretion."[84] This limited role explained the "emphatic language which judges have used in order to drive home the message and the necessity, as judges have seen it, for the act to be so unreasonable that no reasonable minister ... would have come to it."[85] He considered that proportionality could be an indicium of irrationality. But this did not involve an enquiry into "mere" proportionality; rather, to be irrational, the decision would have to be *so much* out of proportion to the needs of the situation as to be *perverse*.[86] Lord Lowry emphasized that there was "*no* authority" for the proposition that the European variant of proportionality was a part of English law and much against.[87] He recited a number of reasons why this was not a cause for regret, all being consonant with the public interest model:[88] (1) Parliament had entrusted the discretion to the decision maker, who was often elected; (2) the judges were not well placed by training or experience, nor furnished with the requisite knowledge or advice, to answer administrative problems where the scales were evenly balanced, but had a much better chance of reaching the right answer – or, put another way, not falling into error – under *Wednesbury*; (3) stability

81 *Smith*, above n 65 at 541.
82 Ibid.
83 *Brind*, above n 67 at 765.
84 Ibid.
85 Ibid.
86 Ibid at 766.
87 Ibid.
88 Ibid at 767.

and certainty would be undermined as, under a proportionality test, something could always be said against an administrative decision, and disappointed parties would be more willing to try their luck through review; and (4) the resultant increase in review applications would lead to increased expenditure by litigants, prolonged uncertainty for all concerned, and increased burdens for courts: "The losers in this respect will be members of the public, for whom the courts provide a service."[89]

Lord Ackner took a similar view, considering that proportionality could be adopted only if Parliament incorporated the Convention.[90] On the other hand, Lords Bridge and Roskill, while not considering *Brind* to be the case for application of proportionality, did not exclude the possibility of future legal development.[91] Lord Templeman did not offer a view on this point.

Thus, the courts resisted back door incorporation and were unwilling to develop a novel proportionality doctrine at common law, albeit some judges showed warmer attitudes than others. However, there was also evident in cases such as *Brind* and *Smith* a judicial unease in applying a perversity standard where basic interests were at stake; a concern to seek to ensure, as far as possible within a supervisory jurisdiction, UK compliance with Strasbourg requirements; and a concern that English law and English courts not be seen to be unable to assist a claimant whose basic interests had been impinged. For example, Lord Bridge emphasized that a refusal to import Convention norms did not leave the courts powerless to prevent human rights infringements,[92] while Lord Templeman, having begun his speech by recalling the United Kingdom's international commitments, considered that the subject matter and date of the *Wednesbury* principles did not make it necessary or appropriate "to judge the validity of an interference with human rights by asking … whether the Home Secretary has acted irrationally or perversely."[93] Similarly, Sir Thomas Bingham M.R. in *Smith*, while accepting that the Convention could not form a substantive limit on executive discretion, nonetheless emphasized that review was a key mechanism for ensuring Convention compliance and that the courts

89 Ibid at 767.
90 Ibid at 763.
91 Ibid at 749, 750.
92 Ibid at 748. See also his dissent in *Attorney General (no 1)*, above n 74 at 1286.
93 Ibid at 751.

had a duty to protect citizens' rights and to do right by all manner of people.[94]

The solution settled upon to meet these concerns was, building on previous jurisprudence,[95] establishment of an "anxious scrutiny" variant of *Wednesbury*. In *Brind*, Lord Bridge described the anxious scrutiny approach as follows:[96]

> The primary judgment as to whether the particular competing interest justified the particular restriction imposed falls to the Secretary of State to whom Parliament has entrusted the discretion. But we are entitled to exercise a secondary judgment by asking whether a reasonable Secretary of State, on the material before him, could reasonably make the primary judgment.

Under this test, the basis for legal intervention remained reasonableness, not proportionality. The added burden upon the decision maker, compared to the ordinary *Wednesbury* test, was that it must take into account the claimant's interests as one relevant consideration and consider whether prejudice to those interests is warranted in the public interest. But if it does this, a court will be unlikely to intervene: "If the Secretary of State has asked himself [whether the impact on the claimant is justifiable] and answered it ... in the light of all relevant evidence, the court cannot interfere."[97] *Anxious scrutiny* is review on "a conventional *Wednesbury* basis adapted to a human rights context,"[98] in that the ultimate question for a court remains whether, having taken an individual's interests into account, the decision maker nonetheless struck a balance that was "perverse."[99] Thus, it was possible for Lord Ackner to observe in *Brind* that anxious scrutiny, despite its name, "in no sense increas[ed] the severity of the *Wednesbury* test."[100] Similarly, in *Smith*, the Master of the Rolls, despite applying anxious scrutiny, maintained,

94 *Smith*, above n 65 at 555–6.

95 Eg *R v Secretary of State for the Home Department, ex parte Bugdaycay* [1987] 1 AC 514 at 531–2; *R v Secretary of State for Transport, ex parte de Rothschild* [1989] 1 All ER 933 at 939.

96 *Brind*, above n 67 at 749.

97 *Bugdaycay*, above n 95 at 532.

98 *Smith*, above n 65 at 540, 554.

99 *Brind*, above n 67 at 758.

100 Ibid at 757.

"[t]he threshold for irrationality is a high one."[101] It is perhaps no surprise then that the Courts in *Brind* and *Smith* declined judicial review.

Importantly, while the anxious scrutiny test recognized the importance of basic interests, the mode of protection adopted did not undermine the coherence of the public interest model. Anxious scrutiny did not, for example, involve the courts recognizing enforceable individual rights at common law equivalent to those under the Convention and adjudicating rights claims on their merits, including determining proportionality for themselves. As Lord Carnwath observed recently, under anxious scrutiny, "the role of the courts is often more about process than merits."[102] The focus is, consonant with the public interest model, on the *manner* of the exercise of the power itself, rather than direct judicial enforcement of substantive entitlements. Indeed, anxious scrutiny carries forward the goals of the public interest model, facilitating good administration and proper exercise of power by requiring a decision maker to turn its mind to all relevant considerations, one of which is prejudice to basic interests.[103] The courts' role under anxious scrutiny remains supervisory as the primary decision over how interests should be balanced is for the decision maker, and the courts will intervene only where the decision maker obviously abuses its power.

Enlisting Parliament: Statutory Interpretation

In *Brind*, Their Lordships flatly rejected the proposition that an obligation to comply with Convention rights could be implied into every empowering provision.

However, in the 1993 case of *Leech*, the Court of Appeal found a way around the ruling in *Brind* and, in doing so, gave a lead to the House of Lords, as we shall see in the next section.[104] The Court found rights equivalent to Convention rights *at common law*, and it held that absent express words or necessary implication to the contrary, an empowering provision could not authorize disproportionate interferences with these basic common law rights. The principle of interpretation – the "principle of legality" – that express words are required to oust vested

101 *Smith*, above n 65 at 558.

102 *Kennedy v Information Commissioner* [2015] AC 455 at [245].

103 See *Secretary of State for the Home Department v MN and KY* [2014] 1 WLR 2064 at [31].

104 *R v Secretary of State for the Home Department, ex parte Leech* [1994] QB 198.

common law rights – was long established, and the Court drew on this tradition. But a novelty in *Leech* was the augmenting of this traditional principle with a proportionality dimension. Further, in *Leech* the principle was applied beyond independently actionable, vested common law rights, such as those in tort, contract, or property. Application of the principle had, in general, been limited traditionally to such established rights,[105] and it did not generally extend to protecting civil liberties – which were traditionally considered of less normative weight than private law rights.[106]

The main right at stake was said to be that of access to court, now branded a *constitutional right*.[107] While this is described as a *right*, there is no actionable right at common law to access court or right not to be impeded in one's access to court – for example, in the law of torts. Rather, in the English tradition access to court is probably best explained as a liberty or privilege at common law; that is, one is free to access a court, but there is no legal duty on another individual or authority, directly correlative to an individual right, not to impede access.[108]

105 See eg *Ledwith v Roberts* [1937] 1 KB 232 at 260 (liberty); *Morris*, above n 5 (property); *Raymond v Honey* [1983] 1 AC 1 (legal professional privilege). See further J.N.E. Varuhas, "Conceptualising the Principle(s) of Legality" (2018) 29 *Public Law Review* 196.

106 See text to above nn 56–8; and see eg *Malone*, above n 52, a case concerning invasion of privacy by wiretapping (privacy not at the time being a recognized private law right), where the Court held that the Post Office (at the request of the police) could lawfully wiretap absent any statutory authorization, whether express or otherwise. Note, however, that there are some earlier examples of the classic, orthodox principle of legality being applied to preserve access to court specifically. See eg *R v Secretary of State for the Home Department, ex parte Anderson* [1984] QB 778.

107 *Leech*, above n 104 at 210.

108 See Varuhas 2013, above n 73 at 405. In his *Commentaries on the Laws of England*, Blackstone said, "A third subordinate right of every Englishman is that of applying to the courts of justice for redress of injuries," Book I (Oxford, Clarendon, 1765–69) 141. The statement is much quoted in support of the idea of a constitutional "right" of access to court (eg *R (Unison) v Lord Chancellor* [2017] UKSC 51 at [75]). But while the malleable term *right* is used by Blackstone and others, what is being described is a freedom or liberty that each person has to bring court proceedings; going to court is one option among many that each person is free to pursue within their personal freedom, to the extent that they are not lawfully prohibited from doing so. Such a liberty is to be distinguished from the *absolute rights* to physical security, liberty, and property identified by Blackstone, the protection of which was, in his view, the principal aim of society and laws (at 123, 129, 141). These absolute rights, as they have been concretized in the common law, are a distinct genus from *liberties*: they are independently actionable, genuine rights that cast correlative duties in private law and have been afforded strong and direct protection through the imposition of damages liability in the law of torts: see eg *Ratcliffe v Evans* [1892] 2 QB 524 at 528. Certain common law doctrines

Turning to the proportionality dimension, Steyn LJ held that a broad provision granting a general power to make rules for the regulation of prisoners authorized, by implication, rules providing for some screening by a prison governor of correspondence between a prisoner and solicitor and, thus, some incursion upon the right of access to court. However, he also held that "[t]he authorised intrusion must ... be the minimum necessary to ensure that the correspondence is in truth bona fide legal correspondence."[109] Thus, a rule allowing all correspondence to or from a prisoner to be read was unjustified. The requirement of *minimum intrusion* is obviously drawn from Strasbourg, and it reflects a core plank of structured proportionality analysis. Elsewhere in his judgment, Steyn LJ articulated another plank of that test: there had to be a "demonstrable need" for the rules.[110]

Several points should be noted. The first relates to the *technique* of rights protection. In *Leech*, the basis of intervention was the *ultra vires* doctrine. It was held that a rule that disproportionately infringed an individual's access to court was *ultra vires* a parent provision that did not expressly provide for such an intrusive rule. In form, this approach is different from substantive review – the court holds that there was no power in the terms of the statute to make the rule, rather than impugning a rule based on its quality. On one view, this approach does not challenge the public interest model as the *ultra vires* ground is geared to keeping decision makers on track – that is, ensuring that powers are exercised within the four corners of the parent statute. But, practically, the result achieved is the same as if the courts were applying proportionality as a substantive review doctrine; as Lord Reed observed recently, this "augmented" legality principle imposes, "in substance, a requirement of proportionality."[111] Further, as we shall see, *Leech* laid the foundation for a potentially broad range of "triggers" for the augmented principle of

---

such as contempt have protected the liberty to access court *through their practical operation*, but they do not seemingly involve recognition of a personal legal right to unhindered access to court – the doctrine of contempt is oriented towards a broader enquiry into whether there has been interference with the due course of justice or lawful processes of the court.

109 *Leech*, above n 104 at 217.

110 Ibid at 212–3.

111 *Pham v Secretary of State for the Home Department* [2015] 1 WLR 1591 at [119]. See further text to below n 207ff.

legality, including other common law liberties or privileges, such as free expression.

In turn, this "augmented" principle of legality with its novel proportionality dimension, potentially posed a far more serious threat to the public interest model than the modest developments in substantive review. In principle, a requirement that intrusions upon private rights or residual liberties should be no more than strictly necessary could be read in as a limit on any statutory power. Given that most powers, if exercised, will intrude upon some right or personal freedom, this development was potentially far reaching. For a decision maker, the interests of the individual subject to the decision would be a primary focus, whereas the public interests for which Parliament had conferred the powers would be demoted from controlling to countervailing interests. Furthermore, courts would, according to the proportionality method, themselves determine whether any limit met a demonstrable need, was the least intrusive, etc., thus making significant inroads into a decision maker's power to determine what would best serve the common good.

Why did the courts feel more able to adopt proportionality in this context than substantive review? The answer probably lies in the form of rights protection. In applying the legality principle, the courts were, at least in form, enquiring into Parliament's intention. If the judicial intervention is grounded in democratic will – however tenuous this might be – it is more difficult to criticize it as illegitimate judicial overreach. The Court in *Leech* stressed that its decision was based on axiomatic principle: "It is important not to lose sight of the precise nature of the question to be answered. The question is simply one of vires."[112]

Also of importance is that the Court's hand was forced in *Leech*. The ECtHR's decision, handed down a year earlier, in *Campbell*, made clear that for officials to read a prisoner's mail without reasonable cause violated Article 8.[113] In *Leech*, the Court deliberately reasoned to its conclusion based on domestic principles, noting at the end of the judgment the happy coincidence that the outcome matched that reached by the ECtHR in *Campbell*.[114] The concerns that the courts ought to have the tools available to protect basic interests and also the "pride" factor further reinforced the aggressive approach to review: "It is a principle of *our* law

112 *Leech*, above n 104 at 208.
113 *Campbell v UK* (1992) 15 EHRR 137.
114 *Leech*, above n 104 at 217.

that every citizen has a right of unimpeded access to a court. ... Even in *our* unwritten constitution it must rank as a constitutional right."[115]

Leech could have had far-reaching implications, yet the augmented legality principle has very rarely been deployed in general and especially outside the prison context (until its very recent reinvigoration).[116] An important factor in explaining this is that there was a pre-existing common law presumption that prisoners retained all "civil rights" other than those necessarily excluded by imprisonment.[117] This default reinforced the view that, in the prison context specifically, Parliament needed to speak very clearly to displace retained rights and liberties. Another factor is that the prison context – including, in particular, prisoner correspondence and access to lawyers – was an area where the United Kingdom had *repeatedly* been found in breach of the Convention, creating *sustained* pressure to ensure compliance.[118]

Last, while the augmented legality principle was a domestic innovation spurred by pressure to ensure Convention compliance, it was arguably inspired, at least in part, by the EU doctrine of indirect effect, which English courts already had experience applying. According to this doctrine, domestic laws would be interpreted to ensure conformity with EU norms, including emergent EU principles of fundamental rights. In this regard, it is difficult to see as coincidence that, in the year preceding the *Leech* decision, Lord Browne-Wilkinson had advocated, in a published article,[119] development of common law techniques of statutory interpretation to protect basic interests, drawing heavily on the developments in EU law.

Pressure Release (2000s)

The Human Rights Act 1998 entered into force in 2000. It rendered enumerated Convention rights actionable in domestic law, enabling English courts to adjudicate claims based directly on these rights and

115 Ibid at 210; emphasis added.

116 See text to below n 207ff.

117 *Leech*, above n 104 at 209; *Raymond*, above n 105 at 10; *R v Board of Visitors of Hull Prisons, ex parte St Germain* [1979] QB 425 at 455.

118 Eg *Golder v UK* (1975) 1 EHRR 524; *Silver v UK* (1983) 5 EHRR 347; *Campbell v UK*, above n 113.

119 Lord Browne-Wilkinson, "The Infiltration of a Bill of Rights" [1992] PL 397. See also his judgments in *Wheeler*, above n 52 at 1064–5; *Marcel*, above n 74 at 1124.

grant remedies for breach. The introduction of a major field dedicated to protection of fundamental, individual rights was a radical change in the public law landscape. The HRA initially had the knock-on effect of precipitating a flurry of activity at common law, the courts seemingly emboldened by its advent to further develop common law rights protections and move common law review away from the public interest model. However, this activity was short-lived, and the overall effect of the Act on the common law was to kill the momentum built up during the previous decade to reorient common law doctrines towards rights. Given that Convention rights were now directly actionable pursuant to a statutory action, a core motivation for so developing the common law fell away. Thus, for over a decade following the entry into force of the HRA, the common law largely developed in conformity with its traditional public interest roots.

A New Rights-Based Field

Such was the hold of the public interest model that rights adjudication under the HRA was initially subordinated to pre-existing, judicial review thinking. Thus, in very early case law under the Act, the courts did not themselves adjudicate whether there had been a rights breach and defences, such as proportionality, on their merits. Rather, they asked, according to the anxious scrutiny method, whether the public authority's decision, pertaining to the claimant's enumerated rights, was irrational.[120]

However, after a period of adjustment, this supervisory approach, according to which determinations over human rights were first and foremost for executive officials, was eschewed. Through a series of decisions from 2007, the House of Lords confirmed that the effect of the Act was that the courts *themselves* should adjudicate on the merits claims of breaches of enumerated rights and defences including proportionality.[121] This would involve the courts exercising value judgments as to whether a particular measure was the least intrusive necessary and over proportionality

---

120 Eg *R (Mahmood) v Secretary of State for the Home Department* [2001] 1 WLR 840.

121 *Belfast City Council v Miss Behavin' Ltd* [2007] 1 WLR 1420 at [12]–[15], [31], [44]; *R (Begum) v Governors of Denbigh High School* [2007] 1 AC 100 at [29]–[31]; *Huang v Secretary of State for the Home Department* [2007] 2 AC 167; *E v Chief Constable of the Royal Ulster Constabulary* [2009] 1 AC 536 at [13], [52]ff; *R (Quila) v Secretary of State for the Home Department* [2012] 1 AC 621 at [46], [61], [91].

between competing interests. The courts would give weight to executive decisions where warranted, but, in every case, the final decisions over the scope of rights, breach, and justifications were for the courts. Thus, rights were to be given direct effect and protection; protection was not to be filtered through pre-existing review grounds. In this way, human rights law was decoupled from the common law of review.

This approach reflects the policies underpinning the HRA of affording strong protection to rights – rights would not be afforded sufficient protection if rights adjudication were subordinated to administrative law thinking – and ensuring compliance with Strasbourg requirements: only by adjudicating rights claims on their merits could domestic courts ensure compliance. More generally, the fact that the courts were exercising a statutory jurisdiction gave them a democratic foundation for an expanded approach.[122] At a deeper level, the approach adopted reflects that, under the HRA, courts are involved in adjudicating statutorily created legal, personal rights. Within the separation of powers, adjudication of rights is for the courts. This adjudicative approach is different from that applied in review proceedings, where the courts exercise a secondary jurisdiction, supervising decisions made by an administrative official who has the primary power of decision. The relevant question in human rights law is not whether a decision maker exercised its powers properly in pursuit of public goals under a parent statute, but whether legal rights, external to the parent statute, were breached by an otherwise proper exercise of public powers.

That human rights law is based in personal legal rights is reflected in other core features of the field, which make up its doctrinal superstructure and which stand in contrast to common law review.[123] For example, standing rules are narrow, with *locus standi* limited to the individual rights holder whose rights have been infringed;[124] this is in contrast to

---

122 Eg *A v Secretary of State for the Home Department* [2005] 2 AC 68 at [42]: "The 1998 Act gives the courts a very specific, wholly democratic, mandate. As Professor Jowell has put it, 'The courts are charged by Parliament with delineating the boundaries of a rights-based democracy' ("Judicial Deference: Servility, Civility or Institutional Capacity?" [2003] *Public Law* 592 at 597)."

123 See further J.N.E. Varuhas, *Damages and Human Rights* (Oxford, Hart Publishing, 2016) chs 3–4; J.N.E. Varuhas, "Against Unification" in H. Wilberg and M. Elliott (eds), *The Scope and Intensity of Substantive Review* (Oxford, Hart Publishing, 2015).

124 HRA, s 7(1). Courts have refused standing to public interest claimants on the basis that their rights had not been affected by the challenged administrative action: *R*

the wide public interest rules at common law, which correspond to the basic norms being public duties. In common with other fields dedicated to protecting basic individual interests, such as tort, damages are available in human rights law,[125] which reflects the law's focus upon protecting against setbacks to personal interests.

Human rights claims are often initiated through ordinary civil procedure, alongside other rights-based claims, such as claims in tort.[126] The judicial review procedure, designed to house claims for exercise of the courts' supervisory jurisdiction, will often be inapt in human rights claims in which courts are primary fact-finders and, thus, may be modified or claims allowed to progress through ordinary procedure so as to allow greater provision for discovery and cross-examination.[127] Further, impediments to access to court, such as the leave requirement within judicial review procedure, seem inapt for claims based in basic individual rights, for which the courts have the primary constitutional responsibility.

Millennium Blip: The HRA's Initial Impact on Common Law Review

Initially, the advent of the HRA precipitated a questioning of the continuing relevance of *Wednesbury* as the test for substantive review at common law and reassertion of the augmented principle of legality.

In the 2001 House of Lords case of *Daly*, it was accepted that adjudication under the HRA and under *Wednesbury*, while they could lead to similar results, were materially different.[128] However, Lord Cooke suggested that the day may come when *Wednesbury* is recognized as an "unfortunately retrogressive decision in English administrative law" and observed, "[i]t may well be … that the law can never be satisfied in any administrative field merely by a finding that the decision under review

---

(Children's Rights Alliance for England) v Secretary of State for Justice [2013] 1 WLR 3667; *In the Matter of An Application for Judicial Review by the Northern Ireland Commissioner for Children and Young People* [2007] NIQB 115.

125 HRA, s 8. See Varuhas 2016, above n 123.

126 Eg *Ruddy v Chief Constable Strathclyde Police* [2012] UKSC 57. See further ibid at 212–18; M. Elliott and J.N.E. Varuhas, *Administrative Law*, 5th edn (Oxford, Oxford University Press, 2017) [13.3.10].

127 Eg *Tweed v Parades Commission* [2007] 1 AC 650. See further Varuhas 2016, above n 123 at 212–18; Elliott and Varuhas, above n 126 at [13.2.3].

128 *R (Daly) v Secretary of State for the Home Department* [2001] 2 AC 532 at 547–8.

is not capricious or absurd."[129] Lord Slynn in the 2001 case of *Alconbury* considered "that even without reference to the Human Rights Act 1998 the time has come to recognise that [the proportionality] principle is part of English administrative law" and that it was "unnecessary and confusing" "to keep the *Wednesbury* principle and proportionality in separate compartments."[130] Dyson LJ, in the 2003 Court of Appeal case of *ABCIFER*, voiced strong support for supplanting *Wednesbury* with proportionality, but considered that it was for the Law Lords to perform *Wednesbury*'s "burial rites."[131]

In its 1999 decision in *Simms*, the House of Lords picked up the augmented legality principle from *Leech*, complete with its proportionality dimension.[132] Their Lordships held a blanket policy prohibiting prisoners from having oral interviews with journalists *ultra vires* the Prison Rules, on the basis that the policy involved a disproportionate interference with freedom of expression, which the Rules did not expressly authorize. In reaching this conclusion, Lord Steyn, who had previously penned the judgment in *Leech*, endorsed the view that there was no difference in principle between English law and Article 10 of the Convention in the field of freedom of expression.[133] Similarly, Lord Hoffmann said that, through the legality principle, UK courts applied "principles of constitutionality little different from those that exist in countries where the power of the legislature is expressly limited by constitutional document."[134] He considered that the HRA would not detract from this power. Indeed, the HRA was described as merely "supplement[ing]" existing common law protections, and Lord Hoffmann observed that much of the Convention reflected the common law in any case.[135]

These are rather bold claims given that this was the very first case in which the House of Lords itself affirmed the augmented legality principle; the principle was hardly an entrenched feature of English jurisprudence, it being hard to find an example of a court applying it since *Leech*, while it remained the case that it had been applied only in prisoner cases. The *realpolitik* of *Simms* was that their Lordships felt

---

129 Ibid at 549.

130 *R (Alconbury Developments Ltd) v Secretary of State for the Environment, Transport and the Regions* [2003] 2 AC 295 at [51].

131 *R (ABCIFER) v Secretary of State for Defence* [2003] QB 1397 at [34]–[5].

132 *R v Secretary of State for the Home Department, ex parte Simms* [2000] 2 AC 115.

133 Ibid at 126.

134 Ibid at 131.

135 Ibid.

capable of embracing the augmented legality principle because they were imminently to be bestowed with similar powers under the HRA in any case. Further, consonant with the "pride" theme in the jurisprudence, underpinning many of these grand statements was an apparent concern to show that the common law, of which the judges were the guardians, was in no way inferior when compared to written constitutions elsewhere, the Convention or the HRA.

Orthodoxy Reaffirmed

However, this initial flurry of activity at common law was soon followed by the sound of silence, there being little development in substantive review or the principle of legality in over a decade following cases such as *Simms* and *Daly*. *Wednesbury* was not interred. The higher courts continued to apply the test at common law without comment.[136] There was no move from anxious scrutiny towards a full-blown proportionality test. Furthermore, the courts clearly distinguished adjudication under the HRA with anxious scrutiny at common law. For example, Lord Hoffmann in *Miss Behavin'*, distinguishing the approach under the HRA from that at common law, said, "the question is ... whether there has actually been a violation of the applicant's Convention rights and not whether the decision maker properly considered the question of whether his rights would be violated or not."[137]

Similarly, Lord Carnwath has said that, in HRA cases, "[t]he court's function ... is to decide for itself whether the decision was in accordance with Convention rights; it is not a purely reviewing function"; "Under the HRA ... the claimant would have a right to full merits review by the court, again on fact and law."[138] The point has been repeated in a series of House of Lords and Supreme Court decisions.[139] Further, as mentioned above, recognition of this difference between the exercise of a primary jurisdiction in human rights claims, and of a supervisory

136 Eg *In re Duffy* [2008] UKHL 4; *R (McDonald) v Kensington and Chelsea RLBC* [2011] 4 All ER 881; *R (KM) v Cambridgeshire CC* [2012] 2 All ER 1218; *R (Lumba) v Secretary of State for the Home Department* [2012] 1 AC 245.

137 *Miss Behavin'*, above n 121 at [15].

138 *Kennedy*, above n 102 at [244]. See similarly regarding the difference between proportionality in EU law and ordinary grounds of review: *R (Sinclair Collis Ltd) v Secretary of State for Health* [2012] QB 394 at [181], [250], *cf* [82].

139 Above n 121.

jurisdiction at common law, has manifested in other ways, including differences in procedural treatment of claims.[140]

The augmented principle of legality was, following *Simms*, applied by Lord Bingham in the 2001 case of *Daly*, notably another prisoner case, but it was not applied again until very recently (see next section). That is, no court, as far as I am aware, and especially not the House of Lords or Supreme Court, applied proportionality analysis in the context of an *ultra vires* enquiry for over fifteen years following *Daly*. The orthodox legality principle, that express words are required to oust rights, was applied, but with no proportionality element.[141] When the House of Lords was, in the 2006 case of *Watkins*, invited to convert the "constitutional" common law rights, invoked in legality cases such as *Leech* and *Simms*, into genuine, free-standing, actionable claim-rights, as opposed to aspects of an interpretive enquiry with no independent application outside such enquiry, the House flatly refused.[142] Not only this, but Lord Rodger admitted that rights-based developments in common law review during the 1990s and early 2000s had been an indirect means of ensuring compliance with the Convention – "a means of incorporation avant la lettre":

> Now that the Human Rights Act 1998 is in place, such heroic efforts are unnecessary: the Convention rights form part of our law ... where the matter is not already covered by the common law but falls within the scope of a Convention right, a claimant can be expected to invoke his remedy under the Human Rights Act rather than to seek to fashion a new common law right.[143]

Because claims for the protection of rights could be made directly under the HRA, there was no need for recourse to the more indirect means of protection afforded by common law, and as the House of Lords acknowledged in *Daly* – contrary to the grand assertions of confluence in *Simms* – there was a risk of non-compliance with the Convention if reliance were placed solely on common law methods.

---

140 Above nn 126–7.

141 Eg *R (Anufrijeva) v Secretary of State for the Home Department* [2004] 1 AC 604; *Ahmed v HM Treasury* [2010] 2 AC 534.

142 *Watkins v Secretary of State for the Home Department* [2006] 2 AC 395.

143 Ibid at [64].

Thus, it was no longer necessary to stretch the coherence of the conceptual framework of common law review, within which the goal of rights protection never fitted particularly comfortably. But it would be a mistake of the first order to conflate this stall in rights-based developments with the common law standing still. Common law review continued to develop vibrantly, *consonant with the public interest framework*, and its two principal concerns. For example, the courts vigorously developed the law of consultation, to ensure that consultations abided by basic tenets of good administrative practice, and the law of legitimate expectations, which was explicitly premised on a concern for good administration.[144] The seeds were sown for the development of a new branch of "systemic" procedural fairness, concerned to ensure the fairness of administrative systems as a whole.[145] The courts elaborated duties on authorities to disclose certain types of information, these duties embodying a "fundamental rule of good public administration."[146] Perhaps the most significant development is the emergence of a law of policy, the courts now requiring in certain circumstances authorities to have policies, publish policies, and adhere to them, while the policies must be clear.[147] These requirements promote good public administration, specifically facilitation of open, certain, and consistent public decision making.

More generally, despite the rights challenges of the 1990s and early 2000s, the basic public interest framework remained intact, and core tenets were strengthened. Improper purposes and relevant considerations remain at the heart of judicial review. Administrative action continues to be presumed lawful.[148] The Supreme Court has reiterated that a "public authority has no self-interest distinct from that of the public it serves";[149] the corollary of this is that to put special interests of officials, individuals, or corporations ahead of the public interests that authorities exist to serve is to abuse public power.

Wide public-interest standing rules have been reaffirmed, the Supreme Court specifically rejecting narrow, rights-based standing on

144 *R (Niazi) v Secretary of State for the Home Department* [2008] EWCA Civ 755 at [30].

145 *R (Refugee Legal Centre) v Secretary of State for the Home Department* [2004] EWCA Civ 1481. See now *R (Howard League for Penal Reform) v The Lord Chancellor* [2017] EWCA Civ 244.

146 *R (X) v Secretary of State for the Home Department* [2013] 1 WLR 2638 at [6].

147 Elliott and Varuhas, above n 126 at [5.3.3].

148 *R (Gujra) v Crown Prosecution Service* [2013] 1 AC 484 at [51].

149 *R (HSE) v Wolverhampton CC* [2012] 1 WLR 2264 at [52]; and see [24]–[5].

the basis that there is an "essential difference between the nature and purpose of the court's supervisory jurisdiction, on the one hand, and its jurisdiction to adjudicate on disputed questions of right, on the other."[150] Review proceedings are "not brought to vindicate a right vested in the applicant, but to request the court to supervise the actings of a public authority so as to ensure that it exercises its functions in accordance with the law."[151] A narrow focus on individual grievances would ignore review's wider public functions.[152]

The courts have affirmed that public duties rather than individual rights are review's basic norms. As Sedley J observed in the late 1990s, "Public law is not at base about private rights; it is about wrongs – that is to say misuses of public power."[153] Thus, common law review concerns itself with "general duties," which "do not confer enforceable rights" or entail "individual or specific dut[ies]."[154] The Court of Appeal in 2011 said that whereas HRA rights are "clearly" "civil or private law rights," a common law challenge did not depend on the existence of a positive right but rather "a sufficient interest in an arguable abuse of power"; the review challenge turns not on rights but "on the propriety of the acts and omissions which have brought about the interference with [the claimant's] interests and rights."[155]

Whereas in rights-based claims the discretion to refuse relief is narrow, recent decisions reaffirm wide, remedial discretion at common law and its importance in safeguarding public administration and public interests.[156]

All this is not to suggest that common law review and HRA law have developed in strict isolation from one another. Invariably, there has been some borrowing and learning among the fields.[157] But each is marked by its own "genetic imprint."[158]

---

150 *AXA General Insurance Ltd v HM Advocate* [2012] 1 AC 868 at [163].

151 Ibid at [159].

152 *Walton v Scottish Ministers* [2013] PTSR 52 at [90].

153 *R v Somerset County Council, ex parte Dixon* [1998] Env LR 111 at 121.

154 *R (R) v Children and Family Court Advisory Support Service* [2012] 1 WLR 811 at [91], [94]; [2013] 1 WLR 163 at [73], [83].

155 *R (Maftah) v Secretary of State for Foreign and Commonwealth Affairs* [2012] 2 WLR 251 at [28]–[9].

156 Eg *Walton*, above n 152 per Lord Carnwath; *R (Champion) v North Norfolk DC* [2015] 1 WLR 3710 at [54]ff; *Youssef v Secretary of State for Foreign and Commonwealth Affairs* [2016] AC 1457 at [61].

157 For some examples of field interaction, see Varuhas 2013, above n 73 at 391–2.

158 R. Rawlings, "Modelling Judicial Review" (2008) 61 *Current Legal Problems* 95 at 121.

Rights Resurgent (2010s)

For over a decade, each of human rights law and common law review largely developed along their own trajectories, consonant with their own discrete, normative concerns. However, unexpectedly over the last four years, the Supreme Court has shown interest in effecting some sort of unification of the two fields, starting with the 2014 decision of *Kennedy*[159] and continuing with the 2015 decision in *Pham*[160] and the 2016 decision in *Keyu*,[161] among others. These developments, in turn, have pushed what had become a relatively stable system of public law during the 2000s into a renewed state of flux.

Drivers

It seems that a number of phenomena may have driven this resurgent judicial interest in developing the common law along rights-based lines.[162] Whereas the previous wave of rights thinking, during the 1990s, was predominantly driven by supranational forces, current trends are seemingly the product of domestic drivers.

First, from 2013, senior ministers have raised the prospect of scrapping the HRA and replacing it with a British bill of rights, these political murmurs crystallizing into a manifesto commitment of the Conservative Party, which won power in 2015,[163] and commitments in successive Queen's speeches to bring forward proposals for a new bill of rights (which have not materialized).[164] It appears that these developments were a key prompt for the courts to reinvigorate rights-based

159 *Kennedy*, above n 102.

160 *Pham*, above n 111.

161 *R (Keyu) v Secretary of State for Foreign and Commonwealth Affairs* [2016] AC 1355.

162 A number of these drivers were hinted at by Lady Hale in her speech, "UK Constitutionalism on the March?," keynote address to the Constitutional and Administrative Law Bar Association Conference 2014, 12 July 2014, 15, https://www.supremecourt.uk/docs/speech-140712.pdf.

163 See Conservative Party, *Protecting Human Rights in the UK* (2014); *The Conservative Party Manifesto 2015* (2015) 60.

164 "Her Majesty's Most Gracious Speech to Both Houses of Parliament at the State Opening of Parliament 2015," 27 May 2015, www.gov.uk/government/speeches/queens-speech-2015; "Her Majesty's Most Gracious Speech to Both Houses of Parliament at the State Opening of Parliament 2016," 18 May 2016, www.gov.uk/government/speeches/queens-speech-2016.

developments at common law – development of a common law rights jurisprudence would fill any gap left by repeal. Of course, whether this was necessary is open to question in light of subsequent events: plans to repeal the HRA are on the back burner for the time being, being overtaken by the huge political fallout from the Brexit referendum; and, in any case, there are significant, perhaps insurmountable political hurdles to repeal.[165]

This illustrates a problem with premising legal development on speculations as to future events – the events may not occur, yet legal changes premised on occurrence of the events remain. In any case, the Conservative Party's proposal was not simply to repeal the HRA but to replace it, and assurances were given more recently that any new charter would not roll back existing rights protections, albeit these reassurances are difficult to assess without concrete proposals. On the other hand, the advent of Brexit and with it the loss[166] of EU Charter rights, as well as the potential loss of, or watering down of, other basic rights formerly derived from EU law, may reinforce the Supreme Court Justices' commitment to developing a common law rights jurisprudence. Brexit will also bring with it a potentially grand expansion in centralized executive power, especially in light of the significant legislative powers conferred on UK ministers under the European Union (Withdrawal) Act. This may further prompt the Justices to "beef up" the judicial toolkit, especially those legal norms relating to the review of secondary legislation; in this regard, the recent case of *Unison* is of significance (discussed below).[167]

Second, recent years have seen a rise in Euro-scepticism in ordinary politics; this culminated in the Brexit referendum, in which a majority favoured UK withdrawal from the EU. It seems that these shifting political mores may have been one prompt for the courts to rely more on English common law norms than HRA rights, which derive from

165 The proposal was absent from the 2017 Queen's Speech, and the 2017 Conservative election manifesto states that the HRA will not be repealed or replaced during the process of Brexit, but that the UK human rights framework will be considered once the process of leaving the EU is complete: "Her Majesty's Most Gracious Speech to Both Houses of Parliament" 21 June 2017, www.gov.uk/government/speeches/queens-speech-2017; *The Conservation Party Manifesto 2017* (2017) 37.

166 On the Charter see European Union (Withdrawal) Act 2018, s 5(4). The extent to which other rights may be watered down or lost remains to be seen.

167 *Unison*, above n 108, discussed below at text to n 207ff.

the Convention, while jurisprudence under the Act has been marked by heavy reliance on Convention decisions. Thus, the Supreme Court's newly discovered "ordinary approach" holds that a court should have recourse first to "domestic law" before having recourse to the HRA.[168]

This move seems underpinned by a belief that "home-grown" common law adjudication will be viewed as more legitimate than adjudication on the basis of rights derived from the Convention and ECtHR jurisprudence. Of course, this is rather odd as the HRA is a domestic statute and the law under it municipal law. Further, the principal reason why the courts have so heavily relied on European material under the HRA is because the higher courts *themselves* chose to mandate this approach. This is despite such an approach not being mandated by the HRA, one rationale for enactment of the HRA being that it offered an opportunity for British courts to make a distinctive contribution to European human rights law. It was open to English courts to forge their own distinctive human rights jurisprudence under the HRA, while taking account of Strasbourg jurisprudence. Instead, by adopting the judicially created *mirror principle*,[169] according to which English courts seek to replicate what the Convention would have decided in any given case, a home-grown law of human rights was rendered impossible. As such, the law under the HRA is open to being characterized in the media and ordinary politics as a "foreign" imposition, rather than – as it is – a core aspect of *domestic* law. Indeed, not only is the HRA a domestic statute, but it is a statute in which Parliament has enumerated those rights it considers fundamental. Difficult questions may arise for the Supreme Court as to why those rights that the community's elected representatives have designated as fundamental should be relegated behind those that the judges have recently "discovered" at common law.

Third, we are seemingly witnessing a new wave of judicial pride in the common law, one that has several dimensions. It is arguably the product of a more general move by the Supreme Court Justices to establish the new Court's centrality in the constitutional order, which has involved the Court not only forging a new rights jurisprudence but also adjudicating review claims according to judicially articulated

168 *Kennedy*, above n 102 at [46]; *R (Osborn) v Parole Board* [2014] AC 1115 at [54]ff.

169 *R (Ullah) v Special Adjudicator* [2004] 2 AC 323. Note that there has been some backtracking on that principle: eg *Manchester City Council v Pinnock* [2011] 2 AC 104 at [48]–[9].

constitutional values.[170] This resurgent common law, constitutionalist jurisprudence, is a "power play," or "flexing of the muscles," a signal to other constitutional actors of the Court's importance and willingness to uphold fundamentals. Thus, whereas during the 1990s lower courts, in *Leech* and *Smith*, played a significant role in leading rights-based developments, the new wave is a Supreme Court initiative. One obvious risk with this strategy is that if the judges push too far, this will induce "strike-back" by government and curtailment of judicial power.[171]

Further, there is a concern among the justices, more or less recorded explicitly in case law,[172] that the common law, of which the judges are the keepers, is being "outshone," or "eclipsed," by the HRA and that its primacy needs to be reasserted – by developing a common law rights jurisprudence.[173] However, questions arise as to whether the concern is well founded. First, the common law has continued to develop vibrantly, in line with its traditional public interest ethos.[174] Second, while the Supreme Court may hear a high proportion of HRA cases,

---

170 Eg *R (Evans) v Attorney General* [2015] AC 1787; *R (Buckinghamshire CC) v Secretary of State for Transport* [2014] 1 WLR 324; *R (Miller) v Secretary of State for Exiting the European Union* [2017] UKSC 5.

171 In this regard, note the recent imposition of further restrictions on the judicial review procedure, and the severe cutting back of legal aid, while the Supreme Court, now more visible in the public eye than the House of Lords, is also subject to greater public scrutiny and criticism (see eg the Judicial Power Project, established by the think tank Policy Exchange: judicialpowerproject.org.uk). Charting a series of recent examples of government strike-back, see (albeit noting that strike-back has always been a feature of the British constitution): C. Harlow and R. Rawlings, "'Striking Back' and 'Clamping Down': An Alternative Perspective on Judicial Review" in J. Bell, M. Elliott, J.N.E. Varuhas, and P. Murray (eds), *Public Law Adjudication in Common Law Systems* (Oxford, Hart Publishing, 2016).

172 *Kennedy*, above n 102 at [46], [133]; *Osborn*, above n 168 at [54]–[63]; and see *Unison*, above n 108 at [64]. Judicial speeches have also voiced this concern: see eg Lord Toulson, "Fundamental Rights and Common Law," keynote address delivered to the "Fundamental Rights Conference: A Public Law Perspective," London School of Economics, 10 October 2015.

173 A linked concern has also been voiced that an undue focus on Convention norms could undermine English courts' standing and influence in the wider common law world: Lord Judge, "The Judicial Studies Board Lecture 2010," Inner Temple, London, 17 March 2010, 8 ("It would be a sad day if the home of the common law lost its standing as a common Law [*sic*] authority"), http://webarchive.nationalarchives.gov.uk/20131202164909/http://judiciary.gov.uk/Resources/JCO/Documents/Speeches/lcj-jsb-lecture-2010.pdf.

174 Above text to n 144ff.

most cases in the Administrative Court continue to revolve around axiomatic common law grounds.[175] Thus, the Supreme Court's view of the public law landscape is likely skewed by its own docket. Third, underlying the concern is an idea that common law review and the HRA are institutional competitors. But this is questionable. Arguably, the fields complement one another, one ensuring the proper exercise of power, the other protecting basic rights. Fourth, the Court's judicial strategy may backfire: if the common law is subordinated to rights thinking, it may become a mere outpost of human rights law, serving no distinctive function.

A Game of Levels

The Supreme Court faces a conundrum. On the one hand, if it were to ignore the wider context, including the risk of the loss of rights posed by Brexit and potential repeal of the HRA, this could risk backsliding in terms of the legal protection afforded to basic rights and the courts' ability to hold government to account. On the other hand, the introduction of a significant rights dimension into common law review in response to the external drivers risks introducing incoherence into the law and undermining the stability and internal rationality of common law review as well as precipitating allegations of judicial overreach and potential "strike-back" by the political branches and media.

The dominant trend has been towards forging a new rights jurisprudence in the face of the aforementioned external drivers – in particular, importing the rights-based proportionality method from HRA law into the common law. However, as we shall see, and as may be expected, there are different views evident among the Justices as to how the law ought to develop and whether it ought to develop. The law is thus in a state of flux, and there is, in consequence, uncertainty over key questions. For example, there is uncertainty over the status of *Wednesbury*, the status and scope of the application of proportionality at common law, and the interrelationship between any common law proportionality test and *Wednesbury*;[176] and there is also now, as we shall see, emergent uncertainty over the approach to HRA adjudication. In light of

175 See Varuhas 2013, above n 73; S. Nason, *Reconstructing Judicial Review* (Oxford, Hart Publishing, 2017).

176 See in particular *Keyu*, above n 161.

this uncertainty, the Court has indicated that a review of the area may be required.[177]

Most new rights-based developments have occurred in substantive review, albeit (as discussed below) Lord Reed has preferred reviving the augmented legality principle ahead of developing substantive review. Marking out the present wave of rights thinking from the previous wave is that there is evidence of rights-based thinking spreading beyond substantive review and statutory interpretation to other areas, such as procedural fairness.[178] The focus here, however, is on substantive review – as this has been the main site of activity – and the principle of legality – which presents an alternative path for substantive protection of rights at common law. I will focus on two main strands of this emergent jurisprudence, which make up a game of levels, and go on to highlight a third strand, which seeks to prioritize legal coherence.

LEVELLING UP SUBSTANTIVE REVIEW

The first strand, "levelling up," involves developing common law substantive review so that it resembles human rights adjudication. A core aspect of legal development under this vision is the application of structured proportionality at common law to test the legality of administrative action where basic rights are at stake.

Justices have, in seeking to justify these developments, articulated a "continuity" narrative. The concern to shore up the legitimacy of current trends by appealing to history is evident in statements such as the following from Lady Hale in 2015: "We are not making it up as we go along, but building upon the centuries of law and jurisprudence which make up our national narrative."[179] We find, for example, a continuity narrative in statements in recent cases relating to the place of rights in judicial review; these statements also evoke the "pride" theme and echo Lord Hoffmann's grand statements of the confluence of common law and human rights law in *Simms*.[180] In *Pham*, Lord Sumption said, "Many [Convention] rights had been recognized at common law for many years, in some cases since the famous opening chapter of Blackstone's Commentaries on the Laws

---

177 *Youssef*, above n 156 at [55]. See also ibid at [131]–[3].
178 *Osborn*, above n 168.
179 Hale, above n 162.
180 Above, n 132.

of England ('The Rights of Persons')."[181] Lord Mance in *Kennedy* similarly observed that Convention rights would generally, if not always, be expected to find their homologue in domestic law, especially given common lawyers' contribution to the Convention's inception.[182]

The common law has, indeed, long protected many basic rights, first and foremost those in person and property. However, these rights were sourced in private law fields such as tort[183] – it was these rights that Blackstone and Dicey saw as constitutional. Indeed, the modern review system was developed in deliberate contradistinction to rights-based fields, with ideas of rights (including human rights) being marginalized. Where modifications have been made, as with the adoption of anxious scrutiny, these did not involve the creation of actionable rights in judicial review, but rather involved tweaks to pre-existing grounds. Further, many rights in the Convention have not been recognized *as rights* at common law, such as free expression, freedom of religion, freedom to marry, and access to court; these were traditional civil *liberties* – not independently actionable legal rights or entitlements. Where, in recent times, genuine rights equivalent to those in the Convention have been recognized at common law, specifically a right to privacy, they have been housed in private law.[184]

We find a similar continuity narrative in relation to the proportionality method. Full-blown proportionality at common law is explained as a natural and modest evolution of anxious scrutiny or as synonymous with anxious scrutiny.[185] However, a move to proportionality as practised under the HRA at common law obviously constitutes a significant shift, and the anxious scrutiny cases explicitly and repeatedly rejected structured proportionality, instead maintaining a manifest irrationality standard, consonant with the public interest model. Further, anxious scrutiny, like *Wednesbury* more generally, was a marginal head seldom deployed – an outlier – whereas current trends present rights and proportionality at the very heart of the review jurisdiction.

Ultimately, if there is any dominant narrative of the modern system of common law review, it is not one characterized by rights and

---

181 *Pham*, above n 111 at [102].

182 *Kennedy*, above n 102 at [46].

183 Noting that the writ of habeas corpus was a prerogative remedy specifically dedicated to protecting the fundamental right to liberty, but ironically does not play a significant role in modern judicial review despite the increased recourse to the notion of fundamental rights within review. Note also that, even in tort, the law historically fastened on remedies, not rights; such was the nature of the writ system.

184 *Campbell*, above n 70; *Vidal-Hall v Google Inc* [2015] 3 WLR 409.

185 Eg *Kennedy*, above n 102 at [46], [51]ff; *Pham*, above n 111 at [93]ff, [104]ff.

proportionality. In this regard, current trends represent change, not continuity, yet strategically, it is unsurprising that the Court should wish to avoid a narrative of radical change.

The Justices have relied on a number of normative arguments to support the move to rights-based proportionality. One such argument is the "no reason why not" argument: "There seems no reason why" the multi-stage proportionality enquiry "should not be relevant in judicial review even outside the scope of Convention and EU law."[186] Another is that it would be arbitrary or inconsistent to treat "essentially similar issues" differently, "depending on the source of law which is invoked as a ground of challenge."[187]

Such arguments may be rhetorically attractive, but they leave deeper issues unresolved. With anxious scrutiny, it was always clear that the courts exercised a secondary judgment over decisions that were first and foremost for the official decision maker to take, intervening only if the balance struck was patently irrational. But under HRA-inspired proportionality, it is for the courts to exercise the primary and final judgment over which interests are relevant to a given exercise of power, the weight that ought to be accorded to each, and how the balance should ultimately be struck; the court itself exercises a determinative value judgment. As Simon Brown LJ observed in *Smith*, the move from anxious scrutiny to proportionality would involve a "shift" in the "constitutional balance."[188]

It is difficult to see how this shift can be reconciled with the axiomatic, long-standing conception of common law review as a supervisory jurisdiction. If a court itself is to strike the balance between competing interests, and this determination binds the official decision maker, can it any longer be maintained that the court is conducting a *review* as such? Yet the idea that the courts were only ever exercising a secondary, supervisory jurisdiction was crucial to maintaining the legitimacy of the courts' role in common law review; among other reasons, Parliament has conferred the power of decision upon the official, not the court. Other arguments advanced by the Supreme Court to support a move to proportionality, such as the old favourite, that proportionality is more structured than *Wednesbury*,[189] similarly pass over the fact that such a doctrinal shift

186 *Kennedy*, above n 102 at [95].
187 *Pham*, above n 111 at [104].
188 *Smith*, above n 65 at 541.
189 *Kennedy*, above n 102 at [54].

involves the transmutation of a supervisory jurisdiction into a primary jurisdiction.

Importantly, by adopting rights-based proportionality, the judges mandate that the primary focus for the executive decision maker is to be the individual's interests. The public interests, for which the official has been conferred their powers, are relegated to secondary, countervailing concerns. They will enter the analysis only as a potential justification for interference with the individual's interests. It is not clear how this ranking of interests can be reconciled with Parliament's intent in conferring the powers, which is, as the courts have reiterated over several decades, that the powers be exercised to serve the public interest. This concern does not arise under the HRA as Parliament itself mandated that officials must comply with the enumerated rights. The "no reason why not," "consistency," and "structure" arguments do not address these legitimacy concerns.

A further issue, implicated by the foregoing analysis, is that to apply proportionality, the courts need to recognize a raft of new rights at common law, to which the proportionality defence would be attached; proportionality requires a "trigger" and a norm against which justifications can be tested. It is also arguably necessary for rights to be recognized as this helps to justify the courts exercising objective judgment over proportionality; if the normative basis of the claim is an actionable legal right, then substantive questions, such as proportionality, are legitimately for the courts to determine. However, any recognition of a host of new rights is likely to be met with claims of judicial overreach. Surely, in a democratic order, it is for the polity or its representatives to identify those rights that are fundamental and constitutive of the polity. It is generally accepted, for example, that, in the law of tort, courts will be very slow to recognize new rights because decisions to confer new rights or entitlements raise complex questions of distributive justice. The judicial creation of a raft of new rights is even more contentious when these rights are apparently to take priority ahead of those rights Parliament has enacted in the HRA.

Thus, for example, in *Pham*, several Justices located a right to reside in one's country or a right to British nationality, which they sought to trace to Blackstone.[190] This "right" was adjudicated and enforced in the same way as an HRA right, including application of full-blown proportionality. But there has never been an actionable right to reside at common

190 *Pham*, above n 111 at [97]–[8]; and see [108].

law, correlative to legal duties on authorities. At best, the right to reside was traditionally a mere liberty or privilege, not subject to positive legal protection.[191] The effect of *Pham*, obscured by the Justices' generic appeals to an undifferentiated notion of rights, is to confer a new set of legal entitlements to which authorities must now give effect.[192] The minting of a new right is itself sufficient to raise legitimacy concerns, and that is before accounting for the fact that nationality and citizenship are matters of high politics.

Lastly, the wider ramifications of a move to rights have not been properly considered, yet they are likely to produce a series of unintended ripple effects, which the Court will, in time, have to address. Damages have not been available in the common law of review, but they are a standard remedy for breaches of basic rights in English law and are available under the HRA. If the courts increasingly hold common law review to be a source of fundamental rights, there will be increased pressure to recognize damages. This is especially so in the light of Lord Sumption in *Pham* analogizing the new breed of common law fundamental rights to long-established rights in the person and property – which have been protected through the imposition of damages liability in the law of torts.

It will be more difficult to sustain wide discretion to refuse relief on review, given that it is a defining feature of English law that where there is a right, there ought to be a remedy: *ubi ius, ibi remedium*. The common law's wide public-interest standing rules, which Lord Diplock saw as a core plank of a comprehensive and effective administrative law system, may become difficult to sustain. If the basis of a claim is an individual's legal right, to allow an unaffected interest group to bring the claim may be objectionable on the basis that this involves an interference with the right-holder's autonomy. In this regard, the adoption of a new, human-rights-inspired conception of common law procedural fairness has already had the effect of narrowing the scope of application of duties of consultation.[193] It will

191 As made clear by the quotations from primary and secondary authorities, ibid – eg at [97]–[8].

192 One can see the same mode of reasoning employed in *Kennedy*, above n 102, in relation to free expression, a traditional liberty that was effectively transformed into a legal entitlement by the majority in that case.

193 *R (Moseley) v Haringey LBC* [2014] 1 WLR 3947; J.N.E. Varuhas, "Judicial Review at the Crossroads" (2015) 74 *Cambridge Law Journal* 215.

also be more difficult to maintain the special protections for authorities provided for in review procedure, given that the courts have previously recognized that where claims are based in legal rights, those restrictions are inappropriate.

On the other hand, if the courts are wedded to maintaining certain of these features, such as wide remedial discretion or standing rules, the model of review will be an unstable one. The field will be characterized by a jumble of features, some drawn from human rights law and underpinned by individual-regarding normative concerns, and some drawn from the public interest model, underpinned by public-regarding normative concerns. But incoherence may well be a cost that the Supreme Court is willing to accept.

LEVELLING DOWN HUMAN RIGHTS LAW

So much for levelling up. The second strand evident in the case law, "levelling down," involves human rights adjudication being subordinated to methods drawn from the supervisory jurisdiction. This strand is seemingly a counter to the "up" strand, supported by Justices who favour a narrower judicial role. Nonetheless, the "down" strand follows from, or takes advantage of, the same idea underpinning the up strand, that human rights and common law review might ultimately be synthesized or, at least, that each field should produce the same result on common facts. But instead of the common law being aligned with human rights law, human rights law is aligned with the common law.

Thus, in *Carlile*, Lord Sumption, a proponent of a narrow judicial role,[194] adopted an approach to HRA adjudication akin to a relevant-considerations or *Wednesbury* approach, on the basis that high policy issues were at stake.[195] In a case involving high matters of state, a decision maker would comply with the HRA if it simply took rights into account and reached a decision that was not perverse. The problem with this approach is evidenced by Lord Sumption's views that some matters are pre-eminently for the executive, the court must not usurp the primary decision maker, and to take an approach other than the one

194 Eg J. Sumption, "Judicial and Political Decision-Making: The Uncertain Boundary – the FA Mann Lecture, 2011" (2011) 16 *Judicial Review* 301.

195 *R (Lord Carlile of Berriew QC) v Secretary of State for the Home Department* [2015] AC 945.

he propounded in *Carlile* would be beyond the functions of a "court of review."[196] Such statements would find a natural home in a claim seeking exercise of the courts' supervisory jurisdiction. But they are out of place in a claim based in legal rights. In a rights-based claim, courts may afford weight to executive decisions, but it is ultimately for the court to decide whether a right has been breached and whether that breach was justified; the court is the primary decision maker and must conduct any balancing. To hold that the courts' role under the HRA is to ensure that decision makers keep broadly on track – that they "set about [their] task rationally, by reference to relevant matters and on the correct legal principle"[197] – is to confuse human rights law for a supervisory jurisdiction and for the courts to abdicate their constitutional responsibilities.

The other Justices in *Carlile* were understandably reticent about Lord Sumption's approach. Lord Neuberger, for example, restated orthodoxy: "once a Convention right is affected by a decision of the executive, the court has a duty to decide for itself whether the decision strikes a fair balance between the rights of an individual ... and the interests of the community as a whole."[198] While a court should be "properly humble about its own capacities," the proportionality assessment is nonetheless "ultimately a task for the court";[199] "the question is whether the decision of the Secretary of State *was right*."[200]

Despite the *Carlile* majority's resistance, the more general, emergent trend towards synthesis leaves open the possibility that some judges, especially those cautious about judicial overreach, will approach human rights claims in the way Lord Sumption did. And there is evidence of such approach in subsequent case law[201] and even in the prior decision of *Kennedy*.[202] This should suggest caution on the part of those,

196 Ibid at [46].
197 Ibid at [49].
198 Ibid at [57].
199 Ibid at [105].
200 Ibid at [115]; emphasis added.
201 For an example of a light-touch approach, see *Beghal v Director of Public Prosecutions* [2016] AC 88 at [75]ff.
202 *Kennedy*, above n 102 at [54] ("proportionality review may itself be limited in context to examining whether the exercise of power involved some manifest error or a clear excess of the bounds of discretion").

including Justices, who support a synthesis of common law review and human rights law on the basis that this will invariably enhance rights protection.

BUSINESS AS USUAL

So much for the game of levels. A third strand evident in the cases, despite presently being overshadowed by the "no reason why not" line of thought, seeks to prioritize coherence and stability, and avoid unintended ripple effects. This is to recognize that human rights law and common law review are discrete fields, which are complementary. Each perform distinctively valuable functions – respectively protection of the common good and protection of basic rights – and neither should be subordinated to the other.[203] On this view, the status quo arrived at during the 2000s should be maintained. Thus, in *Kennedy*, Lord Carnwath observed that even where basic interests are implicated at common law, the law's concern is generally more with the decision-making process (pursuant to the anxious scrutiny test), consonant with the orthodox conception of review as supervisory, whereas a court's role in HRA claims is akin to adjudication on the merits.[204]

In *Pham*, Lord Reed took a careful approach, stating that even if anxious scrutiny at common law and structured, rights-based proportionality under the HRA might lead to the same result in some cases, they are not the same test.[205] He thus avoided the revisionism apparent elsewhere in the case law that anxious scrutiny is equivalent to structured proportionality. That Lord Reed distinguished substantive review at common law from HRA adjudication reflects that his analysis was underpinned by an awareness of doctrinal context: that human rights law is a rights-based field, whereas common law review is concerned with the regulation of public power. Thus, he specifically distinguished structured proportionality, as a justification for breach of a *legal right*, from a "looser" enquiry into means and ends under grounds of review, such as *Wednesbury*, which *confine the exercise of public powers*.[206]

---

203 For a defence of this view, see Varuhas 2015, above n 123; J.N.E. Varuhas, "Taxonomy and Public Law" in M. Elliott, J.N.E. Varuhas, and S.W. Stark (eds), *The Unity of Public Law?* (Oxford, Hart Publishing, 2018).

204 *Kennedy*, above n 102 at [245].

205 *Pham*, above n 111 at [115]–[16].

206 Ibid at [113].

While not apparently in favour of developing substantive review to embrace full-blown proportionality, Lord Reed in *Pham* did recall – in a little noticed passage – the otherwise long forgotten line of cases, starting with *Leech*, in which proportionality *had* been applied under the *principle of legality*.[207] The seed sown in *Pham* came into full bloom in the subsequent 2017 case of *Unison*, where Lord Reed, giving the lead judgment, reinvigorated the augmented legality principle, which had fallen into desuetude for the quarter of a century since the cases of *Simms* and *Daly*, and extended it beyond the prison context.[208] The principle was applied with full force to quash a fees order that impeded the "right" of access to justice in the employment context.[209] The order was *ultra vires* as the parent statute did not explicitly authorize the making of orders that disproportionately intruded upon access to justice.

The re-emergence of the augmented legality principle is suggestive of an alternative approach to protecting basic interests, other than developing substantive review – which has so far been the main site of the latest rights-based developments. The augmented principle is certainly not free from concerns of judicial overreach.[210] But its strength over substantive review is that it ties the court's intervention to the question of what Parliament has authorized in the terms of the parent statute; the courts present their intervention as giving effect to legislative intent. Further, if the issue is one of statutory interpretation, it is squarely within the courts' constitutional sphere of responsibility.[211]

The line of cases from *Leech* onwards also provides a precedential foundation that the courts can point to. Further, the conceptual basis of

---

207 Ibid at [118]. Similarly, in *AXA*, above n 150 at [145]–[53], while rejecting the proposition that substantive review grounds applied to Acts of the Scottish Parliament, Lord Reed nonetheless maintained that the principle of legality applies to limit the Parliament's capacity to interfere with basic rights.

208 *Unison*, above n 108.

209 As discussed above (see text to n 107ff), access to court is probably best conceptualized as a liberty.

210 Text to n 111ff above.

211 See *R (DSD) v Parole Board* [2018] EWHC 694 (Admin). Having articulated the proportionality analysis to be applied under the augmented legality principle, the Court said, "These are matters for the court and not for the decision-maker" (at [190]). Contrast the Court's stated approach to substantive review in the same case: "it is for the decision-maker and not for the court to make the primary judgment as to what should be considered in the circumstances of any given case. The court exercises a secondary judgment, framed in broad *Wednesbury* terms" (at [141]).

intervention is entirely orthodox: simple *ultra vires* (rather than infringement of rights simpliciter).[212] In turn, this basis for judicial intervention is less likely to undermine the formal coherence of common law judicial review. On the other hand, the parent statute was barely mentioned in Lord Reed's analysis in *Unison*, and the suspicion will invariably arise that resting judicial intervention on the intention of Parliament is a fig leaf, and, in substance, intervention based on the augmented legality principle is no different than application of rights-based proportionality as a head of substantive review.

Another question that arises is, why should some "fundamental rights" cases be adjudicated on the basis of substantive review and others on the basis of the legality principle? In this regard, one commonality that stands out among the augmented legality cases is that all concern review of delegated legislation (as opposed to administrative discretion). Strategically, it would be difficult for the Court to deploy intensive substantive review in such cases given that long-standing precedents emphasize a highly deferential approach to substantive review of delegated legislation.[213] It is, perhaps, more than coincidence that the courts have chosen to reinvigorate the augmented principle of legality specifically in the context of review of statutory instruments, just as UK ministers are about to be bestowed with wide-ranging powers to make statutory instruments under Henry VIII clauses contained in the European Union (Withdrawal) Bill.

Conclusion

Over time, different forces have operated to push and pull common law development in different directions, militating against any linear narrative of how the House of Lords and Supreme Court have located the role of rights within common law judicial review. However, placing current trends in the wider context of the development of modern judicial review over four decades offers greater insight into those trends. In particular, the Supreme Court's sudden turn to rights at common law within the last few years seems explicable on the basis of extra-legal factors including government threats to repeal the HRA, the risk of loss of

212 See *Unison*, above n 108 at [87]. That the orders were held *ultra vires* explains why they were automatically *void ab initio* (at [119]).

213 *Kruse v Johnson* [1898] 2 QB 91; *Nottinghamshire*, above n 36.

vested rights through Brexit, trends in ordinary politics, judicial pride in the common law, and the desire of a newly established Supreme Court to establish its place in the constitutional order. The cost of responding to these wider concerns is that the coherence of the law has been compromised and instability introduced into the system of public law, while there are likely to be increasing concerns over judicial legitimacy and politicization as the courts create a new set of rights and intrude deeper into the administrative sphere. There are also risks of unintended side effects; for example, the move to synthesize common law review and human rights law, while seemingly originally motivated by a desire to enhance rights protection at common law, has opened up the possibility that rights protection under the HRA will be downgraded.

If the account of the last forty years offers any lesson, it is that any attempt at speculation as to the trajectory of future legal development would be foolhardy. A number of possible paths lie before the Supreme Court. Which is chosen will depend on how the Court resolves the push of external drivers, the desire to adapt the law in light of changed circumstances, and the pull of internal concerns of legal coherence and rational legal ordering. The reconciliation of these variables will, in turn, precipitate the next episode in the relationship between rights and administrative law.

9 The Continuing Significance of *Dr Bonham's Case*

HAN-RU ZHOU*

Dr Bonham's Case stands as one of the most iconic cases in the common law world. Every constitutional scholar trained in that legal tradition would almost instantly recognize Coke CJ's famous statement regarding the controlling common law and the voidness of statutes. Yet, more than four centuries later, *Bonham*'s significance in modern constitutionalism remains notoriously controversial and uncertain. The search for any subsisting value from the case is fraught with seemingly insurmountable obstacles.

To state the obvious, *Bonham* was decided in times vastly different from ours, and, in any event, whatever Coke meant with regard to the controlling common law would have been superseded by the establishment of Parliamentary sovereignty. However, the advent of judicial review (of legislation), initially in the United States, breathed new life into *Bonham* as many legal commentators have cast the constitutional authority of courts vis-à-vis legislation in the continuity of Coke's idea of the controlling common law. In recent decades, supreme courts from several common law–based systems appear to have expanded the grounds of judicial review to cover norms not necessarily deriving from constitutional instruments, but said to be traced back to the ancient common law constitution invoked by Coke and his contemporaries. With these "new-old" constitutional developments (re-)entering the fray, making sense of *Bonham* today seems as much about what it

* I extend my thanks to Paul Daly, Matthew Harrington, Noura Karazivan, Michel Morin, Luc Tremblay, and the two anonymous reviewers for their comments on earlier drafts; and to Clara Berké and Maya Grabianowska for their excellent research assistance. This research was supported by the Fonds de recherche du Québec – Société et culture.

was intended to mean as about what each generation of jurists believed (or perhaps simply wanted) it to mean.

This chapter proposes another re-examination of *Bonham* and its legacy. Writing about *Bonham* is undoubtedly a risky enterprise, not least given the sheer volume of literature on the subject. But while studies of *Bonham* have typically sought to reconstruct its "original meaning" from a purely historical perspective, the present enquiry aims at integrating the successive interpretations of the case over time into a narrative of the emergence and development of judicial review. Building on *Bonham*'s certainties and uncertainties, the proposed account seeks to connect it to our times and shed a useful light on the practice of judicial review in a way that could also reflect the largely intertwined constitutional histories of the world's different common law–based systems. Ultimately, *Bonham*'s significance in modern constitutionalism depends on how it is and will be reinterpreted and re-appropriated, in the same way that other iconic laws and cases have been reinterpreted and re-appropriated by each generation of jurists.

The first part of the chapter returns to *Bonham* and Coke's times by setting out his reported judicial and extrajudicial statements concerning the controlling common law. But if *Bonham* is to be understood as more than just a historical curiosity, a fresh look at the case's influence on ensuing judicial developments is called for. In this respect, the second part of this chapter seeks to draw a portrait, as near-complete as possible, of the relevant case law from Coke's era until the dawn of parliamentary sovereignty. This examination shows that Coke's idea of the controlling common law and the voidness of statutes was frequently cited and adopted by judges and lawyers well into the eighteenth century, a period longer than what many legal scholars believe. The prevailing position is that the establishment of parliamentary supremacy in the United Kingdom and the adoption of a written Constitution in the United States sounded the death knell for *Bonham*.

The third part of the chapter suggests that the latter development may well have allowed the legacy of *Bonham* to subsist in the background – in particular, through Marshall CJ's famous exposition of the supremacy of the Constitution and the role of the US Supreme Court in *Marbury v Madison*. The part then ties the more recent constitutional developments concerning the rise of unwritten constitutional norms, particularly far reaching in the Canadian context, into the larger, evolving account of the common law and its relationship with statute law over time and across legal systems as a distinctive feature of the common law tradition.

Bonham and the Search for Its "Original Meaning"

In 1606, the Royal College of Physicians, a body incorporated by letters patent twice confirmed by statute, prohibited Thomas Bonham, holder of a Doctor of Physic degree from the University of Cambridge, from practising medicine in London for a month because he did not have a licence issued by the college. When Bonham continued to practise despite the prohibition, he was fined and ordered to cease his medical practice. Upon his continued refusal to comply, he was arrested and imprisoned. Bonham then brought an action for false imprisonment against the college.

In the Court of Common Pleas, Coke CJ held that the college did not have the power to imprison Bonham as neither the statutes nor the letters patent granted the college powers to fine and imprison a person for practising without a license; its powers extended only to malpractice. Even if they had granted such powers, Coke added, the college had not used them correctly. As the letters patent confirmed by statute allowed the college to receive half of all the fines that it imposed, Coke found that the college had benefited from the outcome of the prosecution and had therefore acted contrary to the principle that no one ought to be judge in his own cause. At which point, he famously stated,

> In many cases the common law will controul Acts of Parliament and sometimes adjudge them to be utterly void: for when an Act of Parliament is against common right or reason, or repugnant, or impossible to be performed, the common law will controul it and adjudge such Act to be void.[1]

Some authors have claimed that Coke expressed a contrary view in the very next case of his *Reports*, in which he wrote,

> There are divers customs in London which are against common right, and the rule of the common law, and yet they are allowed in our books, and *eo potius*, because they have not only the force of a custom, but are also supported and fortified by authority of Parliament.[2]

1 *Dr Bonham's Case* (1609) 8 Co Rep 113b at 118a; 77 ER 646 at 652. It has been observed that this statement does not appear in the manuscript report of the case or in its other printed report, Brownlow's; see C.M. Gray, "Bonham's Case Reviewed" (1972) 116 *Proceedings of the American Philosophical Society* 35 at 36, 46.

2 *Case of the City of London* (1609) 8 Co Rep 121b at 126a; 77 ER 658 at 664, discussed in G. Burgess, *Absolute Monarchy and the Stuart Constitution* (New Haven, CT, Yale University Press, 1996) at 187–8.

That Coke would have contradicted himself or changed his mind between two consecutive case reports is a surprising claim. Indeed, his subsequent judgment in *Rowles v Mason* suggests that the apparently contradictory statements have to be understood within his conception of the interaction among the different parts of the law. In Coke's words,

> The Law consists of three parts. First, common law. Secondly, statute law, which corrects, abridges, and explains the common law, the third custom which takes away the common law: but the common law corrects, allows, and disallows, both statute law, and custom, for if there be repugnancy in statute; or unreasonableness in custom, the common law disallows and rejects it, as it appears by *Doctor Bonham's case*, and 8 Coke, 27, H. 6, Annuity.[3]

Coke's other cases and writings help us gain a better sense of his famous statement in *Bonham*. In *Prohibitions Del Roy*, Coke reported his exchange with King James I, in which the two men debated whether the king had the authority to render judgments, the latter arguing that "he thought the law was founded upon reason, and that he and others had reason, as well as the Judges."[4] But for Coke, the king was referring to "every man's natural reason," whereas *reason* in the legal context meant "the artificial reason and judgment of law, which law is an act which requires long study and experience, before that a man can attain to the cognizance of it."[5] As law and reason are *summa ratio*, the "golden met-wand and measure to try the causes of the subjects,"[6] any custom, proclamation, by-law or Act of Parliament "against law and reason" is deemed void – that is, unlawful and of no legal force or effect.[7]

On 17 October 1616, Coke was called before Lord Ellesmere LC, at the direction of King James I, to be told of His Majesty's "distaste" of

---

3 *Rowles v Mason* (1612) 2 Brownl & Golds 192 at 197–8; 123 ER 892 at 895.

4 *Prohibitions Del Roy* (1607) 12 Co Rep 63 at 64–5; 77 ER 1342 at 1343.

5 Ibid. See also Co Litt 62a; 2 Co Inst 97b.

6 *Prohibitions Del Roy* (1607) 12 Co Rep 63 at 65; 77 ER 1342 at 1343. See also 4 Co Inst 41.

7 See *Case of Proclamations* (1610) 12 Co Rep 74 at 75; 77 ER 1352 at 1353; *Bonham* (1609) 8 Co Rep 113b at 118a; 77 ER 646 at 652–3; *Rowles v Mason* (1612) 2 Brownl & Golds 192 at 198; 123 ER 892 at 895; 1 Co Litt 62a. In Coke's earlier reports before his appointment to the bench, see *Lord Cromwell's Case* (1578) 4 Co Rep 12b at 13a; 76 ER 877 at 880; *Chamberlain of London's Case* (1589) 5 Co Rep 62b; 77 ER 150; *Case of Monopolies* (1601) 11 Co Rep 84b at 86a–7a; 77 ER 1260 at 1262–4.

some parts of Coke's reports and asked to revise five cases. The fourth question demanded of Coke was reported as follows:

> In Dr. Bonham's case, what he means by this passage, That in many cases the common law shall control acts of parliament, and sometimes shall judge them to be merely void: For where an act of parliament is against common right and reason, the law shall control it, and adjudge it void.[8]

Four days later, Coke delivered his answer, in which he essentially repeated every word of the contentious part of the case, stating once more that "[t]he words of my report do not import any new opinion, but only a relation of such authorities of law, as had been adjudged and resolved in ancient and former times, and were cited in the argument of Bonham's case."[9] On 15 November of the same year, Coke was removed from the King's Bench. At the swearing-in ceremony of Coke's replacement as the new chief justice, Ellesmere LC reiterated his disapproval of judges who claim "to have power to judge Statutes and Acts of Parliament to be void, if they conceived them to be against common right and reason" except in cases "of impossibilities or direct repugnances."[10] Such a power, Ellesmere LC added, should remain with the king and Parliament.

Rowles v Mason is the only one of Coke's known cases where *Bonham* is cited.[11] While his *Institutes* make a few references to it in passing, some authors argue that, by then, Coke had implicitly recanted his opinion regarding the controlling common law and accepted the absolute legal authority of Parliament.[12]

---

8 "Papers, containing Lord Chancellor Ellesmere's exceptions to Sir Edward Coke's reports, and Sir Edward Coke's answers," 16–22 October 1616.

9 Ibid.

10 *The Lord Chancellors Speech to Sir Henry Mountague, When He Was Sworn Chief Justice of the Kings-Bench* (1616) Moore KB 827 at 828; 72 ER 931 at 932.

11 See also D.C. Smith, *Sir Edward Coke and the Reformation of the Laws: Religion, Politics and Jurisprudence, 1578–1616* (Cambridge, Cambridge University Press, 2014) 173.

12 See eg J.D. Goldsworthy, *The Sovereignty of Parliament: History and Philosophy* (Oxford, Oxford University Press, 1999) 112–13, citing Co Litt 115b ("The Common Law hath no controller in any part of it, but the high Court of Parliament, and if it be not abrogated or altered by Parliament, it remainses still"); 2 Co Inst Proeme ("The highest and most binding Laws are the Statutes which are established by Parliament"); and 4 Co Inst 36 ("Of the power and jurisdiction of the Parliament for making of laws in proceeding by Bill, it is so transcendent and absolute, as it

More than four centuries later, the interpretation of *Bonham* continues to divide legal commentators into two broad camps. In a nutshell, one side has interpreted Coke's words as an exercise of statutory construction, without accepting the existence of a higher common law binding on Parliament, while the other side regards the controlling common law as something closer to a nascent reference to judicial review.[13]

In addition to the relatively limited direct evidence of what Coke meant, the interpretation of the available historical materials, including the drawing of any relation to the modern legal context, is further complicated by the significant differences between Coke's period and our own. For instance, the distinction between statutory construction and the invalidation of statutes did not exist at that time, nor did the notion of judicial review based on a higher law. The concept of separation among the three branches of government was still unfamiliar to English jurists as Montesquieu's masterwork, *The Spirit of the Laws*, would not be published for another 140 years. Parliament passed laws but was also considered the "highest and most honourable Court of Justice."[14] The principle of parliamentary sovereignty had not yet been established, either. Thus, statutes did not have the same authority as today and were often viewed as mere declarations of natural law or of the common law. As Jeffrey Goldsworthy has admitted, "[i]t would be fruitless to attempt to settle this interpretative question here, or even to add to the debate."[15] In one of the more recent studies of *Bonham*, another legal historian remarks that "[u]nless significant new evidence is identified, it seems unlikely that agreement is possible over such an ambiguous passage."[16]

---

cannot be confined either for causes or persons within any bounds"). See also ibid 72 ("And the proceedings in that Court for so long time, & under so many honourable Judges and reverend Sages of the law, hath gotten such a foundation, as cannot now without an Act of Parliament be shaken. And the errors in the Kings Bench cannot be reversed ... but in the High Court of Parliament").

13 See eg R. Berger, "*Doctor Bonham's Case*: Statutory Construction or Constitutional Theory?" (1969) 117 *University of Pennsylvania Law Review* 521; R.A. MacKay, "Coke: Parliamentary Sovereignty or the Supremacy of the Law?" (1924) 22 *Michigan Law Review* 215.

14 4 Co Inst 39.

15 Goldsworthy, above n 12 at 112.

16 I. Williams, "Edward Coke" in D.J. Galligan (ed), *Constitutions and the Classics: Patterns of Constitutional Thought from Fortescue to Bentham* (Oxford, Oxford University Press, 2014) 100.

Besides the obvious historical value of the literature expounding *Bonham*, it is worth questioning the current legal usefulness of pursuing the enquiry over that case's original meaning. The reality remains that it has been used (or, some have argued, misused) to justify judicial review or claims pertaining to a common law constitution. Even if we knew for certain what Coke meant, how would such knowledge affect the study of contemporary constitutional debates? It seems that this purpose could be better served by shifting the focus from the search for the original meaning of *Bonham* to its successive reinterpretations, leading up to today's practice of judicial review in common law–based systems.

Beyond *Bonham*: The Voidness of Statutes from the Late Tudor Period to the Dawn of the Age of Parliamentary Sovereignty

As early as 1581, the King's Bench held in a slander case that the impugned private act on which the plaintiff had based his claim "was against law and reason, and therefore void,"[17] thus ruling in favour of the defendant represented by Coke himself. Following *Bonham*, the notion that statutes were voidable was repeated by other judges of the Court of Common Pleas. The issue in *Day v Savadge*[18] arose from the plaintiff's refusal to make a payment of wharfage of his goods to the City of London on the basis of a custom according to which all freemen were discharged from wharfage payment. Denying the existence of such a custom, the city in turn invoked another custom, allowing it to certify to the justices the existence of any custom of the city. Moreover, the city argued that all its customs, including the custom of certificate, had been confirmed "by authority of Parliament."

Hobart CJ delivered a judgment in favour of the plaintiff, holding that there was no such custom of certificate, before adding that parliamentary support would have been irrelevant, given the partiality of that custom. Echoing both *Calvin's Case* and *Bonham*, Hobart CJ concluded his judgment with the statement that "even an Act of Parliament, made against natural equity, as to make a man Judge in his own cause, is void in it self, for jura naturae sunt immutabilia, and they are leges legum."[19]

17 *Lord Cromwell's Case* (1578) 4 Co Rep 12b at 13a; 76 ER 877 at 880.

18 *Day v Savadge* (1614) Hob 85, 80 ER 235.

19 Ibid, Hob 87, 80 ER 237. See also *Calvin's Case* (1608) 7 Co Rep 1a at 12b–13b; 77 ER 377 at 392–3.

In *Sheffield v Ratcliffe*, decided the following year, Hobart CJ responded thus to a controversy in the case law presented to him regarding the interpretation of the consequences of forfeiture for treason:

> If you ask me then, by what rule the Judges guided themselves in this diverse exposition of the self same word and sentence?
>
> I answer, it was by that liberty and authority that Judges have over laws, especially over statute laws, according to reason and best convenience, to mould them to the truest and best use.[20]

While Hobart CJ did not refer to *Bonham* in those two cases, they have generally been cited as approval of Coke's notion of the controlling common law.[21]

In *Hutchins v Player*, the plaintiff challenged the validity of an act of the common council of the City of London regulating the trade of draperies in Blackwell Hall and Leadenhall. In response to one of the plaintiff's objections that the act was contrary to the Magna Carta, Bridgman CJ cited chapter 9 of the Charter, which preserves the City's "old Liberties and Customs," but then referred to Hobart CJ's statement in *Day v Savadge* in support of the proposition that

> a custom in London against common reason and natural equity (though it be confessed by pleading to be confirmed by Act of Parliament, 7 R. 2) yet it is not allowable; both because it is none of the customs intended, and because even an Act of Parliament made against natural equity, as to make a man judge in his own cause, is void in itself.[22]

---

20 *Sheffield v Ratcliffe* (1615) Hob 334 at 346; 80 ER 475 at 486.

21 See eg A.D. Boyer, "Understanding, Authority, and Will: Sir Edward Coke and the Elizabethan Origins of Judicial Review" (1997) 39 *Boston College Law Review* 43 at 85 fn 151, 90 fn 166; P.A. Joseph, "Beyond Parliamentary Sovereignty" (1989) 18 *Anglo-American Law Review* 91 at 93; T.F.T. Plucknett, "Bonham's Case and Judicial Review" (1926) 40 *Harvard Law Review* 30 at 49–50; J.E.W. Thomas, "The Relationship of Parliament and the Courts: A Tentative Thought or Two for the New Millennium" (2000) 31 *Victoria University of Wellington Law Review* 5 at 17; M.D. Walters, "The Common Law Constitution in Canada: Return of *Lex Non Scripta* as Fundamental Law" (2001) 51 *University of Toronto Law Journal* 91 at 111. But see J. Goldsworthy, "Response to the Commentators" (2002) 27 *Australian Journal of Legal Philosophy* 193 at 195.

22 *Hutchins v Player* (1663) OBridg 272 at 300; 124 ER 585 at 600–1.

Just a few years earlier, in *AG v Mico*, the defendant, charged in the Court of Exchequer for corrupting or attempting to corrupt two customs officers, had attacked the part of the bill compelling discovery against him. In a detailed set of reasons, Widdrington CJ gave judgment for the defendant, finding that no law, reason, or authorities compelled him to answer. Widdrington CJ distinguished among the law of God, the law of nature, and the law of the land. In his discussion of the law of nature, he cited several cases that applied the rule according to which a man is not obliged to condemn himself, before stating the following:

> Now if this be the law and choice of Nature, then is it superior to all positive laws, and is called lex æterna, or the moral law, 7 Rep. 12 b., *Calvin's case*. It is the law that was infused into the heart of man at his first creation; and whatever positive laws are contrary to this law of Nature and reason, they are void in themselves, vide 8 Rep. 118, *Doctor Bonham's case*.[23]

Well before *Bonham*, judges had also asserted the voidness of Acts of Parliament when they were called upon to arbitrate conflicting claims between the Crown and Parliament. In the *Case of Monopolies*, the King's Bench ruled that the letters patent granting the plaintiff a licence to import and sell playing cards amounted to "a monopoly against the common law," given the general prohibition enacted by Parliament *pro bono publico*. However, the Court still recognized that

> forasmuch as an Act of Parliament which generally prohibits a thing upon a penalty, which is popular, or only given to the King, may be inconvenient to divers particular persons, in respect of person, place, time, &c. for this reason the law has given power to the King, to dispense with particular persons.[24]

The rationale for the dispensing power was explained by Coke in the *Case of Non Obstante* to lie in the king's "sovereign power to command his subjects to serve him for the public weal." Because it was "solely and inseparably" annexed to his person, "this Royal power cannot be restrained by any Act of Parliament, neither in *thesi*, nor in *hypothesi*."[25] One example was the royal prerogative of mercy and to pardon,

23 *AG v Mico* (1658) Hard 137 at 140; 145 ER 419 at 421.

24 *Case of Monopolies* (1601) 11 Co Rep 84a at 88a; 77 ER 1260 at 1265.

25 *Case of Non Obstante* (1581) 12 Co Rep 18 at 18; 77 ER 1300 at 1300 [reference omitted].

vis-à-vis which Coke even stated that Parliament knew that if it passed an Act to restrain the prerogative, that Act "shall not bind the King."[26] In the *Case of the Ship-Money*,[27] it was expressly recognized that, under necessity, the king could dispense with an Act of Parliament to raise money for the defence of the kingdom.

In what was probably the leading case of the time on the dispensing power, *Thomas v Sorrell*, the defendant was sued for selling wine without a licence in contravention of an Act of Parliament, against which he invoked the letters patent granting him the right to sell wine notwithstanding the Act. In stating in a dictum that the king might dispense with certain Acts, Vaughan CJ distinguished between *mala in se* and *mala prohibita*, explaining that

> what we call *malum in se* is either that which the very term implies to be unlawful, as murder is unlawful killing, adultery is unlawful copulation; and these can by no law be made lawful, and much less can the King dispense with them; for such laws would certainly be void, because there is a contradiction in the very term; for it is impossible that murder, which is the unlawful killing of man, should be lawful.[28]

The king's exercise of his dispensing power was upheld once more in *Godden v Hales*,[29] before its abolition by the Bill of Rights 1689, subject to statutory exceptions.

The notion of voidable statutes survived the Glorious Revolution, maintaining a degree of judicial support until the Victorian era. In the case of *City of London v Wood*, the defendant appealed the judgment of the court of the mayor and aldermen of London, which ordered him to pay a fine to the city pursuant to a city by-law. In overturning the Mayor's Court judgment, Holt CJ set out the main issue of the case in the following terms:

> But the true great point is, that the Court is held before the mayor and aldermen, and the action brought in the names of the mayor and

26 *Case of Non Obstante* (1581) 12 Co Rep 18 at 18; 77 ER 1300 at 1300. See also *Calvin's Case* (1608) 7 Co Rep 1a at 14a; 77 ER 377 at 393.

27 *Case of Ship-Money* (1637) 3 StTr 825.

28 *Thomas v Sorrell* (1673) 1 Freem 137; 89 ER 100; (1672) Vaugh 330 at 336–7; 124 ER 1098 at 1102.

29 *Godden v Hales* (1686) 2 ShowKB 475; 89 ER 1050.

> commonalty; and that very man, who is head of the city, and without whom the city has no ability or capacity to sue, is the very person before whom the action is brought; and this cannot be by the rules of any law whatever, for it is against all laws that the same person should be party and Judge in the same cause, for it is manifest contradiction. … And what my Lord Coke says in *Dr. Bonham's case* in his 8 Co. is far from any extravagancy, for it is a very reasonable and true saying, that if an Act of Parliament should ordain that the same person should be party and Judge, or, which is the same thing, Judge in his own cause, it would be a void Act of Parliament; for it is impossible that one should be Judge and party, for the Judge is to determine between party and party, or between the Government and the party; and an Act of Parliament can do no wrong, though it may do several things that look pretty odd; for it may discharge one from his allegiance to the Government he lives under, and restore him to the state of nature; but it cannot make one that lives under a Government Judge and party.[30]

In reported cases from as late as 1717 and 1725,[31] some King's Bench judges would still refer approvingly to Hobart CJ's statements in *Sheffield v Ratcliffe* and *Day v Savadge*, cited earlier.

By the time Blackstone published the first volume of his *Commentaries* in 1765, the notion of voidable statutes had dwindled significantly. "[I]f the parliament will positively enact a thing to be done which is unreasonable, I know of no power that can control it,"[32] wrote Blackstone, qualifying judicial control over legislation as "subversive of all government." He insisted that "there is no court that has power to defeat the intent of the legislature, when couched in such evident and express words, as leave no doubt whether it was the intent of the legislature or no."[33] While still acknowledging that "acts of parliament impossible to be performed are of no validity,"[34] Blackstone limited this rule to one of statutory construction. Perhaps betraying an ambivalence reminiscent of Holt CJ's statement in *City of London v Wood*, Blackstone cited *Bonham* approvingly on the one hand, but opined on the other hand that a court

30 *City of London v Wood* (1701) 12 Mod 669 at 687–8; 88 ER 1592 at 1602.

31 See *Thornby v Fleetwood* (1717) 10 Mod 406 at 412; 88 ER 784 at 787; *The Cy of Mercers & Ironmongers of Chester v Bowker* (1725) 1 Str 639; 93 ER 751.

32 1 Bl Comm 91.

33 Ibid.

34 Ibid.

could not "defeat" a statute clearly permitting a man to be a judge in his own cause. While some judges and lawyers would continue to invoke a judicial authority to disregard Acts of Parliament contrary to the law of England as founded in natural law, divine law, or the common law,[35] Blackstone's *Commentaries* are generally regarded as confirming the establishment of parliamentary sovereignty.

In sum, from at least the late Tudor period until the first half of the eighteenth century, the notion of voidable statutes was widely accepted by judges. The study of the case law from that period chronicles an evolution in the interpretation of that notion, ending with the advent of parliamentary sovereignty. The most visible part of this evolution is a decline in the frequency of judicial statements on, and parties' references to, the notion of voidable statutes, combined with an increase in the frequency of judicial statements accepting the supreme legal authority of Parliament. Moreover, the case law shows a tendency to restrict the grounds for voiding statutes.

To restate the relevant part of Coke's judgment in *Bonham*, the common law will control an Act of Parliament and adjudge it to be void when that Act is against common right and reason, *or* repugnant, *or* impossible to be performed. While judicial statements that statutes may be voided abound, there has been no other judicial mention of the entire grounds for voiding statutes, as expressed in *Bonham*, except by Lord Ellesmere LC himself in objecting to Coke's statement.[36] In *City of London v Wood*, cited earlier, Holt CJ even appeared to have endorsed both the notion of voidable statutes and that of legislative supremacy. Thereafter, even the principle that no man can be judge in his own cause, so repeatedly invoked as the archetypal controlling common law principle, would be subject to exceptions.[37]

With parliamentary sovereignty firmly in place, it would *a priori* make sense to assume that Coke's notion of the controlling common law had been laid to rest. However, declaring it dead would be difficult to square with the remarkable attention it has received ever since,

35 See eg *Heathfield v Chilton* (1767) 4 BurrSC 2015 at 2016; 98 ER 50 at 50 (Lord Mansfield); *Stewart v Lawton* (1823) 1 Bing 374, 130 ER 151; *Forbes v Cochrane* (1824) 2 B&C 448 at 471–3; 107 ER 450 at 459–60; *Grand Junction Canal Co v Dimes* (1849) 12 Beav 63 at 65–8; 50 ER 984 at 985–6.

36 *Earl of Oxford's Case* (1615) 1 RepCh 1, 21 ER 485.

37 See eg *Between the Parishes of Great Charte v Kennington* (1742) 2 Str 1173, 93 ER 1107; *Dimes* (1849) 12 Beav 63 at 77; 50 ER 984 at 989; 1 Bl Comm 91.

especially beyond the British Isles. In what may be qualified as an exile rather than a death, *Bonham* and its legacy have found their way back into mainstream constitutional discourse, albeit on other continents through British colonization and decolonization.

Judicial Review and the Modern Controlling Common Law

In the British colonies, a doctrine of statutory voidness, supported by closer judicial oversight, was introduced into colonial law through a combination of imperial legislation, colonial constitutions, and judicial pronouncements.[38] When the colonies achieved independence, the set of legal norms held as superior to statutory law found their way into the new countries' legal systems through their first national constitutions, as expounded by their supreme courts. The paramount example is the United States. In *Marbury v Madison*, Marshall CJ famously defended "certain principles, supposed to have been long and well established."[39] One of these "fundamental principles of our society ... too plain to be contested" was that the Constitution "controls" legislation, and any law "repugnant to the Constitution is void."[40] Sixteen years later, in *McCulloch v Maryland*, Marshall CJ reiterated "[t]his great principle ... that the Constitution and the laws made in pursuance thereof are supreme; that they control the Constitution and laws of the respective States, and cannot be controlled by them."[41] Holding the impugned state law to be "incompatible with, and repugnant to, the constitutional

38 The most widely known legislative example is s 2 of the Colonial Laws Validity Act 1865, but older versions of this provision had been enacted for more than a century back. See eg s IX of An Act for Preventing Frauds, and Regulating Abuses in the Plantation Trade 1696 (7 & 8 Wil 3 c 22), which states that "all laws, by-laws, usages or customs ... in any of the said plantations, which are in any wise repugnant to the before mentioned laws, or any of them, so far as they do relate to the said plantations, or any of them, or which are any ways repugnant to this present act, or to any other law hereafter to be made in this kingdom, so far as such law shall relate to and mention the said plantations, are illegal, null and void, to all intents and purposes whatsoever." On judicial review based on state constitutions in the pre-revolutionary period, see R. Williams, ch 6 in this volume.

39 *Marbury v Madison* (1803) 5 US (1 Cranch) 137 at 176.

40 Ibid at 177–8.

41 *McCulloch v Maryland* (1819) 17 US (4 Wheat.) 316 at 426.

laws of the Union," the Supreme Court declared it "unconstitutional and void."[42]

Anyone reading *Marbury* and *McCulloch* cannot fail to note the presence of the same key terms once used by Coke, with only the *Constitution* substituted for the *common law*.[43] To many constitutional scholars in the United States and elsewhere, the intellectual origins of *Marbury* can be traced back to *Bonham*. As Douglas Edlin has stated, "*Bonham* is widely understood to be the conceptual foundation for the modern doctrine of judicial review, particularly as developed in the United States."[44] One author even suggested that a statue of Coke should be erected in the US Supreme Court building![45] By contrast, other constitutional scholars such as Larry Kramer assert that the US concept of judicial review did not originate in Coke's work.[46]

To be sure, the literature on *Marbury* and on judicial review more generally is extraordinarily rich, and whether Marshall was influenced by *Bonham* and English theories of the voidness of statutes remains sharply contested. Without taking a position on this protracted debate, one can still query how *Bonham* became such a central figure, despite all the ambiguity surrounding that case and the dearth of concrete evidence connecting Coke's notion of the controlling common law to US judicial review. According to some legal historians such as Samuel Thorne,[47] the political theory taken to underlie Coke's judgment in *Bonham* was not, in fact, his own work, but rather that of later generations of judges, commentators, and lawyers, who bestowed on it a content adapted to their own constitutional systems.

As had happened with the interpretation of *Bonham*, the debate over its relationship with judicial review evolved into an assumption. According to one critic of the Cokeian brand of judicial review, that assumption is that, in the overall history or story of judicial review,

42 Ibid at 425, 436.

43 See N. Feldman, "The Voidness of Repugnant Statutes: Another Look at the Meaning of *Marbury*" (2004) 148 *Proceedings of the American Philosophical Society* 27.

44 D.E. Edlin, *Judges and Unjust Laws: Common Law Constitutionalism and the Foundations of Judicial Review* (Ann Arbor, MI, University of Michigan Press, 2008) 73.

45 D.O. McGovney, "The British Origin of Judicial Review of Legislation" (1944) 93 *University of Pennsylvania Law Review* 1 at 47.

46 See L.D. Kramer, *The People Themselves: Popular Constitutionalism and Judicial Review* (New York, Oxford University Press, 2004) 20–4.

47 S.E. Thorne, "Dr Bonham's Case" (1938) 54 *Law Quarterly Review* 543 at 545, 552.

Coke's work represented, at the very least, "the point of intellectual transition between the medieval and the modern worlds."[48] Eventually, *Bonham* also came to be regarded as part of the historical foundations of judicial review in several common law–based systems. To some constitutional observers, *Bonham*'s ideas might even have been revived in the United Kingdom and New Zealand[49] (where courts do not conduct US-style judicial review).

With judicial review having become a staple of most common law–based systems, a more recent illustration of what appears to be yet another reinterpretation of *Bonham*'s legacy is the challenge to the conventional position that the exercise of judicial review must be based exclusively on the terms of the constitutional instrument. In other words, "[a]ny claim about constitutional law has to be connected to the text in some way, however contrived."[50] The adoption of written constitutions in common law–based systems may well have initially limited the debates concerning the exercise of judicial review to the confines of their provisions, thus somewhat overshadowing the subsisting existence and role of constitutional norms not necessarily codified by a country's constitution. One need look no further than judicial review itself, a basic principle now so integral to many countries' legal systems, although it is often not formally stated in their constitutions. And from this first principle, a number of legal principles and rules are drawn as corollaries – for instance, those that are essential to the proper exercise of judicial review, such as judicial impartiality, judicial independence, and, more broadly, the separation of powers.

Despite the unequivocal terms in which the conventional position is framed, several legal systems have developed a practice of judicial

48 G.L. McDowell, "Coke, Corwin and the Constitution: The 'Higher Law Background' Reconsidered" (1993) 55 *Review of Politics* 393 at 399 [reference omitted].

49 See eg R.A. Edwards, "*Bonham's* Case: The Ghost in the Constitutional Machine" (1996) 11 *Denning Law Journal* 63 at 70–2; J. Leclair, "L'avènement du constitutionnalisme en Occident: fondements philosophiques et contingence historique" (2011) 41 *Revue de droit de l'Université de Sherbrooke* 159 at 197; T. Poole, "Back to the Future? Unearthing the Theory of Common Law Constitutionalism" (2003) 23 *Oxford Journal of Legal Studies* 435 at 447; Williams, above n 16 at 89–90.

50 D.A. Strauss, "Foreword: Does the Constitution Mean What It Says?" (2015) 129 *Harvard Law Review* 1 at 21. See also W.N. Eskridge and J.A. Ferejohn, *A Republic of Statutes: The New American Constitution* (New Haven, CT, Yale University Press, 2010) 34, 59–60; P.W. Hogg, *Constitutional Law of Canada*, 5th edn (Toronto, Carswell, 2007) 15–52.

review founded on norms that are more or less loosely connected to the terms of their respective constitutions. These norms are "not derived by normal processes of textual interpretation from the written Constitution."[51] They "form an independent unwritten component of the supreme constitution existing alongside the written texts."[52] Yet, Laurence Tribe adds, their "apparent detachment and distance from the Constitution's text does not prevent any of [them] from being identified by nearly everyone as binding elements of our nation's supreme law."[53]

A well-known Canadian example is the *implied bill of rights* theory. In the period before the adoption of the Canadian Charter of Rights and Freedoms in 1982, one way of securing a measure of protection for individual rights and freedoms was to read them into the Constitution. While the relevant cases of judicial review focused on freedom of expression, it has been argued that the theory extended to freedom of conscience and religion, freedom of assembly, and freedom of political association. The clearest authority in favour of a constitutionally protected, implied bill of rights is *Ontario (AG) v OPSEU*, in which Beetz J, delivering the majority judgment of the Supreme Court, cited with approval the early implied bill of rights cases before stating (in a dictum) that, quite apart from Charter considerations, "neither Parliament nor the provincial legislatures may enact legislation the effect of which would be to substantially interfere with the operation of this basic constitutional structure [which contemplates the existence of the right to freedom of political expression]."[54] However, he held in the end that the impugned statute, which prohibited civil servants' involvement in political activities, did not unduly offend freedom of expression.

A more recent instance of judicial review based on unwritten constitutional principles is *Re Provincial Court Judges*,[55] where the validity of a series of provincial statutes regulating the salaries of provincial statutory court judges was challenged on the grounds that they violated judicial independence. As the Supreme Court acknowledged, the provisions of the Canadian Constitution guarantee judicial independence

---

51 T.C. Grey, "Do We Have an Unwritten Constitution?" (1975) 27 *Stanford Law Review* 703 at 703–4; Hogg, ibid at 15–51.

52 Walters, above n 21 at 101.

53 L.H. Tribe, *The Invisible Constitution* (Oxford, Oxford University Press, 2008) 29.

54 *Ontario (AG) v OPSEU* [1987] 2 SCR 2 at 57.

55 *Re Provincial Court Judges* [1997] 3 SCR 3.

only in proceedings before the superior courts and statutory criminal courts, and some of the appeals in this case did not arise from these courts. Nonetheless, the majority justices of the Supreme Court struck down the impugned statutes as they violated the unwritten constitutional principle of judicial independence. Following this case, more constitutional challenges based on such principles reached the Supreme Court,[56] and some of them were successful.

The idea of unwritten constitutional norms that are judicially enforceable against legislation has also made inroads into several other common law–based systems, as alluded to by Brice Dickson.[57] More broadly, McLachlin CJ once observed that "[t]raditionally at common law, unwritten fundamental principles of constitutional or quasi-constitutional significance have been identified by past usage, chiefly the cases that have been decided by judges in the past," before adding that "[i]f an ordinary law is clearly in conflict with a fundamental constitutional norm, the judge may have no option but to refuse to apply it."[58]

To be sure, these judicial developments have been strongly criticized by many constitutional commentators, whose grievances range from claims that the judges have unjustifiably ignored constitutional history and traditional conceptions of legislative authority to claims that they have arrogated to themselves an unrestrained, undemocratic power of constitutional amendment. The discussion then folds into the perennial debate in modern democracies, which may well be "irresoluble on rational grounds,"[59] as to the proper boundaries of the operation of judicial review. Despite these challenges and the virtually unlimited literature on the subject, this chapter has sought to contribute to the debate by proposing a general account of the development of judicial review that coheres with the relevant historical sources

56 See *Babcock v Canada (AG)* [2002] 3 SCR 3; *Mackin v New Brunswick (Minister of Finance)* [2002] 1 SCR 405; *Ell v Alberta* [2003] 1 SCR 857; *Provincial Court Judges' Assn of New Brunswick v New Brunswick (Minister of Justice)* [2005] 2 SCR 286; *British Columbia v Imperial Tobacco Canada Ltd* [2005] 2 SCR 473; *British Columbia (AG) v Christie* [2007] 1 SCR 873; *Conférence des juges v Quebec (AG)* [2016] 2 SCR 116.

57 See ch 2 in this volume.

58 B. McLachlin, "Unwritten Constitutional Principles: What Is Going On?" (2006) 4 *New Zealand Journal of Public and International Law* 147 at 156–7, 161.

59 M. Tushnet, "How Different Are Waldron's and Fallon's Core Cases for and against Judicial Review?" (2010) 30 *Oxford Journal of Legal Studies* 49 at 70.

since Coke's times. The point is best captured by Mark Walters, who has observed that

> insofar as the theory of unwritten fundamental law is regarded as an assertion of the supremacy of natural law, right reason, or universal principles of political morality and human rights over legislation, it is part of a rich intellectual tradition that has informed common law thinking from medieval times, through the English and American revolutionary ages, and into the high Victorian era of empire out of which Canada's written constitution emerged.[60]

Conclusion

This chapter has explored once more the historical (or historically assumed) relationship between *Dr Bonham's Case* and modern judicial review of legislation in common law–based systems. Much of the voluminous literature on *Bonham* has engaged deeply with the complexities of the period's legal and political systems, including the uncertain relationship among the courts, the Crown, and Parliament. But an exclusive focus on the purely historical context poses the risk of neglecting the considerable body of pre-Blackstonian judicial attitudes towards *Bonham* and the notion of voidness of statutes, both of which have fostered a narrative of reinterpretations of *Bonham* and its evolving legacy.

Almost as soon as *Bonham* was rendered, seventeenth-century judges and lawyers regularly began invoking every man's natural reason and law's artificial reason as grounds for holding statutes void. The eighteenth century saw the rise of parliamentary sovereignty and, with it, much less reference to the idea of voidable statutes. Blackstone severely restricted the grounds for disregarding a statute by admitting such a possibility only when faced with a self-contradictory statute or one impossible to apply. The dawn of the nineteenth century would nonetheless mark the advent of an adapted doctrine of statutory voidness on a new continent, appearing first in the United States before spreading across most of the common law world. And from the second half of the twentieth century, a number of constitutional scholars gradually returned once more to *Bonham* as part of their justification of the expansion of the

60 Walters, above n 21 at 126.

grounds for judicial review to include so-called unwritten norms with little or no connection to the terms of the national constitution.

The reinterpretations of Coke's ideas regarding the relationship between the common law and statute law do not constitute a unique phenomenon. Another example of legal reinterpretation is the common law principles concerning the reception of English law in the colonies. Today, these principles are well settled. The laws of England would come into force immediately in colonies established by settlement. By contrast, in colonies acquired by conquest, the laws of the conquered territories would continue in force until altered by the Crown, except in matters of public law, where English law would apply immediately.[61]

However, the English cases and practice during the colonial era instantiated the long-standing principle according to which, in conquered colonies, "the rules of English public law are not automatically substituted for the old colonial rules which continue to be applied until the will of the King becomes known."[62] In *Blankard v Galdy*, Holt CJ ruled that an English statute against buying offices in the administration of justice did not apply to the purchase of the office of Provost Marshal in Jamaica, a conquered colony. Holt CJ stated that, contrary to settled colonies, conquered colonies "retain their antient laws: and it is impossible the laws of [England], by meer conquest without more, should take place in a conquered country."[63] It is only by the latter half of the seventeenth century that the reception at large of English law in conquered colonies would gain real traction, especially in the United States, through reinterpretations of Coke's "birthright theory," which refers to English subjects' benefit of English law.[64]

Another more recent instance of a continuing process of reinterpretation of common law ideas is the *living tree* metaphor, famously associated with Lord Sankey LC's landmark judgment in *Edwards v A-G*

61 See in general H. Brun, G. Tremblay, and E. Brouillet, *Droit constitutionnel*, 6th edn (Montreal, Yvon Blais, 2014) 9–10; Hogg, above n 50 at ch 2. *Cf* 1 Bl Comm 104–5. Additionally, in most colonies, the reception of English law was declared or confirmed by various imperial and colonial statutes.

62 M. Morin, "Les changements de régimes juridiques consécutifs à la Conquête de 1760" (1997) 57 Revue du Barreau 689 at 692 (trans).

63 *Blankard v Galdy* (1693) Holt KB 341, 90 ER 1089.

64 See B.H. McPherson, *The Reception of English Law Abroad* (Brisbane, Supreme Court of Queensland Library, 2007) 18–20, 30–2, 234–55, 326.

for Canada,[65] concerning whether a woman was a "qualified person" to become a senator under s. 24 of the Constitution Act, 1867. Lord Sankey LC, for the Judicial Committee of the Privy Council, acknowledged that, in England, women had been under a legal incapacity to serve in either house of Parliament (until 1918) and that, in the history of the British North American legislatures, no woman had served or claimed to serve in public office until 1916. In rejecting the view that these considerations were conclusive of the matter, the Privy Council qualified the Constitution as "a living tree capable of growth and expansion within its natural limits" and thus calling for "a large and liberal interpretation."[66]

Despite the broad words, the real scope of the case was rather limited: the Privy Council indeed specified that it was not considering any matter arising under the division of legislative powers between the federal Parliament and the provincial legislatures, which represented the main source of constitutional appeals at the time. In the following decades, *Edwards* was barely mentioned in the Canadian case law or anywhere else in the Commonwealth. However, the expansion of the scope of the living tree metaphor took on an accelerated pace after the adoption of the 1982 Charter. Today, the prevailing position in Canadian law is that "progressive interpretation applies to all constitutional provisions, including the Charter."[67] And with the modern rise of unwritten constitutional principles, the courts have even extended this interpretative approach to that component of the Constitution as well.[68] The living tree metaphor has, furthermore, gained considerable interest in many other common law–based systems as a point of reference for the application of various forms of progressive constitutional interpretation.

More than four centuries later, Coke's famous words in *Bonham* still resonate strongly throughout the common law world, with each generation of jurists revisiting the case in light of their contemporary context and the challenges their societies face. The most recent iteration identified in this chapter may be summed up in the proposition that when an Act is contrary to certain fundamental constitutional principles of the common law, these principles "will control it and adjudge such Act to be void." On a closer look, one could reasonably argue that the

65 *Edwards v A-G for Canada* [1930] AC 124 (PC).

66 Ibid at 136.

67 Hogg, above n 50 at 36-25, 36-27.

68 See *Re Provincial Court Judges*, above n 55 at [106]–[8], [126]; *Prov. Court Judges' Assn*, above n 56 at [2]–[3].

reinterpretations of *Bonham* have remained within that case's spirit and are not so vastly different from one another.

The question of which interpretation is more consistent with what Coke had in mind will probably remain hotly contested, but that should not discourage anyone from engaging with his works and the ideas of that period of history. The value of history should not, by any means, be lessened, but, in expounding a constitution, jurists need not seek at all costs the original meaning of ancient cases or works, however canonical they may be. Constitutional interpretation must strive to fit with history, just as history guides us in helping explain our constitutions so as to make them, all things considered, the best they can be.[69]

69 *Cf* R. Dworkin, *Law's Empire* (Cambridge, MA, Harvard University Press, 1986) 314, 316, 379.

PART III

Common Law Concepts

10 The Development of an Obligation to Perform in Good Faith

ANGELA SWAN AND JAKUB ADAMSKI

If we were able to step back or aside and look at a kind of "natural law" or a "law of nature" of contracts or contractual relations, one of the features of that law – a central feature of it[1] – would be the idea that those who make contracts should perform them in good faith and honestly. From that point of view, a law of contracts that denied or even deprecated the role of good faith would be regarded as weird, as excluding from consideration something that has to be at the heart of any exchange relation.[2] The level, of course, varies with the nature of the relationship but cannot be wholly done away with.[3] The traditional English and Canadian common law of contracts formally denied that the concept of good faith had any role to play outside some specific

1 Some of the most influential figures in the history of the common law have recognized this. Sir Fredrick Pollock, a leading nineteenth-century contract law scholar, noted that "the law of contract is in truth nothing else than the endeavour of the sovereign power, a more or less imperfect one by the nature of the case, to establish a positive sanction for the expectation of good faith which has grown up in the mutual dealings of men of average right-mindedness": *Principles of Contract*, 3rd edn (1881), xx. More than one hundred years earlier, Lord Mansfield, who did much to lay the foundations of a modern commercial law at common law, said that "[t]he governing principle [of good faith] is applicable to all contracts and dealings": *Carter v Boehm* (1766) 3 Burr 1905 at 1910, 97 ER 1162 at 1164 (KB). Of course, this agreement does not entail agreement upon either the proper scope of the doctrine of good faith or the best methods for enforcing it.

2 Trust is an integral part of any vibrant commercial society; and surely a notion of good faith in contract law only serves to protect that trust.

3 Even if some exchange relations have no past and little prospect of a future, most have both a past and at least the hope of a future.

relations (contractual or otherwise). This chapter will explore how that position has now changed. We shall look at three examples where Canadian law imposes obligations of good faith, honesty, and integrity upon the contracting parties.

We are here to write about supreme courts and the common law. It is the job of a supreme court, in developing the law in the common law tradition, to state *general organizing principles*;[4] in fact, it is possible to say that this is precisely what such a court should do in every area of the law, private as well as public.[5] The Supreme Court of Canada has now stated an important general organizing principle[6] in the law of

4 In his noted Maccabean Lecture, Lord Goff remarked, "The primary function of judges is not the formulation of legal principles. Their main task, more workaday, more humdrum, is to try cases: in civil cases, to adjudicate upon disputes between litigants. ... But in the exercise of their functions, judges have from time to time to expound the law. For obvious reasons, this duty falls primarily upon appellate courts": "The Search for Principle" in G. Jones and W. Swadling (eds), *The Search for Principle: Essays in Honour of Lord Goff of Chieveley* (Oxford, Oxford University Press, 2000) 313 at 314. Lord Bingham expressed a similar view when describing one of the proper functions of the House of Lords: "the function of developing and where necessary modifying the common law so as to provide for new situations and ensure that the law broadly reflects the changing standards, values, and needs of society": "The Highest Court in the Land" in T. Bingham, *Lives of the Law: Selected Essays and Speeches 2000–2010* (Oxford, Oxford University Press, 2011) 157 at 168.

5 In the past several decades, the Supreme Court of Canada has preferred an approach to stating its reasons in a wide range of cases spanning both private and public law in what it describes as a "principled approach." This approach eschews the stating of rules in favour of arguments that lay bare the motives underpinning some area of law; while the latter approach is said to be less certain and to favour particularized justice, it is nonetheless worth noting that, in application, it has not produced any wildly unexpected results. See further D. Murynka, "Give Me One Good Reason: The 'Principled Approach' in Canadian Judicial Opinion" (2015) 40:2 *Queen's Law Journal* 609. While this judicial style is certainly more circumscribed in the United Kingdom, where courts are quicker – even at the highest level – to reaffirm or restate rules rather than principles of contract law, there has been an ever growing reliance on adding open-ended exceptions to ensure that justice can be done in individual cases; of course, an approach like the Canadian one undermines the supposed predictability and certainty normally ascribed to rules: see R. Ahdar, "Contract Doctrine, Predictability and the Nebulous Exception" (2014) *Cambridge Law Journal* 39. Both approaches are designed to ensure that the law is flexible enough to provide the appropriate individualized justice that a given case might require.

6 This statement requires some understanding of what a principle of contract is. In *Principle and Policy in Contract Law: Competing or Complementary Concepts?*

contracts. In *Bhasin v Hrynew*,[7] the Court said that there was now in the common law provinces of Canada – in 1994, the Civil Code of Quebec codified this long-standing civilian principle[8] – a general organizing principle of good faith performance.[9]

In contrast to the law in both civilian legal systems, like the Civil Code of Quebec, and in the United States,[10] common law courts in

---

(Cambridge, Cambridge University Press, 2011) at 17, S. Waddams has noted the inherent ambiguity in its meaning:

> But if we ask what *were* these principles [of contract law historically], the answer proves surprisingly elusive. The word has been used in many different senses, the meaning varying according to what is implicitly contrasted with it (principle and rule, principle and policy, principle and precedent, principle and authority, principle and pragmatism, principle and practice, principle and convenience, principle and utility, general principle and particular rule, general principle and particular case).

7 2014 SCC 71, [2014] 3 SCR 494, 379 DLR (4th) 385 ("*Bhasin*"). For an excellent, comprehensive, and interesting comment on the decision, see J.T. Robertson, "Good Faith as an Organizing Principle in Contract Law: *Bhasin v Hrynew* – Two Steps Forward and One Look Back" (2015) 93 *Canadian Bar Review* 809 ("Robertson").

8 Art 6, 7, and 1375. The last article requires good faith when an obligation is created, during its performance, and on its enforcement. The development of these civilian principles before their inclusion in the Civil Code of Quebec is discussed by the Supreme Court in *Banque National v Soucisse* [1981] 2 SCR 339; *Banque National v Houle* [1990] 3 SCR 122, 74 DLR (4th) 577; and *Banque de Montréal v Bail Ltée* [1992] 2 SCR 554, 93 DLR (4th) 490. *Houle* is an example of good faith in enforcement, not performance. That duty is well established in the common law: see eg *Ronald Elwyn Lister Ltd v Dunlop Canada Ltd* [1982] 1 SCR 726, 135 DLR (3d) 1; and *Kavcar Investments Ltd v Aetna Financial Services Ltd* (1989) 70 OR (2d) 225, 62 DLR (4th) 277 (CA). Early precedents of the civilian notion of good faith in contractual relations can be found even in the Roman law of contract: see M.J. Schermaier, "Bona Fides in Roman Contract Law" in S. Whittaker (ed), *Good Faith in European Contract Law* (Cambridge, Cambridge University Press, 2000) 63.

9 We shall not discuss the extent to which Canadian common law has developed a localized set of good faith obligations in the area of construction tendering. Canadian courts have arrogated to themselves the duty of policing the tendering process, including imposing a duty of fair and equal treatment on the parties (*Martel Building Ltd v Canada* [2000] 2 SCR 860 at para 88), which includes the duty to conduct the negotiating process in good faith (*Oz Optics Ltd v Timbercon, Inc* 2011 ONCA 714, 107 OR (3d) 509, 343 DLR (4th) 443 at para 68). While the courts have not made a good job of supervising the tendering process and have increased substantially the costs of public sector procurement, much of the motivation for developing a uniquely Canadian approach to tendering law can be seen as the effort of the courts to create a satisfactory place-holder for the obligations they want to impose on the process in the face of strident authorities denying them.

10 Restatement (Second) of Contracts, s 205, states that "[e]very contract imposes upon each party a duty of good faith and fair dealing in its performance and its

Canada, following the general attitude of the English courts,[11] have had great and surprising difficulty in accepting the idea that a doctrine of good faith performance of contractual obligations could exist.[12] As one of us said a long time ago (and as the Supreme Court noted), "[t]he traditional common law took a kind of perverted pride in the claim that it had no general notion of good faith, as if admitting that the law could be founded in 'good faith' would be admitting to the presence of some kind of embarrassing social disease."[13] Not far off thirty years to the day after that statement was made in a public lecture and published, the Supreme Court in *Bhasin* finally recognized that there was a general organizing principle of good faith performance in Canadian common law.

---

enforcement." Very similarly, s 1-304 of the Uniform Commercial Code (UCC) provides that "[e]very contract or duty within the Uniform Commercial Code imposes an obligation of good faith in its performance and enforcement." The principal scope for this obligation is in the law of sales, Art 2 of the UCC. For a brief overview of the development of the doctrine of good faith in contract law in the United States, see Steven J. Burton, "History and Theory of Good Faith Performance in the United States" in L. DiMatteo and M. Hogg (eds), *Comparative Contract Law: British and American Perspectives* (New York, Oxford University Press, 2016) 210.

11 In 2005, a lord chancellor said,

> [T]he English law of contract is the international law of choice over a wide range of areas, particularly in finance, shipping, and insurance. It contributes significantly to the earnings of the UK and thereby promotes the prosperity of the EU. ... You could say, [*sic*] that the English common law of contract is now a world-wide commodity. It has become so because it is a system that people like. It provides predictability of outcome, legal certainty, and fairness. It is clear and built upon well-founded principles, such as the ability to require exact performance *and the absence of any general duty of good faith.* ... This has made the common law without rival as the law of choice in commercial transactions. It is important for the UK, and important for the EU that it remains so.

Lord Falconer, Opening Speech for the European Contract Law Conference, London, 26 September 2005, www.ec.europa.eu/consumers/cons_int/safe_shop/fair_bus_pract/cont_law/conference092005/falconer2005.pdf; emphasis added. Quoted in C. Mitchell, *Contract Law and Contract Practice: Bridging the Gap between Legal Reasoning and Commercial Expectation* (Oxford, Hart Publishing, 2013) 218.

12 See eg the separate reasons for judgment of the majority and minority in *Peel Condominium Corporation no 505 v Cam-Valley Homes Limited* (2001) 57 OR (3d) 1, 196 DLR (4th) 621 (CA).

13 J. Swan, "Whither Contracts: A Retrospective and Prospective Overview," in *Special Lectures of the Law Society of Upper Canada 1984 – Law in Transition: Contracts* (1984) 125 at 148. This sentence was quoted by Cromwell J in *Bhasin*, above n 7 at para 36.

It will be an argument of this chapter that the recognition of the new general organizing principle merely made obvious what could have been seen for a long time had a kind of ideological blindness – made vividly clear by the quotation in note 11 above and that in note 31 below – not made it very difficult for courts to see it. The ideological nature of the inability to see the role of good faith, honesty, and integrity in the law of contracts can be seen when a broader range of legal principles or standards of conduct is considered. This chapter will explore the development and application of some of those standards.

A Note on the Importance of Judicial Attitude

There is one general point that needs to be kept in mind whenever one considers what judges do. That point is the importance of the attitude that judges bring to what they do. It is almost impossible to overemphasize the importance of judicial attitude. An awareness of the attitude that judges bring to what they do, to the problems they have to deal with and the solutions they find, explains a great deal of how the law is developed. There are a few features of judicial attitude that have to be remembered. The first is that it is virtually impossible to search online for expressions of the attitude that a judge might have to something. A great deal – in fact, an alarmingly large element – of legal research is characterized by serendipity, so a phrase search in an online database may disclose a case, but the chances of finding an express statement of a judge's attitude are very low. It is generally true that expressions of attitude can be found only in texts or articles – and then only if an author considers attitude to be important.

The importance of understanding (or being alive to) the attitude that a judge is likely to bring to a problem is that it very strongly suggests what might be relevant to the decision. A judge who, for example, worries about rewarding a party who has behaved badly is likely to ask herself or himself whether there is a way to avoid that result. Judges who like rules may be unhappy with general principles where, as she or he may believe, the law is uncertain.

A focus on judicial attitude has to recognize the constraints that act upon a judge. She or he functions in a process characterized by two facts or rights: the right of the parties to present proofs – that is, the parties' stories, the facts of the case – and reasoned arguments. A judge may not find facts for herself or himself or decide the case on arguments not raised by counsel. The judicial process situates any expression of a judge's attitude in a context where it is the law, and not the judge's idiosyncratic preferences, that will determine the result. It is, however, important to remember that the law is seldom so clear that a judge's desire to reach a particular result is irrelevant. That desire may, of course, not be determinative of the result.

It is therefore the job of anyone writing about the law to offer judges arguments that will be responsive to their concerns and their responsibilities. This task is particularly important when, as in the case we shall look at, the new general organizing principle appears vague and perhaps uncertain. We shall keep this obligation firmly in mind.

There is another important background fact to consider, one that powerfully determines how judges approach their job. Judges function in the *judicial process*. That process is characterized, as we have just said, by two things: the right of the parties – in practice, of course, their counsel – (1) to make proofs – that is, lead evidence, tell the story – of what happened and (2) to make reasoned arguments. The process precludes a judge from finding facts on her or his own, and the right to make reasoned arguments requires that the standards of what counts as an argument be known in advance of a trial. These characteristics of the process impose real restraints on what a judge can do – the restraints are not materially relaxed before a court of appeal or the Supreme Court – and colour her or his approach to the law. Judgments, particularly at the appellate level, must then reflect how they will be used by trial judges and subsequent courts. It will be important to assess how well the Supreme Court acknowledged these factors in its reasons in *Bhasin*.

A further point, applicable particularly to the Supreme Court, must be noted. That court cannot choose the cases that come before it except in the negative sense that it can deny leave to appeal and not hear the ones it does not want to deal with. While the Court gives no reasons for its leave decisions – and guessing the reasons on leave applications is as much use as examining the entrails of chickens[14] – it is not unimaginable that a member of a leave panel[15] or a staff lawyer briefing the panel may say, "You know, we haven't dealt with good faith before; perhaps we should take this case and deal with the whole notion of

14 Of course, this did not hold back the Romans from having their haruspices, nor does it hold us back from having our court augurs.

15 The panel for *Bhasin* was McLachlin CJ and Abella and Cromwell JJ, a particularly strong panel of common law judges, 2013 CanLII 53400.

good faith performance." The importance of this fact (or possibility) is that the Supreme Court has to make what it can of the materials at hand. It is then inappropriate and unhelpful to analyse the decision as if it were a trial decision; a case before the Supreme Court may have – if we can put it this way – a bigger role to fill than the resolution of that particular dispute.[16]

The Decision in *Bhasin v Hrynew*

The facts in *Bhasin v Hrynew* were complicated but can be shortly stated.[17] Mr Bhasin was an enrolment director working for a corporation called Canadian American Financial Corp. (Canada) Limited (Can-Am), selling registered educational savings plans. The agreement between Mr Bhasin and Can-Am was called a "commercial dealership agreement"; it was not a franchise.[18] Mr Hrynew was another director who also worked for Can-Am on a similar basis. Mr Hrynew coveted Mr Bhasin's business. Can-Am was required by the Alberta Securities Commission to appoint a compliance officer. Can-Am, working with Mr Hrynew and against Mr Bhasin, appointed Mr Hrynew as its compliance officer, called a provincial trading officer (PTO), falsely

---

16 The importance of the case, once leave had been given, was clearly understood by counsel. The principal arguments were made by prominent Toronto litigation firms, both acutely aware of the issues at stake, and Mr Bhasin's counsel included Professor John McCamus, a leading private law scholar in Canada. In this way, the case echoes nineteenth-century cases like *Smith v Hughes* (1871) LR 6 QB 597 and *Parker v South Eastern Railway Co* (1877) 2 CPD 416 (CA), whose doctrinal (and practical) importance far outweighed the actual pecuniary amounts in dispute and led to the parties' cases being argued by leading contract law scholars.

17 We have taken the substance of this statement of the facts and the summary of the Supreme Court's reasons for judgment from A. Swan, "The Obligation to Perform in Good Faith: Comment on *Bhasin v Hrynew*" (2015) 56 *Canadian Business Law Journal* 395.

18 Cromwell J referred, at para 4, to this point and to the Alberta Franchises Act, RSA 2000, c F-23, s 7. That Act, like the Arthur Wishart Act (Franchise Disclosure), 2000, SO 2000, c 3, sub-s 3(1), imposes "a duty of fair dealing in [the] performance and enforcement" of every franchise agreement. The closeness of Mr Bhasin's relation with Can-Am to a franchise agreement and the statutory obligations governing such a relation could easily have been used to justify the duty that Cromwell J imposed, although it was not offered as a basis for imposing the duty of good faith performance on the defendant. Manitoba, The Franchises Act, CCSM c F156, sub-s 3(1) and New Brunswick, the Franchises Act, SNB, 2014, c 111, sub-s 3(1) have equivalent language.

telling Mr Bhasin – who objected strenuously to the appointment – that Mr Hrynew's appointment was required by the commission. Mr Bhasin's objections were based on his lively fear that, with the information Mr Hrynew would now have about his business, Mr Hrynew could easily take it over. It was Mr Bhasin's refusal to allow Mr Hrynew access to his confidential information that led Can-Am to refuse to renew Mr Bhasin's contract. In the result, Mr Hrynew substantially took over Mr Bhasin's business.

The trial judge, Moen J,[19] held both Mr Hrynew and Can-Am liable. Mr Hrynew was liable for inducing Can-Am to breach its contract with Mr Bhasin, Can-Am for breach of contract, and both defendants for civil conspiracy. She awarded damages of some $381,000[20] to Mr Bhasin. The Alberta Court of Appeal allowed the appeal and dismissed Mr Bhasin's claims.[21]

Cromwell J, who gave the reasons for judgment of the Supreme Court, summarized the trial judge's findings:

> [98] The trial judge concluded that Can-Am acted dishonestly with Mr. Bhasin throughout the period leading up to its exercise of the non-renewal clause, both with respect to its own intentions and with respect to Mr. Hrynew's role as PTO. Her detailed findings amply support this overall conclusion.

He said,

> [103] As the trial judge found, this dishonesty on the part of Can-Am was directly and intimately connected to Can-Am's performance of the Agreement with Mr. Bhasin and its exercise of the non-renewal provision. I conclude that Can-Am breached the 1998 Agreement when it failed to act honestly with Mr. Bhasin in exercising the non-renewal clause.

Cromwell J rejected the claim against Mr Hrynew for inducing breach of contract and the claim against Mr Hrynew and Can-Am for civil conspiracy. He held,

> [108] I have concluded that Can-Am's breach of contract consisted of its failure to be honest with Mr. Bhasin about its contractual performance

19 2011 ABQB 637.

20 Robertson, above n 7, points out that formal judgment was entered for $455,064.

21 2013 ABCA 98, 362 DLR (4th) 18, [2013] 11 WWR 459.

> and, in particular, with respect to its settled intentions with respect to renewal. It is therefore liable for damages calculated on the basis of what Mr. Bhasin's economic position would have been had Can-Am fulfilled that duty. While the trial judge did not assess damages on that basis given her different findings in relation to liability, she made findings that permit this Court to do so.
>
> [109] The trial judge specifically held that but for Can-Am's dishonesty, Mr. Bhasin could have acted so as to "retain the value in his agency": paras. 258–59. In reaching this conclusion, the trial judge was well aware of the difficulties that Mr. Bhasin would have in selling his business given the "almost absolute controls" that Can-Am had on enrollment directors and that it owned the "book of business": para. 402. She also heard evidence and made findings about what the value of the business was, taking these limitations into account. These findings, in my view, permit us to assess damages on the basis that if Can-Am had performed the contract honestly, Mr. Bhasin would have been able to retain the value of his business rather than see it, in effect, expropriated and turned over to Mr. Hrynew.

In the result, damages of $87,000 were awarded against Can-Am. It is not entirely clear from the judgment at trial or in the Supreme Court how Can-Am's breach led to this award of damages. The important lesson from the case is not that a particular breach led to a particular award of damages, but that the basis for any remedy was Can-Am's breach of its duty to perform its obligations to Mr Bhasin in good faith.

Cromwell J uses both the phrase "good faith performance" and the phrase "honest performance." We have seen attempts to differentiate them.[22] We do not believe that it is possible or useful to assume or believe that the phrases describe or focus on different things. It seems

---

22 Robertson, above n 7 at 816, distinguishes them and claims that J. McCamus, "The New General Principle of Good Faith Performance in Canadian Contract Law" (2015) 32 *Journal of Contract Law* 103 at 107, agrees with him. We find the distinction elusive and, what is more important, unhelpful. Note that UCC s 1-201(20) provides that "good faith … means honesty in fact and the observance of reasonable commercial standards of fair dealing." Under the UCC, the distinction between honesty in fact and reasonable commercial standards of fair dealing is seen as encapsulating a subjective and an objective standard of good faith, respectively (J.M. Feinman, "Good Faith and Reasonable Expectations" (2014) 67 *Arkansas Law Review* 525 at 533). See also s 2-103(1)(b), where good faith is again equated with honesty and fair dealing, this time "in the trade." Robertson, above n 7 at 821–7 has an extended analysis of the development of the American position.

more fruitful to assume that good faith is or connotes honesty and, of course, vice versa. If both phrases mean that one should not tell lies or behave in bad faith, they must be, in effect, synonyms. Even if the two concepts could be separated for litigation purposes, it is hard to conceive how they could be separated when a solicitor is giving advice to a client.[23]

Cromwell J summarized his conclusion:

> [65] The organizing principle of good faith exemplifies the notion that, in carrying out his or her own performance of the contract, a contracting party should have appropriate regard to the legitimate contractual interests of the contracting partner. While "appropriate regard" for the other party's interests will vary depending on the context of the contractual relationship, it does not require acting to serve those interests in all cases. It merely requires that a party not seek to undermine those interests in bad faith. This general principle has strong conceptual differences from the much higher obligations of a fiduciary. Unlike fiduciary duties, good faith performance does not engage duties of loyalty to the other contracting party or a duty to put the interests of the other contracting party first.

Rather than examining the Supreme Court's reasons in *Bhasin* in detail, we would prefer to focus on three aspects of it:

1. the significance of the decision;
2. the nature of the obligation imposed by the general organizing principle; and
3. the possible application of the new organizing principle to negotiations.

The Significance of the Decision

Cromwell J stated his goal:

> [32] The notion of good faith has deep roots in contract law and permeates many of its rules. Nonetheless, Anglo-Canadian common law has resisted acknowledging any generalized and independent doctrine of good faith

23 They appear to be conjoined in English law, which consistently denies a free-standing contractual duty of good faith: see recently *Braganza v BP Shipping Ltd* [2015] UKSC 17, [2015] 1 WLR 1661. It is also worth noting that trust is an important

> performance of contracts. The result is an "unsettled and incoherent body of law" that has developed "piecemeal" and which is "difficult to analyze": Ontario Law Reform Commission ("OLRC"), *Report on Amendment of the Law of Contract* (1987), at p. 169. This approach is out of step with the civil law of Quebec and most jurisdictions in the United States and produces results that are not consistent with the reasonable expectations of commercial parties.
>
> [33] In my view, it is time to take two incremental steps in order to make the common law less unsettled and piecemeal, more coherent and more just. The first step is to acknowledge that good faith contractual performance is a general organizing principle of the common law of contract which underpins and informs the various rules in which the common law, in various situations and types of relationships, recognizes obligations of good faith contractual performance. The second is to recognize, as a further manifestation of this organizing principle of good faith, that there is a common law duty which applies to all contracts to act honestly in the performance of contractual obligations.
>
> [34] In my view, taking these two steps is perfectly consistent with the Court's responsibility to make incremental changes in the common law when appropriate. Doing so will put in place a duty that is just, that accords with the reasonable expectations of commercial parties and that is sufficiently precise that it will enhance rather than detract from commercial certainty.[24]

Cromwell J adopted[25] John McCamus's argument that there are three broad types of situations in which a duty of good faith performance of some kind has been found to exist: (1) where the parties must cooperate to achieve the objects of a contract, (2) where one party exercises a discretionary power under a contract, and (3) where one party seeks to evade its contractual duties.[26]

---

component of any contractual relation, particularly one that involves a significant investment by the parties or requires extended performance. Actions that might threaten the trust that one party would have in the other are likely to be neither in good faith nor honest. An examination of trust in contractual relations is far beyond the scope of this chapter.

24 Robertson, above n 7, seems to say at 813 that the Supreme Court has *not* adopted a "general rule imposing a duty on all contractual parties to perform their obligations in good faith." We do not agree with him; we think that the Court *has adopted* just such a rule.

25 *Bhasin*, above n 7 at para 47.

26 J. McCamus, *The Law of Contracts*, 2nd edn (Toronto, Irwin Law, 2012) at 835–68.

In the first category, Cromwell J referred to cases like *Dynamic Transport Ltd. v O.K. Detailing Ltd.*[27] In the second category, he placed *Mitsui & Co. (Canada) Ltd. v Royal Bank of Canada*,[28] and in the third, he put *Mason v Freedman*.[29] Cromwell J also referred to cases in Australia and in England, including *Yam Seng PTE Ltd v International Trade Corporation Ltd.*[30] and *Mid Essex Hospital Services NHS Trust v Compass Group UK and Ireland Ltd. (t/a Medirest)*.[31]

In justifying going forward, Cromwell J said,

> [60] Commercial parties reasonably expect a basic level of honesty and good faith in contractual dealings. While they remain at arm's length and are not subject to the duties of a fiduciary, a basic level of honest conduct is necessary to the proper functioning of commerce. The growth of longer term, relational contracts that depend on an element of trust and

---

27 [1978] 2 SCR 1072, 85 DLR (3d) 19, where the cooperation of the parties is necessary to achieve the goal of their arrangement. See also *Mackay v Dick* (1881) 6 App Cas 251 (HL).

28 [1995] 2 SCR 187, 123 DLR (4th) 449, where a party's contractual discretion was limited. See also *Greenberg v Meffert* (1985) 50 OR (2d) 755, 18 DLR (4th) 438, 37 RPR 74, leave to appeal refused: [1986] 1 SCR x, 30 DLR (4th) 768, 64 NR 156; *Canadian National Railway Co v Inglis Ltd* (1997) 36 OR (3d) 410, 153 DLR (4th) 291 (CA).

29 [1958] SCR 483, 14 DLR (2d) 529, where a vendor was not excused from completing the sale of a house on the ground that his wife had not barred her dower when he had made no attempt to have her do so. See also *100 Main Street East Ltd v WB Sullivan Construction Ltd* (1978) 20 OR (2d) 410, 88 DLR (3d) 1 (CA).

30 [2013] EWHC 111, [2013] 1 Lloyd's Rep 526 (QB) ("*Yam Seng*"). The approach to good faith taken by Leggatt J in this judgment is strongly criticized in J.W. Carter and Wayne Courtney, "Good Faith in Contracts: Is There an Implied Promise to Act Honestly?" [2016] 75 *Cambridge Law Journal* 608. Leggatt J continued to refine his approach to good faith in *Sheikh Tahnoon Bin Saeed Bin Shakboot Al Nehayan v Kent* [2018] EWHC 333.

31 [2013] EWCA Civ 200 (CA) Jackson LJ said (para 105),

> In addressing this question [i.e., whether there is a "general overarching duty to co-operate in good faith"], I start by reminding myself that there is no general doctrine of "good faith" in English contract law, although a duty of good faith is implied by law as an incident of certain categories of contract. … If the parties wish to impose such a duty they must do so expressly.

Jackson LJ was referring, *inter alia*, to *Yam Seng*. This comment on Jackson LJ 's reasons, http://ipdraughts.wordpress.com/2013/03/22/as-you-were-duty-of-good-faith-not-implied-into-english-law-contract/, explores the decision in the context of the class-ridden English judiciary!

> cooperation clearly calls for a basic element of honesty in performance, but, even in transactional exchanges, misleading or deceitful conduct will fly in the face of the expectations of the parties.[32]

It is very important to understand what Cromwell J is saying here. He is not saying that an obligation of good faith performance makes an ordinary commercial relation a fiduciary one; he is saying that everyone, *in any contractual relation*, expects the other party to behave in good faith. That is a reasonable expectation, and it does not seem to be an onerous obligation, particularly if it can be translated as "Just don't tell lies!"

We do not believe that just because the cases relied on by Cromwell J did not use the phrase *good faith*,[33] they are not examples of good faith performance and that, as a result, *Bhasin* does not stand for the imposition of a general duty of good faith performance. This argument is reminiscent of the old forms of action – separate claims based on allegations of wrongdoing that did not cumulate into a law of contracts or a law of torts – and is the denial of both the obligation on a supreme court and the value of a case like *Bhasin*. The obligation on a supreme court is often to gather disparate – or apparently disparate – bits of the law and bring them within, or identify, a general organizing principle that treats each case or separate example as an aspect of a broad principle. This process was, of course, exemplified by what the House of Lords did in *Donoghue v Stevenson*.[34] It was, for example, performed by the Supreme Court in *Morguard Investments Ltd. v De Savoye*,[35] when the Canadian law on the enforcement of foreign judgments was set on a wholly new course, and in many other cases.[36] The process has, of course, now been repeated with *Bhasin*.

---

32 Cromwell J referred to A. Swan and J. Adamski, *Canadian Contract Law*, 3rd edn (Markham, ON, LexisNexis, 2012) s 1.24. (We think that the reference should be to s 1.25.)

33 This argument is made by Robertson, above n 7 at 834. Robertson relies on J. McCamus, "The Use of Discretion, Failure to Cooperate and Evasion of Duty: Unpacking the Common Law Duty of Good Faith Contractual Performance" (2004) 29 *Advocates' Quarterly* 72; and McCamus, *Law of Contracts*, above n 26 at 835–8, referred to by Cromwell J, *Bhasin*, above n 7 at para 42.

34 [1932] UKHL 100, [1932] AC 562, [1932] All ER Rep 1.

35 [1990] 3 SCR 1077, 76 DLR (4th) 256, [1991] 2 WWR 217.

36 We would include, looking only at cases where Cromwell J gave the principal judgment: *Galambos v Perez* 2009 SCC 48, [2009] 3 SCR 247, 312 DLR (4th) 220,

An aspect of this argument is that it is neither necessary nor helpful to analyse the Supreme Court's reasons to decide whether some aspect is part of the *ratio decidendi* or *obiter*.

In one obvious sense, the decision in *Bhasin v Hrynew* is very significant. It will no longer be possible for judges to say, as, for example, the Alberta Court of Appeal said,

> We cannot find any good authority in common-law Canada to import into contracts generally a duty to act in good faith, independent of the express terms, and where there is no question of eviscerating the main objectives of the contract.[37]

Before dealing with the extent to which this statement in *Belfield Corporate Risk* is now – and was even, pre-*Bhasin*, in 2013 – incorrect, we would like to examine the statement itself in more detail because it perfectly illustrates the analytical or conceptual problems that courts have had with the concept of good faith performance.

Notice, first, the language that the Alberta Court of Appeal uses: "import into contracts," "independent of the express terms." Each of these phrases reflects the assumptions of the pre-*Bhasin* world, and each is shown by Cromwell J to be or to express an invalid concern.

It is important to see that when the Alberta Court of Appeal said what it said, even as it offered authority for it,[38] it was stating what it believed to be a truism, almost the expression of an ideology, rather than a careful statement of the law, reached after a thorough examination of the case. The principal contribution of the analysis adopted by Cromwell J is his careful demonstration that what the Court of Appeal had said was simply wrong *when it was said* and that the adoption of his general

---

dealing with fiduciary duties; *Kerr v Baranow* 2011 SCC 10, [2011] 1 SCR 269, 328 DLR (4th) 577, dealing with restitutionary claims arising on the breakdown of a marriage; and, with some misgivings, *Tercon Contractors Ltd v British Columbia (Transportation and Highways)* 2010 SCC 4, [2010] 1 SCR 69, 315 DLR (4th) 385, dealing with the doctrine of fundamental breach, as other examples.

37 *Benfield Corporate Risk Canada Ltd v Beaufort International Insurance Inc* 2013 ABCA 200, 365 DLR (4th) 628 at para 120. Côté JA was a member of the panel in both this case and in *Bhasin v Hrynew* at the Alberta Court of Appeal.

38 The Court of Appeal offered *Ko v Hillview Homes Ltd* 2012 ABCA 245; *Wallace v United Grain Growers Ltd* [1997] 3 SCR 707, 152 DLR (4th) 1, [1999] 4 WWR 86; and *Keays v Honda Canada Inc* 2008 SCC 39, [2008] 2 SCR 362, 294 DLR (4th) 577 as authorities to support its statement.

organizing principle reflected the extent to which, *as a matter of fact*, good faith obligations were, and have been for a long time, recognized by Canadian courts.

The statement that an obligation of good faith would "import" something into a contract – that is, plainly something from outside, whatever it is that records the terms of the "contract" – expressed a very common view of the concept of good faith. The point that was obvious long before *Bhasin* and, indeed, for a very long time, going far back into the common law and law merchant,[39] is that it is extremely hard even to conceive of any contractual relation, especially one that involves any kind of extended performance by the parties, as not being infused with at least expectations of good faith performance.[40] No business can expect to have satisfied customers – and hence, in the long run, to stay in business – if its performance of its obligations is niggardly or ungenerous. The performance of a contractual obligation that is measured by a customer's expectations, rather than by the minimum necessary to avoid breach, will be a performance that is in good faith, and sellers, manufacturers (vis-à-vis their distributors or suppliers), employers – even landlords and others – have recognized this fact for a very long time.

There are, of course, many contractual relations where the role of good faith is minimal or almost completely absent: the mortgagor or debtor just has to make its payments on time and in the correct amount. In these cases, the mortgagee or creditor will have fully performed its

39 See eg F. Braudel, *The Wheels of Commerce*, vol 2 of *Civilization & Capitalism 15th – 18th Century* (New York, Harper & Row, 1979, trans S. Reynolds, 1982) for an extremely interesting account of medieval and, later, trading and commercial practices that emphasize the importance of trust, honesty, and good faith. A good example was the good faith shown by Spanish merchants who, in breach of Spanish law, cooperated with non-Spanish merchants in trading with the New World. For a very recent paper along the same lines, see "Going Global: The Secrets of the World's Best Business People" (2015) 417 *Economist* (19 December 2015–1 January 2016) 105.

40 It would be odd if there were a big difference between a purely contractual relation and a partnership in the expectations the members had of the good faith that was the foundation of the relation. The partnership was, of course, the forerunner of the corporation. Both the partnership and the corporation are infused with fiduciary standards of good conduct. Such standards are even imposed on some employees. The imposition of fiduciary duties is a major method that equity adopted to maintain the integrity of certain relations: that of partners but also those of principals and agents and, of course, the relations between lawyers and their clients.

obligations;[41] it remains only for the mortgagor or debtor to perform its obligations. On the other hand, as a matter of commercial practice or simply good business practices, retailers, for example, may well give customers a right to return goods or to some other adjustment that they are not contractually required to give.[42]

In *Yam Seng*,[43] a recent English case on good faith performance, Leggatt J dealt with an argument that the defendant corporation had breached a duty of good faith performance. He said,

> As a matter of construction, it is hard to envisage any contract which would not reasonably be understood as requiring honesty in its performance. The same conclusion is reached if the traditional tests for the implication of a term are used. In particular the requirement that parties will behave honestly is so obvious that it goes without saying. Such a requirement is also necessary to give business efficacy to commercial transactions.[44]

In the result, Leggatt J was able to decide in the plaintiff's favour on narrower grounds – *viz.*, the defendant's breach of a particular term of the contract and misrepresentation. It is nevertheless important, particularly in the context of the generally hostile English attitude to good faith,[45] that he saw honesty or good faith as an integral aspect of contractual performance.

Cromwell J dealt with the "origin" of the obligation of good faith performance by saying that it "inheres" in the parties' relation.[46] This

---

41 It is, of course, possible that a lender might, in bad faith, make payment difficult or impossible: see eg *Çukurova Finance International Ltd v Alfa Telecom Turkey (nos 3 to 5)* [2013] UKPC 2, [2013] UKPC 20, [2013] UKPC 25, [2016] AC 923.

42 The contractual limitation may be used to discourage those who have evil intentions, but waived for those who are honest and reasonable. A good example of this approach occurs with claims against tour operators under *Jarvis v Swan's Tours* [1973] QB 233, [1973] 1 All ER 71. Provided that the claim is less than the deductible on the operator's insurance policy, it is likely to be met, if reasonable; claims above that amount will be handed over to the insurer to deal with, and the insurer will be wholly unconcerned about good business relations with the operator's customers.

43 [2013] EWHC 111.

44 Ibid at para 137.

45 See eg the statement quoted above at n 10.

46 *Bhasin*, above n 7 at para 45, following Swan and Adamski, *Canadian Contract Law*, above n 32, §8.134 at 726. Robertson, above n 7 at 817, seems to ignore this statement and suggests – what we think is mistaken – that an express term of the contract can perhaps trump the obligation to perform in good faith. Robertson's opinion is bound up with the belief that the obligation of good faith performance is still an implied term.

source for the obligation is extremely important and precludes or excludes all the unhelpful analyses of implied terms.[47] The obligation is not something imposed on the parties by a court; it is not some criterion or contractual term external to the parties' relation; it is a part, an integral part, of it. Two consequences follow from this conclusion. The first is that the recognition of such an obligation cannot be one "imposed" on the parties or, as a result, something that threatens their "freedom of contract."[48] The second is that the parties are not free to exclude the obligation of good faith performance by either an inconsistent term or even an express disclaimer.

Cromwell J makes this last restriction express. He said that because "the duty of honesty in contractual performance is a general doctrine of contract law that applies to all contracts, like unconscionability, the parties are not free to exclude it."[49] It follows from this statement and from the fact that the obligation inheres in the parties' relation that the obligation is not caught by an entire agreement clause.[50] Such a clause can invoke the parol evidence rule, but that rule has nothing to do with

47 The idea, prevalent in England, above n 28, that the obligation of good faith can be an "implied term" is unhelpful for all the reasons that the whole concept and traditional analysis of implied terms misunderstands or misstates what is really going on. See eg Swan and Adamski, *Canadian Contract Law*, above n 32, s 8.1.6 at 696–723. We cannot restate our arguments here. The hold on the Canadian legal mind of the idea that the obligation of good faith performance is an *implied term* is extraordinary. See eg the Lexpert seminar given on 2 June 2015, "The Implied Obligation of Good Faith," https://www.bennettjones.com/News_and_Events/Seminars_and_Webinars/Implied_Obligation_of_Good_Faith.

48 Ontario Court of Appeal in *High Tower Homes Corporation v Stevens* 2014 ONCA 911, 123 OR (3d) 81 at para 36, and the British Columbia Court of Appeal in *Moulton Contracting Ltd v British Columbia* 2015 BCCA 89, 381 DLR (4th) 263 at para 67, dealt with the question whether good faith should be thought of as an implied term or as something that cannot be disclaimed. Both courts said that the obligation was not an implied term.

49 *Bhasin*, above n 7 at para 75. Cromwell J made reference to *Civiclife.com Inc v Canada (Attorney General)*, 2006 CanLII 20837, where the Ontario Court of Appeal awarded substantial compensatory and punitive damages against the Crown for an egregious breach of its obligations of good faith towards the plaintiff.

50 There have been worries that an "entire agreement clause" might exclude the obligation; they are misplaced. There is, in any case, widespread confusion over the scope of an entire agreement clause. See eg *Soboczynski v Beauchamp*, 2015 ONCA 148, 385 DLR (4th) 148 for an accurate statement of the effect of such a clause.

or to say to an obligation that simply exists once the parties have created their relation.[51]

Cromwell J does suggest that just as the parties can qualify the standard of reasonableness by defining what would satisfy them, they can similarly qualify what would be the standard to be met with respect to the obligation to perform in good faith or honestly. He refers to the Uniform Commercial Code, §1-302(b), which provides,

> The obligations of good faith, diligence, reasonableness, and care … may not be disclaimed by agreement. The parties, by agreement, may determine the standards by which the performance of those obligations is to be measured if those standards are not manifestly unreasonable.[52]

We have great difficulty in conceiving how an obligation of either honest or good faith performance can be qualified in the sense envisaged by the Uniform Commercial Code (UCC) or Cromwell J. A performance that is only a little bit dishonest or done with just a teeny, little bit of bad faith seems to be one that is neither honest nor in good faith.[53] The image this brings to our mind is of being just a little bit pregnant! Of course, the consequences of a very minor and non-material breach of

51 The parol evidence rule is probably the least understood "rule" in the law of contracts. The so-called rule can *exclude nothing* because the question before the court – whether it understands it or not – is to determine *where* the parties' agreement is to be found. Is it to be found in the collection of pages proffered by one of the parties or in those pages and some other stuff, different pages or even oral statements, proffered by the other? *In answering these questions, no evidence directed at them can be excluded*. Moreover, the fact that the words of one document may be thought to be unambiguous is wholly irrelevant to the question. Of course, once the court has decided that the set of pages proffered by one party *is* the final expression of the parties' agreement, then it is obvious that nothing else matters. If the court then wants to say that the evidence that led to this conclusion was inadmissible, we suppose it can say so – a kind of proleptic inadmissibility – but why bother? The standard statement of the rule is simply silly and, of course, dead wrong.

52 *Bhasin*, above n 7 at para 77.

53 It seems hard to argue that one should be free to tell lies, even little ones, and even if a party were to seek contractual permission to do so, it has been held that it cannot. While in *ABRY Partners v F & W Acquisition, LLC*, 891 A.2d 1032, at 1059 (Del ch 2006) then Strine VC suggested, on the basis of prior law, that an integration and disclaimer clause might be effective even against a claim of fraud so long as the clause contained "language that … can be said to add up to a clear anti-reliance clause by which [a party] has contractually promised that it did not rely upon statements outside the contract's four corners in deciding to sign the contract." But a review of Delaware

the obligation of good faith or honest performance may not be significant or material or even lead to any award of damages.

The other phrase used by the Alberta Court of Appeal, "independent of the express terms," can equally be shown to be incorrect. An obligation that inheres in a contractual relation cannot be conceived as independent of the express terms of the contract when, with the express terms and, we suppose, the necessary implied terms, the obligation constitutes the terms of the contract.

In an important sense, the decision in *Bhasin v Hrynew* does not change the law; it should not change the advice that solicitors give their clients, and it should not lead to different results in the bulk of the cases that come before Canadian courts. It should and, we hope, will change the language the courts use in describing the basis for their decisions and, in doing that, change the attitude that they bring to the cases that come before them. The case will, of course, be waved in the air by barristers but, in our opinion, will not cause many cases to be decided otherwise than they would have been had the decision not existed.[54]

It was and is always the attitude of the courts to examples of bad faith – indeed, as it is to every question that comes before them – that is important. It was the attitude of the Alberta Court of Appeal in *Benfield Corporate Risk Canada Ltd. v Beaufort International Insurance Inc.*[55] to the very

jurisprudence, both before and after *ABRY Partners*, reveals that the argument has never been successful: H. Jiang, "Freedom to Mislead: The Fictitious Freedom to Contract around Fraud under Delaware Law" (2017) 13 *New York University Journal of Law & Business* 393. See also *Plas-Tex Canada Ltd v Dow Chemical of Canada Ltd*, 2004 ABCA 309, 245 DLR (4th) 650, [2005] 7 WWR 419, where a seller, knowing that the goods it was selling were defective, dangerous, and completely unsuitable for the buyer's purposes, was unable to rely on an exemption clause. It always mystifies us that anyone would think that such a seller could succeed in its attempt to shift the risk of loss in the circumstances to the buyer. In civilian systems, the same idea is captured within the scope of the principle that exemption clauses cannot relieve a party against its own gross fault (Art 1474). See eg *ABB Inc v Domtar Inc* 2007 SCC 50, [2007] 3 SCR 461, 287 DLR (4th) 385, and Art 1527.

54 Courts of appeal permitted parties to re-argue cases after *Bhasin v Hrynew* came down, as they did after the decision in *Sattva Capital Corp v Creston Moly Corp* 2014 SCC 53, [2014] 2 SCR 633, 373 DLR (4th) 393, but the results did not change. See eg *High Tower Homes Corporation v Stevens* 2014 ONCA 911. B. Crawford, "The New Contractual Principle of Good Faith and the Banks" (2017) 32 *Banking and Finance Law Review* 407 shows that although arguments based on *Bhasin* have been made in litigation with banks, those arguments have not changed the results that would have been reached had they not been made.

55 Above n 37 and text around n 32.

idea that there could be a general principle of good faith performance that led it to say what was manifestly wrong or, at least, inaccurate.

The Nature of the Obligation Imposed by the General Organizing Principle

Notwithstanding the fact that Cromwell J said at the very beginning of his reasons,

> [1] Finding that there is a duty to perform contracts honestly will make the law more certain, more just and more in tune with reasonable commercial expectations ...

there were, almost immediately after the decision was released, howls of outrage: "The world we knew is collapsing!" "There is no certainty!" "What shall I tell my clients to do?"[56] These cries were motivated by a perception that legal certainty resides, or is found, in rules – and the more precise the better![57] This concept of certainty[58] misunderstands what it

---

56 These claims were made in many law firm posts or comments – eg https://mcmillan.ca/mobile/Lets-Be-Honest-The-New-Duty-of-Good-Faith-in-Contractual-Performance:

> While the Supreme Court embarked on its analysis with the admirable intention of enhancing commercial certainty, the decision is likely to have the opposite effect on the predictability of contract law. Future courts will now have to grapple with what, exactly, "honest performance" entails, and the extent to which that duty may be modified by express contractual terms.

Julius Melnitzer, in "Lexpert's Top 10 Business Decisions of 2015," 11 January 2016, said that the "courts delivered body blows to business positions on some controversial and meaningful issues: the Supreme Court of Canada imputed a duty of good faith into contract law, creating a great deal of controversy and uncertainty in doing so," http://www.lexpert.ca/article/lexperts-top-10-business-decisions-of-2015/.

57 This view is not new. In *Economy and Society*, the great German sociologist Max Weber preferred the formality of rules to the informality of broad principles in a rational legal system, and this has been taken as support for legal certainty, especially to assist rational economic decision making or, more simply, commerce. The perceived superiority of rules over general standards like good faith with respect to certainty is challenged in O. Raban, "The Fallacy of Legal Certainty: Why Vague Legal Standards May Be Better for Capitalism and Liberalism" (2010) 19 *Public Interest Law Journal* 175.

58 For a detailed attempt to understand what uncertainty in commercial law actually means, see I. MacNeil, "Uncertainty in Commercial Law" (2009) 12 *Edinburgh Law Review* 68. It is not obvious how one can evaluate the relative uncertainty between

can look like. Yes, we need to have a clear rule requiring us to drive on the right-hand side of the road – except, of course, when we must not. Solicitors need to know how to control precisely what steps they and their clients must take as the client's relation with another party moves from the non-legal world into a legal relation.[59] Legal certainty may, however, come, not from rules, but from other sources. The requirement that an employer give reasonable notice of termination to an employee is not very precise, but it is not generally hard for a solicitor to advise an employer client what length of notice to give an employee whom the client wants to dismiss without cause. In any case, the sensible solicitor will often suggest that the client err, in the case of an error, on the generous side.

Similarly, it is occasionally difficult to advise a director what she or he should do to comply with a director's fiduciary duty in some broad sense. Advising her or him what to do in a specific situation is much easier, and such practical difficulties have not led to any serious claims denying the existence of these duties or any calls to abolish them – if anything, the clear trend for the past half-century has been to fortify them.[60] For example, the language of the Ontario Business Corporations Act[61] is very broad:

---

complex common law systems (which generally did not have a general obligation of good faith) and civilian systems (which have one) generally or even between individual common law systems: see M. Siems, "Comparative Legal Certainty" in M. Fenwick, M. Siems, and S. Wrbka (eds), *The Shifting Meaning of Legal Certainty in Comparative and Transnational Law* (Oxford, Hart Publishing, 2017) at 115. Finally, it can be asked whether, even if the approach taken in *Bhasin* does actually generate some level of uncertainty, it still produces better results (eg in an economic sense) than alternative methods: see D. Bertolini, "Decomposing *Bhasin v Hrynew*: Towards an Institutional Understanding of the General Organizing Principle of Good Faith in Contractual Performance" (2017), 67 *University of Toronto Law Journal* 348 at 404ff.

59 In *O'Neil v Phillips* [1999] UKHL 24, [1999] 2 All ER 961 at 967, Lord Hoffmann stated that "[i]t is highly desirable that lawyers should be able to advise their clients whether or not a petition is likely to succeed" and that the general principles applicable to an application by a shareholder seeking relief for unfair prejudice are "tolerably well settled" enough to permit solicitors to do so even if they are broadly stated.

60 This understanding of directors' duties is clear in the attitude of Laskin J in *Canadian Aero Service Limited v O'Malley* [1974] SCR 592, 40 DLR (3d) 371, as made evident by the title of a well-known comment on the case: S.M. Beck, "The Quickening of Fiduciary Obligations" (1975) 53 *Canadian Business Review* 771. The Dickerson Report, in response to a perception of lax corporate governance at the time, explicitly expanded and raised the obligations imposed on a corporate director in the exercise of his or her duties (see *Peoples Department Stores Inc (Trustee of) v Wise* 2004 SCC 68, [2004] 3 SCR 461).

61 RSO 1990, c B.16.

> 134(1) Every director and officer of a corporation in exercising his or her[62] powers and discharging his or her duties shall:
>
> (a) act honestly and in good faith with a view to the best interests of the corporation; and
> (b) exercise the care, diligence and skill that a reasonably prudent person would exercise in comparable circumstances.
>
> (2) Every director and officer of a corporation shall comply with this Act, the regulations, articles, bylaws and any unanimous shareholder agreement.

A solicitor is not bothered by the broad language in the legislation in giving a client advice. Certainty comes not from knowing precisely where the line will be drawn, but from the knowledge that the client should be kept far away from it. In fact, the prudent solicitor will not – or at least should not – advise a client to sail close to whatever line there may be. Courts of equity have imposed fiduciary duties (or their precursors) for a very long time,[63] and it has not been argued – at least not for several centuries – that those duties have prevented people from carrying out those duties efficiently.[64] Solicitors have not had difficulty advising

---

62 We can hardly bear to reproduce s 122 of the Canada Business Corporations Act. It provides: "Every director and officer of a corporation in exercising *their* powers and discharging *their* duties shall ..." The mindless computer search for a singular, masculine personal pronoun and its automatic replacement by a plural pronoun is an example of absolutely horrible writing. It is not an excuse that this usage has now become common; it is still horrible and wholly unnecessary. The odd thing is that, at several other points, the Act uses the phrase "he or she."

63 The Court of Chancery has imposed such duties on directors (or committee members) since at least 1742 and the case *The Charitable Corporation v Sutton* (1742) 2 Atk 400, 26 ER 642. See also *Keech v Sandford* (1726) Sel Cas T King 61, 25 ER 223 (Ch).

64 If anything, the argument has been made that these features are strengths in the promotion of business: see eg the arguments of one of the most famous Delaware Chancery judges (W.T. Allen, "Ambiguity in Corporation Law" (1997) 22 *Delaware Journal of Corporate Law* 894). More broadly, Chancery developed its flexible, general principles – the fiduciary principle being the most important one for this chapter – to protect the integrity of diverse relationships, including various business associations. It designed those rules to protect these relations from behaviour by one of the parties to them that is likely to hurt or undermine the relation. Such behaviour is sometimes called *opportunistic* in academic literature. Thus, "[f]iduciary duty and the duty of good faith are variations on a theme. Both are judicially imposed loyalty obligations

fiduciaries what to do, even if there is the occasional case where the line is very hard to draw or discern,[65] and surprising and unexpected results occur.[66] There may be cases, like *Hodgkinson v Simms*,[67] where one can

---

designed to attack the potential for opportunism in relationships" (D. Gordon Smith, "The Critical Resource Theory of Fiduciary Duty" (2002) 55 *Vanderbilt Law Review* 1399 at 1487–8). Yet because such behaviour is difficult to detect, it also created presumptions about where such behaviour is present (see further H.E. Smith, "Why Fiduciary Law Is Equitable" in A. Gold and P. Miller (eds), *Philosophical Foundations of Fiduciary Law* (Oxford, Oxford University Press, 2014) at 261). Moreover, to allow these principles to be effectively applied to new, and often unforeseeable, circumstances and to make it difficult to circumvent them, and thereby undermine their purpose, they were (and still are) stated in broad, general terms. This is true even where those principles were later codified. Thus, it is not just coincidence that eg the test whether a partnership or corporation should be wound up depends on what is "just and equitable." See eg Partnerships Act, RSO 1990, c P.5, cl 35(1)(f) and Ontario Business Corporations Act, subcl 207(1)(b)(iv).

65 See eg *Boardman v Phipps* [1966] UKHL 2, [1967] 2 AC 46, [1966] 3 All ER 721.

66 A famous example of such a surprising consequence of a breach of directors' duties occurred in *Smith v Van Gorkom* 488 A 2d 858 (Del 1985).

67 [1994] 3 SCR 377, 117 DLR (4th) 161, [1994] 9 WWR 609. See P.C. Wardle, "Playing the Market: An Exploration of Stockbrokers' Liability for Client Losses" (1996) 27 *Canadian Business Law Journal* 323. More specifically, the obligations that might have seemed unexpected with respect to brokers in *Hodgkinson* are now becoming not only expected but required. The obligations that investment advisers owe to their clients are now, of course, getting a significant workout: see eg the Canadian Securities Administrators' discussion paper, "Canadian Securities Regulators Seek Comment on Proposals to Enhance the Obligations of Advisers, Dealers and Representatives toward Their Clients," 28 April 2016, http://www.osc.gov.on.ca/en/NewsEvents_nr_20160428_csa-seek-comment-enhance-obligations-advisers-dealers-representatives.htm. We shall return to this issue. Thus, the particular duties imposed on the investment advisers have, if anything, been strengthened post-*Hodgkinson*. More generally, *Hodgkinson* can be seen as part of a series of cases through the Commonwealth where, in the absence of an express doctrine of good faith, commercial parties mostly unsuccessfully attempted to rely on equitable principles, especially the fiduciary principle, to enforce cooperation in commercial transactions (see further A. Mason, "Contract, Good Faith and Equitable Standards in Fair Dealing" (2000) 116 *Law Quarterly Review* 66 at 84–7). In *Hospital Products Ltd v United States Surgical Corporation* (1984) 156 CLR 41, eg, a majority of the High Court of Australia refused to find that a relationship between a distributor and a manufacturer was a fiduciary relationship on facts that would easily breach the *Bhasin* honesty requirement. The wide approach to recognizing fiduciary duties adopted by the majority in *Hodgkinson* was significantly drawn back in *Professional Institute of the Public Service of Canada v Canada (Attorney General)* 2012 SCC 71, [2012] 3 SCR 660.

be surprised that a relation was characterized as a fiduciary one, but that surprise has nothing to do with uncertainty over the scope of the duty. And, of course, solicitors can so manage their practices that they, too, stay far from whatever lines or dangerous rocks and shoals there may be.

An example of the difficulties that can arise when a broad fiduciary duty is pushed in surprising directions is provided by the conflict of interest rules governing lawyers, particularly as those rules have been developed by the Supreme Court. The Supreme Court has expressed itself in four cases. The first was *MacDonald Estate v Martin*,[68] where the court held that a lawyer, having worked, as a student, at a firm that represented one client, had tainted the firm to which she moved when that firm represented a client adverse in interest to the first. The second case was *R. v Neil*,[69] which dealt with a different problem – *viz.*, the extent of the obligation of loyalty that a lawyer and, by extension, her or his firm – owes to two clients when the lawyer's obligations to the two clients may conflict.

The third case is *Canadian National Railway Co. v McKercher LLP*,[70] where the court returned to the issues raised by *Neil* – *viz.*, the obligation on a law firm that represents two clients adverse in interest. In the fourth case, *Strother v 3464920 Canada Inc.*,[71] the Supreme Court largely protected a firm that had behaved properly from the consequences of the acts of a rogue partner in breach of his obligations to his client.

The majority in *MacDonald Estate* allowed for the creation of "ethical walls" and invited Canadian law societies and the Canadian Bar Association to develop rules to deal with the need to protect clients. The dissent would have virtually prevented any lawyer moving from one firm to another. *Neil* stated a rule that is so wide as to be unworkable; *McKercher* suggests that the Supreme Court may have resiled from the very expansive position it took in both *MacDonald Estate* and *Neil*. The plain fact is that lawyers do their best, both with the principles stated by the Supreme Court and the Rules of Professional Conduct of their several law societies, to do what they should, but perfect compliance is not always possible, and trial judges and courts of appeal are generally

68 [1990] 3 SCR 1235, 77 DLR (4th) 249, [1991] 1 WWR 705.
69 2002 SCC 70, [2002] 3 SCR 631, 218 DLR (4th) 671.
70 2013 SCC 39, [2013] 2 SCR 649, 360 DLR (4th) 389.
71 2007 SCC 24, [2007] 2 SCR 177, 281 DLR (4th) 640.

reasonable. *Strother* probably caused more of a great sigh of relief than surprise.

So it is with compliance with the obligation of good faith performance. We do not need to know where the line has to be drawn; it is not hard to tell a client, "Just don't tell lies." The function of a principle like good faith performance is to discourage bad faith or dishonest performance; and, while it may be hard to define *bad faith* in advance of some projected action, it is not that hard to say on which side of the line some action or statement falls. It is this aspect of the new general organizing principle that most vividly demonstrates the pointlessness of worrying about the exact scope of the principle or whether there is, in fact, a new obligation of good faith performance as opposed to some more limited obligation.

It is a mistake to believe that the imposition of a duty of good faith or honest performance will make the law or, to be more precise, commercial law undesirably uncertain. We can turn the argument around: What might certainty look like, or how might we attain it?[72] Solicitors need to know what they have to do to make a valid contract for a client. They have to know how to apply the rules of offer and acceptance, how to make sure that there is consideration – if there could be any doubt that it would exist – and how to avoid such traps and pitfalls as there may be. It is generally not hard for a law of contracts to satisfy these needs.

Certainty looks quite different from other points of view. A solicitor who wants to draft an employee non-competition clause will be told by the law, the cases, and the text writers that such a clause has to be reasonable. In fact, with respect to employees, such a clause is *prima facie* void. This knowledge does not prevent the solicitor from telling a client what temporal and geographical limits on the clause are likely to be considered reasonable by a court. The solicitor's advice will be: Do not overreach, and ask only for what you really have to have and can easily defend before a judge. In other words, the content of the word

72 It is important to remember what Oliver Wendell Holmes said ("The Path of the Law" (1897) 10 *Harvard Law Review* 457; emphasis added):

> The language of judicial decision is mainly the language of logic. And the logical method and form flatter that longing for certainty and for repose which is in every human mind. *But certainty generally is illusion, and repose is not the destiny of man.*

reasonable, when told to the client, will be informed by the solicitor's knowledge of the cases where non-competition clauses were (or were not) upheld and by the general recognition of the fact that overreaching is dangerous.

Words like *reasonable, good faith,* and *best and commercially reasonable efforts* (or *endeavours*), when used in contractual language, cannot be replaced by a rule. Those words set, or define, a standard of conduct against which a party's actions will be tested. It is foolish to expect that the general organizing principle of good faith performance imposed by the Supreme Court in *Bhasin v Hrynew* can be reduced to a rule. Yet this expectation seems to be held by some civil litigators. A case comment of *Bhasin v Hrynew*, for example, said this:

> It remains to be seen in the common law jurisprudence how courts can develop the law to finally settle the debate surrounding the source of good faith and to establish a principled approach towards what constitutes bad faith in order to resolve the lack of coherence and commercial certainty in the world of contract law.[73]

The authors seem to have an expectation of what the courts can do that is very unlikely to be met. The source of the obligation of good faith performance is precisely stated by Cromwell J to *inhere* in the parties' relation: it is just there; it is not an implied term; it is not imposed by the court. If *good faith* is "defined," as it probably has to be, as an absence of bad faith, we do not need to know more about what is bad faith than that it is, or includes, dishonesty; dissimulation, failing to disclose what has to be disclosed;[74] or mean, stingy performance. There are other adjectives that could be used, but the important points are two: (1) we do not actually need much precision; it is important to know only that there is a line that should not be crossed; and (2) it is not usually hard to determine when the line has been crossed. A careful solicitor does not advise a client to sail close to any line, whether it be the good faith line or the fiduciary line, that is dangerous to cross.

---

73 N. Effendi, H. Pessione, and O.V. Nguyen, "*Bhasin v Hrynew*: Towards Clarity and Coherence with respect to Good Faith in Contract Performance" (2016) 46 *Advocate's Quarterly* 94 at 122.

74 It is not uncommon for agreements of purchase and sale, or agreements by which an investor will put money into a business, to include a clause that says, "There is no fact undisclosed that, if disclosed, would be material."

When the senior author discussed *Bhasin v Hrynew* in her firm, the "deal" lawyers, the solicitors, were not overly concerned about the "new" requirement to perform in good faith or even about the possibility that there may be a duty to negotiate in good faith. They recognized that it is simply bad practice for a client or a solicitor to lie, and being dishonest is a bad and very foolish way to begin a relation that is to be a framework for future cooperation. In other words, *Bhasin* changed nothing. The litigators might have become briefly excited over a novel judicial pronouncement, but then they always do when they have a new argument to make or a new cause of action to pursue.

The further argument that parties' freedom of contract is improperly limited by their inability to exclude the duty of good faith performance from their agreement is equally mistaken and, if taken seriously, very unpleasant. The parties' power to do all kinds of things is denied by the law: as we have mentioned, an employee non-competition clause is *prima facie* void as contrary to public policy, and a vendor non-competition clause will be unenforceable if it is not reasonable. A party guilty of fraud is both liable in deceit and to have the contract rescinded. It is absurd to imagine that the courts, whether or not there were a recognized obligation of good faith performance, would uphold a contractual provision that permitted one party to lie to the other, and, as we have mentioned, such a power has been explicitly denied as contrary to public policy.[75]

As Cromwell J specifically noted, no party will ever be successful in arguing that a contract can exclude the defence of unconscionability, and if a solicitor drafted such a clause, the courts' response would be immediate: the clause would be void as contrary to public policy. In one sense, of course, the whole law of illegal contracts is one long refutation of the idea that the parties can do whatever they want.[76] *Freedom of contract* means no more than that the parties are free, *within the limits set by the law*, to do what they want. Like the immunity of the argument

75 See above n 48.

76 The statutory examples – the Interest Act, RSC 1985, c I-15, ss 4 and 8; the criminal interest provisions of the Criminal Code, RSC 1985, c C-46, s 347; and, of course, many others in particular industries and trades – catch parties and their solicitors all the time. It scarcely needs to be said that no drafting technique will insulate the contracting party from the consequences of such legislation.

based on unconscionability to a claim based on freedom of contract, so, too, is the argument based on the obligation to perform in good faith.

There is another important fact to consider. A clause disclaiming an obligation to perform in good faith would have to be very clearly drafted; it would be some kind of exemption clause. How likely would it be that one party would accept the other party's offer if that offer said, "We hereby disclaim any obligation to perform our contractual obligations in good faith"? Who could possibly know the consequences of such a disclaimer: what is the other party actually undertaking to do? It is almost inconceivable that any contract would arise if such a clause were in the draft agreement.

Finally, the idea that the decision in *Bhasin v Hrynew* somehow *increases* commercial uncertainty misunderstands or misperceives the pre-*Bhasin* law.[77] Cromwell J and those like us, who have argued for years for a general duty of good faith performance, note that such duties have actually existed for a very long time.[78] We are, for example, certain that the old law merchant would have recognized such a duty. As we have said, all that Cromwell J did was to gather the existing cases, placed in various subcategories of the law of contracts, into one general organizing principle. Important cases like *Dynamic Transport Ltd. v O.K. Detailing Ltd.* have been "dismissed" as "condition precedent" cases

---

77 In "Good Faith, Good Conscience, and the Taking of Unfair Advantage" in A. Dyson, J. Goudkamp, and F. Wilmot-Smith (eds), *Defences in Contract* (Oxford, Hart Publishing, 2017) at 63, S. Waddams argues that there was a wide, equitable jurisdiction to control unconscionable contractual performance, which could be subsumed into the doctrine of good faith as laid out in *Bhasin v Hrynew* if the doctrine was given an objective meaning.

78 One example can stand for many: In *Mackay v Dick* (1881) 6 App Cas 251 at 263 (HL), Lord Blackburn said,

> I think that I may safely say, as a general rule, that where in a written contract it appears that both parties have agreed that something shall be done, which cannot effectually be done unless both concur in doing it, the construction of the contract is that each agrees to do all that is necessary to be done on his part for the carrying out of that thing, though there may be no express words to that effect.

Lord Blackburn found support for this statement in a case decided in 1469! It would be silly and unhelpful to claim that he – one of the greatest common law commercial judges of the nineteenth century, if not the greatest, and hardly a radical judge – was not recognizing that there was an obligation to perform in good faith, an obligation that, moreover, looks very much like one that simply inheres in the contractual relation the parties had.

and so, we assume, are somehow outside the *good faith* canon.[79] Such a dismissive characterization of that case can only justify some belief – or ideology – that an obligation of good faith performance must not be recognized as a general principle of the law of contracts. To which we can only ask, "Why on earth not?"

The Oppression Remedy

Consider the obligation to perform in good faith from another point of view. Canadian courts and solicitors have had to live with the oppression remedy under the Canada Business Corporations Act and provincial business corporations Acts[80] for several decades. That remedy can easily be seen to be based on an obligation of good faith performance. The Ontario Business Corporations Act provides:

> 248(1) A complainant and, in the case of an offering corporation, the Commission may apply to the court for an order under this section.
>
> (2) Where, upon an application under subsection (1), the court is satisfied that in respect of a corporation or any of its affiliates,
>
> (a) any act or omission of the corporation or any of its affiliates effects or threatens to effect a result;
> (b) the business or affairs of the corporation or any of its affiliates are, have been or are threatened to be carried on or conducted in a manner; or
> (c) the powers of the directors of the corporation or any of its affiliates are, have been or are threatened to be exercised in a manner, *that is oppressive or unfairly prejudicial to or that unfairly disregards the interests of any security holder, creditor, director or officer of the corporation*, the court may make an order to rectify the matters complained of.

79 See eg G. Hall, *Canadian Contractual Interpretation Law*, 3rd edn (Toronto, LexisNexis, 2016) 41. See also *100 Main Street East Ltd v WB Sullivan Construction Ltd* (1978) 20 OR (2d) 410, 88 DLR (3d) 1 (CA), a case that could be similarly "dismissed."

80 All modern provincial corporate legislation, except that of Prince Edward Island, provides for an oppression remedy. The legislative provisions are not, however, uniform across Canada. While the Quebec Civil Code has a wide-ranging and mandatory good faith obligation, see above n 8, the recent Quebec Business Corporations Act offers the remedy to a narrower class of potential claimants (see the definition of *security* in art 2 and arts 439, 450). The wider protection of the Civil Code from bad faith could explain this difference as the excluded parties are those who would have contractual claims for relief.

Actions that trigger the oppression remedy, the emphasized part of ss. 234(2), can easily be characterized as actions that are not done in good faith.

Canadian courts have not had great difficulty in dealing with applications under the oppression remedy.[81] We shall not go through the very many cases where a remedy for oppression has been given. What is interesting is that the test for oppression is whether a respondent's actions have disappointed or failed to protect the complainant's reasonable expectations that she, he, or it had when investing in the corporation as a shareholder, engaging with the corporation as a creditor,[82] or acting as a director.[83]

The lesson from the oppression remedy cases is simply that courts have, in effect, been applying a test that is very similar to one that they would have to apply in working out the scope and application of the general organizing principle of good faith or honest performance – and

---

81 See eg the very interesting discussion of the early decisions on the oppression remedy by S. Block, "Corporate Matrimonial Law: An Unofficial History of the Oppression Remedy" in *Selected Topics in Corporate Litigation* (Queen's Annual Business Law Symposium, Queen's University, Kingston, ON, 2000) 41. It is possible to read this paper, written by a leading litigator, as expressing some surprise that the law is not more uncertain than it actually is!

82 In *BCE Inc v 1976 Debentureholders* 2008 SCC 69, [2008] 3 SCR 560, 301 DLR (4th) 80, the Court said (emphasis added),

> [61] Lord Wilberforce [in *Ebrahimi v Westbourne Galleries Ltd.* [1973] AC 360 (HL), at 379, interpreting S 222 of the UK *Companies Act, 1948*] spoke of the equitable remedy in terms of the "rights, expectations and obligations" of individuals. "Rights" and "obligations" connote interests enforceable at law without recourse to special remedies, for example, through a contractual suit or a derivative action under S 239 of the *CBCA*. It is left for the oppression remedy to deal with the "expectations" of affected stakeholders. *The reasonable expectations of these stakeholders is the cornerstone of the oppression remedy.*
>
> [62] As denoted by "reasonable," the concept of reasonable expectations is objective and contextual. The actual expectation of a particular stakeholder is not conclusive. In the context of whether it would be "just and equitable" to grant a remedy, the question is whether the expectation is reasonable having regard to the facts of the specific case, the relationships at issue, and the entire context, including the fact that there may be conflicting claims and expectations.

See also *Lee v To* [1998] 9 WWR 1 (Sask CA), *101114752 Saskatchewan Ltd v Devonian Potash Inc* 2012 SKCA 64, following *Naneff v Con-Crete Holdings Limited* (1995) 23 OR (3d) 481 (CA) and *Sieminska v Boldt*, 2013 SKCA 136.

83 See eg *Wilson v Alharayeri* 2017 SCC 39, [2017] 1 SCR 1037.

Canadian law or corporate law, in particular, has not collapsed as the remedy has been given.[84]

The Ubiquity of Concerns for Integrity

It is impossible in a chapter of this scope to deal with more than a very few examples where a person's integrity or good character is relevant to her or his qualification for a job or, putting the point the other way round, where a lack of integrity may lead to unpleasant consequences for the person. *Good faith, honesty,* and *integrity* are functional synonyms and, whichever one was used, would lead to the same advice being given by a solicitor.

We mentioned[85] the developing concern that those who act for clients or customers in guiding their investments or advising them what to do with their money act primarily for the client or customer. Those who act on the industry side of the investment business must now act with integrity. We also note briefly that the discretionary or residual power granted to Canadian securities regulators to protect the integrity and honesty in the capital markets is impressive.[86]

The Ontario Securities Act provides:

> 27(1) On receipt of an application by a person or company and all information, material and fees required by the Director and the regulations, the Director shall register the person or company, reinstate the registration of the person or company or amend the registration of the person or company, unless it appears to the Director,
>
> (a) that, in the case of a person or company applying for registration, reinstatement of registration or an amendment to a registration, the person or company is not suitable for registration under this Act; or
> (b) that the proposed registration, reinstatement of registration or amendment to registration is otherwise objectionable.

---

84 It is worth noting that several jurisdictions that have been hostile to the notion of good faith performance, like England, above nn 11 and 31, have the oppression remedy as part of their corporate law: see United Kingdom Companies Act, s 994; Australia, Corporations Act 2001, s 234; and Singapore, Companies Act, s 216.

85 Above n 67.

86 See eg Securities Act, RSO 1990, c S.5, s 127. In one recent, well-reported instance, this power was used by the Ontario Securities Commission to prohibit several individuals from serving as corporate directors as a result of their being convicted in

(2) In considering for the purposes of subsection (1) whether a person or company is not suitable for registration, the Director shall consider,

(a) whether the person or company has satisfied,
  (i) the requirements prescribed in the regulations relating to proficiency, solvency and *integrity*, …

116 Every investment fund manager,

(a) shall exercise the powers and discharge the duties of their office *honestly, in good faith and in the best interests of the investment fund*; and
(b) shall exercise the degree of care, diligence and skill that a reasonably prudent person would exercise in the circumstances. …

61(2) The Director shall not issue a receipt for a prospectus or an amendment to a prospectus if it appears to the Director that …

(e) *the business of the issuer may not be conducted with integrity and in the best interests of the security holders of the issuer* because of the past conduct of,
  (i) the issuer,
  (ii) any of the issuer's officers, directors, promoters, or control persons, or
  (iii) the investment fund manager of the issuer or any of the investment fund manager's officers, directors or control persons.[87]

The policies developed by the Canadian Securities Administrators emphasize the importance of the possession of integrity as a necessary quality for a registrant.[88] Similarly, the Dealer Member Rules of the Investment Industry Regulatory Organization of Canada (IIROC) provide:

29.1. Dealer Members and each partner, Director, Officer, Supervisor, Registered Representative, Investment Representative and employee of a Dealer Member (i) shall observe high standards of ethics and conduct in the transaction of their business, (ii) shall not engage in any business

---

a foreign jurisdiction of various criminal offences when they did not discharge their director's duties in good faith: see *In Re Black* 2015 ONSEC 4.

87 RSO 1990, c S.5; emphasis added.

88 See eg Canadian Securities Administrators, Consultation Paper 33-403 and Companion Policy 31-103CP; and Ontario Securities Commission, Staff Notices 33-742 and 33-746.

> conduct or practice which is unbecoming or detrimental to the public interest, and (iii) shall be of such character and business repute and have such experience and training as is consistent with the standards described in clauses (i) and (ii) or as may be prescribed by the Board.[89]

The point to be made by including these examples of (ultimately) legislatively imposed standards of good faith or integrity is that there is nothing new in the principles that *Bhasin v Hrynew* impose on contracting parties. In other words, both corporate law, in the duties on directors and in the oppression remedy, and the entire securities industry, with its emphasis on integrity, are simply saying that people have to perform – that is, do their jobs, conduct or run their businesses – in good faith and honestly. How can these developments be other than a very good thing? It would be extremely odd if the general law of contracts were, notwithstanding these developments, to deny that an obligation of good faith performance or honest performance existed.

The Possible Application of the New Organizing Principle to Negotiations

We shall deal with this topic summarily. It is the heart of Cromwell J's development of his general organizing principle that existing cases had demonstrated the widespread acceptance of an obligation to perform in good faith.[90] That claim has been the senior author's argument for at least thirty years.[91] We have similarly argued in our textbook that there is a recognized obligation to negotiate in good faith.[92] We acknowledge

89 IIROC is the body that supervises (and disciplines) the participants in the investment industry. Provincial securities commissions and bodies like the Toronto Stock Exchange perform the same function with respect to Canada's capital markets. The annual reports published by these bodies illustrate the extent of the enforcement of the obligation on participants in Canadian capital markets to behave with integrity.

90 See above text with nn 27–31 for a short list of the important cases.

91 See Swan and Adamski, *Canadian Contract Law*, above n 32, s 8.1.7.

92 Ibid s 4.2.2. Others are now making this argument on the basis of *Bhasin*: see eg T. Buckwold, "The Enforceability of Agreements to Negotiate in Good Faith: The Impact of *Bhasin v Hrynew* and the Organizing Principle of Good Faith in Common Law Canada" (2016) 58 *Canadian Business Law Journal* 1; L.E. Tarkman and K. Sharma, "The Binding Force of Agreements to Negotiate in Good Faith" (2014) 73 *Cambridge Law Journal* 598. For a recent, careful exploration of the issue of the

that those cases may not use the phrase *negotiate in good faith*; however, the point is not the trivial one that some other words are used or not, but the fact that obligations indistinguishable from, or coincident with, an obligation to negotiate in good faith have been recognized for a very long time.

Our argument with respect to that obligation is that the pattern in the cases is the same. Yes, there are many judicial statements denying that there cannot be an obligation to negotiate in good faith, but, like the statement by the Alberta Court of Appeal that we quoted earlier,[93] and as we have said, they are better understood as statements of an ideology than as the result of a careful examination of the cases.

The cases that are principally offered as authority for the proposition that there is no duty to negotiate in good faith are *Walford v Miles*,[94] *Martel Building Ltd. v Canada*,[95] *Peel Condominium Corp. No. 505 v Cam-Valley Homes Ltd.*,[96] and *978011 Ontario Ltd. v Cornell Engineering Co. Ltd.*[97] In contrast, there are many cases that have imposed obligations, which may as well be called obligations of good faith in negotiations as anything else: the enforceability of an amendment to a contract requires the change to have been brought to the other side's attention;[98] an offer known to have been made by mistake cannot be accepted;[99] statements

obligation to negotiate in good faith under Quebec civil law, see the judgment of Hamilton J in *Goulet v Carrière* 2014 QCCS 5801; and see *SIGA Techologies, Inc v PharmAthene, Inc* 67 A 3d 330 (2013 Del) – eg, for such an obligation being enforced under American law.

93 See above n 37.

94 [1992] 2 AC 128, [1992] 1 All ER 453, [1992] 2 WLR 174 (HL).

95 2000 SCC 60, [2000] 2 SCR 860, 193 DLR (4th) 1.

96 (2001) 53 OR (3d) 1, 196 DLR (4th) 621, 14 BLR (3d) 169 (CA), rev'g (1999) 28 RPR (3d) 186.

97 (2001) 53 OR (3d) 783, 198 DLR (4th) 615 (CA).

98 *Walton v Landstock Investments Ltd* (1976) 13 OR (2d) 693 at 696, 72 DLR (3d) 195 (CA), leave to appeal refused [1976] 2 SCR ix; *AMJ Campbell Inc v Kord Products Inc* (2003) 63 OR (3d) 375, 32 BLR (3d) 90 (SCJ); *Big Quill Resources Inc v Potash Corp of Saskatchewan Inc*, 2000 SKQB 332, [2000] 10 WWR 465, aff'd 2001 SKCA 31. See Swan and Adamski, *Canadian Contract Law*, above n 32, ss 4.128, 4.129.

99 *McMaster University v Wilchar Construction Ltd* [1971] 3 OR 801, 22 DLR (3d) 9; aff'd, (1973) 12 OR (2d) 512n, 69 DLR (3d) 400n (HCJ & CA); *Stepps Investments Ltd v Security Capital Corporation* (1976) 14 OR (2d) 259, 73 DLR (3d) 351 (HCJ); *Stevens v Stevens* 2013 ONCA 267, 114 OR (3d) 721 (CA).

or actions made in the context of negotiations may bind the person making them, even if no contract arises.[100]

In our opinion, it is only a matter of time before an argument that there is a duty to negotiate in good faith is accepted by Canadian courts. As with the argument that the decision in *Bhasin v Hrynew* created uncertainty, there will be yells and screams that it is the end of civilization as we know it. The recognition of any obligation of good faith, whether in performance or negotiations, simply recognizes what the parties expect: do not tell lies; do not mislead.

Conclusion

The justification for the new general organizing principle, for the oppression remedy, and for the new and stringent standards of conduct for investment advisers is that such developments, by bringing integrity into contractual relations, protect the reasonable expectations of those involved, particularly those who might be at a disadvantage with respect to the other party. Of course, exactly similar or parallel justifications apply to the imposition on professionals of all kinds – lawyers, accountants, engineers, etc. – of fiduciary duties or simply obligations of integrity in the performance of their jobs.[101]

The importance of the claim that underlying the developments that have been discussed is the idea of protecting the reasonable expectations of the parties involved is that it provides a powerful basis for

---

100 *Waltons Stores (Interstate) Ltd v Maher* [1988] HCA 7, 164 CLR 387, 88 AJLR 110 (HCA). The basis for the decision, imposing liability on the defendant, appellant, for the costs thrown away by the plaintiff, respondent, in preparing a building to be leased to the defendant, was that it was unconscionable for the defendant not to have told the plaintiff that it (the defendant) had had second thoughts about the lease. It is fairly clear that the defendant's solicitor gave it very bad advice.

101 It was, of course, the compromised integrity of accounting firms like Arthur Anderson that led, *inter alia*, to the débâcle at Enron and the demise of the firm itself. This event demonstrated that professional integrity has an important public function in maintaining properly functioning markets. See eg J.C. Coffee, "Understanding Enron: It's about the Gatekeepers, Stupid" (2002) 57 *Business Lawyer* 1403. It could be argued that the shift represented in recent cases like *Deloitte & Touche v. Livent Inc. (Receiver of)*, 2017 SCC 63, [2017] SCR 855, 416 DLR. (4th) 32, and settlements between accounting firms and investors, challenge the justification for the result in *Hercules Managements Ltd v Ernst & Young* [1997] 2 SCR 165, 146 DLR (4th) 577, [1997] 8 WWR 80.

generalizing the law – that is, exactly what Cromwell J did in *Bhasin*. The importance, in turn, of a generalized approach to the law – and we shall focus particularly on the law of contracts – is that it makes the job that judges do easier and provides a basis for those who advise clients, comment on the law, or try to foresee what it might become or how it might develop.[102]

A focus on the expectations of the parties is a focus on things that exist in a way that a focus on, for example, the intentions of the parties is either a focus on things that do not exist or, if they do, are simply unhelpful in dealing with the problem that may have arisen. When courts say, for example, that the interpretation of a contract requires an examination of the parties' intentions,[103] they simply ignore what has to be the proper focus of their enquiry. What are the intentions of a householder who takes out an insurance policy on her house? How could those intentions – they have to be no more precise than "I want insurance coverage if something terrible happens" – be in any way useful to understanding the coverage of the policy? What is important are her expectations – reasonable ones, of course – and the extent to which the insurer did or did not meet them. This focus is the basis for the approach to the interpretation of an insurance policy that gives coverage provisions a broad interpretation, exclusions from coverage a narrow interpretation, and exceptions or limitations on exclusions a wide interpretation.[104] The separate approaches, of course, reflect what each of the insured and insurer must establish.

---

102 A continuing professional development program offered by Lexpert on 10 May 2016 advertised these topics on the duty of good faith: History of the Duty of Good Faith, Subsequent Case Law, What Your Employees and Agents Need to Know, Good Faith in Insurance Contract, Good Faith in Intellectual Property, Good Faith and Leasing, Good Faith and Employment, Good Faith in Franchising, Good Faith in Insolvency. So much for the development of a generalized approach!

103 *Eli Lilly & Co v Novopharm Ltd; Eli Lilly & Co v Apotex Inc* [1998] 2 SCR 129, 161 DLR (4th) 1. We develop this idea in greater detail in J. Adamski and A. Swan, "Contractual Interpretation in the Supreme Court: Confusion Reigns Supreme" in M. Harrington (ed), *Private Law in Canada: A 150-Year Retrospective* (Markham, ON, LexisNexis, 2017) 115.

104 See eg *Amos v Insurance Corp of British Columbia* [1995] 3 SCR 405, 127 DLR (4th) 618, [1995] 9 WWR 305; *Progressive Homes Ltd v Lombard General Insurance Co of Canada* 2010 SCC 33, [2010] 2 SCR 245, 323 DLR (4th) 513, [2010] 10 WWR 573.

The resistance of barristers to the idea that what matters is the reasonable expectations of the parties is extraordinary.[105] Some academics (and practitioners) are equally hostile.[106] A focus on reasonable expectations deals with or satisfies two important values or goals of the law of contracts: it provides a justification for the law of contracts[107] and offers a criterion for the resolution of the problems that come before the courts. The importance of this goal is that it is likely to offer a judge a basis for deciding a case in a manner that is consistent with her or his attitude to the law or the particular problem before the court. In other words, the criterion that the judge can adopt can reflect what she or he believes should be done. In saying that a judge may do what she wants to do, we are not subverting the law; we are recognizing that every difficult decision reflects values that are in conflict and that a choice must be made between them. That choice must reflect what the judge believes is the right thing to do *in the context in which she or he is functioning*.

In our textbook, we say,

> It is the argument of this work that principles do matter, that how courts approach a problem is at least, if not more, important than what they do because, regardless of the result in the previous case, an unprincipled result may lead other courts astray. It is hoped that a focus on principles, on the analysis of the cases, may do something to counteract the harmful and unhelpful proliferation of findable decisions. Where, however, the Supreme Court – and it is particularly on the Supreme Court that the

---

105 For a vivid example, see *Onex Corporation v American Home Assurance Company* 2013 ONCA 117, 114 OR (3d) 161 at paras 165–74. The case was reheard before a different trial judge and came back to the Court of Appeal, 2015 ONCA 573, application of leave to appeal dismissed, 14 April 2016, where, dismissing the appeal, the claim of the plaintiff was allowed.

106 See eg G. Hall, "A Study in Reasonable Expectations" (2007) 45 *Canadian Business Law Journal* 150; B.J. Reiter, "A Study in Reasonable Expectations: A Rebuttal to Geoff Hall" (2008) 46 *Canadian Business Law Journal* 95; S.A. Smith, "'The Reasonable Expectations of the Parties': An Unhelpful Concept" (2010) 48 *Canadian Business Law Journal* 366; and R. Bigwood, "Book Review, Swan & Adamski, *Canadian Contract Law*, 3rd ed." (2014) 55 *Canadian Business Law Journal* 313.

107 See eg A.L. Corbin, *Corbin on Contracts*, vol 1 (St Paul, MI, West Publishing, 1963), s 1 at 2:

> That portion of the field of law that is classified and described as the law of contracts attempts the realization of reasonable expectations that have been induced by the making of a promise.

burden falls – lifts the analysis of a problem out of the morass in which it had lain for a long time, even though its original basis for doing so may have been weak, other courts can quickly discern clearer and more satisfactory principles and produce better decisions.[108]

We see Cromwell J's decision in *Bhasin v Hrynew* as an example of the Supreme Court doing exactly what it should be doing – *viz.*, taking a high-level view of the state of the law, discerning important aspects or doctrinal threads within it, and using that insight to craft a new and important principle. The decision brings together closely related aspects of the law that too many people have seen as being unrelated to each other; it provides now a basis for the further development of the law to reflect the values that are both inherent in it and very important. The court takes a small step – and is careful to demonstrate that it is a small step – that brings several disparate areas of the law into harmony.[109] The arguments for the step are carefully and cogently made, and the obvious problems that might be foreseen or raised are examined and found wanting or are shown to be unjustified.[110] In short, the decision is a very good one.

Almost exactly thirty years before the decision in *Bhasin* was released, the senior author had argued for the development that has now occurred and offered the same arguments for it that the Supreme

108 Swan and Adamski, *Canadian Contract Law*, above n 32, s 1.50.

109 Consistent with our argument, D. Murynka, above note 5 at 613, points outs that "[d]espite its popularity in judicial discourse, I suggest that explicitly 'principled' judicial reasoning has not had a revolutionary effect on the actual *outcomes* of Canadian cases in the last three decades."

110 This view is consistent with the careful approach to the principles that ought to be guiding judicial reform of the common law, which Bastarache J laid out in *Friedmann Equity Developments Inc v Final Note Ltd* 2000 SCC 34, [2000] 1 SCR 842 at 42ff and followed in *Durham Condominium Corporation no 123 v Amberwood Investments Limited* (2002) 58 OR (3d) 481, 211 DLR (4th) 1 (CA). At the expense of oversimplification, it must be also said that the Canadian Supreme Court in the area of private law reform in the last twenty years has consistently sought to articulate broad principles rather than narrow rules. Two well-known examples of this have been its attempt to lay out the principles of unjust enrichment and fiduciary duties. Another contributor to this volume, Professor Steve Hedley, casts doubt on the search for principles of unjust enrichment and, consequently, would probably question the utility of the Supreme Court's methodology (see ch 12).

Court has adopted.[111] She concluded her case comment on *Bhasin*[112] by saying, "it is with a strong sense of satisfaction (and vindication) that I say, 'Now, what was so hard about that?'" She also asked, "What took you so long?"

111 J. Swan, "Whither Contracts: A Retrospective and Prospective Overview" in *Special Lectures of the Law Society of Upper Canada 1984 – Law in Transition: Contracts* (Don Mills, ON, De Boo, 1984) 125.

112 A. Swan, "The Obligation to Perform in Good Faith," above n 17 at 395.

11 Cause and Courts

SANDY STEEL

Common law tort laws recognize this general rule: to obtain substantial compensatory damages in respect of an injury from a defendant, the claimant must demonstrate that the defendant's wrongful conduct was a cause of that injury on the balance of probabilities.[1]

The central question that apex courts across the common law have had to answer over the last fifty years or so is whether any exception should be made to the general rule. Apex courts in the United Kingdom, Canada, and the United States have answered in the affirmative. The exceptions have proved controversial, and some consider that the inevitable result of exceptions in this area is incoherence, uncertainty, and injustice.

In the first part of the chapter, I briefly set out the current state of the law in relation to these exceptional rules. In the second part, I suggest that we can draw five lessons about when exceptions should be made to basic rules in tort law from the development of these exceptions. These are the lessons of (1) transparency – the exception must be recognized as such and its scope clearly defined; (2) necessity – an exception should be recognized as such only if it is not simply a covert application of the general rule; (3) non-arbitrariness – the exception must apply to all cases within its rationale; (4) the exception cannot undermine the rationality of the general rule in all cases; (5) competence – the exception

1 By *common law*, I will mean England and Wales, Canada, Australia, and the United States. The United States refers to the proof standard as the *preponderance of the evidence*, but this is only a different label for the same idea. Not all conduct before it is causative of injury is *wrongful* (in tort law). I will ignore this complication. By *cause*, I will mean only what is referred to as *factual* cause.

should be respectful of certain institutional constraints. In the final part of the chapter, I briefly question whether, lessons learned, apex courts should still be willing to make exceptions to the general rule.

The Law on Causal Proof Exceptions

This exception to the general rule is recognized by England, Canada, and most US states, but not by Australia:

> (1) *Multiple negligent actors (defendant indeterminacy).* D1, D2, D*n* each behave negligently in relation to C, one or more DDs have been causative of a personal injury risked by each D's negligence, but no D can be proved to be a cause on the balance of probabilities of C's personal injury. Here England, Canada, and many US states permit C to recover against any D either in full or in proportion to a roughly estimated probability that the D was causative of their injury.

This rule originates in the famous decision of the California Supreme Court in *Summers v Tice*.[2] In that case, the claimant was struck by a single bullet in the eye. It could not be determined which of the two defendants, who had negligently fired in the claimant's direction during a hunting trip, had fired the bullet causative of the eye injury. The court held that unless each defendant could prove that it had not been the cause of the eye injury, it would be held fully liable in respect of it. The crux of the court's reasoning was that, as between an innocent plaintiff and two negligent defendants, it was fairer that the defendants bore the risk of uncertainty over causation.

On almost identical facts, the Supreme Court of Canada, in *Cook v Lewis*, also reached the conclusion that both defendants should be held liable *in solidum*.[3] Cartwright J, relying upon *Summers v Tice*, made much the same fairness argument as the Californian court.[4] Rand J ingeniously argued that the defendant whose negligence had not caused the physical injury had nonetheless interfered with the plaintiff's evidential right to establish the violation of its primary right: by firing, that defendant had deprived the claimant of the ability to establish its claim

2 (1948) 33 Cal 2d 80.
3 [1951] SCR 830.
4 Ibid at 842.

against the defendant who was causative of the physical injury.[5] In virtue of this, it was apt to reverse the burden of proof, with the result that, failing causal proof, each defendant was held liable in full.

The rule in *Cook v Lewis* was recently reaffirmed by the Supreme Court in *Clements v Clements*.[6] In one of the most lucid judgments in this area, the Court explained that the Canadian law's exceptions to the general rule are limited to the situation where a claimant would not have suffered its injury had no one behaved wrongfully in relation to it.[7] The exceptions are designed to prevent claimants from having no rights to compensation where it is clear on the balance of probabilities that they would not have suffered their injury had no one breached a duty in relation to them. Canada's exceptional rules are thus largely limited to the situation envisaged in (1).

Despite being no less keen, and probably no more careful, hunters, English law's exceptional rules, unlike those in the United States and in Canada (and France and Germany), did not develop out of a situation of multiple negligent shooters.[8] I will discuss that development in a moment. However, it is reasonably clear that English law recognizes liability in the *multiple negligent actors* situation, albeit this is not in virtue of a rule conceptualized as geared distinctly towards this type of situation, as it largely is in the United States and Canada, and it may be restricted to cases where the uncertainty is somehow attributable to a gap in *scientific* knowledge.[9]

English law, but not Canadian or Australian law, recognizes the following, further, exception:

> (2) *Negligent actor(s), scientific impossibility of proof.* D's negligence may have been a cause of C's personal injury, but it is impossible to determine whether this is so on the balance of probabilities because of the current state of scientific knowledge, C's personal injury may have been caused entirely by one or more non-wrongful causes, and the other salient potential causes of C's injury would have caused the injury in the same way

---

5 Ibid at 833–4.

6 [2012] 2 SCR 181.

7 Ibid at paras 43, 45.

8 Canada, the United States, Germany, and France seem to have developed such rules in response to hunting accidents. See S. Steel, *Proof of Causation in Tort Law* (Cambridge, Cambridge University Press, 2015) ch 4.

9 *Sanderson v Hull* [2008] EWCA Civ 1211, although compare *Fitzgerald v Lane* [1987] 2 All ER 455, where no such restriction seems envisaged.

as D's negligent conduct. If C's injury is *mesothelioma*, then C can recover against D in full. If the injury is *not mesothelioma*, and D is not a medical professional, then C can recover in proportion to the roughly estimated probability that D's negligence was a cause of C's injury.

This baroque rule requires some explanation. This branch of English law's causal exceptionalism grew out of cases involving industrial accidents and diseases, where the causal uncertainty related to whether a defendant's breach of duty played a causal role in the occurrence of the injury or disease, or whether it was entirely due to non-tortious conditions, it therefore being uncertain whether the injury was caused by a breach of duty at all. (This is an uncertainty not present in the multiple negligent actors situation.)

In the 1940s, the Court of Appeal had flirted with the idea that where a defendant had breached a statutory duty designed to protect the safety of workers, and an employee had suffered an injury within the risk against which the duty was geared to protect, the employer had to prove that the risk would have materialized in any event.[10] The reasoning was interesting. It was the idea – attributed to Parliament's intention – that this was one of the risks that should be attributed to the employer as a cost of doing business, being one in respect of which the employer could readily be expected to obtain insurance.

This development was firmly rejected by the House of Lords in *Bonnington Castings v Wardlaw*, where Their Lordships unanimously affirmed the position that the claimant bore the burden of proof on causation in the tort of negligence and for breach of statutory duties geared to protect workers' safety.[11] In affirming one orthodoxy, however, the court might have been taken to be departing from another. In holding that it was sufficient for the pursuer to prove that the defender's breach *materially contributed* to its injury (pneumoconiosis), was it recognizing that causation could be established without proof of *but-for* causation? The better view is that it probably was since Their Lordships seemed unconcerned about whether but-for causation had been established in relation to what was treated as an indivisible injury.[12] Strictly, then,

10 See eg *Roberts v Dorman Long & Co Ltd* [1953] 2 All ER 428.

11 [1956] AC 613.

12 With the possible exception of Lord Keith. See J. Stapleton and S. Steel, "Causes and Contributions" (2016) 132 *Law Quarterly Review* 363. Cp S.H. Bailey, "Causation in Negligence: What Is a Material Contribution?" (2010) 30 *Legal Studies* 167.

Bonnington did not establish an exception to the substantive causal requirements of liability. Nor did it establish any exception to *proof* of causation: causation, in the guise of material contribution to damage, was established on the balance of probabilities.

The first case seemingly to recognize a genuine exception to the general rule of proof was *McGhee v National Coal Board*, where D negligently failed to provide showers for the use of its workers after they had worked in D's brick kiln.[13] Due to the absence of showers, P, D's employee, cycled home, caked in dust. P contracted dermatitis as a result of exposure to the dust. The causal question, as formulated by the House of Lords, was whether the provision of showers would have prevented P from contracting dermatitis. This could not be determined on the balance of probabilities: the dermatitis might have been wholly caused while P was working in the kiln, his exposure to dust during that time not being wrongful. The House of Lords held that, in the circumstances, a material increase in the risk of P's contracting dermatitis could be equated with a material contribution to P's dermatitis.

Lord Reid's judgment is obscure. It is not clear why His Lordship considered it permissible to equate two obviously different things: namely, materially increasing a risk and materially contributing to an injury. If the fiction was justified on normative grounds, they were not expressed. Lord Simon was more explicit: "To hold otherwise would mean that the respondents were under a legal duty which they could, in the present state of medical knowledge, with impunity ignore."[14] One reasonable way of understanding this claim is as a deterrence argument: in circumstances where medical knowledge over a causal mechanism is undeveloped, but it is known that the agent in question increases the risk of a certain type of injury, employers can expose employees to that risk without fear of sanction. In short, in those circumstances, employers have no tort-given incentive to take sufficient care of their employees. Lord Wilberforce was explicit, too, about the normative, rather than epistemic, foundation of the decision: as between the negligent employer and the employee, it was fairer that the latter bore the risk of causal uncertainty where causation is scientifically impossible to prove.[15]

13 [1973] 1 WLR 1.

14 Ibid at 9. It can also be given a Kantian spin: that a legal duty that is unenforceable is somehow a source of illicit normative control over another, with one person "unilaterally" setting the terms of an interaction.

15 Ibid at 6–7.

At a time of when, among senior judges, there was a perceived sense that the boundaries of liability in negligence were too widely drawn, the House of Lords, in *Wilsher v Essex Area Health Authority*, asserted that *McGhee* had established no new principle of law.[16] In *Wilsher*, a premature baby became blind. It could not be established whether the blindness was causally attributable to the defendant doctor's negligence, which had materially increased the risk of the blindness, or one or more of several other factors, which had also increased the risk. The claimant attempted to rely upon *McGhee* to leap this evidential gap. The House of Lords held that *McGhee* was based upon an inference of fact and no such inference could be drawn on the facts of *Wilsher*, given the number of other alternative risk sources.[17] Although this interpretation of *McGhee* has been skilfully defended, it cannot be sustained: Lord Wilberforce's and Lord Simon's judgments stand against this, and Lord Reid's judgment amounts to an acceptance of a fiction.[18] In this first of many rewritings of previous decisions in this area, the House of Lords emphasized the simplicity and certainty of the general rule.[19]

The real *McGhee* was resurrected by the House of Lords in *Fairchild v Glenhaven Funeral Services Ltd*.[20] Mr Fairchild had died from mesothelioma, which was caused by exposure to asbestos dust. Three of his former employers had exposed him to asbestos dust, in breach of their duties of care. Scientific uncertainty surrounding the mechanism by which asbestos causes mesothelioma was taken to preclude the attribution of causation to any particular defendant's breach on the balance of probabilities. The cancer could have been caused by a small number of fibres or by the cumulative effect of a large number of fibres. The House of Lords held that each employer was liable to the victim's estate. The formulations of the scope of the exception varied, but *Wilsher* was distinguished on the basis that the other possible causes of the claimant's injury were different in kind, or operated in different ways, to the risk created by the defendant's negligence.[21]

---

16 [1988] AC 1074.

17 One of those *very* robust inferences of fact with which Canadian tort lawyers will be familiar.

18 For the skilful defence: A. Beever, *Rediscovering the Law of Negligence* (Oxford, Hart Publishing, 2007) 465–72.

19 [1988] AC 1074 at 1092.

20 [2003] 1 AC 32.

21 Ibid at 57, 95. It seems that the exception may still apply, even if there are other possible causes that operate in a different way to that provided by the defendant's

In *Barker v Corus*, it was clarified that each defendant would be liable, under *Fairchild*, only in proportion to the roughly estimated risk that it had negligently imposed upon the claimant.[22] Three members of the majority achieved this result by treating the gist of the claim as being for the risk of mesothelioma.[23] Baroness Hale, also in the majority, rather held that, in virtue of the departure from the general rule of proof of causation, fairness to the defendants required suspension of joint and several liability, but without conceptualizing the damage in respect of which the claimant recovered as the risk itself.[24]

Barker was immediately reversed by s. 3 of the Compensation Act 2006, but only in relation to mesothelioma caused by asbestos. It follows that, at common law, proportional liability remains the law in relation to cases to which the *McGhee/Fairchild* rule applies. This liability is now conceptualized as permitting *causation* of the *personal injury* to be established by proof of a material increase in risk, rather than as liability for risk-as-damage.[25] The Court of Appeal has held that the rule applies to other lung cancers where there is a similar scientific uncertainty over the causal mechanism by which they are contracted.[26] But it seems highly unlikely that the rule applies in medical negligence.[27]

Lessons

Exceptions Should Be Transparent and Clear

Decisions that can be justified only by departures from the general rule should not be described as applications of the general rule. Moreover, they should be clearly described as departures therefrom. This is one of the simple lessons of *McGhee*. By suggesting that the

---

breach, so long as it is known that the type of agent provided by the defendant's breach played a causative role. This, at least, is one way of reconciling the decision in *Heneghan v Manchester Dry Docks Ltd* [2016] EWCA Civ 86 with the existence of the restriction described in the text.

22 [2006] 2 AC 572.

23 Lord Hoffmann, Lord Scott, and Lord Walker.

24 *Barker*, above n 22 at 615–17.

25 *Durham v BAI (Run off)* [2012] UKSC 14 at paras 65, 84.

26 *Heneghan v Manchester Dry Docks Ltd* [2016] EWCA Civ 86. See also *Zurich Insurance v International Energy Group* [2015] UKSC 33 at paras 109, 127.

27 *Gregg v Scott* [2005] 2 AC 176.

liability in that case could be based upon material contribution to the injury itself, given the way that the but-for question was formulated in that case, the decision gave rise to two main problems. First, if the rules are not applied as stated, then it becomes unclear when the general rule will, in fact, be applied. One is no longer necessarily judged according to the law itself. Second, it means that the outcomes in cases are not properly justified. Departures from proof of causation call for justification. The call goes unanswered where the departure operates covertly under the shadow of the general rule. English law has, in *Fairchild*, addressed this problem with *McGhee*: material increase in risk is now clearly recognized as an exception to the general rule. However, although the exception is now described as such, its scope is still far from clear. The rule of law demands that if an apex court introduces a novel exceptional rule into the law, the scope of the exception should be reasonably clear. If the exception cannot be formulated with any clarity, this must count significantly against its introduction.[28]

Exceptions Should Be Necessary

Exceptions should be recognized only if the general rules are incapable of reaching the result one seeks to realize by creating the exception. If the facts can be analysed as a *genuine* application of the general rule, then no exception is necessary. This is a demand of analytical clarity or parsimony.[29]

It might be argued that the pursuer in *McGhee* could have shown orthodox but-for causation on the balance of probabilities, not by an illicit inference from contribution to risk to contribution to injury, but by reconfiguring the counterfactual question fed into the but-for test. Instead of asking, "Would P's injury have been avoided if showers had been provided?," one asks, "Would P's injury have been avoided if P had not been exposed to dust by D in the brick kiln?" The answer to this question is that it is more probably true than not that P would not have contracted dermatitis.

28 Compare the law on material contribution to injury, which may not have reached this minimal level of transparency. See J. Stapleton and S. Steel, "Causes and Contributions" (2016) 132 *Law Quarterly Review* 363.

29 In a sense, this could be understood simply as a requirement of transparency.

Compare the difficult South African case of *Lee v Minister of Correctional Services*.[30] The plaintiff had contracted tuberculosis while in a prison, operated by the defendant, which had inadequate systems in place to reduce the risk of contracting tuberculosis. The plaintiff could not demonstrate that had the defendant behaved non-negligently and put in place appropriate precautions to reduce the risk, his tuberculosis would not have occurred. The Constitutional Court held that, in exceptional circumstances, it would be sufficient for plaintiffs to prove that, but for D's *conduct*, the injury would not have occurred. Thus, had P not been *detained*, P would not have contracted tuberculosis. *Lee* is structurally similar to *McGhee* in that the defendant's conduct imposed an innocent risk upon the plaintiff (the background, inevitable risk of tuberculosis from prisoners with unidentified infections) and a negligent risk.

Clearly, it is a non-starter to suggest that, generally, it suffices as proof of but-for causation in the tort of negligence that, but for D's *conduct*, the injury would not have occurred.[31] It must be that but for D's *negligence*, C's injury would not have occurred. So, for example, even if it is true that D drove negligently, and true that C would not have suffered injury had D not driven, C will not succeed on but-for causation if the *negligence* made no difference to the occurrence of the injury.

But, sometimes, it can be negligent for D to engage in a general activity of a certain type, call it A, as well as being negligent by doing some particular token act within A, call it A*p*. Typically, although specific acts of driving (A*p*) may be negligent, it will not be the case that the driver was negligent to drive at all (A). Indeed, even though it is quite foreseeable, perhaps inevitable, that I will at some point in my life drive negligently, it does not follow (from that fact alone) that any particular decision of mine to drive is negligent. But persons who are drunk should choose not to drive at all. Their decision to A is itself negligent, even if (surprisingly) none of their A*p* acts is negligent.

Weinrib has argued that *McGhee* has a structure like the drunk driver case.[32] In a recent article, he writes,

---

30 [2012] ZACC 30.

31 See generally A. Fagan, "Causation in the Constitutional Court: *Lee v Minister of Correctional Services*" (2013) 5 *Constitutional Court Review* 105.

32 I should stress that Weinrib does not draw this particular analogy, but I find it helpful to put the point this way.

> The risk-creating segment of the defendant's activity remains innocent only when accompanied by risk-alleviating measures. One cannot, accordingly, segregate the innocence of creating the risk from the culpability of not alleviating it.[33]

The idea seems to be that the defendant's decision to have his employees work in the kiln becomes a negligent decision in itself because there were no showers available. It is like putting someone in your care behind the wheel of a car that you know, or ought to know, has defective brakes.[34]

So, if the decision to have the workers work in the kiln is itself, in the circumstances, negligent, we might think that the relevant counterfactual is one that asks, Had the defendant not done that negligent act (have the workers work in the kiln), would the claimant's injury have been avoided?

Interestingly, Weinrib does not actually make this move – the move of modifying the counterfactual. He says,

> In the absence of more specific evidence about the causal efficacy of the various segments of the defendant's conduct, causation of the injury can be attributed to the defendant's negligent risk-creating conduct as a whole.[35]

Weinrib, rather, takes himself to have justified a rebuttable presumption that the defendant's failure to provide showers was a cause of the claimant's injury. If the defendant shows that the injury would have happened anyway with the provision of showers, then the defendant avoids losing the causal issue.

It is not clear to me why a rebuttable presumption that the failure to provide the showers was a cause of dermatitis is the rational upshot of Weinrib's argument. If the presumption is based upon epistemic grounds – namely, that the breach materially increased the risk of the claimant's injury – then the inference that the defendant's negligence was a cause should apply in any case where a defendant's breach materially increases the risk of a claimant's injury, regardless of whether

33 E. Weinrib, "Causal Uncertainty" (2016) 36 *Oxford Journal of Legal Studies* 135 at 154.
34 Again, this is my analogy.
35 Weinrib, above n 33 at 155.

it increases risk in relation to a risk source innocently caused by the defendant or by some condition not caused by the defendant. Why does the causal source of an innocent risk make an *epistemic* difference to the question whether the defendant's negligence made a difference to the occurrence of the injury?

In truth, it cannot. It can make only a normative difference. But why does it make the normative difference that Weinrib suggests – namely, that it justifies a rebuttable presumption of causation? It is difficult to say. What really seems to concern Weinrib is the desire to "[prevents] the defendant from taking advantage of an uncertainty that is entirely the product of the interplay of the components of his own activity."[36] This argument is unrelated to the argument that starts from the idea that the whole activity is wrongful.

If one really believed that the whole activity was wrongful – the activity of having the pursuer work in the kiln with no showers – the but-for counterfactual should ask *what would have happened had that act not occurred?* In the same way, we should ask of the person who puts someone behind the wheel of a car with defective brakes – what would have happened had they not put the person behind the wheel of this car?

This would solve one problem in *McGhee* (but-for causation) but give rise to another. For example, it cannot be right that a drunk driver is liable when his drunkenness made no difference to the occurrence (or process by which) the injury came about.[37] The reason is not that the decision to drive while drunk is not a factual cause of the claimant's injury. It is. The reason is that the risks associated with driving while drunk are not the risks that materialized. Similarly, in *McGhee*, the reason that makes it negligent (if it is) to have the employees work in the kiln is precisely the exposure to risks associated with the absence of showers, but it is unknown whether *these* risks materialized. If the risks that made the defendant's conduct negligent made no difference to the occurrence of the particular injury, the injury was not within the scope of the risks that made the conduct negligent in the first place. If the burden of proof is on the claimant to prove this, then the claimant loses on this issue, even if he succeeds on factual causation.[38]

---

36 Ibid at 157.

37 See also G. Turton, *Evidential Uncertainty in Causation in Negligence* (Oxford, Hart Publishing, 2016) 203.

38 This appears to be the case. See *BPE Solicitors and Another v Hughes-Holland* [2017] UKSC 21 at [53].

Although Weinrib's argument fails to provide a justification for the decision in *McGhee*, the general lesson is true. If genuine but-for causation will do the job, there is no need for exceptional rules.

Exceptions Should Be Non-arbitrary

If an exception to the general proof rule is recognized, its scope should be non-arbitrary. By *non-arbitrary*, I mean simply that its scope should be sensitive to the reasons for recognizing the exception in the first place.[39]

If those reasons relate primarily to the diminished incentives that recurrent causal uncertainty presents to defendants, then (it is extremely likely that) an exception cannot be limited to, for example, a particular disease. This is one reason that statements that the rule in *Fairchild* is limited to mesothelioma are open to criticism.[40] One of the justifications offered by the House of Lords for the exception in that case was that the defendants' duties of care would have been empty of content had their breach not been sanctioned in this context due to the recurrent inability of the claimants to prove their case on causation. But recurrent causal uncertainty exists in a variety of situations.

If those reasons relate to the greater injustice of depriving a claimant who has certainly been wrongfully injured of a claim compared to the lesser chance of inflicting an injustice upon a culpable defendant, then the exception cannot be limited to cases where the defendants have culpably used *similar* agents as English law holds, at least in relation to the second type of exception, described in the first section of this chapter (so long as proof of individual causation remains impossible).[41]

If there is no consistency among the exceptional rules recognized, then those who fall outside the special enclaves, when the reasons underpinning the enclaves would extend to their case, can legitimately complain that they are unfairly treated.

39 See generally S. Steel, "Causation in English Tort Law: Still Wrong after All These Years" [2012] 31 *University of Queensland Law Journal* 243.

40 See eg the judgment of Lord Brown in *Sienkiewicz v Greif (UK) Ltd* [2011] UKSC 10.

41 The requirement that the agents be similar is, at best, a rough guideline for satisfying the requirement that proof be impossible on the balance of probabilities.

Exceptions Should Not Undermine the General Rule in All Cases

A pragmatic conflict is introduced into the law where one rule is recognized whose justificatory underpinning (J2) is in conflict with that of another rule (J1).[42] The effect of such conflicts can be unfairness: if J2 supports a broader rule than J1, then those whose case was judged by the rule justified by J1 can complain that they were unfairly treated differently from those within the rule justified by J2. It can have other bad effects. Such conflicts give rise to uncertainty, too, as the possibility of the general rule being entirely eclipsed becomes real.

Here is an example of a justification for an exceptional rule that undermines the general rule in all cases and, thus, may introduce such a conflict. It is a "moral luck" argument. Lord Rodger made a version of this argument in *Fairchild*.[43] It is just luck that negligent conduct does not cause harm. Luck should not matter to the moral assessment of a person or their actions. Causative and non-causative defendants are equally culpable if negligent. If liability should be luck-insensitive, too, then it does not matter very much if a claimant cannot prove causation in a *multiple negligent defendants* situation. Fairly obviously, though, the claimant can make the same argument in any case where the defendant is negligent. The very nature of causation is that it makes liability luck-sensitive. An exception based on this reasoning alone utterly undermines the general rule.

The lesson is that the justification for an exceptional rule must satisfy one of two constraints. It must either show that the justification for the general rule, although generally applicable, is subject to a *cancelling* condition such that its rationale does not apply in a particular kind of case. Or it must show that although the general rule is applicable in the particular kind of case at hand, the reasons for the general rule are *outweighed* by the reasons for recognizing an exception, and those reasons are restricted to a particular kind of case.[44]

---

42 I borrow "pragmatic conflict" from J. Raz, "Law and Value in Adjudication" in his *The Authority of Law: Essays on Law and Morality*, 2nd edn (Oxford, Oxford University Press, 2011) 201.

43 *Fairchild*, above n 20 at [155].

44 On reasons being cancelled and being outweighed, see J. Raz, *Practical Reason and Norms* (Oxford, Oxford University Press, 1999) ch 1.

Exceptions Should Be Respectful of Institutional Constraints

By *institutional constraints*, I refer to reasons that apply to the courts under the ideal of the rule of law and constraints relating to the competence of courts. Each is considered in turn.

The rule of law demand of clarity has already been mentioned. The *Fairchild* exception has been criticized as a flagrant violation of this demand.[45] Another obvious rule of law pressure point is the demand of prospectivity. Almost any change in the common law, whether it be to recognize an exception or otherwise, amounts to a retrospective change in the law.

An important point should be made, however, about the nature of these demands.[46] The demands of the rule of law have varying weight depending on the type of legal issue at stake. There are three subpoints here. First, a defendant who is retrospectively placed under a primary obligation and sanctioned for its breach normally has far greater cause for complaint than one who is subject to a retrospective alteration in the remedial structure of the breach of an already existing primary obligation (at least where the alteration would prevent the defendant from escaping the effects of that duty).[47] The latter has at least had some warning as to the law's requiring him or her not to act in the way that is now being redressed. There seems to be less moral urgency to providing a defendant with assurance as to the precise consequence of the breach of duty than telling defendants in advance what those duties are.[48] Second, the zero-sum nature of tort law means that rule of law benefits to defendants *eo ipso* curtail the rights of claimants, which is not true of the criminal law.[49] In determining the legal

45 See R. Stevens, "The Proper Limits of Judicial Law-Making," accessed October 2016, http://judicialpowerproject.org.uk/robert-stevens-the-proper-limits-of-judicial-law-making/.

46 It might also be noted that different rule of law considerations need to be balanced against each other: a decrease in clarity might be outweighed by greater consistency in the law (or the opposite).

47 See especially T. Endicott, "Adjudication and the Law" (2007) 27 *Oxford Journal of Legal Studies* 311 at 318.

48 *Cf Patel v Mirza* [2016] UKSC 42 at [113]: "The same considerations [of certainty in the law] do not apply in the same way to people contemplating unlawful activity."

49 See J. Gardner, "Some Rule-of-Law Anxieties about Strict Liability in Private Law" in L.M. Austin and D. Klimchuk (eds), *Private Law and the Rule of Law* (Oxford, Oxford University Press, 2014) 211–13.

consequences of a breach of an existing legal duty in tort law, then, the rule of law imposes less rigorous demands than the criminal law or, at least, the demands of the rule of law need to be tempered by other considerations. Third, to the extent that the retrospectivity problem is based upon a concern to avoid disrupting justified expectations, it is much weaker in hard or controversial cases where no such expectations can arise.[50]

There are other institutional constraints. First, courts have only limited law-making powers. Their main, and perhaps only, law-making power exists by *application* of legal rules and through the *ratio* of their decisions. This legal fact is relevant to the moral decision that courts face in exercising their law-making power. If some change in the law would immediately require a large number of further changes in order for the law to be in a (fully) desirable condition, the courts would face the problem that those further changes could not be achieved in the case before them. Initiating a partial reform in those circumstances can have at least two adverse consequences. On the one hand, it may lead to significant uncertainty over whether and when those changes will be made and their precise effect on other areas of law. On the other, it can introduce (albeit potentially only temporarily) rules with conflicting rationales into the law until all the relevant changes have been made. Thus, in situations where one legal change would necessitate wide-ranging further changes, courts should be wary of making the initial change.

Second, there is the familiar point that there is reason to believe that even apex courts are, as a general matter, less promising fora than legislatures, in which empirical evidence as to the effects of liability can be gathered and assessed. This, too, is partly a function of the focus of litigation on a single issue or a set of relatively narrow issues.[51]

---

50 Raz, above n 42 at 198: "Such an objection to judicial law-making has no force at all when unregulated disputes or any hard and controversial legal case is concerned."

51 Although see J. Morgan, "Policy Reasoning in Tort Law: The Courts, the Law Commission, and the Critics" (2009) 125 *Law Quarterly Review* 215 at 221: "the real question requires a *comparison* of the judicial and legislative processes' suitability for handling such arguments. The Law Commission's evident difficulty in estimating the impact of its proposals for reforming public authority liability throws into doubt any assumption that the legislative process must necessarily be superior."

Third, there is usually taken to be a democratic objection to judicial law-making that amounts to *judicial legislation*.[52] The distinction between permissible judicial development of the law and impermissible judicial legislation has been described as "subtle and elusive."[53] On one view, the distinction, in very broad terms, is between law-making that is based firmly on existing, past commitments within the legal system and law-making that is based upon a judgment about the best rule for governing a situation in the future, with the past being relevant largely only as context.[54] The complexities of this extremely loose formulation cannot be explored here. Two points must suffice. First, on this view, the democratic objection applies particularly to wide-ranging changes in the law that have little basis in existing legal commitments, rather than incremental ones. Second, given the inherent vagueness of the idea of an incremental change based upon existing commitments and one that is more extensive and novel, there is clearly room for reasonable disagreement about where the line between permissible and impermissible judicial law creation is to be drawn in a particular case.

Learning the Lessons

I believe that apex courts could accept this rule without falling foul of the lessons described in the previous section:

> *Multiple negligent actors*. If D1, D2, D*n* each behave negligently in relation to C, the negligent conduct of one or more DDs has been causative of an injury risked to C by each D's negligence (an injury in respect of which each D owed a duty of care), but no individual D can be proved to be a cause on the balance of probabilities of C's injury, then each D should be liable to C in full in respect of C's injury.

Consider three positive arguments in favour of the rule before I present a brief defence of this claim. First, this rule can be justified, with Rand J, on the ground that each D's negligence either causes C's injury

52 For a recent statement of this objection (*inter alia*), see J. Finnis, "Judicial Power: Past, Present and Future," lecture given 20 October 2015, Gray's Inn Hall, accessed October 2016, http://judicialpowerproject.org.uk/wp-content/uploads/2015/10/John-Finnis-lecture-20102015.pdf.

53 Ibid at 6.

54 This is drawn loosely from Finnis's discussion: ibid.

or prevents C from establishing its claim in respect of that injury against the other defendants.[55] In a two-defendant case, one defendant's negligence causes the injury itself, while the other's negligence prevents the claim from being established in respect of that injury.[56] Call this the "prevention argument."

Second, the claimant faces a 100 per cent risk of injustice, while each defendant is subject only to a 50 per cent risk. It is true that there is a 100 per cent risk of injustice, whether liability is created or denied. But while the claimant individually faces a 100 per cent risk, each defendant individually faces only a 50 per cent risk. Call this the "relative injustice" argument.[57]

Third, the law is generally anxious to avoid a claimant being without a legal right in respect of an injury that would not have happened without wrongful conduct, simply by virtue of being the victim of more than one negligent act.[58]

This rule can be formulated reasonably clearly (Lesson 1). It does not rely upon unclear concepts such as the notion of a "single causative agent" or "scientific impossibility of proof," currently found in English law. Certainly it does not resolve all questions of application, but there does not seem to be a particularly great lack of clarity about the scope of the rule. The exceptional rule applies to cases in which it is impossible to establish liability on an orthodox but-for causation basis in respect of the injury, so it is in that sense "necessary" for liability to be established at all (Lesson 2).

Is the rule arbitrary (Lesson 3)? The most difficult case for the rule is:

> *Modified Cook v Lewis*. D1 negligently fires in C's direction. D2 simultaneously, but non-negligently, fires in C's direction.[59] C is injured by one of the bullets.

It might seem odd that each defendant's liability hinges upon whether the other has behaved negligently. Why is D1 liable where D2

---

55 This argument seems first to emerge in French law in the late nineteenth century: Steel, above n 8 at 157 fn 89.

56 For a *much* longer treatment of this, see ibid at 175–83.

57 This argument applies regardless of the number of defendants: the probability of injustice against a particular defendant will always be less than the certainty of injustice against the claimant.

58 See *Baker v Willoughby* [1970] AC 467; *Wright v Cambridge Medical Group* [2013] QB 312.

59 Imagine that D2's gun fires for reasons fully beyond D2's control.

is negligent, but not if D2 fires innocently? Intuitively, it seems odd that one's liability should vary in this way depending on whether someone, for whom one is not responsible, has behaved negligently. The negligence of a third person seems not to add to the case for saying that you are responsible to another.[60]

Yet, on reflection, this can be explained. We do not know in this example that the defendants have either negligently caused C's injury or deprived C of a claim in respect of that injury. Nor can we say that C faces a 100 per cent risk of injustice compared to only a 50 per cent risk against each defendant. Finally, the law draws a distinction between tortious and non-tortious events in other causal contexts.[61] This also establishes that the exception does not undermine the rule in every case (Lesson 4). If the rule applied to the revised *Cook v Lewis*, it would, in effect, apply to every case where proof of causation is impossible. But that is just to deny the defendant the advantage of the general burden of proof rule in every case.

Last, do institutional considerations point against the recognition of this rule? There are four points here. First, in rule of law terms, the law is not prohibiting any new conduct in recognizing the exceptional rule; it is only altering the proof required for it to be accepted that a prohibition has been breached. It is not clear how much protection defendants who reasoned that they could breach their duty of care without sanction deserve (this is one category of defendants whose expectation would be upset by the introduction of the rule). Admittedly, however, this argument does not apply to third parties, such as liability insurers, who might well have (unobjectionably) taken into account the precise proof threshold at which a negligent defendant would be made liable.

Second, the multiple negligent actors situation is a classic hard case, which gives rise to powerful intuitions of fairness on both sides. This weakens the claim that, *ex ante*, persons have a legitimate expectation that the law will not be altered here.

Third, in terms of one dimension of the institutional competence considerations adverted to above, the arguments for the exceptional rule do not depend directly upon the assessment of any empirical arguments. The argument for the rule is not, for instance, premised on the claim that it will lead defendants to take optimal levels of care.[62]

60 See R. Stevens, *Torts and Rights* (Oxford, Oxford University Press, 2007) 151.

61 Compare *Baker*, above n 58, with *Jobling v Associated Dairies* [1982] AC 794.

62 There may, of course, be negative, adverse effects of adopting the rule (or positive ones).

Finally, would the introduction of the rule amount to judicial legislation? This seems to me the most difficult question. On the one hand, it can be said that the rule does resound with the established legal concern to avoid a wronged victim falling between two stools. To that extent, the innovation draws on a reasonably close analogy to an existing legal doctrine within the law on causation.

On the other hand, it can be said that the satisfactory introduction of the rule, at least in the context of mass industrial disease, requires a large number of changes in the law. This last point seems to be vindicated by the English experience. After *Fairchild*, *Barker v Corus* settled the question of the extent of a defendant's liability, rendering it proportionate rather than joint and several. After *Barker*, *Sienkiewicz* was needed to determine whether the rule was limited to multiple negligent defendants.[63] After *Sienkiewicz*, two further cases were needed to determine the effect of the *Fairchild* exception on employers' liability insurance policies – in particular, whether the exception could be relied upon to satisfy a causation-based trigger in those policies and whether insurers could claim contribution from each other. In resolving the latter question, the Supreme Court in *Zurich* has created a further, novel, exceptional principle in insurance law, the scope of which is also open to question.[64]

It is difficult to argue that these changes would not better have been achieved by a single piece of legislation.[65] However, had the normative arguments for the *Fairchild* exception been more clearly identified, with the focus being on the fact that the claimant had been the victim of an established legal wrong, then at least *Sienkiewicz* could have been avoided as well as much of the uncertainty about the scope of the exception itself. Furthermore, given the argument of existing legal principle for recognizing the exception, it might be said that the judicial development of the law would not be an *illegitimate* use of an apex court's law-creating powers, albeit the avoidance of uncertainty for peripheral parties, such as insurers, is a reason why legislation is desirable.

63 *Sienkiewicz v Greif (UK) Ltd* [2011] UKSC 10.

64 See *Zurich*, above n 26.

65 See also Lord Hoffmann, "Fairchild and After" in A. Burrows, D. Johnston, and R. Zimmermann (eds), *Judge and Jurist: Essays in Memory of Lord Rodger of Earlsferry* (Oxford, Oxford University Press, 2013); "Publication Review: Proof of Causation in Tort Law" (2017) 133 *Law Quarterly Review* 516 at 519–20.

Now consider again:

> *Negligent actor(s), scientific impossibility of proof.* D's negligence may have been a cause of C's personal injury, but it is impossible to determine whether this is so on the balance of probabilities because of the current state of scientific knowledge, C's personal injury may have been caused entirely by one or more non-wrongful causes, and the other salient potential causes of C's injury would have caused the injury in the same way as D's negligent conduct. If C's injury is *mesothelioma,* then C can recover against D in full. If the injury is *not mesothelioma,* and D is not a medical professional, then C can recover in proportion to the roughly estimated probability that D's negligence was a cause of C's injury.

This exceptional rule is harder to justify (a mesothelioma exception, impossible: Lesson 3). If it is not going to fail Lesson 3 – that exceptions must not be arbitrary – some reason will have to be found for limiting the rule to scientific uncertainty. If no reason can be found, then this rule – unrestricted to *scientific* uncertainty, but expanded to uncertainty in general – will violate Lesson 4 since it should then displace the orthodox burden of proof in all cases – a burden of proof situation is simply a situation where proof of causation is *impossible* on the balance of probabilities.

Scientific uncertainty could have at least two possible sources of normative significance. First, it might be argued that such uncertainty is particularly likely to have implications for *deterrence.* If the state of scientific knowledge is such that there could, in current circumstances, be no specific evidence of causation linking a defendant's breach to a claimant's injury, then defendants can ignore their duties of care with impunity, so far as tort law is concerned. Second, it might be argued that such uncertainty has a *fairness* implication: culpable individuals who have caused injury are the ones who always gain from the fact that scientific knowledge is at a particular stage of development.

Neither the deterrence argument nor the fairness argument seems powerful.[66] Any "unfairness" is just an implication of a commitment to the burden of proof being on the claimant. It is odd to assert as a justification for altering the burden of proof the very condition in which the burden of proof is supposed to apply: namely, where proof of causation

66 See further Steel, above n 8, ch 5, and fn 38.

is impossible. Scientific uncertainty may mean that there will be many burden of proof situations, but this does not itself provide a reason for departing from the rule. It is tempting to say, "negligent defendants are privileged as a *group* as against innocent claimants." That is quite true. But, again, this is simply an implication of the burden of proof – presumably, if one notionally counted the number of burden of proof situations before *Fairchild*, there would be a large number of cases where innocent claimants would lose against culpable defendants. The deterrence argument leads to injustice between claimants, some of whom receive an entitlement to damages simply because of the happenstance that their injury will produce good consequences in the future.[67]

Objections

1. The prevention argument faces an array of problems.[68] First, preventing a person establishing a legal claim against another is akin to causing a pure economic loss, and, thus, absent a special relationship, a duty of care would not normally arise in respect of it. Second, this loss is a remote consequence of the negligence since the reasonable person would consider it a far-fetched consequence of that negligence.

In response to the first objection, I would say that preventing a claim in respect of a personal injury, while still distant from inflicting physical injury, brings the claim somewhat closer to personal injury than economic loss.[69] In response to the second, the boundaries of reasonable foreseeability in relation to remoteness are broad.[70] It does not seem far-fetched, for instance, to suppose that exposing an employee, in an

67 Admittedly, if there were evidence that the deterrent impact of tort law were significant, above and beyond other forms of regulation, then the good consequences may be sufficient to outweigh this injustice.

68 See N.J. McBride and S. Steel, "Suing for the Loss of the Right to Sue: Why Wright Is Wrong" (2012) 28 *Professional Negligence* 27.

69 A response already made by Ariel Porat and Alex Stein, *Tort Liability under Uncertainty* (Oxford, Oxford University Press, 2001). For more ambitious arguments that one's secondary right to damages is *identical* to one's primary right that others not negligently damage one and that this justifies treating negligence in relation to the body as negligence in relation to secondary rights in relation to the body as one and the same thing here, see Beever, above n 18 at 459–65 and Weinrib, above n 33 at 140–8.

70 See *Haxton v Phillips Electronics* [2014] EWCA Civ 4, which accepts that such a loss could be reasonably foreseeable in the asbestos mesothelioma context.

industrial context, to a toxic agent in a fluid labour market would lead to difficulty in establishing causation if the employee were exposed to a similar agent by a subsequent employer. If subsequent negligence by a doctor is taken to be a reasonably foreseeable consequence for the purpose of remoteness, why not subsequent negligence by a future employer?

A rejoinder to my response to the first objection is that it necessarily implies that we owe duties of care not carelessly to produce conditions such that a person is incapable of establishing a legal claim against another. This implication might be thought implausible, or at least in need of substantial defence. This implication is not quite right: the implication, more precisely, might be that one would owe duties of care not carelessly to produce conditions such that a person is incapable of establishing a legal claim in respect of personal injury in relation to another. If one unreasonably endangers another's body and one produces this consequence, which affects another's interest in bodily integrity, if this consequence is foreseeable, it does not seem unfair that one be liable in respect of it.[71]

2. The relative injustice argument can be objected to in at least two ways. First, is not the 100 per cent risk to the claimant just an artefact of the way the claim moves procedurally? Suppose that the claimant sues only D1 in *Cook v Lewis*. As against D1, there is only a 50 per cent risk of injustice to C and a 50 per cent risk of injustice to D1. Given the choice of inflicting an injustice and failing to alleviate one, a court should choose the latter. It seems odd that if C procedurally joins D1 and D2, then the justice of the case is fundamentally shifted.

This objection is right to state that whether D1 and D2 are both joined should not matter. But even if D2 is not joined, the court can still know that the long-run effect of denying liability to D1 will be certainly to inflict injustice on C in particular. Nothing similar can be said of either defendant individually.

A more powerful objection is that this reasoning is objectionably consequentialist. It asks us essentially to minimize the expected injustice in the situation. This is not quite right, however, since, on a purely

71 If this argument were accepted, there would be a need, perhaps, to revisit other negligent endangerments of one's physical integrity that produce losses currently classed as *purely economic* and in respect of which, in English law, no duty of care is owed: *Murphy v Brentwood District Council* [1991] 1 AC 398.

consequentialist view, the parties stand equally: there is a 100 per cent risk of injustice either way. It is rather a matter of fairness that the defendants cannot individually reasonably reject being subject to a 50 per cent risk of injustice to avoid the 100 per cent risk of injustice to the claimant.

Conclusion

This contribution has drawn several lessons from the development of the law on exceptions to proof of causation in tort. It has been shown that, in several respects, these developments were regrettable in lacking clarity, transparency, and principled limits. However, it has also been suggested that these defects are avoidable and that causal exceptionalism need not be an illegitimate use of the law-making power of an apex court.

12 What Is Happening to the Law of Unjust Enrichment?

STEVE HEDLEY

The Canadian Supreme Court has stated that there is a principle of *unjust enrichment*, whereby benefits may be recovered if there is an enrichment, a corresponding deprivation, and the absence of any juristic reason for the enrichment. That was stated clearly in *Pettkus v Becker* in 1980,[1] and it was restated in *Garland v Consumers' Gas Co.* in 2004.[2] Yet there is continuing controversy over this, particularly over fundamental questions of coverage (Where does "equity" stop and "unjust enrichment" begin? Are cohabitation cases really examples of unjust enrichment? What about public law cases?) and about the core concept of *juristic reason* (Is the law really to be stated in terms of *absence of juristic reason* or rather in terms of *presence of a factor rendering the enrichment unjust*?).

It seems beneficial to pause and consider why the simple, clear, and apparently definitive statements of the Supreme Court on the issue have not settled the law. Most of the reasons for this are variants on a single theme – that the question of the status and main elements of unjust enrichment is too big an issue to be resolved by a few Supreme Court rulings, no matter how authoritative. If there is a broad and clear doctrine of unjust enrichment, it has many implications across a wide variety of contexts, and simple statements by the Supreme Court in a limited number of those contexts are not going to be enough to suppress all other approaches. It would take a large number of such statements across a wide variety of contexts, by a Supreme Court

1 *Pettkus v Becker* [1980] 2 SCR 834 at 849, Dickson J.
2 *Garland v Consumers' Gas Co* [2004] 1 SCR 629 at para 30, Iacobucci J.

absolutely determined to impose a broad, justification-based law of unjustified enrichment on the lower courts. For a number of reasons, that has not happened. But while the Supreme Court's support for unjust enrichment in a case like *Garland* is genuine enough, the Court is simply not prepared to take that line in *all* disputes where unjust enrichment is in issue.

Of course, much of the work of the higher courts has to do with difficulties in applying general principles, and this is hardly the first area in which the Supreme Court has laid down a principle and then found that it is the work of years, or even decades, to settle the implications of that original ruling. We must, however, distinguish between what are mere teething troubles of unfamiliar doctrines and more fundamental disagreements, which typically occur when the supposed general principle is inconsistent with *other* principles to which we also adhere. For example, the long-running dispute over whether good faith forms part of the law of contract is not because that concept is particularly complicated or obviously undesirable, but because it seems to run counter to the classical understanding of freedom of contract, a principle no one proposes to abandon in its entirety[3] – however that dispute is resolved, it has nothing to do with a reluctance to formulate general principles, and it goes beyond mere difficulties of application. Or, again, a supposed principle may be so formless that it does not, in practice, help lower courts very much, and so they resort to other, perhaps inconsistent, principles that yield more definite answers. I suggest that the continuing controversies around unjust enrichment reflect problems with the principle itself and that, in fact, it is most unlikely that the Canadian law of unjust enrichment will settle down any time soon; the uncertainties around the subject amount to a permanent state of disarray.[4]

3 See Angela Swan and Jakub Adamski's contribution to this volume (ch 10) fn 110.

4 For a variety of views, see J.D. McCamus, "Mistake, Forged Cheques and Unjust Enrichment: Three Cheers for *BMP Global*" (2009) 48 *Canadian Business Law Journal* 76; M. McInnes, "Revising the Reason for Restitution: *Garland* Ten Years After" (2015) 57 *Canadian Business Law Journal* 1; L. Smith, "The State of the Law of Unjust Enrichment in Common Law Canada" (2015) 57 *Canadian Business Law Journal* 39; Z. Sinel, "The Methods and Madness of Unjust Enrichment" in A. Robertson and M. Tilbury (eds), *Divergences in Private Law* (Oxford, Hart Publishing, 2016) ch 10; and R. Chambers, "The Future of Unjust Enrichment in Common Law Canada" [2017] *Restitution Law Review* 3.

Origins

Each area of law has its peculiarities. One of the major peculiarities of restitution is in the nature of the academic input to it. Legal academics are, as a rule, quite reactive, calling attention to interesting legal phenomena after they have happened and trying to determine their significance, but rarely attempting to produce any themselves. But, in this area, there has been a concerted, and in many respects successful, movement to change the face of the topic, to turn it into something it was not already.

It was unpromising territory, and in the early stages, the Supreme Court played relatively little part in it. To be sure, much was made of the 1950s decision in the *Deglman* case,[5] which can be said to have recognized a principle against unjust enrichment (considerably predating its rise in other common jurisdictions), inasmuch as the Court referred to "the principle of restitution against what would otherwise be an unjust enrichment of the defendant at the expense of the plaintiff"[6] in coming to its decision. But the Court's judgment was vague on what the principle was or even on whether there truly was such a principle, and it was left to a few academic enthusiasts to say that the decision was an important one and that it exemplified a key principle.

The problem, if it is a problem, is that restitution cases are not the sort of stuff from which grandeur emanates. Restitution is what non-lawyers call "lawyer's law" and lawyers call a mass of technical rules, most of which lie on the fringes of important areas, and which for understandable reasons are neglected by all but the deeper specialists. For the most part, restitution concerns legal dealings that have misfired for some reason, achieving not the result their authors intended but some more confused result; or cases where one litigant seeks an unusual remedy, either because the usual one is unexpectedly blocked or because, in the peculiar circumstances of the case, it seems inadequate. Such situations are likely to be one-off, and while, no doubt, a court will do its best to achieve a satisfactory resolution of each case, it hardly sounds as if any deep principle is likely to be involved.

So, in one sense, restitutionary material must often have seemed unpromising from the point of view of those seeking to create a new

5 *Deglman v Guaranty Trust Co of Canada* [1954] SCR 725.
6 [1954] SCR 728 at 788, *per* Rand J.

legal topic. It was also unpromising in a second sense: much of its subject matter was already claimed by other areas of law, whether contract law, equity, or property. Indeed, most of the academics who were unenthusiastic about the establishment of unjust enrichment based their opinions on those other areas, seeing little point in re-categorizing what was already adequately understood.

Why Does Restitution Matter?

What, then, is the interest in the area? Only two reasons appear in the literature with any frequency.

The first is the insistence of many academics that there *is* a principle immanent in the ways the courts have dealt with such situations – a principle that many have named the principle against unjust enrichment. While the rulings of these cases often seem pretty diverse, in fact the same sorts of reasons are given again and again, and these reasons can be restated as a legal doctrine and applied in novel situations as well. This is always a complicated argument to make, however, because unjust enrichment is such a latecomer in private law, both to civilian legal systems and to common law systems. Private law got by very well for most of its history by focusing on notions of agreements, wrongs, and property, with unjust enrichment playing (in civilian systems) a minimal role and (in common law systems) no role at all. The stance of those seeking to promote unjust enrichment was, therefore, frequently not so much promoting just solutions to novel problems as trying to prove that the law's *existing* solution could be better understood through the language of unjust enrichment.

The second reason for interest in the area is that while most of its subject matter seems quite marginal, changes in attitudes may turn what was once marginal into something central. There have, for example, always been couples who, for one reason or another, never married but nonetheless lived together much as married couples do. Cohabitation is not new, but, in the past, it was socially marginal and always treated on the fringes of legal doctrine. In more modern times, however, the rise in the frequency and the respectability of cohabitation makes the traditional legal approach quite inadequate: legal change was clearly called for, and for those judges willing to heed that call, unjust enrichment was the best tool available. Again, the increasing juridification of politics means that many claims against the state would, in earlier years, not have been through legal channels, if indeed they would have been made at all. The restitutionary perspective is, therefore, a spur not merely to rationalizing the law but also to doctrinal innovation: it identifies a major problem with the law and proposes a solution.

So the recent history of the Supreme Court's engagement with restitution is really two histories: first, of how the Court has reacted to the growing *theorization* of restitution law; and second, how it has reacted to demands to *innovate* and develop the law for new situations. In this, it is not so different from other major common law jurisdictions.

Yet, in practice, these two possible agendas are in conflict. In theory, this is not so: there seems to be no reason why a wish to state the law rigorously and systematically should necessarily be inconsistent with a wish to act fairly in novel situations. In practice, however, the conflict is rather obvious. Attempts to systematize the law are inevitably backwards-looking, giving a hard look at the problems of yesteryear and setting out what, after decades or perhaps centuries of thought, seems to be the optimal solution. And a lot of the time, this works, to the extent that we continue to face the same problems, or new problems that require similar solutions. But we would be very lucky indeed if the old solutions *always* worked, even for new problems, and there is inevitably tension when we find that they do not. Most of the problems of the older law of restitution were problems between legally sophisticated commercial parties; it should be no big surprise to find that the solutions proposed do not always work when applied in less formal settings or in contexts that are more about government and administration than they are about commerce.

This may be why the emerging Canadian law of unjust enrichment has not really achieved either object to the satisfaction of all. The urge to innovate (and so to apply the law to new situations) does not sit well with the urge to consolidate and theorize (which is almost invariably backwards looking). Use of theory has advanced a great deal, but the resulting law is extremely complex; the suggestion that a principle of unjust enrichment is supposed to *simplify* the law strains plausibility. And the use of unjust enrichment as a tool with which to innovate has not received unanimous applause, either.

Innovation through Restitution

Most restitution cases are, as I have said, deeply uncontroversial: no doubt, the occasional issue or case seems to lead to strong arguments over its merits, but for the most part, no. Nor do they change much:

a lawyer of a century ago would feel pretty much at home with what was being argued over, if not necessarily with all the terminology being used in the argument.

There are two obvious exceptions to this generalization.

The first category is cases involving wrongly demanded taxes or duties, where payments are made but where it is subsequently clearly demonstrated that there was no good, legal ground for demanding them. The second category covers the cohabitation cases, where couples have lived together for a number of years without marriage, and then a question arises as to their mutual entitlements, either on the death of one of them or on relationship breakdown. These are cases where liability would traditionally have been denied outright; cases of these sorts have been pivotal for the development of unjust enrichment, not simply in Canada but also in some other common law jurisdictions: the existing law was clearly wanting, and unjust enrichment was used as a tool to fill an obvious gap.

In relation to both categories, there is no real consensus that the Court has any business trying to achieve this object in the first place. Many would think that it is not the job of the courts, even the Supreme Court, to be making major adaptations to the law to achieve a just result – that is trespassing on the legislature's territory. Such decisions are ultimately community decisions and should be made by legislatures. But these objections are hardly conclusive; they assume a rigid division of intellectual labour, by which a legislature always deals with developing the law and never shirks its duty so as to leave it to other institutions. In the real world of messy, overlapping roles, we can agree that the Court is not always the ideal forum for developing the law, but it may be better than allowing the law not to be developed at all.

It has to be said, however, that there is no very satisfactory answer to this constitutional question. In areas where the legislatures have refused to act to correct a particular injustice, there will always be some who say that the courts should take up the burden and others who say that the legislatures' role should be respected, not merely when they act but also when they refuse to act – in other words, that the failure to act should be treated as a deliberate and authoritative rejection of the claim of injustice. It may, perhaps, be because of the obscure nature of much restitutionary argument that constitutional objections have had relatively little traction in developing the subject. The classic UK defence of *judicial* development of the law is Lord Goff's defence of introducing a right to reclaim taxes wrongly paid, in a passage quite well known in restitutionary circles, although I am unaware of any commentary on it from a constitutional point of view:

> [T]here are particular reasons which impel me to that conclusion. The first is that this opportunity will never come again. If we do not take it now, it will be gone forever. The second is that I fear that, however compelling the principle of justice may be, it would never be sufficient to persuade a government to propose its legislative recognition by Parliament; caution, otherwise known as the Treasury, would never allow this to happen.[7]

But such bold declarations, which start from the premise that a plaintiff deserves a remedy and come perilously close to saying that a legislature can be trusted only with issues that it will approach fairly, are rather rare. The more usual, cautious approach is exemplified by McLachlin J (as she then was) a few years earlier:

> There are sound reasons supporting this judicial reluctance to dramatically recast established rules of law. The court may not be in the best position to assess the deficiencies of the existing law, much less problems which may be associated with the changes it might make. The court has before it a single case; major changes in the law should be predicated on a wider view of how the rule will operate in the broad generality of cases. Moreover, the court may not be in a position to appreciate fully the economic and policy issues underlying the choice it is asked to make. Major changes to the law often involve devising subsidiary rules and procedures relevant to their implementation, a task which is better accomplished through consultation between courts and practitioners than by judicial decree. Finally, and perhaps most importantly, there is the long-established principle that in a constitutional democracy it is the legislature, as the elected branch of government, which should assume the major responsibility for law reform.[8]

Most of the time, considerations of that sort discourage common law judges from anything too openly innovative in unjust enrichment and elsewhere. A further and more context-specific factor has been the unwillingness of leading unjust enrichment academics to embrace the

---

7 *Woolwich Building Society v Commissioners of Inland Revenue* (1992) 65 *Tax Cases* 265 at 372H.

8 *Watkins v Olafson* [1989] 2 SCR 750, McLachlin J.

need for innovation because it would undermine their case that unjust enrichment provides an accurate picture of the law *as it already is*. "No enrichment can be regarded as unjust, disapproved or reversible unless it happens in circumstances in which the law provides for restitution. The answer to the fear of uncertainty is not to reject the word [*unjust*] but to deal firmly with any argument which attempts to detach it from the law."[9] The rise of unjust enrichment in recent decades thus relies on a curious confluence of motives, as the theorists insist that they are consolidating and rationalizing the law rather than changing it, whereas "[t]he last thing the courts needed was an idea of unjust enrichment that reflected what [the] authorities already said and no more."[10]

Development of Theory

Both the itch to theorize and the itch to innovate have had their influence on the law. And in relation to both of them, the Supreme Court came late to the argument. By the time we come to the major decisions dominating the current debate – *Garland*,[11] *Kingstreet*,[12] *Kerr*[13] – the academic argument has already been in full swing for some decades – the academics are making the weather, so to speak. Which is not to say that the Court decided the cases as the academics would have wanted – quite the contrary, in fact. But the issues to be decided are seen in a framework that derives mostly from the academics – it is taken for granted that there is a law of unjust enrichment, and the Court is simply deciding the detail of how it is applied. Again, the major areas in which restitution led to innovation were not chosen by the Court – the social changes that led both to a rise in the extent of cohabitation, and the increased willingness to raise the resulting legal issues in the courts, cannot realistically be laid at the door of the Supreme Court.

But the academics who so earnestly promoted the introduction of unjust enrichment were also late to the party, in a wider sense. Most of private law had already been thoroughly mapped out by the time there

---

9 P. Birks, *An Introduction to the Law of Restitution* (Oxford, Oxford University Press, 1985) 19.

10 C. Webb, *Reason and Restitution, A Theory of Unjust Enrichment* (Oxford, Oxford University Press, 2016) 49.

11 *Garland v Consumers' Gas Co* [2004] 1 SCR 629.

12 *Kingstreet Investments Ltd v New Brunswick* [2007] 1 SCR 3.

13 *Kerr v Baranow* [2011] 1 SCR 269.

was serious scholarship on unjust enrichment; so unjust enrichment scholars were continually in the position of having to argue with others of their colleagues about the scraps left over from larger doctrinal entities. Where did "genuine" implied contract end and "fictitious" implied contract (now to be regarded as an example of unjust enrichment) begin? Was the prospect of an unjust enrichment simply one matter that might weigh with a court when considering the equities of a given situation, or was a "doctrine" of unjust enrichment something that a court either applied or did not apply? Some of the earlier unjust enrichment scholarship was happy to leave such questions in the air, but at least from the time of Peter Birks's *Introduction*,[14] the academic tendency was to argue for a relatively rigid doctrine – an assumption not shared by much of the case law they sought to corral into a definite formation.

Why Is Unjust Enrichment Still So Controversial?

Why have the various declarations by the Supreme Court, favouring the existence of a law of unjust enrichment based on factors of justification, not settled the issue? Why is it still a matter of controversy? There are a number of dimensions to this.

Occasion

First, it is not very likely that the Supreme Court will often receive the opportunity for such pronouncements – and the other occasions when restitutionary issues are before the Court may have an entirely different focus. The framing of issues is largely in the hands of counsel, who are only occasionally interested in supplying the upper courts with interesting opportunities to reorganize the law. How often, after all, does it happen that the dispute between the parties turns straightforwardly on the extent of the law of unjust enrichment or how that law is to be structured? If the issue is in those simple terms, then the Court can give a clear ruling. But often, matters are otherwise: all parties are happy to argue on the basis of a different understanding of the law.

BMP Global, decided only a few years after *Garland*, is a case in point.[15] Here we have a classic restitutionary dispute, over the right to recover

14 Birks, *Introduction to the Law of Restitution*, above n 9.
15 *BMP Global Distribution Inc v Bank of Nova Scotia* [2009] 1 SCR 504.

funds mistakenly paid on the strength of a cheque that turns out to have been forged. This is a much argued issue of civil liability, and the case was argued and resolved on the basis of the many authorities on restitutionary liability for mistake. So very far from relying on an unjust enrichment analysis, the judgment, in fact, nowhere mentions even the words *unjust* and *enrichment* (although it does refer to various academic writings from scholars who use those concepts). It was left to commentators after the case was decided to point out that this was all quite contrary to the *Garland* approach and, indeed, that if *Garland* were taken to prescribe the entire Canadian law of unjust enrichment, then there *was* no "law of mistake" – mistake as such was not a ground of recovery, but simply part of the factual pattern that should lead to a determination of whether there was or was not a juridical basis for the payment.

Some are more pleased about this than others, of course. John McCamus has pointed out that the *BMP Global* approach, if taken consistently, effectively confines *Garland* to novel cases, where the existing authorities give no satisfactory idea of how a case is to be approached at all; in the more common areas, the general pattern of the law is already well established and unlikely to be challenged, no matter how far it departs from the *Garland* doctrine. Thus, the law has, for the most part, reached a stable state, and "[t]he common law branch of the Canadian legal profession may draw a long breath and breathe a heavy sigh of relief."[16] Zoë Sinel, while critical both of *BMP Global* and of the argument that McCamus bases on it,[17] nonetheless concludes that "Canadian law appears for the most part to retain the common law's emphasis on the prima facie justness of entitlements ... despite its foray into the language of juristic reasons."[18] Others are unconvinced. Mitchell McInnes, noting much the same features of the Court's judgment, described it as "on any reckoning, curious" and complains that it "reads like something from an earlier era." "It seems most likely that the court simply followed the lead of counsel who, perhaps relying upon out-dated textbooks or older cases, drafted pleadings without regard to *Garland*."[19]

Wherever we stand on this, the main point here is that Canadian law gets to this position not through a reasoned decision that it is the best

16 McCamus, "Mistake, Forged Cheques and Unjust Enrichment," above n 4 at 101.

17 Sinel, "Methods and Madness," above n 4 at 187.

18 Ibid at 195.

19 McInnes, "Revising the Reason for Restitution," above n 4 at 34 fn 104.

approach, but simply by the ordinary dynamics of litigation: the *Garland* doctrine is a Pandora's box, which neither side in litigation will open except in cases of need, and that need does not seem to arise very often. And if counsel have a choice between presenting the dispute in a way that a court is likely to find familiar, or in a different way, which law professors will deem more up to the minute, it is clear which approach better serves their clients' interests and which they are more likely to adopt. (There are distinct similarities with the position in Australia, where academics enthusiastic for unjust enrichment routinely accuse practitioners of "pleading errors" in such cases, yet with no evidence that the courts within which those practitioners are working regard them as errors.)[20] There is no legal, professional duty to promote academic projects, even if those projects have, in other contexts, generated judicial approval or even enthusiasm.

The Range of Other Considerations

Second, structural, doctrinal considerations are not going to be the only ones to influence the Court. *Where the Court's attention is drawn to the point*, its members may well consider that Canadian law is best organized if it includes a principle of unjust enrichment based on juristic reasons. But even in the leading cases, that is unlikely to be the only matter of concern, and other concerns are likely to pull in different directions. And it simply is not very likely that the sorts of considerations relevant in (say) commercial property cases are going to be of the same type as those relevant in (say) disputes between former cohabitants.

Unsurprisingly, therefore, the case law is actually quite equivocal on structural questions; even cases very supportive of a general principle of unjust enrichment contain statements that tend in a different direction. Opinions that unequivocally state that unjust enrichment is to be based on justificatory factors[21] may also state that restitution is "an equitable remedy that will necessarily involve discretion and questions of fairness."[22] To academics intent on the question of doctrinal structure, this looks like a serious internal inconsistency; justificatory factors are a

20 See eg K. Barker and H. Tait, "Regional Digest: Australia" [2015] *Restitution Law Review* 141 at 142.

21 Eg *Garland v Consumers' Gas Co* [2004] 1 SCR 629 at para 30, Iacobucci J.

22 Ibid at para 44, Iacobucci J.

key part of a doctrinal structure meant to minimize, and perhaps even eliminate, judicial discretion in restitution. "[T]here is no warrant for treating the action in unjust enrichment as a licence for *ad hoc* decision-making. ... There is nothing inherent in the nature of the action in unjust enrichment that marks it for discretionary treatment."[23] If so, it is surprising that the judges so quickly, and apparently instinctively, invoke discretion when it comes to applying the doctrine; the academic denial that discretion is called for suggests a faith in unjust enrichment's conceptual integrity, which the judges do really not share.

In this connection, it is worth noting that even legal systems that unequivocally support the idea of unjustified enrichment – such as the German system – are beginning to find that, in the actual application of the law, a quite different approach emerges. As Thomas Krebs has long pointed out, in principle German law denies the existence of *unjust factors*, but, in practice, it recognizes something very much like them;[24] and as Nils Jansen has recently argued, German *unjustified enrichment* is, in practice, divided into a number of smaller units, no one of which can be wholly explained by reference to unjust enrichment, if indeed unjust enrichment plays any significant role at all in relation to them. The policies of contract law may have more to say in the area than theories of unjust enrichment.[25] This is not to deny the importance of general statements of principle; but they are the *start* of the analysis, not the whole of it, and a completed analysis may lead in very different directions. Recognition of unjust enrichment as an important concept is one thing; allowing it to dictate the entire terms of the legal analysis quite another.

Viewed against the backdrop of the Supreme Court's wider role, this confusion is a relatively clear example of different aspects of that role pulling in different directions. If, as in *Garland*, the issue is framed for the Court as being one whether the Canadian law of restitution should be organized around unjustified enrichment, it is obvious enough why the Court would accept that challenge and produce a clear ruling on the matter. It is, after all, an important question that clearly falls within judicial competence. But

23 M. McInnes, *The Canadian Law of Unjust Enrichment and Restitution* (Toronto, LexisNexis, 2014) 47 (fns omitted).

24 For the interplay of the two approaches, see particularly T. Krebs, *Restitution at the Crossroads: A Comparative Study* (London, Cavendish Publishing, 2001) ch 11.

25 See N. Jansen, "Farewell to Unjustified Enrichment?" (2016) 20 *Edinburgh Law Review* 123; S. Hedley, "'Farewell to Unjustified Enrichment?' A Common Law Response" (2016) 20 *Edinburgh Law Review* 326.

there is a straightforward clash with another thing that the Court is supposed to be doing, which is resolving the actual dispute between two litigants in a fair manner. The former calls for a clear choice between different structures of legal thought; the latter tends to subvert those very structures by allowing multiple opportunities for the fairness and reasonableness of the claim to influence the way in which it is resolved.

Leading cases such as *Garland*, therefore, pose a very real difficulty for those who would reduce the law of restitution to a definite set of rules. On the one hand, they lend considerable support to academics seeking to do that – propositions for which those academics have argued eloquently and in detail are judicially endorsed. On the other, those very same opinions embrace a willingness to look to the equities of the case and, at the margins at least, to decide the dispute in accordance with those equities, so that the general propositions in which the academics place so much confidence turn out to be of lesser importance. And so we find that *Garland* is praised for its far-sighted view of the law but also criticized as harking back to the benighted period before unjust enrichment was regarded as a fully fledged doctrine of the law. And propositions that would go very far to ensuring a failing grade for law students rash enough to propose them – such as that a claim in unjust enrichment may, in a court's discretion, fail where the plaintiff does not merit a remedy or that fault by one party or other may turn out to be the deciding factor – have to be accepted by academic writers when they come from the bench – albeit with considerable protest.[26]

It is interesting to compare this aspect of the law with the English position, which, as a matter of formal law, accepts that unjust enrichment is based on rules rather than on judicial discretion, but is finding this stance hard to live with. The recent decision in *Benedetti*[27] seems to have brought matters to a head, with one of the law lords who decided it subsequently protesting extrajudicially at the formalistic abstraction of the doctrine on which the court relied[28] and some commentators suspecting that the Supreme Court's apparent adherence to doctrine in the case was merely a cover for something quite different.[29] And the more

26 Eg see McInnes, *Canadian Law of Unjust Enrichment*, above n 23 at 25–8, 45–50.

27 *Benedetti v Sawiris* [2013] UKSC 50.

28 R. Reed, "Theory and Practice" in A. Dyson, J. Goudkamp, and F. Wilmot-Smith (eds), *Defences in Unjust Enrichment* (Oxford, Hart Publishing, 2016) ch 13.

29 Eg C. Webb, *Reason and Restitution* (Oxford, Oxford University Press, 2016) 117.

free-and-easy approach of the same court in *Menelaou*,[30] including a willingness to declare an enrichment "unjust" without any substantial analysis, has rung alarm bells in some commentators' minds ("judging in the twenty-first century at its flexible, flabby worst").[31] Judges always need a certain amount of wiggle room if doctrine is to be used to achieve just results. And attempting to deny it to them simply pushes judicial discretion underground, less obvious to observers and harder to discuss. It is a mistake to see cases such as *Menelaou* as a judicial failure; on the contrary, they are a warning not to define judicial techniques in ways that limit the judges' freedom of action.

Too Many Issues

Third, there are too many issues and sub-issues for any single case or even succession of cases simply to root out established approaches to restitutionary issues and substitute an approach based on unjust enrichment. So along with cases proclaiming the unjust enrichment principle, refusing to apply it to selected areas – *Kingstreet*, for example, which insists that claims for wrongly paid taxes are *not* matters of unjust enrichment[32] – and cases such as *Kerr*, which accept an unjust enrichment analysis of their area only on the understanding that it is applied quite differently from other areas of unjust enrichment.[33] Academics committed to a doctrinaire version of unjust enrichment have naturally been disdainful of this – indeed, one UK academic gives *Kingstreet* as an example to other jurisdictions of what *not* to do[34] – but the judiciary is not likely to be moved.

It is notable that the two areas where the rise of unjust enrichment has, in fact, made a substantial practical difference to the law – wrongly paid taxes and the cohabitation cases – are the two areas where the strict academic approach to unjust enrichment has been expressly rejected,

30 *Bank of Cyprus UK Ltd v Menelaou* [2015] UKSC 66.

31 G. Virgo, "Restitution and Unjust Enrichment in the Supreme Court: Reflections on *Bank of Cyprus UK Ltd v Menelaou*," January 2016, http://ssrn.com/abstract=2724024 at 23.

32 *Kingstreet Investments Ltd v New Brunswick* [2007] 1 SCR 3.

33 *Kerr v Baranow* [2011] 1 SCR 269.

34 R. Chambers, "Restitution of Overpaid Tax in Canada" in S. Elliott, B. Häcker, and C. Mitchell, *Restitution of Overpaid Tax* (Oxford, Hart Publishing, 2013) 303 at 311.

in the former instance in favour of public law principles[35] and, in the latter, in favour of a modified and context-specific version of unjust enrichment.[36] In most contexts, most of the time, there is a considerable distance between the academic approach and the judicial approach. But when the area is particularly prominent – considerable practical importance, much injustice done if the principles are not right, much case law – then the divergence is overtly recognized.

Some might say that it is surprising, or even ironic, that the areas where unjust enrichment so obviously does something positive for the law – providing a useful and important remedy where the older law denied one – are also the areas where academic analysis has been found most wanting. But this is not, in fact, surprising at all. The solutions proposed by academics have been rigid and neglectful of the level of discretion that judges have always said that they need. It is, therefore, only to be expected that it is precisely in those areas that the rejection of academic approaches has been so noticeable.

An Unresolvable Dispute?

In summary, therefore, the controversy over the nature and extent of unjust enrichment is not one that can be resolved simply by authoritative rulings from the highest court. I appreciate that this makes no democratic or constitutional sense – that it is for the legislatures and the courts to lay down the law, and the academics' role is simply to establish what that law is. Nor do I deny that, in some abstract sense, the courts have a *right* to insist on their view of the law. My point is rather that, as a practical matter, the courts are unlikely to consistently apply such an abstract framework.

It would require a huge judicial effort to identify every case potentially falling within the scope of unjust enrichment and to insist that each one was argued rigorously in those terms, whether or not it would otherwise have occurred to counsel to do so; mixed messages were always a more likely outcome, and they have, in fact, occurred. What we see in the cases is what we should expect to see: a variety of conceptual approaches to restitutionary issues, with most parties happy to resolve their dispute without raising issues of the structure of restitution law. There will, therefore,

35 *Kingstreet Investments Ltd v New Brunswick* [2007] 1 SCR 3.

36 *Kerr v Baranow* [2011] 1 SCR 269.

be raw material to support a variety of versions of the law, which the academics will do their fractious best to pull together into coherent patterns of liability. No one is really in a position to impose a clear doctrinal structure, and so no clear doctrinal structure manifests itself.

It has been suggested that much of the divergence of views here simply comes down to individual intellectual predilections as to the degree of ordering that is appropriate – that some lawyers prefer everything neat and tidy, whereas others love every last little nuance of the case law and are not much bothered by the chaotic overall pattern left. So, in the writings here, you inevitably have a divide between the "lumpers" and the "splitters" (or, if you prefer, the "hedgehogs" and the "foxes").[37] There is some truth in this, but I think it would be a mistake to take this argument *entirely* outside the realm of rational argument by making it merely one of idiosyncratic personal preferences. One point is that many of the so-called splitters and foxes are unenthusiastic about the supposed intellectual unity of unjust enrichment – not because they oppose intellectual order, but because unjust enrichment threatens a different sort of order, which they favour: such as a properly broad statement of the principles of equity, property, or contract. Another point is that *judicial* statements are almost invariably made in the context of individual cases and so are tied to those cases in ways that academic statements will not be; so judicial theories are almost guaranteed to be "foxier" than their academic counterparts.

As for the controversy over the appropriate framework for restitutionary issues – to what extent we postulate common principles in restitutionary cases and what those common principles should be taken to be – it is difficult to see that debate ending any time soon, as no one point of view has any "killer" arguments at its disposal. The problem for those who seek a more rigorous framework here is always that restitution is something of a latecomer to private law – restitution often, then, is reduced to filling in gaps in the law that the major theories (property, contract, tort/delict, etc.) cannot adequately explain. And while the scholarship has been rather more cosmopolitan than is usual

37 Smith, "State of the Law of Unjust Enrichment," above n 4. The maxim that "the fox knows many things, but the hedgehog knows one big thing" (πόλλ' οἶδ' ἀλώπηξ, ἀλλ' ἐχῖνος ἓν μέγα) is ascribed to the poet Archilochus (?680–?645 BC); its modern popularity derives from Isaiah Berlin's *The Hedgehog and the Fox: An Essay on Tolstoy's View of History* (London, Weidenfeld and Nicolson, 1953).

in private law, the law of restitution has, nonetheless, become something quite different in different common law nations precisely because the gaps to be filled and priorities for filling them are so different.

Unjust versus Unjustified

As to the issue that so agitates the common law scholarship at the moment – whether we should define unjust enrichment in terms of unjust factors (any of which can lead to recovery) or in terms of unjust*ified* enrichment (so that *any* enrichment can lead to liability unless its receipt is justified by the defendant) – it has to be said that those in the former camp are getting the better of the academic argument for now. Approaching the matter from a legal-historical point of view rather than as a partisan, it seems clear that the hurdles that the latter camp must surmount are not impossibly high, but their problems are substantial.

The first reason is historical: the *unjust factors* approach is a great deal closer to the way that restitutionary liability was approached before the modern fashion for unjust enrichment took hold. It is plausible to tell lawyers that there is a "law of mistake" or a "law of compulsion," and (initially at least) it seems artificial and needlessly technical to say that there are no such legal entities, the cases representing merely different facets of the true rule, to be discerned by using a "pyramid of reconciliation."[38] I am never very happy when the unjust factors approach is referred to as "traditional" – anything that counts as a real tradition has to go back a little beyond 1985, in my view[39] – but it is absolutely true that stating the law as based on unjust factors is not so great a change from earlier accounts, whereas rewriting the law on the basis of justificatory factors changes the face of the discipline – a much harder sell. "[T]he shift from unjust factors to juristic reasons leaves the courts, at least in the short term, ill-equipped to resolve interesting cases. *Garland* put the basic civilian model into place, but a great deal remains to be done before the gaps are filled and the pieces are held firmly in place. That is simply the cost of change."[40] Whether the courts are prepared

38 On the "pyramid," see eg P. Birks, *Unjust Enrichment*, 2nd edn (Oxford, Oxford University Press, 2005) 116–17.

39 For the first proper account of the "unjust factors," see Birks, *Introduction to the Law of Restitution*, above n 9 at chs 6–9.

40 McInnes, "Revising the Reason for Restitution," above n 4.

to pay this cost, which seems to buy them relatively little, remains to be seen.

The second reason is structural: the unjust factors approach allows for a great deal of flexibility in expounding the law, whereas stating the law on the basis of unjustified enrichment seems a great deal more rigid. The unjust factors approach was never as unitary as it seemed: textbooks tended to be organized on the basis of the factors, and while the same framework of ideas of *enrichment* and *at the plaintiff's expense* was used in each chapter, they were used in rather different ways. An unjustified enrichment approach moves away from that, attempting to insist on uniformity, with destabilizing results. Of course, the rigidity of the new approach is only apparent: reframing the law as based on justificatory factors rather than unjust factors does not actually make it simpler, it merely moves the difficulties around. So under the unjust factors approach, we must ask which mistakes lead to legal liability, whereas under the unjustified enrichment approach, we ask when a justificatory factor such as contract or gift is invalidated by the existence of a mistake. This intellectual work may turn out to be easy or hard, we do not yet know; the main point is that, either way, it is *work* merely to restate the law in terms we feel happy with. Like the Red Queen, we would have to run pretty fast simply to stay where we are. This is likely to make the unjustified enrichment approach seem unattractive.

The third reason is that if the law is stated in terms of unjustified enrichment, then it is inherently expansionist – in key areas, either a greater range of liability has to be accepted, or novel defences must be postulated to keep the law in check. The much discussed hypothetical to illustrate this is a Scottish one,[41] whereby an apartment owner spends a great deal of money to keep his central heating going, but then is struck by the realization that much of the heat does not stay where it is but goes to warm the apartments above him. Can he sue those higher apartment owners, claiming that they are unjustly enriched at his expense? Our instinctive reaction is that, of course, he cannot, and this result is easy to justify on an unjust factors approach: there is no obvious factor or ground pointing to recovery. On an unjustified enrichment approach, by contrast, it is far from obvious why there is no liability: the folks upstairs are clearly enriched (having been saved the expense

41 Loosely based on an example discussed in *Edinburgh Tramway Co v Courtenay* 1909 SC 99.

of heating their apartments themselves), and there is no very obvious justificatory factor to deny recovery.

Those who support an unjustified enrichment approach can escape liability only by postulating new defences with no obvious merits, such as deeming the enrichment to be a gift.[42] There can, of course, be no objection to legal fictions as such; we are denying much of our legal history and much of the present law by doing so. But no very convincing reason why *this* legal fiction is appropriate here has been given. It looks suspiciously as if the theory of liability selected is simply too broad.

And that is the problem. The sentiment in favour of theories of unjust enrichment has not, for the most part, been driven by a feeling that the law is too narrowly drawn; it has always been, rather, that the law is too chaotic in form and, thus, in need of a more rigorous restatement. Indeed, one of the reasons why reconsideration of the theoretical basis of restitution is largely an *academic* pursuit is that most of the theories proposed would leave the law's coverage pretty much as it is, albeit stated in different language. Yet every area of law needs periodic review, and the question remains whether the language of unjust enrichment is a good way of doing it.

Conclusion

It would be surprising, therefore, if the disputes over the basis of restitutionary liability were authoritatively resolved any time soon. And it is particularly unlikely that this will happen if, as has been the case up to now, the debate is dominated by incompatible demands, the leading academics insisting on a high level of conceptual certainty and clarity, while the judiciary demands significant room for creativity and sensitivity to the facts.

We should also be wary of what is becoming the leading excuse for this confusion – namely, that unjust enrichment is a young doctrine that needs time to sort itself out. Six decades after *Deglman*,[43] this is already rather thin as excuses go, but in any event, it ignores the difficulties that plague the doctrine even in jurisdictions where it is respectably antiquated. Unjust enrichment is everywhere a marginal category, resorted

42 Eg Birks, *Unjust Enrichment*, 2nd edn, above n 38 at 158.
43 *Deglman v Guaranty Trust*, above n 5.

to only for problems that the more mainstream doctrines have shown themselves unable to solve. Those problems are likely to change over time as the mainstream doctrines change and as the wider society asks different things of the law. Doctrinal rigidity is, therefore, not what we want.

13 The Supreme Court, Fundamental Principles of Property Law, and the Shaping of Aboriginal Title

BRUCE ZIFF

The central theme of this collection concerns the influence of supreme courts in the development of the common law. With that in mind, I am going to make the brash (and unempirical) claim that, with regard to the common law principles of property in Canada, the impact of the Supreme Court has been minimal. While views may differ, I can think of only four rulings that can be said to have affected the composition of the law of property, and hence the lives of Canadians, in profound and enduring ways.[1]

There are several reasons why this might be so. In general, a cautious approach has long been a hallmark of the way in which novel property law interests have been judicially validated. A court should be restrained in the creation of new property interests.[2] Borrowing from the lexicon of civilian systems, in recent years this has been described as the *numerus clausus* principle of property law.[3] This can be seen as a

---

1 These are *Harrison v Carswell* [1976] 2 SCR 200 (affirming a private property owner's right of exclusion in the common areas of a shopping mall); *Semelhago v Paramadevan* [1996] 2 SCR 415) (reordering remedies in real estate transactions); *Pettkus v Becker* [1980] 2 SCR 834 (establishing the doctrine of unjust enrichment with the remedial constructive trust in aid); *Highway Properties Ltd v Kelly, Douglas & Co* [1971] SCR 562 (reconceptualizing landlord and tenant remedies).

2 *Keppell v Bailey* (1834) 2 Myl & K 517, 39 ER 1042 (Ch).

3 Bernard Rudden popularized the adoption of this term in the context of the common law: see B. Rudden, "Economic Theory v Property Law: The *Numerus Clausus* Problem," in J. Eekelaar and J. Bell (eds), *Oxford Essays in Jurisprudence*, 3rd Series (Oxford, Oxford University Press, 1987) 239. See also J.H. Merryman, "Policy, Autonomy, and the *Numerus Clausus* in Italian and American Property Law" (1963) 12 *American Journal of Comparative Law* 224.

form of precautionary principle. Property rights, once recognized, can become widespread and entrenched. Because of this, abolishing dysfunctional rules becomes difficult. Hence, it is thought to be wise to move with caution when novel property claims are advanced.[4]

In addition, to the extent to which the received English common law has been altered over time,[5] those changes have come through legislative reform. Unlike other private law spheres (contracts, torts, and restitution), a good deal of the common law has been supplanted or altered by statute. For example, in most, if not all, provinces, there has been a radical revision of the law governing residential tenancies and matrimonial property. Systems of land registration are statute-based, as are the laws governing condominiums, patents, trademarks, and copyrights. And unlike constitutional instruments, these statutes contain highly detailed regimes, which, accordingly, leave the courts with an interpretive role.

So, when the Supreme Court was called upon to decide whether a fishing licence was property for bankruptcy law purposes, the issue was treated as purely one of statutory interpretation. The Court refrained from considering "the concept of 'property' in the abstract."[6] It offered only that "the notion of 'property' is ... a term of some elasticity that takes its meaning from the context."[7] Of course, by the same token, this interpretive function does not completely foreclose a consideration of high principle. In the last two decades, the Supreme Court has been called upon to grapple with some weighty questions involving the law of intellectual property. So, it has been decided that genetically modified plants are patentable,[8] although higher life forms, such as mice with special properties, are not.[9] But such moments are rare.

4 See B. Ziff, "Yet Another Function for the Numerus Clausus Principle of Property Rights, and a Useful One at That," ssrn.com/abstract=2026088. See, however, *Bank of Montreal v Dynex Petroleum Ltd* 2002 SCC 7, where a new form of security interest was recognized.

5 See B. Ziff, "Warm Reception in a Cold Climate: English Property Law and the Suppression of the Canadian Legal Identity" in J. McLaren et al (eds), *Despotic Dominion: Property Rights in British Settler Societies* (Vancouver, UBC Press, 2005) 103 (demonstrating that, in an overwhelming majority of cases in which the matter was in issue, Canadian courts found in favour of the reception of the relevant English property law).

6 *Saulnier (Receiver of) v Saulnier* 2008 SCC 58, para 16 (*per* Binnie J).

7 Ibid.

8 *Monsanto Canada Inc v Schmeiser* 2004 SCC 34.

9 *Harvard College v Canada (Commissioner of Patents)* 2002 SCC 76.

Since the coming into force of the Constitution Act, 1982 and the Canadian Charter of Rights and Freedoms,[10] relatively few private law matters have appeared on the Supreme Court docket. Instead, Charter cases have dominated, especially in the two decades immediately following its enactment. That is to be expected. The Charter has imposed an extraordinary burden on the Court. The language of any bill of rights is designed to be open textured. It was expected that the Supreme Court would shape its contours and do so in a principled and coherent fashion. The demands of that undertaking have meant that less attention can be paid to other areas of the law. Property law was a likely candidate for limited treatment. Because the common law has been supplanted in key areas, the opportunity for issues of national importance has been reduced. Moreover, the absence of a full-blown property law protection in the Charter has meant that the potential for property cases to engage Charter issues has likewise been circumscribed. As a result, for many private property disputes, the provincial courts of appeal have become final appellate tribunals.

Still, the post-Charter docket has not been completely devoid of private law cases, and some of these have involved property rights. There have been a handful of decisions on the remedial constructive trusts,[11] an important development in the law governing specific performance in land sales,[12] and a ruling on the scope of regulatory takings.[13] A number of pivotal cases involving intellectual property have also been resolved by the Court.[14]

In all common law jurisdictions, there is an ill-defined, indeed elusive, line that delineates the law-making roles of courts and legislatures. It is present in both the public law and the private law spheres, including the law of property. In the celebrated case of *International News Service v Associated Press*,[15] a majority on the United States

10 Canadian Charter of Rights and Freedoms, Part I of the Constitution Act, 1982, being Schedule B to the Canada Act 1982 (UK), 1982, c 11.

11 See most recently *Kerr v Baranow* 2011 SCC 10 and the earlier cases cited there.

12 *Semelhago v Paramadevan*, above n 1.

13 *Canadian Pacific Railway v Vancouver (City)* 2006 SCC 5.

14 See especially *Monsanto Canada Inc v Schmeiser*, above n 8; *Harvard College v Canada (Commissioner of Patents)*, above n 9; *CCH Canadian Ltd v Law Society of Upper Canada* 2004 SCC 13; *Galerie d'art du Petit Champlain Inc v Théberge* 2002 SCC 34; *Re Public Performance of Musical Works* 2012 SCC 34; *Mattel USA Inc v 3894207 Canada Inc* 2006 SCC 22; *Sanofi-Synthelabo Canada Inc v Apotex Inc* 2008 SCC 61.

15 248 US 215 (1918).

Supreme Court held that the collection of news created a form of *quasi*-property for the benefit of the collecting wire service. In a famous dissent, Brandeis J argued that the courts were ill-equipped to resolve a question of this complexity. Two decades later, the Australian High Court confronted the issue whether there could be property in something as amorphous as a "spectacle." A majority of the Court declined to extend the common law to recognize such a property right. The *Associated Press* case was cited, and Brandeis J's dissent was adopted in a *majority* opinion.[16]

There have been occasions in which the Supreme Court has resisted engaging broad issues when engagement seemed warranted. For example, in the well-known case of *Re Noble & Wolf*,[17] the validity of a restrictive covenant that prohibited the sale or occupation of certain land to blacks and Jews was at issue. The covenant had been upheld by the Ontario Court of Appeal. That decision was reversed. However, rather than addressing whether such a provision contravened public policy, the Supreme Court instead chose a collateral attack. The reasons for judgment focused on the questions whether a restriction tied to the choice of *occupant* and not to the *use* of a parcel of land was capable of binding a new owner, whether the language used was void for uncertainty, and whether the terms constituted an excessive restraint on the power of alienation.

By the same token, the Court has, on occasion, ventured further than seems warranted. I believe that is true of *Semelhago v Paramadevan*,[18] which I listed above as one of the four most transformative property law decisions of the Supreme Court of Canada. The Court radically altered the law governing remedies for breach of an agreement to purchase land. It was said that the assumption that land was unique was no longer tenable and that, therefore, specific performance should not be awarded as a matter of course when a vendor wrongfully refused to convey title. That statement was *obiter*; even so, it has been faithfully followed in hundreds of lower court judgments. Significantly, argument on this critical issue was not presented to the Court, and the empirical assessment about the nature of real estate was unsubstantiated. It is by no means clear that this ruling has improved the law;

16 *Victoria Park Racing & Recreation Grounds Ltd v Taylor* (1937) 58 CLR 479 (HCA).
17 [1951] SCR 64.
18 Above n 1.

I think it has not.[19] In my view, fundamental property law doctrines should not be resolved in such circumstances.[20]

So far, I have advanced two main points. One is that the impact of the Supreme Court of Canada on the law of property, in recent years at least, has been limited. The second observation, more general in nature, is that the role of apex courts is inevitably influenced by the breadth of the controversy before it. With these ideas in mind, my chapter will now turn to what I regard as the sphere of property law doctrine in which the Supreme Court has had – contrary to the general pattern that I have described – a remarkable and extensive impact on the shape of the law and that it has forged fundamental principles designed to have enduring impact in a way that seems entirely within the warrant of an apex court. I am referring here to the decisions of the Supreme Court governing Aboriginal title and related jural concepts.

Over the last four decades, the courts have been used as a vehicle for change by Aboriginal litigants. The Constitution Act, 1982,[21] which gives constitutional protection to Aboriginal rights, provided added potency to that approach. The result has been a torrent of litigation at the Supreme Court level. In this chapter, I consider that jurisprudence. In doing so, one observation is, I think, incontestable. What emerges from the case law concerning Aboriginal rights is a jurisprudential architecture that is second only in scope and significance to the Charter edifice constructed during roughly the same period. Before 1982, there was little authority on Aboriginal title, and the extant authorities roughed out the law in only a most general way. By contrast, in the last thirty years, the Supreme Court has assumed the role of an activist final appellate body in this field.

Given the breath of this enterprise, it is not surprising that this jurisprudence has been subjected to myriad commentaries and critiques.[22] In this chapter, I will try to make a modest contribution to this discussion,

---

19 For my reasons, see B. Ziff, "Death to *Semelhago*!" (2016) 39 *Dalhousie Law Journal*. However, the Supreme Court implicitly reaffirmed the holding in *Southcott Estates Inc v Toronto Catholic District School Board* [2012] 2 SCR 675.

20 In a short opinion in *Semelhago*, LaForest J expressed a similar concern.

21 Constitution Act, 1982, above n 10 at s 35.

22 See most recently P. Macklem and D. Sanderson (eds), *From Recognition to Reconciliation: Essays on the Constitutional Entrenchment of Aboriginal and Treaty Rights* (Toronto, University of Toronto Press, 2016); M. Asch, *On Being Here to Stay: Treaties and Aboriginal Rights in Canada* (Toronto, University of Toronto Press, 2014).

one that has so far escaped the attention of other commentators. I suspect that this is so because attention has been paid to the constitutional dimensions of Aboriginal law. My claim is that the jurisprudence is marred by an imprecise, unsubtle, and unhelpful approach when principles of Canadian property law have been engaged in the creation of a distinct set of legal principles applicable to Aboriginal rights claims. I do not regard these as fatal flaws; but flaws they are. Before addressing those matters, the core features of the newly crafted framework of Aboriginal property rights will be adumbrated.

An Outlier: Aboriginal Rights in Canada

Before constitutional reform in 1982, there were only two decisions of note as to the nature of Aboriginal rights in Canada. In the first of these, decided in 1888 by the Privy Council,[23] the board described Aboriginal land rights as being personal and usufructuary in nature. That somewhat perplexing characterization stood as law for a century, but has now been abandoned. The second case is *Calder v Attorney General of British Columbia*,[24] circa 1972. That decision is especially noteworthy because it connects with the central theme of this collection – the role of supreme courts.

Calder involved an action brought by the Nisga'a peoples of British Columbia for a declaration of Aboriginal title. Of the seven justices who sat on the appeal, six ruled that Aboriginal land rights had survived the assumption of British sovereignty. However, there was disagreement as to what kinds of subsequent state action could result in the extinguishment of that title. These six justices were evenly divided on that point. The deciding vote was cast by Justice Louis-Philippe Pigeon. He opposed the claim on procedural grounds – namely, that the applicant had not sought a fiat from the province. In British Columbia at that time, a fiat was required whenever a challenge was made to Crown property. The Crown was at liberty to deny the request, and no appeal from that decision was tenable. Pigeon J concluded that the Court was "bound by high authority to hold that the granting of a fiat, when required, is a condition of jurisdiction."[25] In the result, then, the Nisga'a lost (4–3).

23 *St Catharine's Milling & Lumber Co v The Queen* (1888) 14 App Cas 46.
24 [1973] SCR 313.
25 Ibid at para 187.

It is troubling that this defect was the deciding consideration. It is outrageous enough to mandate that permission be required at all. In any event, one would have thought that this concern should have been resolved at a preliminary stage and the appeal stayed pending an application for the fiat. (It was not denied; it had never been sought.)[26] Moreover, the three justices who rejected the claim also supported Pigeon J's position, but chose nevertheless to rule on the merits of the application. Justice Pigeon was not oblivious to the hardship that his ruling entailed.[27] Nevertheless, because he chose not to address the main issue, *Calder* failed to produce a substantive outcome one way or the other.

Calder represents a missed opportunity, and almost a quarter of a century would pass before a definitive ruling on Aboriginal title would be rendered. In 1997, in *Delgamuukw v British Columbia*,[28] the Supreme Court authoritatively laid out the requirements for recognizing Aboriginal title and the quality of a title so recognized.

The contrast between the pronouncements in *Delgamuukw* and those in *Calder* is stark. The opinion of the minority in *Calder* (which supported the Nisga'a claim) is carefully reasoned and has a cautious tone. It hews close to existing Commonwealth and American authorities. By contrast, the majority judgment of Chief Justice Lamer engages the issues from an altitude of 20,000 feet. Based on *Delgamuukw* and the law

---

26 But why not? Several years ago, Thomas Berger, counsel for the Nisga'a, offered this explanation: "The policy of the government ... was that where you were suing the estate of the Crown – that is, you wanted Crown land or Crown resources – they would not issue a fiat. They would in tort cases but not in contract cases, and not in cases where you were trying to ... 'impeach the estate of the Crown.' My argument was, 'We're not impeaching the estate of the Crown. All we want is a declaration. We're not asking for damages. We're not asking that you deliver the Nass Valley to us by five o'clock on Thursday. We just want a declaration that our aboriginal title has never been extinguished, so we aren't caught by this fiat rule.' But Justice Pigeon was off and running with this and decided that we were impeaching the estate of the Crown and, therefore, we should have obtained a fiat. The policy of the government was not to issue a fiat in those circumstances. That's my recollection. I know I spent a lot of time figuring out how to answer the question, 'Are we impeaching the estate of the Crown?' I thought I had the answer, and it turns out I didn't, but it didn't matter anyway'": H. Foster et al (eds), *Let Right Be Done: The* Calder *Case, and the Future of Indigenous Rights* (Vancouver, UBC Press, 2007) 48.

27 Above n 24, para 192.

28 *Delgamuukw v British Columbia* [1997] 3 SCR 1010. An important precursor is *Guerin v R* [1984] 2 SCR 335.

as it has since developed, the following propositions describe the most central features of the current law.

First, the common law will recognize Aboriginal title to land where those lands were exclusively occupied by a claimant nation at the time of the assertion of Crown sovereignty. Present occupation can serve as proof of title provided that there is an element of continuity between past and present occupation. Second, land for which such recognition exists confers a right of use and occupation. Third, even where Aboriginal title is not recognized, a claimant group can assert a non-title right for those significant cultural practices (whether site-specific or otherwise) that existed at the time of first European contact. Fourth, at common law, these rights can be extinguished though surrender or by virtue of otherwise valid unilateral state action, provided such action manifests a clear and plain intention to do so. Fifth, following the enactment of s. 35 of the Constitution Act, 1982, rights cannot be extinguished but can only be infringed (abridged), and then only if such measures are shown to satisfy a stringent justificatory test.[29] Even inchoate rights claims can be protected against unilateral state action.[30]

In the course of framing these rules, the Supreme Court has described a set of guiding meta-principles. Hence, it has been said that in dealing with the Aboriginal peoples of Canada, the honour of the Crown must always be upheld.[31] In addition, the governing law is based on a reconciliation of Aboriginal and non-Aboriginal perspectives.[32] That characterization is said to flow from the special relationship between the Crown and Canada's First Nations. Arising out of that confluence is another important meta-principle – the law governing Aboriginal property rights is *sui generis* – that is, unique. That is true from top to bottom: it describes the principles governing title, reserves, treaties,[33] and the fiduciary obligations owed by the Crown.[34]

---

29 *R v Van der Peet* [1996] 2 SCR 507 at para 28; *R v Marshall* 2003 NSCA 105; *R v Bernard* 2005 SCC 43 at para 39. Provincial law can validly infringe Aboriginal rights, although a province's capacity to do so is limited by the federal structure of Canadian governance.

30 *Haida Nation v British Columbia (Minister of Forests)* 2004 SCC 73; *Carrier Sekani Tribal Council v British Columbia (Utilities Commission)* 2010 SCC 43.

31 *R v Marshall*, above n 29; *R v Bernard*, above n 29 at paras 49ff.

32 *R v Bernard*, above n 29 at paras 45–7.

33 *Simon v R* [1985] 2 SCR 387; *R v Sioui* 1990 CarswellQue 103; *R v Badger* 1996 CarswellAlta 587 (SCC) at para 78.

34 *Guerin v R*, above n 28 at para 104; *Wewaykum Indian Band v R* 2002 SCC 79.

The Supreme Court of Canada has identified five built-in, unique elements of Aboriginal title: (1) title predates the assumption of British sovereignty and so does not derive from a sovereign dispensation of the land, (2) lands are held communally, (3) title is inalienable except by surrender to the Crown, (4) title lands may not be used in a way that is incompatible with traditional uses, and (5) title is immune from expropriation.[35] In addition, the *sui generis* label serves as a filter, limiting, where sensible, the application of any number of common law rules of property. In essence, the *sui generis* label sends a signal that one should not assume that a given property law doctrine applies to such lands. Do not assume that the law governing easements, airspace, or any given rule of construction, etc. will govern title lands.[36]

Sui Generis Considered

I am not convinced that the *sui generis* label is particularly helpful. For the term to be coherent at a theoretical level, we need to know the baseline concept against which uniqueness is to be measured; but we do not. The core meaning of the idea of property in law continues to be debated. Some liken the idea of property to a bundle of rights, a common but not universally accepted metaphor. Accepting this description for the sake of current argument, it is still necessary to determine what counts as the necessary minimum content of the bundle. What is the irreducible core absent which we can no longer call a right one of property?

Among the most helpful academic treatments of that question is the one developed by the American scholar Thomas Merrill.[37] In reviewing the American jurisprudence, Merrill identified three ways in which American courts define property. One of these is described as *single-variable essentialism*. Adherents to that approach argue that the only essential element of the concept is a right of exclusion that is good against the world. A second approach is described as *multi-variable essentialism*. On this view, the core might include not just a right of exclusion but also such other necessary elements as a right of transfer, or use, etc. A third approach is labelled *nominalism*. Under that version, no common core can be discerned. Instead, property is entirely

35 See above n 29.

36 *Tsilquot'in Nation v British Columbia* 2014 SCC 44 at para 72.

37 T.W. Merrill, "Property and the Right to Exclude" (1988) 77 *Nebraska Law Review* 730.

malleable and purposive. Property is that which the law so decrees. It is not clear where things stand in Canada. To date, the Supreme Court of Canada has not engaged in that debate.[38]

Putting this aside, it is apparent that the common law is full of *sui generis* interests. There are dozens of land law rights, each possessing discrete elements. A fee simple is not a life estate; a lease is distinct from a licence; a covenant is not an easement; a patent is not a copyright; and none of these rights is the same as a chose in possession. In short, it is not unique to describe property rights as unique.

In addition, in an effort to stress the differences between Aboriginal rights and general principles of property law, there may be a tendency to misrepresent the common law, to portray it as being more rigid than, in fact, is the case. Consider the decision in *St. Mary's Indian Band v Cranbrook.*[39] This dispute involved an interpretation of a surrender of reserve lands by the St. Mary's Indian Band to the City of Cranbrook. The grant provided that the lands would revert to the band if they "ceased to be used for public purposes." The case turned on whether the surrender was conditional or absolute.

Under the general law, the language used suggests that one of two forms of conditional disposition had been created: either a grant subject to a condition subsequent or a determinable limitation. Under either reading, the transfer would be regarded as conditional. However, the Supreme Court held that the surrender was absolute. In doing so, it stressed the *sui generis* nature of Aboriginal rights.[40] It cautioned that the outcome should not be resolved "by strict reference to intractable real property rules,"[41] the "usual restrictions,"[42] or "the minutiae of the language employed."[43] Hence, the conventional distinction between determinable limitations and conditions was not controlling. Instead, the Court purported to examine afresh the respective intentions of the St. Mary's Indian Band and the Crown at the time of the surrender. It

---

38 Compare the decision of the High Court of Australia in *Yanner v Eaton* [1999] HCA 53.

39 *St Mary's Indian Band v Cranbrook (City)* [1997] 2 SCR 657.

40 "[N]ative land rights are in a category of their own, and as such, traditional real property rules do not aid the Court in resolving this case," ibid at para 14 (*per* Lamer CJC). See also *Blueberry River Indian Band v Canada* [1995] 4 SCR 344.

41 *St Mary's Indian Band v Cranbrook (City),* above n 39 at para 15.

42 Ibid.

43 Ibid.

was held that, having regard to the document as a whole, an absolute transfer was intended. Substance trumped form.

I find it difficult to get past the conditional language used in the surrender. It does seem to suggest that a residual right to reclaim the land was contemplated. But, putting that aside, my principal critique is that there is nothing unique about the Court's analysis. The reasoning adopted here could equally be applied in a non-Aboriginal setting. The language used might denote a condition subsequent or a determinable limitation – or neither. The use of particular language does not mandate iron-clad interpretations, and it will not do so where the substance of the transaction, on balance, suggests otherwise. In construing property dispositions, substance is always supposed to prevail over form.

The Adoption of Analogies

Generally

Although the Supreme Court has repeatedly stressed the *sui generis* nature of Aboriginal rights, there is a noticeable gravitational pull that brings the concept close to the common law. The Supreme Court has offered that analogies to other forms of Canadian property law can assist in understanding Aboriginal property rights. Such analogues are thus supposed to help flesh out the end product of the reconciliation of Aboriginal and common law perspectives. The resort to analogies reflects a perceived need to ground Aboriginal rights concepts in a lexicon that is intelligible by lawyers and judges operating within the framework of the Canadian legal system. This creates an intriguing tension: Aboriginal rights are at once treated as distinct from, but nonetheless similar to, generic Canadian property law.

For an analogy to be helpful in this context, it should satisfy two criteria. First, and most obviously, it must be apt. It must be suited to the role, which means that it should describe the *sui generis* principles as accurately as possible. Second, there must be a useful body of learning about the analogue to enable it to provide guidance on the ground. Usually, this means that there should exist a body of case law that allows one to see how the concept has been applied within the common law context from which it emanates. On two occasions, the Supreme Court has looked to property law analogues in relation to pivotal Aboriginal title concepts. I believe that, in both instances, it has chosen analogies that fail to provide useful guidance. One of these relates to the concept of waste. The second concerns the meaning of occupation of land as applied to title claims. I will deal with each in turn.

Waste

As mentioned above, Aboriginal lands must not be used in a way that is irreconcilable with the manner in which the land was used at the time of sovereignty.[44] In *Delgamuukw,* two examples of this limitation are offered: strip mining on hunting grounds and transforming a site of cultural significance into a parking lot. As a way of describing this restriction in general terms, the majority in *Delgamuukw* turned to the ancient common law concept of waste.

The doctrine of waste applies where two or more people have an interest in a given piece of land. It is most prominent in the context of a property held under a settlement within which one party holds a life estate, while one or more people hold an interest in the remainder.[45] The law of waste provides one mechanism to balance the rights of present and future owners. In essence, waste is designed to prevent the life tenant(s) from altering the land by some physical transformation that would diminish the inheritance for those entitled to the remainder.

Four kinds of waste are applicable when a life tenant–remainderer relationship exists: ameliorating, permissive, voluntary, and equitable. *Ameliorating waste* refers to conduct that enhances the value of property. *Permissive waste* applies where a property holder neglects in taking positive action to maintain a property and applies only where the document of transfer imposes such an obligation. *Voluntary waste* captures a situation in which the life tenant has reduced the value of the land, such as by felling trees or razing a building. *Equitable waste* can be

---

44 *Delgamuukw v British Columbia,* above n 28. The effect of a failure to abide by this restriction has not yet been spelled out. In *Delgamuukw,* Lamer CJ stated that a group that wished to use the land in violation of this inherent limitation is obliged to surrender it to the Crown, presumably seeking a re-grant on terms that are freed from the restriction. But what if the group simply violates the limitation? Presumably it will be subject to an injunction. Another view would be that the irreconcilable use is to be treated as a deemed surrender.

45 The concept has also been applied to tenants in tail after possibility of issue extinct; tenants in common and joint tenants; mortgagor and mortgagee; tenant in fee subject to an executory devise over; rector or vicar as regards the rectory or glebe lands, partners, and a purchaser who is in possession prior to closing: *New Westminster (City) v Kennedy* 1918 CarswellBC 5 (SC) at para 10.

understood as a more severe form of voluntary waste. Equitable waste refers to *unconscientious* acts that alter the property – that is, action that a *prudent* owner would not normally undertake. This is the touchstone of liability for equitable waste.[46]

It was equitable waste that the chief justice saw as the relevant analogue. Here, in full, is what Chief Justice Lamer wrote:

> I am cognizant that the *sui generis* nature of aboriginal title precludes the application of "traditional real property rules" to elucidate the content of that title (*St. Mary's Indian Band v. Cranbrook (City)*, [1997] 2 S.C.R. 657, at para. 14). Nevertheless, a useful analogy can be drawn between the limit on aboriginal title and the concept of equitable waste at common law. Under that doctrine, persons who hold a life estate in real property cannot commit "wanton or extravagant acts of destruction" (E. H. Burn, *Cheshire and Burn's Modern Law of Real Property* (14th ed. 1988), at p. 264) or "ruin the property" (Robert E. Megarry and H. W. R. Wade, *The Law of Real Property* (4th ed. 1975), at p. 105). This description of the limits imposed by the doctrine of equitable waste capture the kind of limit I have in mind here.[47]

At a very general level, the law of waste seems a sensible doctrine to invoke in this context for it shares a common cause with recognized Aboriginal land rights – both seek to preserve land for future generations. But, beyond that, however, resort to the law of waste, and equitable waste in particular, is misleading.

As noted, the law of waste contains different forms. The province of equitable waste is limited. A document granting a life estate might provide that the life tenant is not to be held liable (unimpeachable) for waste. If so, there is no liability *inter alia* for voluntary (destructive) waste. Even when this is so, courts of equity will still intervene in extreme cases: even a tenant unimpeachable for waste remains liable for equitable waste unless the granting document has *explicitly* waived that form of liability. That being so, the line between voluntary and equitable waste becomes quite crucial.

There are very few authorities (especially modern ones) on the meaning of equitable waste, which, on its own, creates difficulties in using the law to describe the limitation in *Delgamuukw*. The chief justice seems

46 Ibid at para 9.
47 *Delgamuukw v British Columbia*, above n 28 at para 131.

to have in mind a massive transformation of the property. However, the case law on equitable waste demonstrates that even some trifling acts can, in context, amount to equitable waste. It has been held, for example, that the felling of a few ornamental trees for use as lumber constitutes equitable waste if the trees are located near the "mansion-house."[48] At the same time, those cases involving large-scale destruction seem to have hinged on the malicious intention of the party in possession to drain the value of the inheritance for purely personal gain.[49] Neither of these scenarios describes a decision of an Aboriginal group to alter the use of all (or some) traditional lands for the benefit of members of a band, present and future. Likewise, all else being equal, strip-mining land is not necessarily imprudent or unconscientious. In fact, a life tenant may exhaust the minerals on an estate if the mine has already been opened. Further, paving a hunting ground is not necessarily equitable waste, as understood in the old English case law. From a purely dollars-and-cents point of view, it might prove to improve the yield of the land. If anything, it might amount to ameliorating waste. In sum, the analogue is inappropriate: it does not comport with the examples provided in *Delgamuukw*.

Occupation

An Aboriginal title claim must be based on exclusive occupation at the time of the assertion of sovereignty. Just what would suffice to meet that standard was not extensively described in *Delgamuukw*, but it has been focal in subsequent Supreme Court of Canada case law.[50] The principal concern in the follow-on cases has been to define the nature and quality of occupation that would suffice when the claimant nation was nomadic or semi-nomadic. An Aboriginal society that is fundamentally

---

48 See further W.A. Bewes, *The Law of Waste: A Treatise on the Rights and Liabilities Which Arise from the Relationship of Limited Owners of the Inheritance with Reference to the Tenements* (London, Sweet & Maxwell, 1894).

49 The leading authority is *Vane v Lord Barnard* (1716) 2 Vern 738, 23 ER 1082, where the life tenant, unimpeachable for waste, was attempting to strip a castle of all valuable materials. His actions were held to constitute equitable waste. See also *New Westminster (City) v Kennedy*, above n 45, where the owners of a house to be seized by the municipality for taxes tried to adopt the same strategy. They, too, were found liable.

50 See especially *R v Marshall*, above n 29, and *Tsilquot'in Nation v British Columbia*, above n 36.

structured on hunting and gathering, without fixed settlements, should be able to show a sufficient occupation to support a title claim, for to deny territorial claims to such groups would be perverse and ethnocentric. Mindful of this concern, the Supreme Court has made it clear that such societies are capable of establishing occupation within the rules of recognition.[51]

As with all other concepts, the meaning of *occupation* is arrived at by drawing on Aboriginal and common law perspectives. The Aboriginal perspective will vary from nation to nation. A court must examine the claimant's laws, practices, size, and technologies as well as the character of the land claimed.[52] What about the common law ingredients?

Occupation (or possession) is a concept of great importance in the common law, but it comes in many forms. At core, possession in law entails two elements – an intention to control and sufficient acts of dominion. However, the application of the two components to solve disputes reveals that the law does not always require a perfect subjective awareness; nor is there a uniform standard for the kinds of physical acts demanded to demonstrate control. The law sets one threshold for the acquisition of possession of an object and another for its retention; less is required in the latter case. The acts required to show possession of land differ dramatically from those pertinent to occupation of land.

In *Tsilquot'in*, the Supreme Court took stock of suitable common law analogies to help shape the requirement of exclusive occupation. Three candidates were identified. One was the law of adverse possession. An adverse possessor may acquire title superior even to the party holding paper title by means of long-term occupation. In general, the possession required to acquire this possessory title must be open and notorious, actual, continuous, exclusive, adverse, and peaceful, and it must continue throughout the mandated period (such as ten years). By the same token, it must be shown that the true owner is out of possession. Overall, we require a greater presence by a squatter than that demanded of the true owner. Importantly, a true owner in possession of some of a parcel will be treated as in constructive possession of the remainder.

51 "The notion of occupation must ... reflect the way of life of the Aboriginal people, including those who were nomadic or semi-nomadic": *Tsilquot'in Nation v British Columbia*, above n 36 at para 38 (*per* McLachlin CJC).

52 Ibid at para 35.

That is generally not sufficient for an adverse possessor.[53] In *Tsilquot'in*, the Court adopted the view that the quality of possession sufficient to ground a title claim can be notionally understood as the middle ground between the minimal occupation of an owner and the more onerous standard required of a squatter.[54]

The second analogue involves cases in which the ownership of a parcel is in dispute. Unlike cases of adverse possession, here the law is concerned with determining which of two rival claimants is the rightful owner of the disputed land. Acts such as enclosing, cultivating, mining, building, maintaining, warning trespassers, felling trees, cutting grass, fishing, and even simple perambulation are potentially germane. The weight given to such acts depends partly on the nature of the land and partly on the purposes for which it can reasonably be used.

The third analogue involves the concept of *general occupancy*. Here is what is said in *Tsilquot'in* about that term:

> In *R. v Marshall* ... Cromwell J.A. (as he then was), in reasoning I adopt, likens the sufficiency of occupation required to establish Aboriginal title to the requirements for general occupancy at common law. A general occupant at common law is a person asserting possession of land over which no one else has a present interest or with respect to which title is uncertain. Cromwell J.A. cites (at para. 136) the following extract from K. McNeil, *Common Law Aboriginal Title* (1989), at pp. 198–200:
>
> What, then, did one have to do to acquire a title by occupancy? ... [I]t appears ... that ... a casual entry, such as riding over land to hunt or hawk, or travelling across it, did not make an occupant, such acts "being only transitory and to a particular purpose, which leaves no marks of an appropriation, or of an intention to possess for the separate use of the rider." There must, therefore, have been an actual entry, and some act or acts from which an intention to occupy the land could be inferred. Significantly, the acts and intention had to relate only to the occupation – it

---

53 Actual possession on one area of a parcel by a squatter will support constructive possession of the rest when the squatter enters the property under colour of title, such as a flawed transfer document: *Bentley v Peppard* (1903) 22 SCR 444.

54 *Tsilquot'in Nation v British Columbia*, above n 36 at para 40, adopting, it would appear, the conclusions of Cromwell JA (as he then was) in *R v Marshall*, above n 29 at para 137.

was quite unnecessary for a potential occupant to claim, or even wish to acquire, the vacant estate, for the law cast it upon him by virtue of his occupation alone.[55]

I can see the sense of using the law of adverse possession in the manner adopted by the Court. I can also follow the logic of engaging the case law on the determination of title in the absence of adequate documentation. However, resort to the law of general occupancy is, with respect, ill advised.

Despite its name, the concept of general occupancy had a very limited scope at common law. It applied only, and only sometimes, to the situation of an unexpired portion of a life estate *pur autre vie*. An estate *pur autre vie* arises when land is given to A for the life of B. The entitlement will terminate on B's death and not before. If A were to predecease B, there would remain some portion of the life interest. Today, that unexpired estate devolves in accordance with general succession law. At common law, however, the estate would pass based on first occupancy. When the grant of the life estate to A included a reference to A's heirs, the first heir to assume occupation of the land on the death of A was entitled to the reminder of the life estate. An heir in this context was described as a *special* occupant. In all other instances, it was the first occupant, whoever that might be, who could take the estate by occupation, as a *general* occupant.

There are several reasons why this is a terrible analogy. If we were to look at the case law on both general and special occupancy (for both are equally useful) on the question of what counts as sufficient possession, we will find very few guiding authorities. Moreover, the concept of general occupancy was implicitly abolished by virtue of provisions of the Statute of Frauds, 1677,[56] so one will not find any cases applying that concept over the last 350 years.

And there is an even more important defect. When factual enquiries about possession-taking by a general occupant arise, the boundary of the land involved is not per se at issue. The question is whether the general occupation has entered onto some part of Blackacre, where Blackacre has predetermined boundaries. In the context of Aboriginal title,

55 Ibid at para 39 (*per* McLachlin CJC).

56 Statute of Frauds, 29 Car II, c 3, s 12. See further R. Megarry and H.W.R. Wade, *The Law of Real Property*, 5th edn (London, Stevens & Son, 1984) 94.

the fact that there are no pre-existing boundaries is a central concern. It is occupation itself that is used to draw those lines.

Conclusion

In the introduction to this chapter, I alluded to the vague demarcations of the law-making competencies of courts, especially apex courts. It is not always clear when a court should grasp the nettle of reform or defer to the legislative branch. I expressed a concern that sometimes the courts seem to resist engagement with policy, while, on other occasions, may pronounce in broad terms where restraint might have been warranted. I do not think that either of these criticisms – too little engagement with policy or too much – can be levelled at the Supreme Court's approach to Aboriginal rights. These issues came to the courts through a strategy of Aboriginal rights advocates, who sought and achieved constitutional protection and then invoked the judicial process to assert those rights. The issues, having a constitutional dimension, invited the kind of principled approach that had developed from the earliest days of Charter rulings and so seemed within the warrant of Canada's highest court.

One of the great challenges that this structure of rights poses concerns the ways in which Aboriginal perspectives can be meaningfully and accurately proved in judicial proceedings. In that light, it has been argued that there is insufficient evidence to date of Aboriginal components in the rules that have been formulated.[57] For its part, the Supreme Court understands that the differences in Aboriginal and common law conceptions are real,[58] and it has warned that courts should be "careful not to lose or distort the Aboriginal perspective by forcing ancestral practices into the square boxes of common law concepts."[59] I have tried to show that one must be equally vigilant to ensure that the common law is invoked in a way that is consonant with its essence.

I am doubtful that the adoption of common law analogies (especially the archaic principle of first occupancy) increases our understanding of the kind of occupation needed to support a claim to Aboriginal title.

---

57 See eg A. Walkem, "An Unfulfilled Promise: Still Fighting to Make Space for Indigenous Legal Traditions," in M. Morellata (ed), *Aboriginal Law since Delgamuukw* (Aurora, ON, Canada Law Book, 2009) ch. 15, passim.

58 *R v Marshall*, above n 29 at para 47.

59 *Tsilquot'in Nation v British Columbia*, above n 36 at para 32 (*per* McLachlin CJC).

If we are to glean anything at all from the common law's approach to possession, it cannot be more than that the concept is necessarily plastic. Possession, as a juridical concept, is dramatically affected by the legal context in which it operates. It is an inherently purposive concept, adapting to the relevant factual and legal settings. Those ideas are recognized in the Supreme Court's most recent pronouncement on this issue; that is probably the most that can be said.

Put another way, the role of an apex court is to provide broad and principled guidance, using language that is as precise as the concepts described can allow. The Supreme Court has held that proof of Aboriginal title requires a real connection with the land being claimed. In addition, it has been held that Aboriginal title cannot be used in a way that undermines the connection with ancestral uses. Whether these are appropriate principles can be a matter of debate. What I suggest is that these guidelines are consonant with the role of an apex court shining a light on the road ahead. The use of analogies such as the law of equitable waste and general occupancy add nothing and, indeed, may obscure what the Supreme Court has decided.

It may even be correct to say that the treatment of Aboriginal rights as *sui generis* is theoretically problematic and prone to inducing unwarranted distinctions between common law and Aboriginal perspectives. However, in several respects, the label is undoubtedly appropriate. The Canadian law of Aboriginal rights is designed to be a blending of the common law and Aboriginal perspectives. That is distinctive. Moreover, the body of law that emerges is unlike any other found in the rest of the common law world and beyond. In a polity that can claim very few special legal creations, this is a noteworthy achievement.

The law on Aboriginal land rights is also unique when viewed against the limited contributions of the Supreme Court to other fundamental principles of property law. It has placed its mark here far beyond any other area of property. In effect, starting from a single premise – the holding in *Calder*[60] that Aboriginal title survived the assumption of sovereignty – over the last thirty years, the Supreme Court has created a body of rules essentially from whole cloth.

As is well known, the majority judgment in *Delgamuukw* ends with this rather remarkable sentence: "Let us face it, we are all here to stay."

60 Above n 24.

To me, this acknowledges that the law created by the Supreme Court of Canada is patently – overtly – a mediation of competing political positions. I find it hard to read the judgment in any other way. Such a sentiment in the body of a legal opinion concerning principles of property law (at least) is, in my experience, also unique.

Afterword

WILLIAM B. EWALD

Rather than repeat Paul Daly's excellent overview in his introduction, and rather than comment on the contributions one by one, let me make three general observations about this collection that may help to point the way forward to future research.

My first observation is that the title, *Apex Courts and the Common Law*, deploys the definite article before the words *common law*. It is striking, however, first, that almost every paper deploys the phrase *the common law* in several distinct senses and, second, that those senses vary from contributor to contributor, often in subtle ways that reflect the vagaries of the legal system under discussion. This is not the place to attempt a comprehensive taxonomy of the way in which this phrase is used around the world. But let me sketch the point with a (necessarily oversimplified) example.

It will be helpful to begin by differentiating three widespread and familiar usages of *the common law*. (1) Sometimes the term is used to designate a substantive body of *legal rules* (as when one speaks of "the common law of contracts" or, as several of the contributions do, of "the role of apex courts in the development of the common law"). (2) Sometimes the phrase is used to classify entire *legal systems* (as when one speaks about Australia as a "common law system" or speaks of "the common law tradition"). Here it might be helpful to quote from the definition of *common law* in the 2017 *CIA World Factbook*, which is fairly typical of what one finds in the scholarly literature of comparative law:

> **Common Law** – A type of legal system, often synonymous with "English common law," which is the system of England and Wales in the UK, and is also In force in approximately 80 countries formerly part of or influenced

> by the former British Empire. English common law reflects Biblical influences as well as remnants of law systems imposed by early conquerors including the Romans, Anglo-Saxons, and Normans. Some legal scholars attribute the formation of the English common law system to King Henry II (r.1154–1189). Until the time of his reign, laws customary among England's various manorial and ecclesiastical (church) jurisdictions were administered locally. Henry II established the king's court and designated that laws were "common" to the entire English realm. The foundation of English common law is "legal precedent" – referred to as *stare decisis*, meaning "to stand by things decided." In the English common law system, court judges are bound in their decisions in large part by the rules and other doctrines developed – and supplemented over time – by the judges of earlier English courts.[1]

The idea is that the common law systems are those that are *historically descended* from English law: that they belong to a common legal *tradition*. (3) A third usage deploys the phrase to refer to a *method*: to the way in which bodies of *case law* are built up by judges in reliance on precedent. Thus one speaks of "common law adjudication" or of "common law reasoning" – it often being said that common law judges reason "from the bottom up" rather than "from the top down."

But now consider these three usages as they are employed in two prominent common law systems: the United States and England. (For the sake of brevity, I shall use *England* as shorthand for "England and Wales.")

(1) *Substantive law*. Let us begin with Oliver Wendell Holmes's influential early work, *The Common Law*, which was published in Boston in 1881. Holmes is almost entirely concerned with a historical exposition and analysis of the *substantive* common law. He has little to say about common law methodology and is not much interested in the contrast with codified systems. (It should be remembered that, in 1881, most of today's civilian systems were still uncodified or only partly codified: the influential German *Bürgerliches Gesetzbuch* was still two decades away.) Holmes's chapter headings are instructive. They are "Early Forms of Liability," "Criminal Law," "Torts" (two chapters), "The Bailee

1 United States, Central Intelligence Agency, *2017 CIA World Factbook*, xxi. Electronic version available at https://www.cia.gov/library/publications/resources/the-world-factbook/docs/notesanddefs.html.

at Common Law," "Possession," "Contracts" (three chapters), "Successions" (two chapters).

In present-day American usage, if you refer to "the common law" as a *substantive* body of law, you most likely intend to refer to the three subjects of tort, contract, and property, which every first-year law student studies under the rubric of *the common law subjects*. So Holmes's list has shrunk: bailments and successions have diminished in importance, and criminal law is no longer considered a common law subject. What about the rest of the first-year curriculum? Americans would not refer to civil procedure as a "common law subject," presumably because American procedures were not inherited from England. As for constitutional law, although some scholars refer to "common law constitutionalism," this is primarily intended to refer to the Supreme Court's *method* of constitutional interpretation: that is, it employs the third sense of *common law*. It would be intelligible, although unusual, to refer to the Supreme Court's substantive body of case law as "constitutional common law" and highly deviant to speak of it as "part of the common law."

In England, in contrast, the substantive sense is broader than in the United States. *The common law* encompasses not only tort, contract, and property but also (as several of the contributions in this volume make clear) large tracts of public law, including much of the law of judicial review.

(2) *The English legal tradition*. What about the historical sense? In the United States, Holmes's list no doubt reflects the fact that the private law subjects he discusses were directly inherited from English law. (Indeed, in 1881, it was still standard to think of the common law as something that Holmes was later to ridicule as a "brooding omnipresence" – that is, as a common body of substantive laws being developed cooperatively by judges in England and America.) Likewise, part of the thought behind the current American usage seems to be this: "Tort, contracts, and property are judge-made subjects historically inherited from England; so it is appropriate to refer to them as 'common law subjects.'"

But here it is necessary to be careful. *How much* of the English legal tradition is encompassed by *the common law*? Are Coke, and the Revolution of 1688, and Blackstone, and Bagehot, and Dicey, and parliamentary sovereignty part of *the common law tradition*? In England (and in some parts of the Commonwealth), it would make little sense to exclude these portions of English law from the tradition. But in the United States, the Constitution was explicitly conceived as a rejection of the very idea of parliamentary sovereignty. That fact leaves us with an awkward choice. If parliamentary sovereignty is not an essential part of the common law, then the English usage is mistaken: but if it is, then the United States (again, contrary to standard usage) is not a common law system. It is, of course, not my point that these usages cannot be made precise: clearly they can be. The point is rather that the phrase *the common law* is too coarse and that it obscures fundamental differences. Note, too, that the questions "What belongs to the common law tradition?" and "What parts of the substantive law are to be classified as common law subjects?" are interdependent: specifically, the adoption of the US Constitution has a large effect on the way in which Americans conceptualize the common law. Invoking Henry II at this point does little to clarify matters, and the legal system of the Plantagenets is best left to the medieval historians.

(3) *Method.* The third standard usage relies on the contrast between "judge-made" law and statutory law: the common law, in this usage, is principally the method whereby judges build up a body of case law and precedents from the bottom up.

I shall set aside jurisprudential questions about legal reasoning and not try to settle whether the contrast with the civil law systems is as great as is often supposed. But here, too, it needs to be emphasized that the methods of apex courts in the English and the US systems are starkly different, and the differences are related to the substantive and historical differences I have just mentioned.

The US Supreme Court considers itself constitutionally a fully coequal branch of the US government. It moreover operates in a cultural environment where state-court judges are elected and where the judiciary is seen as an integral part of the political system. Partly as a result of these facts, the Supreme Court is accustomed to ruling on highly incendiary political matters – racial discrimination, abortion, school prayer, campaign finance, gay marriage – often resolving the matter (as in the 2000 presidential election) by a vote of 5–4.

As for *the development of the common law* (in the American sense of the term), that task falls, not to the Supreme Court, but to the state supreme courts, whose judges are frequently elected and rarely of the intellectual stature of senior judges in England. There is a great willingness to improvise, to backtrack, to borrow from other states, to take a loose attitude towards the principle of *stare decisis*. All of this is, of course, very different in England, and the point I wish to emphasize is that these are primarily differences of *method*, of the manner in which apex courts approach the business of judging.

These points could obviously be elaborated at much greater length. But for now, I merely wish to observe that whether we consider *substantive* classifications, or historical *tradition*, or *methods* of adjudication, there are large differences between the United States and England, and it is not helpful to push them all under the single blanket of *the common law*. (I leave to one side the complexities that would arise from attempting to incorporate into the analysis the legal systems of Scotland, and Northern Ireland, and Great Britain, and the United Kingdom. The legal system of England (inclusive of Wales) is quite complicated enough. But that is my point.) The problems multiply if one attempts to expand the term to cover all eighty countries in what the Central Intelligence Agency (CIA) considers to be the common law world.

I proceed now to my second observation. Although the fact is not emphasized in the chapters, a strikingly large number of the concepts discussed by the contributors – the relationship between public law and private law, "good faith" in the law of contract, the development of administrative law in England, proportionality analysis, the horizontal effect of constitutional law on private law doctrine, multi-factor tests – have their origins in the continental legal systems. None of these concepts had much place in the English law of, say, 1970 – to say nothing of the time of Dicey. Brian Simpson long ago pointed out that the fundamental categories of tort and contract are of Roman origin and were imported into English law from the continental European jurists early in the nineteenth century. In effect, they displaced the common law classification based upon the system of writs.[2] Evidently, the tradition of borrowing from European sources continues today.

What is the relationship between these two observations? For much of the past one hundred years, the legal map of the world has been divided (as the *CIA World Factbook* divides it) into a few broad categories. There are the common law systems, and the civilian systems, and the religion-based systems, and "mixed" systems, and "Indigenous" systems. But the facts I have noted put pressure on these categories, both from the inside and from the outside. Internally, the "common law family" is far from a unity – and that is true even if we leave non-Western

2 A.W.B. Simpson, *Innovation in Nineteenth-Century Contract Law* (1975) 91 *Law Quarterly Review* 247.

systems (India, Kenya, Malaysia) to one side. And externally, there has been a significant importation. The effect of the two tendencies has been to scramble the categories. For some purposes, it makes sense to group together the legal systems of the Commonwealth, while excluding the United States. For others, it makes sense to group together (say) the United States and Germany (which have politically interventionist constitutional courts) and to contrast them with the United Kingdom and France (which do not). These groupings have little to do with Henry II or *stare decisis*.

What are the forces driving the scrambling of the categories? And why are those forces active *now*? That is evidently a large question, but clearly, globalization and the growth of international legal practice has something to do with it. So do changes in international legal education and, in particular, the changes induced by the advent of the European Union (EU). Fifty years ago, the Oxford law curriculum was almost entirely focused on traditional English law. Constitutional law and administrative law were intellectually stagnant; European Community law was a small part of the curriculum; there was no Human Rights Act; "Craig and de Búrca" did not exist; nor did the specialized treatises on various aspects of EU law.

But if you go into Blackwell's Bookshop today, the bookshelves look very different. Works on EU law, international law, comparative private and public law abound. They are essential parts of the law curriculum and of scholarly research (even in what Americans would call "the common law subjects" of tort and contract). Moreover, it has become common for ambitious law students to spend time studying abroad. Some of them end as judges or academics. A law student from Ireland, for example, might take an advanced degree in the United States, then teach at a French-speaking university in Quebec, then transfer to Cambridge to teach alongside faculty from Australia or New Zealand or Germany. This sort of trajectory was far less common in 1972. Inevitably, legal ideas have trickled back into the analysis of "domestic" English law and been exported, in particular, to other members of the Commonwealth.

My third observation is extremely brief. Less than a month after the conclusion of the conference from which this collection developed, in June 2016, the United Kingdom voted to leave the EU. That decision ended a close relationship with the legal systems of continental Europe, which had lasted nearly half a century.

What are likely to be the consequences for the future? My surmise is that, after Brexit, after nearly half a century of close interaction, the momentum in favour of cross-border exchanges within Europe is too great to be easily reversed. There will continue to be demand for lawyers who understand EU law; and in any case, British law faculties have a vested interest in continuing to develop what is now a well-established program of scholarship, if only as a vehicle for continuing to attract bright legal minds from overseas. So I do not expect the law faculties to become narrowly national, whatever happens to the formal relations with the European courts in Luxembourg and Strasbourg.

This collection, I believe, demonstrates the increasingly rapid exchange of legal ideas, not just within the world of English-speaking legal systems but also more generally. It opens the door to a large number of questions about the international transmission of legal ideas, and also calls into question the very distinction between common law systems and civilian systems; but that is a topic for another occasion.

Contributors

Jakub Adamski is adjunct professor, Faculty of Law, McGill University.

Peter Cane is Yorke Distinguished Visiting Fellow at the Faculty of Law, University of Cambridge and a Senior Research Fellow of Christ's College, Cambridge.

Paul Daly is senior lecturer in public law, University of Cambridge and the Derek Bowett Fellow in Law, Queens' College, Cambridge.

Brice Dickson is emeritus professor, Queen's University Belfast.

William B. Ewald is professor of law and philosophy, University of Pennsylvania.

Steve Hedley is professor of law, University College Cork.

James Lee is reader in English law, King's College London.

Audrey Macklin is professor of human rights law, University of Toronto.

Carissima Mathen is associate professor and vice-dean, Faculty of Law (Common Law Section), University of Ottawa.

Beverley McLachlin was a puisne justice of the Supreme Court of Canada from 1989 to 2000 and chief justice of Canada from 2000 to 2017.

Sandy Steel is associate professor, University of Oxford and fellow and tutor in law, Wadham College, Oxford.

Angela Swan is counsel, Aird & Berlis LLP.

Jason N.E. Varuhas is professor of law, Melbourne Law School.

Robert F. Williams is distinguished professor of law and director of the Center for State Constitutional Studies at Rutgers Law School.

Han-Ru Zhou is associate professor of public law, Université de Montréal.

Bruce Ziff is professor of law, University of Alberta.

www.ingramcontent.com/pod-product-compliance
Lightning Source LLC
LaVergne TN
LVHW090146080826
844660LV00013B/690/J

* 9 7 8 1 4 8 7 5 0 4 4 3 4 *